The Complete Ninja Foodi Book for Beginners

Simple, Delicious & Foolproof Ninja Foodi Recipes for Everyone to Cook Pressure Cooker and Air Fryer Delicacies

Joshua Read

© Copyright 2022 - All Rights Reserved

This document is geared towards providing exact and reliable information with regards to the topic and issue covered. The publication is sold with the idea that the publisher is not required to render accounting, officially permitted, or otherwise, qualified services. If advice is necessary, legal, or professional, a practiced individual in the profession should be ordered. - From a Declaration of Principles which was accepted and approved equally by a Committee of the American Bar Association and a Committee of Publishers and Associations. In no way is it legal to reproduce, duplicate, or transmit any part of this document in either electronic means or in printed format. Recording of this publication is strictly prohibited, and any storage of this document is not allowed unless with written permission from the publisher.

All rights reserved. The information provided herein is stated to be truthful and consistent, in that any liability, in terms of inattention or otherwise, by any usage or abuse of any policies, processes, or directions contained within is the solitary and utter responsibility of the recipient reader.

Under no circumstances will any legal responsibility or blame be held against the publisher for any reparation, damages, or monetary loss due to the information herein, either directly or indirectly. Respective authors own all copyrights not held by the publisher.

The information herein is offered for informational purposes solely and is universal as so. The presentation of the information is without contract or any type of guarantee assurance. The trademarks that are used are without any consent, and the publication of the trademark is without permission or backing by the trademark owner.

All trademarks and brands within this book are for clarifying purposes only and are owned by the owners themselves, not affiliated with this document.

CONTENT

1 Introduction

2 Fundamentals of Ninja Foodi XL Pressure Cooker Steam Fryer

10 4-Week Diet Plan

12 Chapter 1 Breakfast Recipes

28 Chapter 2 Vegetable and Sides Recipes

44 Chapter 3 Poultry Mains Recipes

60 Chapter 4 Meat Mains Recipes

80 Chapter 5 Soup, Stew, and Chili Recipes

87 Chapter 6 Fish and Seafood Recipes

100 Chapter 7 Snack and Appetizer Recipes 57

107 Chapter 8 Dessert Recipes

122 Conclusion

123 Appendix 1 Measurement Conversion Chart

124 Appendix 2 Air Fryer Cooking Chart

125 Appendix 3 Recipes Index

Introduction

So far, Ninja Foodi XL Pressure Cooker Steam Fryers haven't been used as much as they could be in integrated cooking systems that work well. They are usually made of thick aluminum or stainless steel, which makes them heavier and more expensive than regular pots. They could also be hard to make in a lot of developing countries. Prices are rarely less than 20 US dollars, and high-end items can easily cost more than 200 US dollars. In places where Ninja Foodi XL Pressure Cooker Steam Fryers aren't used very often, their relatively high prices make it hard for them to spread. People use Ninja Foodi XL Pressure Cooker Steam Fryer more in cities, where fuel has to be paid for in cash, and in rural areas, where they can quickly cook local food. This is especially true in Asia (China, Nepal, and India).

Markets all over the world sell different models of pressure cookers. To find the best model, you must consider price, size, the primary type of stove used (electric, gas, or fire), durability, and maintenance.

This cookbook is the best way to learn how to use a pressure cooker and cook with it. This cookbook will help you get the variety of tasty recipes and instructions on how to clean it after use. In short, you will find precise information along with you need to know about your pressure cooker in this book.

Fundamentals of Ninja Foodi XL Pressure Cooker Steam Fryer

Ninja Foodi XL Pressure Cooker Steam Fryers are unique pots that can be sealed so that air can't get in. It lets pressure inside build up. The pot lid is firmly attached to the pot body by a mechanical device with screws or parts that fit together. A silicone ring or seal between the cover and the pot keeps steam from escaping. When you increase the temperature, the pressure of the moisture inside the pot builds up until it is higher than atmospheric pressure. This lets the temperature go well above the boiling point. With this design, you can save time, energy, and materials. In a pressure cooker, food cooks faster because the temperature can quickly go above 110°C. Also, less steam gets out between the pot and the lid, so less water is needed to cook the food.

What Is Ninja Foodi XL Pressure Cooker Steam Fryer

A fireless cooker, like a heat-retaining bag or box, can also be used with a pressure cooker (discussed later). A test done in Tajikistan found that this combination saved 80% of fuel. If the pot is put into a bag or box that keeps heat in before the pressure valve lets the steam out, no steam energy is lost. For example, instructions for boiling water, how long it takes to cook after the water boils, and how long the pot needs to stay in the heat bag. This information depends on the altitude, the food to be cooked, and the type of pressure cooker and heat retention bag.

Ninja Foodi XL Pressure Cooker Steam Fryer can also be used to make traditional dishes. But users need user training and awareness training to learn how to cook traditional dishes with the new equipment. One best way to do this would be to give out a pressure cooker cookbook with traditional recipes. As the air pressure is lower at higher altitudes, the temperature at which water boils is more down there. So, cooking takes longer and more fuel, or the food doesn't get done. Depending on the altitude, the food must boil for between one-fourth and one-fifth of the average time to soften it.

Benefits of Ninja Foodi XL Pressure Cooker Steam Fryer

The steam and air fry can't perform both at the same time, which is a really hectic task (the moisture would counteract the super crisp technology of the air fryer, obviously). The air fry setting on this appliance is said to have "the perfect balance of temperature control and hot air flow for crispy, golden results with little or no added oil."

It also has a unique steam function, so you can roast a chicken and potatoes in it and then quickly steam some vegetables while the chicken and potatoes rest. But it's not just for quickly steamed greens. The water tank holds 1.1 liters, enough to steam for up to 85 minutes (hello, dumplings, fish, and more!). Oh, and it can also be "BBQ." The deluxe reversible rack makes meat and vegetables as juicy and tender as you want with different position with no smoke and smell.

It has an extra-large, family-sized capacity and can pressure cook, air fry, and steam, all under one SmartLid. It makes meals faster with up to 70% faster than slow cooking, 40% faster than traditional cooking methods, and 25% faster for artisan bread and cakes. Attached Deluxe Reversible Rack cook twice as much or make 3-part full meals at the touch of a button—you can get mains, sides, and desserts. Its advanced Steamcrisp technology make it even easier to steam and crisp simultaneously for faster and juicier results that don't dry out. Slide to open the 14 functions and 3 cooking modes in one lid with the SmartLid slider.

Ninja Foodi XL Pressure Cooker Steam Fryer with SmartLid, an 8-quart Cooking Pot, a 5-quart Cook & Crisp Basket, and a Deluxe Reversible Rack.

Healthier Cooking

Most people buy a Ninja Foodi XL Pressure Cooker Steam Fryer because they want to cook healthier food. Since the cooking process uses very little oil, this is a great way to replace unhealthy deep-fried foods with something more beneficial.

Fried foods, like breaded chicken tenders and fried fish, still need to be sprayed with a bit of oil so that the breading gets evenly crispy as it cooks, but you use a lot less fat. Also, you don't have to fry French fries or tater tots deep to make them nice and crispy.

Rapid, Secure, and User-Friendly

At first, the Ninja Foodi XL Pressure Cooker Steam Fryer was meant to replace a deep fryer. Even though that was great, it wasn't enough to convince most people who needed one since they often don't use a deep fryer at home.

We all wish we had more time to cook, while we don't. This is why ready-made meals and takeout are so popular, even though we all know they are bad for us. If you frequently prepare frozen and breaded dishes like onion rings and chicken tenders, you will appreciate this the most. In order to avoid a soggy mess, the food you prepare in the Ninja Foodi XL Pressure Cooker Steam Fryer gets crisped up.

A light misting of cooking oil on the surface of the dish before cooking is all that's required to create a crunchy, crispy crust.

This method is ideal for cooking frozen breaded or fried foods. You can reheat pizza, so give it a shot! As it warms the slice through, it crisps the bottom crust and properly revitalizes the toppings. It's as good as the first day it was released.

Very Versatile

A healthy alternative to deep frying is the Ninja Foodi XL Pressure Cooker Steam Fryer, which is capable of much more. With this device, you can prepare practically anything, including curries, desserts, whole spaghetti squash, and fried chicken. Yes, it's a terrific way to prepare store-bought frozen items like French fries, tater tots, and pizza rolls. It's so easy that even kids can complete it. Dinner is taken care of.

Faster Than Oven Cooking

One of the best things about a Ninja Foodi XL Pressure Cooker Steam Fryer is that it heats up quickly and gets hot. The moving air also helps the food cook evenly, brown, and crispy without having to do much. This means that you'll be able to cook faster. A Ninja Foodi XL Pressure Cooker Steam Fryer is faster than an oven because it can get hot quickly and is smaller than an oven. Most ovens take up to 10 minutes to heat up, but the Ninja Foodi XL Pressure Cooker Steam Fryer doesn't need to be heated up before most recipes.

Put your food in the basket, slip it into the air fryer, choose your cooking time, and in 10 to 15 minutes you'll have a delicious meal. It's an excellent tool for making snacks quickly and easily. For a party or a snack after school, it's easy to turn it on, put in your favorite snack, and wait a few minutes for it to be done.

Easy and Efficient Reheat

You can cook anything in a Ninja Foodi and use it to reheat food, making it even more helpful. You might want to use a Ninja Foodi XL Pressure Cooker Steam Fryer to reheat food for several reasons.

It's an easy and quick way to reheat food. It keeps food from overcooking or burning. It's simple. It keeps food crispy and fresh tasting. No one in the world likes cleaning up after cooking, right? This unpleasant job can take away a lot of the pleasure of a great meal. So, you'll be happy to know that a good Ninja Foodi XL Pressure Cooker Steam Fryer is also very easy to clean after use.

Easy to Clean

Cleaning up after cooking is the worst thing in the world. This unpleasant job can take away a lot of the pleasure from a great meal. So, you'll be glad to hear that a good Ninja Foodi XL Pressure Cooker Steam Fryer is also very easy to clean after use.

You can clean it every time using it for cooking, you won't have to clean it as often as other pots and pans. Just put soapy water in the basket and use a sponge that won't scratch to clean the inside and outside. Some of the baskets that come with the Ninja Foodi XL Pressure Cooker Steam Fryer can even be cleaned in the dishwasher.

You should also clean it more thoroughly once or twice a month, including the cooking coil, depending on how often you use it. Cleaning the oven is not complicated or time-consuming if you do it often.

Users' Guide

Cooking Functions

Pressure: Quickly cook food while preserving softness.

Steam & Crisp: It allows you to make whole meals with just one touch, vegetables, and proteins that are juicy and crisp, and fresh artisan bread.

Steam & Bake: Bake cakes and quick breads with less fat and more fluffiness with steam.

Air Fry: This method allows food to maintain its crispiness and crunchiness while using very little to no oil.

Broil: Apply intense heat from above in order to brown and caramelize the surface of the meal.

Bake/Roast: Treat the appliance like an oven and use it to make tender meats, baked treats, and a variety of other foods.

Dehydrate: For wholesome snacks, dehydrate meats, fruits, and veggies.

Proof: Establish a setting in which the dough can rest and rise before being used.

Sear/Sauté: Use the appliance as a burner to simmer sauces, sauté vegetables, and brown meats.

Steam: Cook delicate items at a high temperature while being gentle.

Sous Vide: What literally translates to "under vacuum," is a function that allows food to be cooked more slowly while being contained in a plastic bag and placed in an expertly controlled water bath.

Slow Cook: Cook your food for a more extended time at a lower temperature. Yoghurt is manufactured by pasteurizing and fermenting milk to make it creamy.

Yogurt: Get creamy homemade yogurt by pasteurizing and fermenting milk in the unit.

Keep Warm: When the steam, slow cook, or pressure cooking cycle is complete, the appliance will automatically transition to the keep warm setting. After the function has begun, you can stop this transition from happening automatically by pressing the button labelled "stay nice."

If the timer runs for one hour or less, it will count for minutes and seconds. Only minutes will be counted if the clock runs for longer than an hour. After 12 hours, this function will stop functioning.

Operating Buttons

SMARTLID SLIDER: The available features for each set will light up as you move the slider.

DIAL: After deciding on a mode with the slider, you can use the dial to go between the various functions until the one you want is highlighted. Once this is done, the mode you choose will be highlighted.

LEFT ARROWS: To change the temperature of the cooking process, use the up and down arrows.

RIGHT ARROWS: To change the amount of time spent cooking, use the up and down arrows located to the right of the display.

START/STOP button: Press to start cooking, and pressing the button while the unit cooks will stop the current cooking function.

POWER: The Power button pauses all cooking modes and turns off the appliance.

Step-By-Step Instructions

Accessory Assembly Instructions

Deluxe Reversible Rack

Arrange the Deluxe Reversible Rack such that the lower layer is at the bottom. Ingredients should be placed in the lower section of the rack. Pass the deluxe layer through the standard layer's grips. If you need extra counter space for cooking, move the remaining components to the top secret tier.

Cook & Crisp Basket

To clean the diffuser, first remove two of the diffuser's fins from the groove on the basket, then firmly pull the diffuser down on itself. To put together the Cook & Crisp Basket, position the basket so that it is sitting atop the diffuser, and then press down firmly.

Lid Opening and Closing Instructions

To open and shut the lid, pull down on the handle that is located above the slider. When the slider is in the position for the Ninja Foodi XL Pressure Cooker Steam Fryer and AIR FRY/ STOVETOP function, the top can be opened and closed at your convenience. The lid can't be opened when the slider is under PRESSURE.

The lid won't open until the whole unit is no longer under pressure. The smart slider won't move to the right until the pressure is gone from the unit. When the unit is no longer under pressure, it will show "OPN LID" on the screen.

Before First Use

1. Take off and throw away the unit's packaging, stickers, and tape.
2. Pay close attention to the instructions, warnings, and essential safety measures to avoid getting hurt or damaging your property.
3. Use warm soapy water to clean the silicone ring, removable cooking pot, Cook & Crisp Basket, deluxe reversible rack, and condensation collector, and then thoroughly rinse and dry each of these components. Under NO circumstances should the dishwasher be used to clean the bottom of the range.
4. The silicone ring can be put in either way because it has two sides. Place the silicone ring around the outside edge of the lid on the bottom of the rack. Make sure it's in and lays flat under the silicone ring rack.

Take Out the Condensation Collector and Put It Back In Place.

The condensation collector should be inserted into the cooker base's slot. Slide it out each time you use it so you may wash your hands with it.

Take the Anti-Clog Cap Off and Putting It Back On.

The anti-clog cap keeps the valve inside the lid from getting clogged and keeps food from splattering on the user. It should be cleaned with a cleaning brush after every use. To take it off, hold the anti-clog cap with your thumb and bent index finger, then turn your wrist in a clockwise direction. To put it back in, put it where it belongs and press down on it. Before using the unit, ensure the anti-clog cap is correct.

Water Test Beginning the Process of Cooking Under Pressure

New users should perform a water test to get comfortable with pressure cooking.

1. Put the pot in the cooker base and fill it with 3 cups of water at room temperature.
2. Put the lid back, lock it, and move the slider to the PRESSURE setting.
3. Ensure the pressure release valve is in the SEAL (or Pressure functions) position.
4. When the valve is put in place, it will be loose. This is fine.
5. High (Hi) pressure will be the default for the unit. Use the down arrow on the right to change the time to 2 minutes. To start, press START/STOP.
6. The word "PrE" and progress bars will appear on this display to indicate that the device is increasing its pressure.
7. When all of the members of the unit are under pressure, the timer will begin counting down. When the cooking time runs out, the unit will beep and show "End" before letting the pressured steam out quickly. When the pressure release valve is about to open, an alarm will go off. When the pressure release valve is opened, steam will come out. Move the slider to the right when the screen says "OPN Lid" to open the lid. Then take off the top.

Quick Pressure Release & Natural Pressure Release

The Natural Pressure Release

When the cooking is done under pressure, the steam will naturally come out of the unit as it cools. The release time will depend on the food and liquid. The Ninja Foodi will switch to Keep Warm mode during this time. If you want to turn off Keep Warm mode, press the KEEP WARM button. When the pressure has been released naturally, the unit will show "OPN Lid."

Quick Pressure Release

ONLY use if your recipe says to. When the cooking is done under pressure, and the KEEP WARM light is on, rotate or turn the pressure release valve or rotator to the VENT position to immediately let the stress out of the pot. Even after letting the pressure out naturally or using the pressure release valve, there will still be some steam in the unit. When the lid is going to be opened, this steam will escape.

Using Pressure Function

Pressure

1. Press the Power button after inserting the power cord into a wall outlet to turn on the device.
2. Put the ingredients and at least 1 cup of liquid, as well as any other needed items, in the pot. DO NOT fill the jar up past the line "PRESSURE MAX."
3. Close the lid. Next, turn the pressure release valve to the SEAL setting. Move the slider to the PRESSURE setting. To choose Hi or LO, use arrows buttons. Then use the up and down arrows to adjust the cook time.
4. To begin the cooking process, press the START/STOP button. When you turn the Ninja Foodi on, the pressure within will start to build. On the screen, you will see the letters "PrE" as well as progress bars. When the unit has pressurized, the timer will begin counting down.

5. When the allotted amount of time for cooking has passed, switch the pressure release valve to the VENT position. The unit will beep and switch automatically to Keep Warm mode. The timer will also start counting up.

6. When the unit shows "OPN Lid," the pressure has been released, and you can open the lid by moving the slider to the right.

Using Steamcrisp Functions

After you have connected the power cord to an available outlet in the wall and pressed the Power button, the device will begin to operate.

Steam & Crisp

1. Put in the ingredients based on the recipe. Move the slider to STEAMCRISP. The STEAM & CRISP function will be chosen by default. The time and temperature will be set to their defaults. Use arrows on the left side of the screen to select a temperature between 300°F and 450°F in 5-degree increments.

2. To make changes to the cooking time in increments of one minute, up to an hour long, use the arrows buttons. To begin the cooking process, press the START/STOP button. The "PrE" and progress bars on the screen show that the unit is making steam. How long something needs to moisture depends on how many things are in the pot. When the unit has reached the right level of smoke, the display will show the temperature you set, and the timer will start to count down. When the cooking time runs out, the unit will beep and say "End" for 5 minutes. Use the up arrow to add more time if your food needs more time. The unit will not heat up first. Now, we know how to make recipes from Ninja Foodi XL Pressure Cooker Steam Fryer. Let us make try to make anything with steps.

Bake/Roast

1. Equip the pot with all of the necessary implements and components. Put the lid back on. Then, using the dial, choose BAKE/ROAST after moving the slider to the AIR FRY/STOVETOP position. The temperature will automatically be set to the present value. Choose a temperature in increments of 5 degrees by using the arrow buttons to select a value between 250 and 400 degrees Fahrenheit.

2. To modify the cook time, use the arrow buttons to go from up to 1 hour in increments of 1 minute, and then from 1 hour to 4 hours in intervals of 5 minutes.

3. Press START/STOP to begin cooking

4. The unit will beep when cook time reaches zero, and "End" will flash 3 times on the display.

Dehydrate

1. Position the deluxe reversible rack in the lower position, and after that, add a layer of ingredients to the shelf.
2. While still holding it by its handles, position the deluxe layer so that it rests on the reversible rack. After that, add another layer of ingredients on top of the first layer, and cover the container with the lid.
3. To dehydrate the food, turn the dial to DEHYDRATE after moving the slider to the AIR FRY/STOVETOP position. The temperature will automatically be set to the present value. Choose a temperature between 80 and 195 degrees Fahrenheit using the arrow buttons to make adjustments in 5-degree increments.
4. To alter the cook time in 15-minute increments from 1 hour to 12 hours, use the arrow buttons.
5. To start the cooking process, press the START/STOP button.
6. The unit will beep when cook time reaches zero, and "End" will flash 3 times on the display.

Proof

1. Put the dough in the pot or the Cook & Crisp Basket, and then cover it with the lid.
2. Using the dial, select PROOF after first moving the slider to the AIR FRY/STOVETOP position.
3. The temperature will automatically be set to the preset value. Choose a temperature in increments of 5 degrees by using the arrows buttons to select a value between 75 and 95 degrees Fahrenheit.
4. To modify the proof time in minute increments between 20 minutes and 2 hours, use the arrow buttons. The minimum proof time is 20 minutes, and the maximum proof time is 2 hours. Press START/STOP to begin cooking.
6. The unit will beep when cook time reaches zero, and "End" will flash three times on the display.

Sear/Sauté

1. Put the ingredients in the cooking pot. Either open the lid of the appliance or use the slider to select AIR FRY/STOVETOP, or use the dial to select SEAR/SAUTÉ.
2. The default temperature setting will display. To choose "Lo1," "2," "3," "4", or "Hi5", use the arrows for that.
3. Press START/STOP button to begin cooking and end the function after cooking. To switch to another cooking function, use the slider and select your cooking method.

Frequently Asked Questions

Why does it take so much time for the unit to build up its pressure? How much time passes before the pressure starts to rise?

Cooking times vary based on the temperature, the cooking pot's current temperature, and the temperature or quantity of the ingredients. Check that the silicone ring is completely seated and that it is flush against the lid. You should be able to spin the call by giving it a light tug, provided that it was put appropriately.

Inadequate liquid prevents the unit from pressurizing. Why does the time go so slowly?

You can also set hours rather than minutes. When selecting the time, the display window will show HH: MM and the time will also change by increase/decrease in minute increments.
How will I know when the machine starts to pressurize?
The display will show a progress bar of building pressure. The letters "PrE" and flashing lights appear on the screen whenever you use the Pressure function or Steam function. This indicates the machine is generating pressure when using PRESSURE or STEAM. When the main unit has build pressure, your cook time will start. A lot of steam comes from the unit when using the Steam function. Smoke is customary which release through the valve during cooking so don't panic for that.

Why can't I open the lid while releasing pressurizing?

The lid will not unlock before the appliance is depressurized as a safety measure. Set the pressure release valve to VENT to swiftly discharge the pressurized steam. Steam will suddenly erupt from the pressure release valve. The unit will be ready to open when the smoke is finally let out.

Is it normal for the pressure release valve to be slack?

Yes. The loose fit of the pressure release valve is deliberate; it makes switching from SEAL to VENT quick and straightforward and helps regulate pressure by releasing a tiny quantity of steam during cooking to produce outstanding results. When cooking under pressure, please make sure it is in the SEAL position, and when fast releasing, confirm that is turned as far as possible toward the VENT position. The

device hisses and cannot build pressure. A pressure release valve should be turned to the SEAL setting, so double-check this. After doing this, if you still hear a loud hissing sound, the silicone ring may not be entirely in place. To halt cooking, press START/STOP, VENT if necessary, and lift the lid. Please ensure the silicone ring is placed correctly and flatly underneath the rack by applying pressure on it. Once everything is put in place, you should be able to spin the call by giving it a slight tug. Instead of counting down, the device is counting up. The Ninja Foodi is in "Keep Warm" function after the cooking is finished.

How much time does it take the unit to depressurize?

The pressure release depends on the food quantity in the cooking pot and can vary from recipes. If the unit takes longer time than usual to depressurize, Switch off and release all the pressure before opening the lid.

Helpful Tips for Users

Make sure that the ingredients are spread out in the bottom of the cooking pot in an even layer without overlapping one another so that the browning will be consistent. It is important to remember to shake the pan halfway through the allotted cooking time if the elements overlap.

To prevent smaller items from being lost through the deluxe reversible rack, we advise first placing them in a pouch made of parchment paper or aluminum foil and then wrapping them.

After the food has been cooked, select the Keep Warm option to keep it at a warm temperature that is still safe for consumption. To avoid the food inside from drying out, we suggest keeping the lid closed and use this function just before serving it. To reheat meals, use the function labelled "Reheat."

After each usage, the appliance needs to be thoroughly cleaned.
1. Unplug the appliance from the wall outlet before beginning the cleaning process.
2. To clean the cooker base and the control panel, clean them with a damp cloth.
3. With some water and dish soap, you may clean the pressure release valve and anti-clog cap.
4. If food residue is stuck on the cooking pot, fill the pot with water and allow it to soak before cleaning. DO NOT use scouring pads. If scrubbing is required, use liquid dish soap or a non-abrasive cleaner with a nylon pad or brush.
5. Air-dry all parts after each use.

4-Week Diet Plan

Week 1

Day 1:
Breakfast: Parmesan Bread
Lunch: Parmesan Green Bean Casserole
Snack: Parsley Olives Fritters
Dinner: Grilled Salmon with Capers
Dessert: Cranberry Cake

Day 2:
Breakfast: Artichoke Pizza
Lunch: Cheese Broccoli Pizza
Snack: Tacon Mexican Muffins
Dinner: Korean Wings
Dessert: Chocolate Cake

Day 3:
Breakfast: Hush Puffs
Lunch: Parmesan Potatoes
Snack: Mushroom Basil Bites
Dinner: Muffin Burgers
Dessert: Clafoutis

Day 4:
Breakfast: Baked Eggs
Lunch: Refreshing Steamed Broccoli
Snack: Bacon Chaffle
Dinner: Dijon Glazed Pork Loin
Dessert: Soft Raisin Muffins

Day 5:
Breakfast: Bacon Knots
Lunch: Turnips with Greens
Snack: Crispy Courgette Chips
Dinner: Beef Steak Nuggets
Dessert: Macadamia Cookies

Day 6:
Breakfast: Broccoli Quiche
Lunch: Potato Salad
Snack: Cheddar Cheese Rounds
Dinner: BBQ Baby Ribs
Dessert: Orange Cake

Day 7:
Breakfast: Ham Polenta Muffins
Lunch: Colourful Ratatouille Stew
Snack: Avocado Wraps
Dinner: Fried Prawns
Dessert: Pudding with Sultanas

Week 2

Day 1:
Breakfast: Toast Sticks
Lunch: Bacon Red Cabbage with Cheese
Snack: Cheese Sticks
Dinner: Mayo Chicken Salad
Dessert: Pineapple with Macadamia Batter

Day 2:
Breakfast: Ham Eggs
Lunch: Delicious Portobello Pot Roast
Snack: Bacon Sprouts Wraps
Dinner: Pork Cutlets
Dessert: Cranberry Brownies

Day 3:
Breakfast: Oat Muffins
Lunch: Pearl Couscous Salad
Snack: Crusted Courgette Chips
Dinner: Bacon Cups
Dessert: Prune Cookies

Day 4:
Breakfast: Breakfast Scotch Eggs
Lunch: Garlicky Mashed Vegetables
Snack: Bacon Bites
Dinner: Beef Meat Loaf
Dessert: Apricots in Whiskey Sauce

Day 5:
Breakfast: Strawberry Morning Toast
Lunch: Maple Carrots with Dill
Snack: Pickled Bacon
Dinner: Chicken with Mushrooms
Dessert: Cinnamon Pear Clafoutis

Day 6:
Breakfast: Smoked Salmon and Veggie Quiche Cups
Lunch: Paprika Cabbage Steaks
Snack: Coconut Granola
Dinner: Cajun Lemon Salmon
Dessert: Chocolate Egg Rolls

Day 7:
Breakfast: Tropical Oats
Lunch: Mushroom Cheese Loaf
Snack: Beef Smokies
Dinner: Lobster with Butter Sauce
Dessert: Flaxseed Carrot Cake

Week 3

Day 1:
Breakfast: Cranberry Nutty Grits
Lunch: Artichoke Stuffed Aubergine
Snack: Avocado Balls
Dinner: Pork Bun Thit Nuong
Dessert: Vegan Apple Pies

Day 2:
Breakfast: Classical Hard-Boiled Eggs
Lunch: Szechuan Beans
Snack: Air-Fried Pork Rinds
Dinner: Beefy Poppers
Dessert: Raspberry Pineapple Sundaes

Day 3:
Breakfast: Cheesy Meaty Sausage Frittata
Lunch: Sesame Carrots
Snack: Prawn Balls
Dinner: Mushroom Burgers
Dessert: Carrot Cake

Day 4:
Breakfast: Bacon and Sausage Omelet
Lunch: Parmesan Cauliflower
Snack: Turmeric Chicken Bites
Dinner: Short Rib Bibimbap
Dessert: Berries Mug Cake

Day 5:
Breakfast: Mayo Egg Salad
Lunch: Corn on The Cob
Snack: Cashew Dip
Dinner: Delicious Seafood Gumbo
Dessert: Spiced Pumpkin Pudding

Day 6:
Breakfast: Omelet Cups
Lunch: Crusted Aubergine
Snack: Duck Wraps
Dinner: Prawns Scampi
Dessert: Sweet Quiche

Day 7:
Breakfast: Ham Casserole
Lunch: Crispy Sweet Potatoes
Snack: Salmon Bites
Dinner: Hamburgers
Dessert: Creamy Raspberry Jam

Week 4

Day 1:
Breakfast: Cheesy Bacon Quiche
Lunch: Roasted Broccoli
Snack: Aubergine Chips
Dinner: Lemon Chicken with Herbed Potatoes
Dessert: Sweet Raspberry Curd

Day 2:
Breakfast: Delightful Eggs
Lunch: Green Beans Salad
Snack: Meatballs
Dinner: Indian Lamb Steaks
Dessert: Yellow Marmalade

Day 3:
Breakfast: Porridge
Lunch: Spicy Potatoes
Snack: Sushi
Dinner: Beef Carne Asada
Dessert: Regular Chocolate Pudding

Day 4:
Breakfast: Tasty Tomato Spinach Quiche
Lunch: Roasted Broccoli
Snack: Chicken Meatballs
Dinner: Prawns with tangy Risotto
Dessert: Nutty Chocolate Candy

Day 5:
Breakfast: Shakshuka
Lunch: Roasted Country-Style Vegetables
Snack: Crusted Hot Dogs
Dinner: Parmesan Cod
Dessert: Delicious Blueberries Yogurt

Day 6:
Breakfast: Spinach- Rollups
Lunch: Air-Fried Brown Mushrooms
Snack: Beef and Tomatillo Stew
Dinner: Spicy Buffalo Wings
Dessert: Sweet Pecans

Day 7:
Breakfast: Spelt with Berries and Walnuts
Lunch: Roasted Peppers
Snack: Avocado Wraps
Dinner: BBQ Baby Ribs
Dessert: Red Cherry Compote

Chapter 1 Breakfast Recipes

13	Parmesan Bread	20	Oat Muffins
13	Peach Vanilla Fritters	21	Spelt with Berries and Walnuts
13	Pita Bread	21	Flaxseed Muffins
14	Ham Eggs	21	Egg Quesadillas
14	Bacon Knots	21	Boiled Eggs
14	Bacon and Sausage Omelet	22	Porridge
14	Air Fried Grapefruit	22	Tropical Oats
15	Ham Polenta Muffins	22	Smoked Salmon and Veggie Quiche Cups
15	Broccoli Quiche		
15	Hush Puffs	22	Soft Eggs
15	Artichoke Pizza	23	Delightful Eggs
16	Sweet Potato Toast	23	Traditional French Eggs
16	Pepper Bread	23	Cheesy Meaty Sausage Frittata
16	Turkey Sausage Roll-Ups	23	Jelly stuffed Muffins
16	Toast Sticks	24	Healthy Blueberry Oat Mini Muffins
17	Classical Hard-Boiled Eggs	24	Cranberry Nutty Grits
17	Chocolate Rolls	24	Delicious Mushroom Frittata
17	Pepperoni Cheese Pizza	24	Healthy Egg Muffins
17	Spinach- Rollups	25	Tomato and Spinach Healthy Breakfast
18	Breakfast Scotch Eggs	25	Baked Cheesy Hash Brown Bake
18	Baked Eggs	25	Mayo Egg Salad
18	Walnut Apple Muffins	25	Eggs Dish
18	Strawberry Morning Toast	26	Ham Casserole
19	Blueberry Morning Muffins	26	Cheesy Bacon Quiche
19	Mushroom Boat Eggs	26	Tasty Tomato Spinach Quiche
19	Classical Poached Eggs	26	Fried PB&J Sandwich
19	Cheesy Bacon Muffins	27	Pork Quiche Cups
20	Omelet Cups	27	Shakshuka
20	Spinach-Feta Cups	27	Baked Egg
20	Pepper Cups		

Parmesan Bread

Prep Time: 10 minutes | Cook Time: 30 minutes | Serves: 6 to 8

- 115g unsalted butter, melted
- ¼ teaspoon salt
- 75g grated Parmesan cheese
- 3 to 4 cloves garlic, minced
- 1 tablespoon chopped fresh parsley
- 455g frozen bread dough, defrosted
- Olive oil
- 1 egg, beaten

1. Mix the melted butter, salt, Parmesan cheese, garlic and chopped parsley in a suitable bowl. 2. Roll the prepared dough out into a rectangle that measures 20 cm by 43 cm. 3. Spread the butter mixture over the prepared dough, leaving a 1 cm border un-buttered along one of the long edges. Roll the prepared dough from one long edge to the other, ending with the un-buttered border. Pinch the seam shut tightly. Shape the log into a circle sealing the ends by pushing one end into the other and stretching the prepared dough around it. 4. Cut out a circle of aluminum foil that is the same size as the Ninja Foodi Pressure Steam Fryer basket. Brush the foil circle with oil and place an oven safe ramekin or glass in the center. 5. Transfer the prepared dough ring to the aluminum foil circle, around the ramekin. This will help you make sure the prepared dough will fit in the basket and maintain its ring shape. Use kitchen shears to cut 8 slits around the outer edge of the prepared dough ring halfway to the center. Brush the prepared dough ring with egg wash. 6. Brush the sides of the Cook & Crisp Basket with oil and transfer the prepared dough ring, foil circle and ramekin into the basket. 7. Slide the Cook & Crisp Basket back into the Pressure Steam Fryer, but do not turn it on. Let the prepared dough rise inside the Pressure Steam Fryer for around 30 minutes. 8. After the bread has proofed in the Ninja Foodi Pressure Steam Fryer for around 30 minutes. 9. Put on the Smart Lid on top of the Ninja Foodi Steam Fryer. 10. Move the Lid Slider to the "Air Fry/Stovetop". Select the "Air Fry" mode for cooking. 11. Cook the bread ring on the "Air Fry" mode at 170°C for 15 minutes. Flip the bread over by inverting it onto a plate or cutting board and sliding it back into the cook & crisp Basket. 12. Air-fry for another 15 minutes. Serve Warm.
Per serving: Calories: 334; Fat: 10.9g; Sodium: 354mg; Carbs: 20.5g; Fiber: 4.1g; Sugar 8.2g; Protein 06g

Peach Vanilla Fritters

Prep Time: 10 minutes | Cook Time: 6 minutes | Serves: 8

- 185g bread flour
- 1 teaspoon active dry yeast
- 50g sugar
- ¼ teaspoon salt
- 120ml warm milk
- ½ teaspoon vanilla extract
- 2 egg yolks
- 2 tablespoons melted butter
- 310g small diced peaches
- 1 tablespoon butter
- 1 teaspoon cinnamon
- 1 to 2 tablespoons sugar
- **Glaze**
- 95g icing sugar
- 4 teaspoons milk

1. Mix the flour, yeast, sugar and salt in a suitable bowl. Add the milk, vanilla, egg yolks and melted butter and mix until the prepared dough starts to come together. Transfer the prepared dough to a floured surface and knead it by hand for around 2 minutes. Shape the prepared dough into a ball, place it in a suitable oiled bowl, cover with a clean kitchen towel and let the prepared dough rise in a warm place for around 1 to 1½ hours, or until the prepared dough has doubled in size. 2. While the prepared dough is rising, melt one tablespoon of butter in a suitable saucepan on the stovetop. Add the diced peaches, cinnamon and sugar to taste. Cook the peaches for about 5 minutes, or until they soften. Set the peaches aside to cool. 3. Place the Cook & Crisp Basket in your Pressure Cooker Steam Fryer. 4. When the prepared dough has risen, transfer it to a floured surface and shape it into a 15 cm circle. Spread the peaches over half of the circle and fold the other half of the prepared dough over the top. With a knife or a board scraper, score the prepared dough by making slits in the prepared dough in a diamond shape. Push the knife straight down into the prepared dough and peaches, rather than slicing through. You should cut through the top layer of dough, but not the bottom. Roll the prepared dough up into a log from one short end to the other. It should be 20 cm long. Some of the peaches will be sticking out of the prepared dough – don't worry, these are supposed to be a little random. Cut the log into 8 equal slices. Place the prepared dough disks on a floured cookie sheet, cover with a clean kitchen towel and let rise in a warm place for around 30 minutes. 5. Put on the Smart Lid on top of the Ninja Foodi Steam Fryer. 6. Move the Lid Slider to the "Air Fry/Stovetop". Select the "Air Fry" mode for cooking. 7. Air-fry 2 or 3 fritters at a time at 185°C, for around 3 minutes. Flip them over and continue to air-fry for another 2 to 3 minutes, until they are golden brown. 8. Mix the icing sugar and milk in a suitable bowl. Mix vigorously until smooth. Allow the fritters to cool for at least 10 minutes and then brush the glaze over both the bottom and top of each one. 9. Serve warm or at room temperature.
Per serving: Calories: 334; Fat: 7.9g; Sodium: 704mg; Carbs: 6g; Fiber: 3.6g; Sugar 6g; Protein 18g

Pita Bread

Prep Time: 10 minutes | Cook Time: 48 minutes | Serves: 8

- 2 teaspoons active dry yeast
- 1 tablespoon sugar
- 360ml warm water
- 405g plain flour
- 2 teaspoons salt
- 1 tablespoon olive oil
- Salt, to taste

1. Dissolve the yeast, sugar and water in the bowl of a stand mixer. Let the mixture sit for around 5 minutes to make sure the yeast is active. Mix the flour and salt in a suitable bowl, and add it to the water, along with the olive oil. Mix with the prepared dough hook until mixed. 2. Knead the prepared dough until it is smooth. Transfer the prepared dough to an oiled bowl, cover and let it rise in a warm place until doubled in bulk. 3. Place the Cook & Crisp Basket in your Pressure Cooker Steam Fryer. 4. Divide the prepared dough into 8 portions and roll each portion into a circle about 10 cm in diameter. Don't roll the balls too thin, or you won't get the pocket inside the pita. 5. Brush both sides of the prepared dough with olive oil, and sprinkle with salt if desired. 6. Put on the Smart Lid on top of the Ninja Foodi Steam Fryer. 7. Move the Lid Slider to the "Air Fry/Stovetop". Cook one at a time on "Air Fry" Mode at 200°C for 6 minutes, 8. flipping it over when there are two minutes left in the cooking time.
Per serving: Calories: 284; Fat: 9g; Sodium: 441mg; Carbs: 7g; Fiber: 4.6g; Sugar 5g; Protein 19g

Ham Eggs

Prep Time: 5 minutes | Cook Time: 6–7 minutes | Serves: 1

| 1 slice bread | 1 egg | 1 tablespoon shredded Cheddar | 2 teaspoons diced ham |
| 1 teaspoon soft butter | Black pepper and salt | cheese | |

1. Place the Cook & Crisp Basket in your Pressure Cooker Steam Fryer. 2. Using a 6 cm biscuit cutter, cut a hole in center of bread slice. 3. Spread softened butter on both sides of bread. 4. Lay bread slice in the Cook & Crisp Basket and crack egg into the hole. Top egg with black pepper and salt to taste. 5. Put on the Smart Lid on top of the Ninja Foodi Steam Fryer. 6. Move the Lid Slider to the "Air Fry/Stovetop". Select the "Air Fry" mode for cooking. 7. Cook at 165°C for 5 minutes. 8. Turn toast over and top it with shredded cheese and diced ham. 9. Cook for around 1 to 2 more minutes or until yolk is done to your liking.
Per serving: Calories: 372; Fat: 20g; Sodium: 891mg; Carbs: 29g; Fiber: 3g; Sugar 8g; Protein 7g

Bacon Knots

Prep Time: 10 minutes | Cook Time: 8 minutes | Serves: 6

| 455g maple smoked center-cut bacon | 80g maple syrup | Cracked black peppercorns |
| | 55g brown sugar | |

1. Place the Cook & Crisp Basket in your Pressure Cooker Steam Fryer. 2. Tie each bacon strip in a loose knot and place them on a suitable the Cook & Crisp Basket. 3. Mix the maple syrup and sugar in a suitable bowl. Brush each knot generously with this mixture and sprinkle with coarsely cracked black pepper. 4. Put on the Smart Lid on top of the Ninja Foodi Steam Fryer. 5. Move the Lid Slider to the "Air Fry/Stovetop". Select the "Air Fry" mode for cooking. 6. Air-fry the bacon knots in batches. Place one layer of knots in the Ninja Foodi Pressure Steam Fryer basket. Cook on the "Air Fry" mode at 200°C for around 5 minutes. Turn the bacon knots over. Cook on the "Air Fry" mode for 2 to 3 minutes. 7. Serve warm.
Per serving: Calories: 282; Fat: 19g; Sodium: 354mg; Carbs: 15g; Fiber: 5.1g; Sugar: 8.2g; Protein 12g

Bacon and Sausage Omelet

Prep time: 5 minutes | Cook time: 55 minutes | Serves: 6

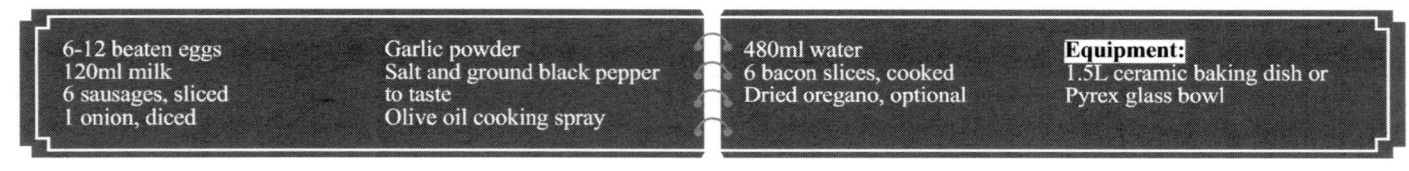

6-12 beaten eggs	Garlic powder	480ml water	**Equipment:**
120ml milk	Salt and ground black pepper	6 bacon slices, cooked	1.5L ceramic baking dish or
6 sausages, sliced	to taste	Dried oregano, optional	Pyrex glass bowl
1 onion, diced	Olive oil cooking spray		

1. In a medium bowl, whisk together the eggs and milk, until well combined. 2. Add the sausages and onion. Season with garlic powder, salt, and pepper. Stir well. 3. Grease Pyrex glass bowl with cooking spray. 4. Pour the egg mixture into the Pyrex and wrap tightly with foil all over. 5. Prepare the Ninja Foodi XL Pressure Cooker Steam Fryer with SmartLid cooking pot by adding the water to the pot and placing the Deluxe Reversible Rack in it. 6. Place the bowl on the Deluxe Reversible Rack and secure the lid. 7. Lock lid; move slider towards PRESSURE. Adjust pressure release valve in the SEAL position. Close pressure-release valve. The cooking temperature will default to HIGH, which is accurate. Set the time for 25 minutes. Select START/STOP and start cooking. 8. When cooking is complete, let pressure naturally release for 10 minutes by turning it into VENT position. Open the lid. Remove the foil. The egg may pop-out of the bowl; just push it back. 9. Lay the cooked bacon on top and cover with shredded cheese. 10. Lock lid; move slider towards PRESSURE. Adjust pressure release valve in the SEAL position. Set the cooking time for 5 minutes at HIGH pressure. Press START/STOP to begin cooking. 11. When the timer beeps, use a Quick Release by turning it into VENT position. Carefully unlock the lid. 12. Take the dish out from the Ninja Foodi XL Pressure Cooker Steam Fryer with SmartLid. If you like, top with dried oregano and serve.
Per Serving: Calories 270; Fat 15g; Sodium 411mg; Carbs 5g; Fiber 3g; Sugar 2g; Protein 9g

Air Fried Grapefruit

Prep Time: 10 minutes | Cook Time: 4 minutes | Serves: 2

| 1 grapefruit | 2 to 4 teaspoons brown sugar |

1. Cut the grapefruit in half. 2. Slice the bottom of the grapefruit to help it sit flat on the counter if necessary. Using a sharp paring knife, cut around the grapefruit between the flesh of the fruit and the peel. 3. Then, cut each segment away from the membrane so that it is sitting freely in the fruit. 4. Place the Cook & Crisp Basket in your Pressure Cooker Steam Fryer. 5. Sprinkle 2 teaspoons of brown sugar on each half of the prepared grapefruit. 6. Transfer the grapefruit half to the "cook & crisp basket". 7. Put on the Smart Lid on top of the Ninja Foodi Steam Fryer. 8. Move the Lid Slider to the "Air Fry/Stovetop". Select the "Air Fry" mode for cooking. 9. Air-fry at 200°C for 4 minutes. 10. Remove and let it cool for just a minute before enjoying.
Per serving: Calories: 82; Fat: 10.9g; Sodium: 354mg; Carbs: 20.5g; Fiber: 4.1g; Sugar: 8.2g; Protein 6g

Ham Polenta Muffins

Prep Time: 10 minutes | Cook Time: 8 minutes | Serves: 8

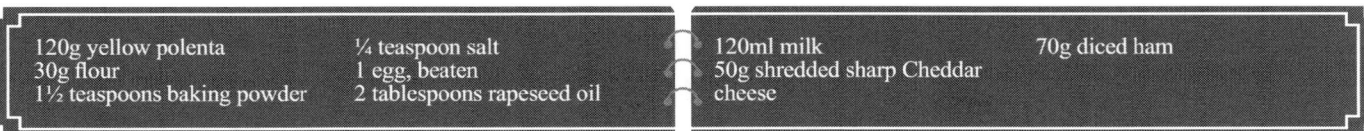

120g yellow polenta
30g flour
1½ teaspoons baking powder
¼ teaspoon salt
1 egg, beaten
2 tablespoons rapeseed oil
120ml milk
50g shredded sharp Cheddar cheese
70g diced ham

1. Place the Cook & Crisp Basket in your Pressure Cooker Steam Fryer. 2. In a suitable bowl, stir the polenta, flour, baking powder, and salt. 3. Add egg, oil, and milk to dry recipe ingredients and mix well. 4. Stir in shredded cheese and diced ham. 5. Divide batter among the muffin cups. 6. Place 4 filled muffin cups in "cook & crisp basket". Put on the Smart Lid on top of the Ninja Foodi Steam Fryer. Move the Lid Slider to the "Air Fry/Stovetop". Select the "Air Fry" mode for cooking. Air-fry 200°C for around 5 minutes. 7. Reduce temperature to 165°C and cook for around 1 to 2 minutes or until toothpick inserted in center of muffin comes out clean. 8. Repeat to cook remaining muffins.
Per serving: Calories: 284; Fat: 9g; Sodium: 441mg; Carbs: 7g; Fiber: 4.6g; Sugar 5g; Protein 19g

Broccoli Quiche

Prep Time: 10 minutes | Cook Time: 4 minutes | Serves: 4

90g broccoli florets
125g chopped roasted red
peppers
140g grated mozzarella cheese
6 eggs
180g heavy cream
½ teaspoon salt
Black pepper

1. Place the Cook & Crisp Basket in your Pressure Cooker Steam Fryer. 2. Grease the Cook & Crisp Basket. Place the broccoli florets and roasted red peppers in the Cook & Crisp Basket and top with the grated Fontina cheese. 3. Mix the eggs and heavy cream in a suitable bowl. Season the beaten eggs with salt and black pepper. Pour the egg mixture over the cheese and vegetables and cover the basket with aluminum foil. Transfer the basket to the Ninja Foodi Pressure Steam Fryer. 4. Put on the Smart Lid on top of the Ninja Foodi Steam Fryer. 5. Move the Lid Slider to the "Air Fry/Stovetop". Select the "Air Fry" mode for cooking. 6. Air-fry at 180°C for around 60 minutes. Remove the aluminum foil for the last two minutes of cooking time. 7. Unmold the quiche onto a platter and cut it into slices to serve with a side salad or perhaps some air-fried potatoes.
Per serving: Calories: 221; Fat: 7.9g; Sodium: 704mg; Carbs: 6g; Fiber: 3.6g; Sugar 6g; Protein 18g

Hush Puffs

Prep Time: 10 minutes | Cook Time: 8 minutes | Serves: 20

240ml buttermilk
55g butter, melted
2 eggs
185g plain flour
240g polenta
65g sugar
1 teaspoon baking soda
1 teaspoon salt
4 spring onions, minced
Vegetable oil

1. Place the Cook & Crisp Basket in your Pressure Cooker Steam Fryer. 2. Mix the buttermilk, butter and eggs in a suitable mixing bowl. In a second bowl mix the flour, polenta, sugar, baking soda and salt. Add the dry recipe ingredients to the wet recipe ingredients, stirring just to mix. Stir in the minced spring onions and refrigerate the prepared batter for around 30 minutes. 3. Shape the prepared batter into 5 cm balls. Brush or grease the balls with oil. 4. Put on the Smart Lid on top of the Ninja Foodi Steam Fryer. 5. Move the Lid Slider to the "Air Fry/Stovetop". Select the "Air Fry" mode for cooking. 6. Air-fry the hush puffins in two batches at 180°C for around 8 minutes, turning them over after 6 minutes of the cooking process. 7. Serve warm with butter.
Per serving: Calories: 349; Fat: 2.9g; Sodium: 511mg; Carbs: 12g; Fiber: 3g; Sugar 8g; Protein 17g

Artichoke Pizza

Prep Time: 10 minutes | Cook Time: 18 minutes | Serves: 2

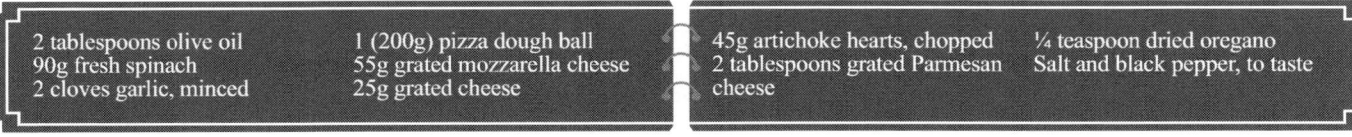

2 tablespoons olive oil
90g fresh spinach
2 cloves garlic, minced
1 (200g) pizza dough ball
55g grated mozzarella cheese
25g grated cheese
45g artichoke hearts, chopped
2 tablespoons grated Parmesan cheese
¼ teaspoon dried oregano
Salt and black pepper, to taste

1. Heat the oil in a suitable sauté pan on the stovetop. Add the spinach and half the garlic to the pan and sauté for a few minutes, until the spinach has wilted then transfer to a bowl. 2. Place the Cook & Crisp Basket in your Pressure Cooker Steam Fryer. 3. Line the Ninja Foodi Pressure Steam Fryer basket with aluminum. Brush the foil with oil. Shape the prepared dough into a circle and place it on top of the foil. 4. Brush the prepared dough with olive oil and transfer it into the Ninja Foodi Pressure Steam Fryer basket with the foil on the bottom. 5. Put on the Smart Lid on top of the Ninja Foodi Steam Fryer. 6. Move the Lid Slider to the "Air Fry/Stovetop". Cook the prepared pizza dough on "Air Fry" mode at 200°C for around 6 minutes. 7. Turn the prepared dough over, remove the aluminum foil and brush again with olive oil. Air-fry for 4 minutes. 8. Add the mozzarella and Fontina cheeses over the prepared dough. Top with the spinach and artichoke hearts. Sprinkle the Parmesan cheese and dried oregano on top and drizzle with olive oil. 9. Put on the Smart Lid on top of the Ninja Foodi Steam Fryer. Move the Lid Slider to the "Air Fry/Stovetop". Cook on "Air Fry" mode at 175°C for around 8 minutes, until the cheese has melted and is browned. 10. Serve.
Per serving: Calories: 372; Fat: 20g; Sodium: 891mg; Carbs: 29g; Fiber: 3g; Sugar 8g; Protein 17g

Sweet Potato Toast

Prep Time: 5 minutes | Cook Time: 8 minutes | Serves: 8

- 1 small sweet potato, cut into ¾ cm slices
- Oil for misting
- Cinnamon

1. Place the Cook & Crisp Basket in your Pressure Cooker Steam Fryer. 2. Spray both sides of sweet potato slices with oil. Sprinkle both sides with cinnamon to taste. 3. Place potato slices in "cook & crisp basket" in a single layer. 4. Put on the Smart Lid on top of the Ninja Foodi Steam Fryer. 5. Move the Lid Slider to the "Air Fry/Stovetop". Select the "Air Fry" mode for cooking. 6. Cook at 200°C for around 4 minutes. Turn and cook for around 4 more minutes until potato slices are barely fork tender.
Per serving: Calories: 284; Fat: 9g; Sodium: 441mg; Carbs: 7g; Fiber: 4.6g; Sugar 5g; Protein 19g

Pepper Bread

Prep Time: 10 minutes | Cook Time: 7 minutes | Serves: 8

- 18 cm round bread boule
- Olive oil
- 120g mayonnaise
- 2 tablespoons butter, melted
- 115g grated mozzarella
- 25g grated Parmesan cheese
- ½ teaspoon dried oregano
- 70g black olives, sliced
- 70g green olives, sliced
- 75g coarsely chopped roasted red peppers
- 2 tablespoons minced red onion
- Black pepper, to taste

1. Place the Cook & Crisp Basket in your Pressure Cooker Steam Fryer. 2. Cut the bread boule in half horizontally. If your bread boule has a rounded top, trim the top of the boule so that the top half will lie flat with the cut side facing up. Brush both sides of the boule halves with olive oil. 3. Place one half of the boule into the Ninja Foodi Pressure Steam Fryer basket with the center cut side facing down. 4. Put on the Smart Lid on top of the Ninja Foodi Steam Fryer. Move the Lid Slider to the "Air Fry/Stovetop". Select the "Air Fry" mode for cooking. 5. Air-fry at 185°C for around 2 minutes to toast the bread. Repeat with the other half of the bread boule. 6. Mix the mayonnaise, butter, mozzarella cheese, Parmesan cheese and dried oregano in a suitable bowl. Fold in the black and green olives, roasted red peppers and red onion and season with black pepper. Spread the cheese mixture over the untoasted side of the bread, covering the entire surface. 7. Put on the Smart Lid on top of the Ninja Foodi Steam Fryer. 8. Move the Lid Slider to the "Air Fry/Stovetop". Select the "Air Fry" mode for cooking. 9. Air Fry bread at 175°C for 5 minutes until the cheese is melted and browned. Repeat with the other half. Cut into slices and serve warm.
Per serving: Calories: 389; Fat: 11g; Sodium: 501mg; Carbs: 28.9g; Fiber: 4.6g; Sugar 8g; Protein 6g

Turkey Sausage Roll-Ups

Prep Time: 10 minutes | Cook Time: 24 minutes | Serves: 3

- 6 links turkey sausage
- 6 slices of white bread, crusts removed
- 2 eggs
- 120ml milk
- ½ teaspoon cinnamon
- ½ teaspoon vanilla extract
- 1 tablespoon butter, melted
- Icing sugar (optional)
- Maple syrup

1. Place the Cook & Crisp Basket in your Pressure Cooker Steam Fryer. 2. Place the sausage links in the Ninja Steam Fryer. 3. Put on the Smart Lid on top of the Ninja Foodi Steam Fryer. 4. Move the Lid Slider to the "Air Fry/Stovetop". Select the "Air Fry" mode for cooking. 5. Air-fry the sausage links at 195°C for 8 to 10 minutes, turning them a couple of times during the cooking process. 6. Roll each sausage link in a piece of bread, pressing the finished seam tightly to seal shut. 7. Mix the eggs, milk, cinnamon, and vanilla in a shallow dish. Dip the sausage rolls in the egg mixture and let them soak in the egg for around 30 seconds. Grease the bottom of the "cook & crisp basket" with oil and transfer the sausage rolls to the basket, seam side down. 8. Put on the Smart Lid on top of the Ninja Foodi Steam Fryer. 9. Move the Lid Slider to the "Air Fry/Stovetop". Select the "Air Fry" mode for cooking. 10. Air-fry the rolls at 185°C for around 9 minutes. Brush melted butter over the bread, flip the rolls over. Cook on the "Air Fry" mode for an additional 5 minutes. 11. Remove the French toast roll-ups from the basket and dust with icing sugar, if using. Serve with maple syrup and enjoy.
Per serving: Calories: 284; Fat: 9g; Sodium: 441mg; Carbs: 7g; Fiber: 4.6g; Sugar 5g; Protein 19g

Toast Sticks

Prep Time: 5 minutes | Cook Time: 5–7 minutes | Serves: 4

- 2 eggs
- 120ml milk
- ⅛ teaspoon salt
- ½ teaspoon pure vanilla extract
- 30g crushed cornflakes
- 6 slices sandwich bread, each slice cut into 4 strips
- Oil for misting or cooking spray
- Maple syrup or honey

1. Place the Cook & Crisp Basket in your Pressure Cooker Steam Fryer. 2. In a suitable bowl, beat eggs, milk, salt, and vanilla. 3. Place crushed cornflakes on a plate or in a shallow dish. 4. Dip bread strips in egg mixture, shake off excess, and roll in cornflake crumbs. 5. Spray both sides of bread strips with oil. 6. Place bread strips in "cook & crisp basket" in single layer. 7. Put on the Smart Lid on top of the Ninja Foodi Steam Fryer. 8. Move the Lid Slider to the "Air Fry/Stovetop". Select the "Air Fry" mode for cooking. 9. Air Fry the strips at 200°C for 5 to 7 minutes or until they're dark golden brown. 10. Repeat to cook remaining toast sticks. 11. Serve with maple syrup or honey for dipping.
Per serving: Calories: 282; Fat: 19g; Sodium: 354mg; Carbs: 15g; Fiber: 5.1g; Sugar 8.2g; Protein 12g

Classical Hard-Boiled Eggs

Prep time: 5 minutes | Cook time: 10 minutes | Serves: 4

5-15 eggs	240ml water

1. Pour the water into the Ninja Foodi XL Pressure Cooker Steam Fryer with SmartLid cooking pot and insert a Cook & Crisp Basket. Put the eggs in the basket. 2. Lock lid; move slider towards PRESSURE. Adjust pressure release valve in the SEAL position. Close pressure-release valve. The cooking temperature will default to HIGH, which is accurate. Set time to 5 minutes. Select START/STOP and start cooking. 3. When cooking is complete, let pressure release naturally for 5 minutes, then quick-release any remaining pressure by turning it into VENT position. 4. Transfer the eggs to the bowl of cold water. Wait 2-3 minutes. If you like, you can peel immediately.
Per Serving: Calories 116; Fat 8.4g; Sodium 542mg; Carbs 0.9g; Fiber 0.2g; Sugar 0.1g; Protein 9.1g

Chocolate Rolls

Prep Time: 10 minutes | Cook Time: 8 minutes | Serves: 6

1 (200g) tube of puff pastry	chocolate chunks	25g sliced almonds	Butter or oil
110g semi-sweet or bittersweet	1 egg white, beaten	Icing sugar, for dusting	

1. Unwrap the thawed puff pastry and separate it into triangles with the points facing away from you. Place a row of chocolate chunks along the bottom edge of the prepared pastry. 2. Roll the prepared pastry up around the chocolate and then place another row of chunks on the prepared pastry. Roll again and finish with one or two chocolate chunks. Be sure to leave the end free of chocolate so that it can adhere to the rest of the roll. 3. Brush the tops of the pastry with the beaten egg white and sprinkle the almonds on top, pressing them into the pastry so they adhere. 4. Place the Cook & Crisp Basket in your Pressure Cooker Steam Fryer. 5. Brush the bottom of the Ninja Foodi Pressure Steam Fryer basket with butter or oil and transfer the crescent rolls to the basket. 6. Put on the Smart Lid on top of the Ninja Foodi Steam Fryer. 7. Move the Lid Slider to the "Air Fry/Stovetop". Select the "Air Fry" mode for cooking. 8. Air-fry rolls at 175°C for 8 minutes. 9. Remove and let the pastries cool before dusting with icing sugar and serving.
Per serving: Calories: 372; Fat: 20g; Sodium: 891mg; Carbs: 29g; Fiber: 3g; Sugar 8g; Protein 17g

Pepperoni Cheese Pizza

Prep Time: 10 minutes | Cook Time: 18 minutes | Serves: 2

1 (200g) pizza dough ball	85g grated mozzarella cheese	peppers
Olive oil	70g thick sliced pepperoni	¼ teaspoon dried oregano
120g pizza sauce	50g sliced pickled hot banana	2 teaspoons honey

1. Place the Cook & Crisp Basket in your Pressure Cooker Steam Fryer. 2. Cut out a piece of foil the same size as the bottom of the Ninja Foodi Pressure Steam Fryer basket. Brush the foil circle with olive oil. Shape the prepared dough into a circle and place it on top of the foil. Dock the prepared dough by piercing it several times with a fork. Brush the prepared dough with olive oil and transfer it into the "cook & crisp basket" with the foil on the bottom. 3. Put on the Smart Lid on top of the Ninja Foodi Steam Fryer. Move the Lid Slider to the "Air Fry/Stovetop". Select the "Air Fry" mode for cooking. 4. Air-fry the plain pizza dough at 200°C for around 6 minutes. Turn the prepared dough over, remove the aluminum foil and brush again with olive oil. Air-fry for an additional 4 minutes. 5. Spread the pizza sauce on top of the prepared dough and sprinkle the mozzarella cheese over the sauce. Top with the pepperoni, pepper slices and dried oregano. 6. Put on the Smart Lid on top of the Ninja Foodi Steam Fryer. Move the Lid Slider to the "Air Fry/Stovetop". Select the "Air Fry" mode for cooking. Adjust the cooking temperature to 175°C. 7. Cook for around 8 minutes, until the cheese has melted and browned. Transfer the prepared pizza to a cutting board and drizzle with the honey. Slice and serve.
Per serving: Calories: 354; Fat: 10.9g; Sodium: 454mg; Carbs: 10g; Fiber: 3.1g; Sugar 5.2g; Protein 10g

Spinach- Rollups

Prep Time: 5 minutes | Cook Time: 8–9 minutes | Serves: 4

4 flour tortillas (18 cm size)	4 slices Swiss cheese	30g baby spinach leaves	4 slices turkey bacon

1. Place the Cook & Crisp Basket in your Pressure Cooker Steam Fryer. 2. On each tortilla, add one slice of cheese and 5–10g of spinach. 3. Roll up tortillas and wrap each with a strip of bacon. Secure each end with a toothpick. 4. Place rollups in "cook & crisp basket", leaving a little space in between them. 5. Put on the Smart Lid on top of the Ninja Foodi Steam Fryer. 6. Move the Lid Slider to the "Air Fry/Stovetop". Select the "Air Fry" mode for cooking. 7.Cook at 200°C for around 4 minutes. Turn and rearrange rollups (for more even cooking). Cook for around 4 to 5 minutes longer, until bacon is crisp.
Per serving: Calories: 372; Fat: 12.9g; Sodium: 414mg; Carbs: 11g; Fiber: 5g; Sugar 9g; Protein 11g

Breakfast Scotch Eggs

Prep Time: 10 minutes | Cook Time: 20–25 minutes | Serves: 4

2 tablespoons flour, extra for coating	4 hardboiled eggs, peeled	oil for misting or cooking spray	90g flour
455g breakfast sausage	1 raw egg	**Crumb Coating**	
	1 tablespoon water	80g panko breadcrumbs	

1. Mix flour with sausage and mix thoroughly. 2. Divide into 4 equal portions and mold each around a hardboiled egg so the sausage completely covers the egg. 3. In a suitable bowl, beat the raw egg and water. 4. Dip sausage-covered eggs in the remaining flour, then the egg mixture, then roll in the crumb coating. 5. Place the Cook & Crisp Basket in your Pressure Cooker Steam Fryer. 6. Put on the Smart Lid on top of the Ninja Foodi Steam Fryer. 7. Move the Lid Slider to the "Air Fry/Stovetop". Select the "Air Fry" mode for cooking. 8. Air Fry at 180°C for around 10 minutes. Spray eggs, turn, and spray other side. 9. Continue air frying for another 15 minutes or until sausage is well done.
Per serving: Calories: 289; Fat: 14g; Sodium: 791mg; Carbs: 8.9g; Fiber: 4.6g; Sugar 8g; Protein 16g

Baked Eggs

Prep Time: 10 minutes | Cook Time: 12 minutes | Serves: 1

1 teaspoon olive oil	oregano	Salt and black pepper	Fresh parsley, chopped
2 tablespoons finely chopped onion	Pinch crushed red pepper flakes	2 slices of bacon, chopped	
1 teaspoon chopped fresh	1 (350g) can crushed or diced tomatoes	2 large eggs	
		25g grated Cheddar cheese	

1. Start by making the tomato sauce. Preheat a suitable saucepan over medium heat on the stovetop. Add the olive oil and sauté the onion, oregano and pepper flakes for around 5 minutes. Add the tomatoes and bring to a simmer. Season with salt and black pepper. Cook for on a simmer for around 10 minutes. 2. Place the Cook & Crisp Basket in your Pressure Cooker Steam Fryer. 3. Meanwhile, place the prepared bacon in the "cook & crisp basket". 4. Put on the Smart Lid on top of the Ninja Foodi Steam Fryer. 5. Move the Lid Slider to the "Air Fry/Stovetop". Select the "Air Fry" mode for cooking. 6. Cook on the "Air Fry" mode at 200°C for 5 minutes, shaking the basket every once in a while. 7. When the bacon is almost crispy, remove it to a paper-towel lined plate and rinse out the Ninja Foodi Steam Fryer, draining away the bacon grease. 8. Transfer the tomato sauce to a shallow 18 cm pie dish. Crack the eggs on top of the sauce and scatter the cooked bacon back on top. Season with salt and black pepper and transfer the pie dish into the Ninja Foodi Pressure Steam Fryer basket. 9. Air-fry eggs at 200°C for 5 minutes until the eggs are almost cooked to your liking. Sprinkle cheese on top. Cook on the "Air Fry" mode for 2 minutes. 10. Sprinkle with a little chopped parsley and let the eggs cool for a few minutes.
Per serving: Calories: 289; Fat: 14g; Sodium: 791mg; Carbs: 8.9g; Fiber: 4.6g; Sugar 8g; Protein 16g

Walnut Apple Muffins

Prep Time: 10 minutes | Cook Time: 11 minutes | Serves: 8

125g flour	¼ teaspoon salt	1 egg	½ teaspoon vanilla extract
65g sugar	1 teaspoon cinnamon	4 tablespoons pancake syrup	30g chopped walnuts
1 teaspoon baking powder	¼ teaspoon ginger	4 tablespoons melted butter	30g diced apple
¼ teaspoon baking soda	¼ teaspoon nutmeg	185g unsweetened applesauce	

1. In a suitable bowl, stir flour, sugar, baking powder, baking soda, salt, cinnamon, ginger, and nutmeg. 2. In a suitable bowl, beat egg until frothy. Add syrup, butter, applesauce, and vanilla and mix well. 3. Place the Cook & Crisp Basket in your Pressure Cooker Steam Fryer. 4. Pour the prepared egg mixture into dry recipe ingredients and stir just until moistened. 5. Gently stir in nuts and diced apple. 6. Divide batter among the 8 muffin cups. 7. Place 4 muffin cups in "cook & crisp basket". 8. Put on the Smart Lid on top of the Ninja Foodi Steam Fryer. 9. Move the Lid Slider to the "Air Fry/Stovetop". Select the "Air Fry" mode for cooking. 10. Air fry at 165°C for around 9 to 11 minutes. 11. Repeat with remaining 4 muffins or until toothpick inserted in center comes out clean.
Per serving: Calories: 289; Fat: 14g; Sodium: 791mg; Carbs: 8.9g; Fiber: 4.6g; Sugar 8g; Protein 16g

Strawberry Morning Toast

Prep Time: 10 minutes | Cook Time: 8 minutes | Serves: 4

4 slices bread, 1 cm thick	Butter-flavored cooking spray	165g sliced strawberries	1 teaspoon sugar

1. Place the Cook & Crisp Basket in your Pressure Cooker Steam Fryer. 2. Grease one side of each bread slice with butter-flavored cooking spray. Lay slices sprayed side down. 3. Divide the strawberries among the bread slices. 4. Sprinkle evenly with the sugar and place in the Ninja Foodi Pressure Steam Fryer basket in a single layer. 5. Put on the Smart Lid on top of the Ninja Foodi Steam Fryer. 6. Move the Lid Slider to the "Air Fry/Stovetop". Select the "Air Fry" mode for cooking. 7. Air Fry toast at 200°C for 8 minutes. The bottom should look brown and crisp and the top should look glazed.
Per serving: Calories: 282; Fat: 19g; Sodium: 354mg; Carbs: 15g; Fiber: 5.1g; Sugar 8.2g; Protein 12g

Blueberry Morning Muffins

Prep Time: 10 minutes | Cook Time: 14 minutes | Serves: 8

155g flour	¼ teaspoon salt	120ml milk
100g sugar	80ml rapeseed oil	100g blueberries, fresh or frozen and thawed
2 teaspoons baking powder	1 egg	

1. In a suitable bowl, stir flour, sugar, baking powder, and salt. 2. In a separate bowl, mix cooking oil with egg, and milk and mix well. 3. Add egg mixture to dry recipe ingredients and stir just until moistened. 4. Gently stir in blueberries. 5. Spoon batter evenly into muffin cups. 6. Place the Cook & Crisp Basket in your Pressure Cooker Steam Fryer. 7. Place 4 muffin cups in "cook & crisp basket". 8. Put on the Smart Lid on top of the Ninja Foodi Steam Fryer. 9. Move the Lid Slider to the "Air Fry/Stovetop". Select the "Air Fry" mode for cooking. 10. Air fry at 165°C for around 12 to 14 minutes or until tops spring back when touched lightly. 11. Repeat previous step to cook remaining muffins.
Per serving: Calories: 219; Fat: 10g; Sodium: 891mg; Carbs: 22.9g; Fiber: 4g; Sugar 4g; Protein 13g

Mushroom Boat Eggs

Prep Time: 10 minutes | Cook Time: 10 minutes | Serves: 4

4 postulate rolls	½ teaspoon dried onion flakes	¼ teaspoon dried dill weed
1 teaspoon butter	4 eggs	¼ teaspoon dried parsley
25g diced fresh mushrooms	½ teaspoon salt	1 tablespoon milk

1. Place the Cook & Crisp Basket in your Pressure Cooker Steam Fryer. 2. Cut a small rectangle in the top of each roll and scoop out center, leaving 1 cm shell on the sides and bottom. 3. Place butter, mushrooms, and dried onion in the Cook & Crisp Basket. 4. Put on the Smart Lid on top of the Ninja Foodi Steam Fryer. Move the Lid Slider to the "Air Fry/Stovetop". Select the "Air Fry" mode for cooking. Cook at 200°C for around 1 minute. Stir and cook for 3 more minutes. 5. In a suitable bowl, beat the eggs, salt, dill, parsley, and milk. Pour mixture into basket with mushrooms. 6. Put on the Smart Lid on top of the Ninja Foodi Steam Fryer. 7. Move the Lid Slider to the "Air Fry/Stovetop". Select the "Air Fry" mode for cooking. 8. Air Fry the eggs at 200°C for 2 minutes. Stir. Continue cooking for around 3 or 4 minutes, stirring every minute, until eggs are scrambled to your liking. 9. Remove basket from Pressure Cooker Steam Fryer and fill rolls with scrambled egg mixture. 10. Place filled rolls in "cook & crisp basket". Put on the Smart Lid on top of the Ninja Foodi Steam Fryer. Move the Lid Slider to the "Air Fry/Stovetop". Select the "Air Fry" mode for cooking. Air Fry at 200°C for 2 to 3 minutes or until rolls are browned.
Per serving: Calories: 334; Fat: 12.9g; Sodium: 414mg; Carbs: 11g; Fiber: 5g; Sugar 9g; Protein 11g

Classical Poached Eggs

Prep time: 5 minutes | Cook time: 5 minutes | Serves: 4

Nonstick cooking spray	4 large eggs	

1. Lightly spray 4 cups of a 7-count silicone egg bite mold with the nonstick cooking spray. Crack each egg into a sprayed cup. 2. Pour 240ml water into the Ninja Foodi XL Pressure Cooker Steam Fryer with SmartLid cooking pot. Place the Deluxe Reversible Rack and carefully lower it into the pot. 3. Lock lid; move slider towards PRESSURE. Adjust pressure release valve in the SEAL position. Close pressure-release valve. The cooking temperature will default to HIGH, which is accurate. Set QUICK RELEASE and time to 5 minutes. Select START/STOP and start cooking. When cooking is complete, let pressure release quickly by turning it into VENT position. 4. Run a small rubber spatula or spoon around each egg and carefully remove it from the mold. The white should be cooked, but the yolk should be runny. 5. Serve immediately.
Per Serving: Calories 160; Fat 8.2g; Sodium 266mg; Carbs 12.6g; Fiber 7.1g; Sugar 4g; Protein 8.6g

Cheesy Bacon Muffins

Prep Time: 10 minutes | Cook Time: 9 minutes | Serves: 4

4 eggs	Olive oil	100g shredded cheddar cheese
Black pepper and salt	4 English muffins, split	4 slices ham or bacon

1. Place the Cook & Crisp Basket in your Pressure Cooker Steam Fryer. 2. Beat eggs and add black pepper and salt to taste. Spray the Cook & Crisp Basket with oil and add eggs. Put on the Smart Lid on top of the Ninja Foodi Steam Fryer. 3. Move the Lid Slider to the "Air Fry/Stovetop". Select the "Air Fry" mode for cooking. Cook at 200°C for around 2 minutes, stir, and continue cooking for around 3 or 4 minutes, stirring every minute, until eggs are scrambled to your preference. Remove the Cook & Crisp Basket. 4. Place bottom halves of English muffins in "cook & crisp basket". Take half of the shredded cheese and divide it among the muffins. Top each with a slice of ham and one-quarter of the eggs. Sprinkle remaining cheese on top of the eggs. Use a fork to press the cheese into the egg a little so it doesn't slip off before it melts. Transfer the basket to Pressure Cooker Steam Fryer. 5. Put on the Smart Lid on top of the Ninja Foodi Steam Fryer. 6. Move the Lid Slider to the "Air Fry/Stovetop". Select the "Air Fry" mode for cooking. 7. Air Fry at 180°C for around 1 minute. Add English muffin tops. Cook for around 2 to 4 minutes to heat through and toast the muffins.
Per serving: Calories: 221; Fat: 7.9g; Sodium: 704mg; Carbs: 6g; Fiber: 3.6g; Sugar 6g; Protein 18g

Omelet Cups

Prep time: 5 minutes | Cook time: 15 minutes | Serves: 2

- ½ teaspoon olive oil
- 3 eggs, beaten
- 240ml water
- Salt and freshly ground black pepper to taste
- 1 onion, chopped
- 1 jalapeño pepper, chopped

1. Prepare two ramekins by adding a drop of olive oil in each and rubbing the bottom and sides. In a medium bowl, whisk together the eggs, water, salt and black pepper until combined. Add the onion and jalapeño, stir. 2. Transfer egg mixture to the ramekins. Prepare the Ninja Foodi XL Pressure Cooker Steam Fryer with SmartLid by adding the water to the pot and placing the Deluxe Reversible Rack in it. Place the ramekins on the Deluxe Reversible Rack. 3. Lock lid; move slider towards PRESSURE. Adjust pressure release valve in the SEAL position. Close pressure-release valve. The cooking temperature will default to HIGH, which is accurate. Set the time for 5 minutes at HIGH pressure. Select START/STOP and start cooking. 4. When cooking is complete, let pressure release quickly by turning it into VENT position. 5. Carefully unlock the lid. Serve hot.

Per Serving: Calories 220; Fat 13g; Sodium 321mg; Carbs 6g; Fiber 4g; Sugar 2g; Protein 12g

Spinach-Feta Cups

Prep time: 5 minutes | Cook time: 15 minutes | Serves: 4

- 240ml water
- 30g chopped baby spinach
- 6 beaten eggs
- 1 chopped tomato
- 55g mozzarella cheese, shredded
- 60g feta cheese, cubed
- 1 teaspoon black pepper
- ½ teaspoon salt

1. Pour the water into the Ninja Foodi XL Pressure Cooker Steam Fryer with SmartLid cooking pot and insert a Deluxe Reversible Rack. Lay the spinach in two heatproof cups. 2. In a bowl, whisk together the eggs, mozzarella cheese, feta cheese, tomato, salt and pepper until combined. Pour the mixture into the cups, leaving ½ cm of head room. Place the cups on the Deluxe Reversible Rack. 3. Lock lid; move slider towards PRESSURE. Adjust pressure release valve in the SEAL position. Close pressure-release valve. The cooking temperature will default to HIGH, which is accurate. Set the time for 8 minutes at HIGH pressure. Select START/STOP and start cooking. 4. When cooking is complete, let pressure release quickly by turning it into VENT position. Carefully unlock the lid. 5. Serve the dish warm.

Per Serving: Calories 175; Fat 8g; Sodium 326mg; Carbs 5g; Fiber 0.2g; Sugar 0.3g; Protein 1g

Pepper Cups

Prep time: 5 minutes | Cook time: 15 minutes | Serves: 4

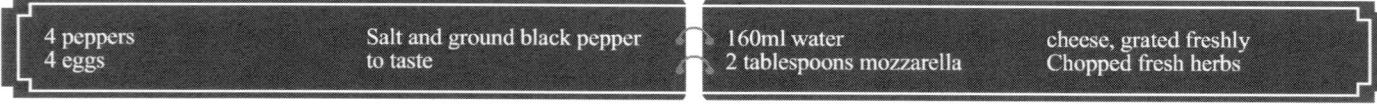

- 4 peppers
- 4 eggs
- Salt and ground black pepper to taste
- 160ml water
- 2 tablespoons mozzarella cheese, grated freshly
- Chopped fresh herbs

1. Cut the peppers ends to form about 4 cm high cup. Remove the seeds. Crack 1 egg into each pepper. Season with salt and black pepper. Cover each pepper with a piece of foil. 2. Pour the water into the Ninja Foodi XL Pressure Cooker Steam Fryer with SmartLid cooking pot and insert a Cook & Crisp Basket. Place the peppers in the basket. 3. Lock lid; move slider towards PRESSURE. Adjust pressure release valve in the SEAL position. Close pressure-release valve. The cooking temperature will default to HIGH, which is accurate. Set the time for 4 minutes at HIGH pressure. Select START/STOP and start cooking. 4. When cooking is complete, let pressure release quickly by turning it into VENT position. Carefully unlock the lid. Transfer the pepper cups onto serving plates. 5. Sprinkle with mozzarella cheese and chopped fresh herbs of your choice. Serve.

Per Serving: Calories 226; Fat 9.3g; Sodium 324mg; Carbs 8.7g; Fiber 3g; Sugar 2g; Protein 12.6g

Oat Muffins

Prep Time: 10 minutes | Cook Time: 12 minutes | Serves: 8

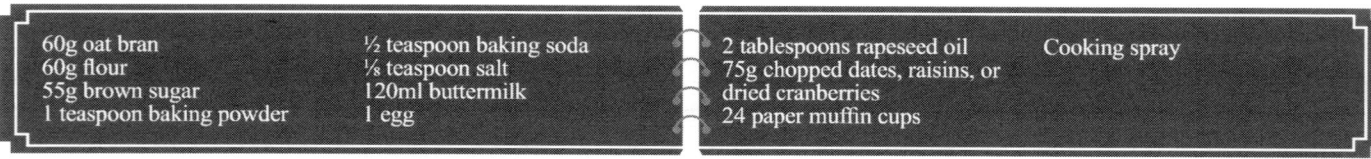

- 60g oat bran
- 60g flour
- 55g brown sugar
- 1 teaspoon baking powder
- ½ teaspoon baking soda
- ⅛ teaspoon salt
- 120ml buttermilk
- 1 egg
- 2 tablespoons rapeseed oil
- 75g chopped dates, raisins, or dried cranberries
- 24 paper muffin cups
- Cooking spray

1. Place the Cook & Crisp Basket in your Pressure Cooker Steam Fryer. 2. In a suitable bowl, mix the oat bran, flour, brown sugar, baking powder, baking soda, and salt. 3. In a suitable bowl, beat the buttermilk, egg, and oil. 4. Pour the prepared buttermilk mixture into bowl with dry recipe ingredients and stir just until moistened. Do not beat. 5. Gently stir in dried fruit. 6. Use baking cups to help muffins hold shape during baking. Grease them with cooking spray, place 4 sets of cups in "cook & crisp basket" at a time, and fill each one ¾ full of batter. 7. Put on the Smart Lid on top of the Ninja Foodi Steam Fryer. 8. Move the Lid Slider to the "Air Fry/Stovetop". Select the "Air Fry" mode for cooking. 9. Cook at 165°C for around 12 minutes, until top springs back when touched and toothpick inserted in center comes out clean. 10. Repeat for remaining muffins.

Per serving: Calories: 334; Fat: 10.9g; Sodium: 454mg; Carbs: 10g; Fiber: 3.1g; Sugar 5.2g; Protein 10g

Spelt with Berries and Walnuts

Prep time: 8 minutes | Cook time: 10 minutes | Serves: 6

175g spelt, rinsed and drained	¼ teaspoon salt	1 tablespoon pure maple syrup	6 tablespoons chopped walnuts
240ml unsweetened almond milk	½ teaspoon pure vanilla extract	220g fresh blueberries, raspberries, or strawberries	
	1 teaspoon ground cinnamon		

1. In the Ninja Foodi XL Pressure Cooker Steam Fryer with SmartLid cooking pot, combine the spelt, almond milk, 240ml of water, salt, vanilla, cinnamon, and maple syrup. 2. Lock lid; move slider towards PRESSURE. Adjust pressure release valve in the SEAL position. Close pressure-release valve. The cooking temperature will default to HIGH, which is accurate. Set time to 10 minutes. Select START/STOP and start cooking. 3. When cooking is complete, let pressure release naturally for about 10 minutes, then quickly release any remaining pressure by turning it into VENT position. 4. Unlock and remove the lid. Stir the spelt. Spoon into bowls and top each serving with 35 g of berries and 1 tablespoon of walnuts.
Per Serving: Calories 241; Fat 11g; Sodium 266mg; Carbs 5g; Fiber 4g; Sugar 2g; Protein 12g

Flaxseed Muffins

Prep Time: 15 minutes | Cook Time: 11 minutes | Serves: 8

60g 2 tablespoons whole-wheat flour	½ teaspoon baking powder	½ teaspoon pure vanilla extract	16 foil muffin cups, paper liners removed
25g oat bran	¼ teaspoon salt	50g grated carrots	Cooking spray
2 tablespoons flaxseed meal	½ teaspoon cinnamon	30g chopped pecans	
55g brown sugar	120ml buttermilk	30g chopped walnuts	
½ teaspoon baking soda	2 tablespoons melted butter	1 tablespoon pumpkin seeds	
	1 egg	1 tablespoon sunflower seeds	

1. Place the Cook & Crisp Basket in your Pressure Cooker Steam Fryer. 2. In a suitable bowl, stir the flour, bran, flaxseed meal, sugar, baking soda, baking powder, salt, and cinnamon. 3. In a suitable bowl, beat the buttermilk, butter, egg, and vanilla. Pour into the prepared flour mixture and stir just until dry recipe ingredients moisten. Do not beat. 4. Gently stir in carrots, pecans, nuts, and seeds. 5. Double up the foil cups so you have 8 total and spray with cooking spray. 6. Place 4 foil cups in "cook & crisp basket" and divide half the prepared batter among them. 7. Put on the Smart Lid on top of the Ninja Foodi Steam Fryer. 8. Move the Lid Slider to the "Air Fry/Stovetop". Select the "Air Fry" mode for cooking. 9. Air-fry at 165°C for around 9 to 11 minutes or until toothpick inserted in center comes out clean. 10. Repeat to cook remaining 4 muffins.
Per serving: Calories: 349; Fat: 2.9g; Sodium: 511mg; Carbs: 12g; Fiber: 3g; Sugar 8g; Protein 7g

Egg Quesadillas

Prep Time: 10 minutes | Cook Time: 12 minutes | Serves: 4

4 eggs	Oil for misting or cooking spray	4 tablespoons salsa	sliced
2 tablespoons skim milk		50g Cheddar cheese, grated	
Black pepper and salt	4 flour tortillas	½ small avocado, peeled and	

1. Beat eggs, milk, salt, and pepper. 2. Place the Cook & Crisp Basket in your Pressure Cooker Steam Fryer. 3. Spray the Cook & Crisp Basket with cooking spray and add egg mixture. 4. Put on the Smart Lid on top of the Ninja Foodi Steam Fryer. 5. Move the Lid Slider to the "Air Fry/Stovetop". Select the "Air Fry" mode for cooking. 6. Cook at 130°C for 8 to 9 minutes, stirring every 1 to 2 minutes, until eggs are scrambled to your liking. Remove and set aside. 7. Spray one side of each tortilla with oil or cooking spray. Flip over. 8. Divide eggs, salsa, cheese, and avocado among the tortillas, covering only half of each tortilla. 9. Fold tortilla in half and press down lightly. 10. Place 2 tortillas in "cook & crisp basket". 11. Put on the Smart Lid on top of the Ninja Foodi Steam Fryer. 12. Move the Lid Slider to the "Air Fry/Stovetop". Select the "Air Fry" mode for cooking. 13. Air fry at 200°C for 3 minutes or until cheese melts and outside feels crispy. Repeat with remaining two tortillas. 14. Cut each cooked tortilla into halves or thirds.
Per serving: Calories: 382; Fat: 10.9g; Sodium: 354mg; Carbs: 20.5g; Fiber: 4.1g; Sugar 8.2g; Protein 06g

Boiled Eggs

Prep time: 2 minutes | Cook time: 15 minutes | Serves: 9

9 large eggs	

1. Pour 240ml water into the Ninja Foodi XL Pressure Cooker Steam Fryer with SmartLid cooking pot and insert Deluxe Reversible Rack. Gently stand the eggs in the rack, fat ends down. 2. Lock lid; move slider towards PRESSURE. Adjust pressure release valve in the SEAL position. Close pressure-release valve. The cooking temperature will default to HIGH, which is accurate. Set time to 2 minutes. Select START/STOP and start cooking. 3. When cooking is complete, let pressure release naturally. 4. Using tongs, carefully remove the eggs from the pressure cooker. Peel or refrigerate the eggs when they are cool enough to handle.
Per Serving: Calories 210; Fat 12g; Sodium 174mg; Carbs 5g; Fiber 3g; Sugar 1g; Protein 8g

Porridge

Prep time: 5 minutes | Cook time: 20 minutes | Serves: 7

40g steel cut oats	70g wild rice	Ground cinnamon	walnuts
95g short-grain brown rice	40g polenta	Unsweetened almond milk	
75g millet	3 tablespoons ground flaxseed	Berries	
75g barley	½ teaspoon salt	Sliced almonds or chopped	

1. In the Ninja Foodi XL Pressure Cooker Steam Fryer with SmartLid cooking pot, combine the oats, brown rice, millet, barley, wild rice, polenta, flaxseed, salt, and 1.9L of water. 2. Lock lid; move slider towards PRESSURE. Adjust pressure release valve in the SEAL position. Close pressure-release valve. The cooking temperature will default to HIGH, which is accurate. Set time to 20 minutes. Select START/STOP and start cooking. 3. When cooking is complete, let pressure release naturally for about 10 minutes, then quickly release any remaining pressure by turning it into VENT position. 4. Once the pin drops, unlock and remove the lid. Stir. 5. Serve with any combination of cinnamon, almond milk, berries, and nuts.
Per Serving: Calories 251; Fat 16g; Sodium 235mg; Carbs 6g; Fiber 3g; Sugar 2g; Protein 11g

Tropical Oats

Prep time: 5 minutes | Cook time: 5 minutes | Serves: 4

80g steel cut oats	480ml coconut water or water	1 (5 cm) vanilla bean, scraped (seeds and pod)	35g chopped unsalted macadamia nuts
240ml unsweetened almond milk	190g frozen chopped peaches	Ground cinnamon	
	120g frozen mango chunks		

1. In the Ninja Foodi XL Pressure Cooker Steam Fryer with SmartLid cooking pot, combine the oats, almond milk, coconut water, peaches, mango chunks, and vanilla bean seeds and pod. Stir well. 2. Lock lid; move slider towards PRESSURE. Adjust pressure release valve in the SEAL position. Close pressure-release valve. The cooking temperature will default to HIGH, which is accurate. Set time to 3 minutes. Select START/STOP and start cooking. 3. When cooking is complete, let pressure release naturally for about 10 minutes, then release quickly any remaining pressure by turning it into VENT position. Unlock and remove the lid. 4. Discard the vanilla bean pod and stir well. 5. Spoon the oats into 4 bowls. Top each serving with a sprinkle of cinnamon and 1 tablespoon of the macadamia nuts.
Per Serving: Calories 220; Fat 14g; Sodium 211mg; Carbs 5g; Fiber 2g; Sugar 1g; Protein 11g

Smoked Salmon and Veggie Quiche Cups

Prep time: 15 minutes | Cook time: 15 minutes | Serves: 2

Nonstick cooking spray	2 tablespoons finely chopped onion	and boneless), chopped	¼ teaspoon dried dill
4 asparagus spears, cut into 1 cm pieces	75g smoked salmon (skinless	3 large eggs	Pinch ground white pepper
		2 tablespoons low-fat milk	

1. Pour 360ml water into the Ninja Foodi XL Pressure Cooker Steam Fryer with SmartLid cooking pot and insert Deluxe reversible rack. 2. Lightly spray the bottom and sides of the ramekins with nonstick cooking spray. Divide the asparagus, onion, and salmon between the ramekins. 3. In a measuring cup with a spout, whisk together the eggs, milk, dill, and white pepper. Pour half of the egg mixture into each ramekin. Loosely cover the ramekins with aluminum foil. 4. Carefully place the ramekins inside the pot on the rack. 5. Lock lid; move slider towards PRESSURE. Adjust pressure release valve in the SEAL position. Close pressure-release valve. The cooking temperature will default to HIGH, which is accurate. Set time to 15 minutes. Select START/STOP and start cooking. When cooking is complete, let pressure release quickly by turning it into VENT position. 6. Carefully remove the ramekins from the pot. Cool, covered, for 5 minutes. 7. Run a small silicone spatula or a knife around the edge of each ramekin. Invert each quiche onto a small plate and serve.
Per Serving: Calories 240; Fat 8g; Sodium 235mg; Carbs 6g; Fiber 3g; Sugar 1g; Protein 12g

Soft Eggs

Prep time: 5 minutes | Cook time: 5 minutes | Serves: 2

4 eggs	2 English muffins, toasted	to taste
240ml water	Salt and ground black pepper	

1. Prepare the Ninja Foodi XL Pressure Cooker Steam Fryer with SmartLid cooking pot by adding the water to the pot and insert the Cook & Crisp Basket. Put the eggs in the basket. 2. Lock lid; move slider towards STEAMCRISP. Select STEAM & BAKE, set temperature to 200°C, and set time to 4 minutes. Press START/STOP to begin cooking. 3. When cooking is complete, transfer the eggs to the bowl of cold water. Wait 2 to 3 minutes. Peel the eggs. 4. Serve one egg per half of toasted English muffin. Sprinkle with salt and pepper to taste.
Per Serving: Calories 160; Fat 11.8g; Sodium 255mg; Carbs 9.6g; Fiber 3.9g; Sugar 2g; Protein 7.6g

Delightful Eggs

Prep time: 5 minutes | Cook time: 5 minutes | Serves: 4

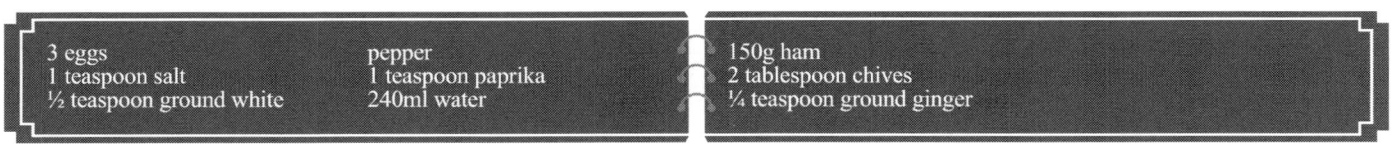

3 eggs	pepper	150g ham
1 teaspoon salt	1 teaspoon paprika	2 tablespoon chives
½ teaspoon ground white	240ml water	¼ teaspoon ground ginger

1. Beat the eggs into the small ramekins. Season with the salt, pepper, and paprika. Prepare the Ninja Foodi XL Pressure Cooker Steam Fryer with SmartLid cooking pot by adding the water to the pot and placing the Deluxe Reversible Rack on top. Place the ramekins on the Deluxe Reversible Rack. 2. Lock lid; move slider towards STEAMCRISP. Select STEAM & BAKE, set temperature to 175°C, and set time to 4 minutes. Press START/STOP to begin cooking. Meanwhile, chop the ham and chives and combine the ingredients together. Add ground ginger and stir the mixture. Transfer the mixture to the serving plates. 3. When cooking is complete, carefully unlock the lid. 4. Serve the eggs over the ham mixture.
Per Serving: Calories 221; Fat 14g; Sodium 221mg; Carbs 6g; Fiber 4g; Sugar 1g; Protein 11g

Traditional French Eggs

Prep time: 5 minutes | Cook time: 15 minutes | Serves: 4

½ teaspoon olive oil	4 slices bacon	4 tablespoon chives, chopped
4 eggs	Salt to taste	240ml water

1. Prepare the ramekins by adding a drop of olive oil in each and rubbing the bottom and sides. Crack an egg in each, add a bacon slice on top, season with salt and top each with chives. 2. Pour the water into the Ninja Foodi XL Pressure Cooker Steam Fryer with SmartLid cooking pot and insert a Cook & Crisp Basket. Place the ramekins in the basket. 3. Lock lid; move slider towards PRESSURE. Adjust pressure release valve in the SEAL position. Close pressure-release valve. The cooking temperature will default to HIGH, which is accurate. Set QUICK RELEASE and time to 8 minutes. Select START/STOP and start cooking. 4. When cooking is complete, let pressure release quickly by turning it into VENT position. 5. Serve immediately.
Per Serving: Calories 200; Fat 5g; Sodium 269mg; Carbs 4g; Fiber 1g; Sugar 1g; Protein 5g

Cheesy Meaty Sausage Frittata

Prep time: 5 minutes | Cook time: 35 minutes | Serves: 2

360ml water	4 beaten eggs	25g cheddar cheese, grated	Salt and ground black pepper
1 tablespoon butter	2 tablespoons sour cream	90g cooked sausage meat	to taste

1. Prepare the Ninja Foodi XL Pressure Cooker Steam Fryer with SmartLid by adding the water to the pot and placing the Deluxe Reversible Rack on top. 2. Grease 15-18 cm soufflé dish with butter. In a bowl, whisk together the eggs and sour cream until combined. 3. Add the cheese, sausage, salt and pepper, stir well. Pour into the dish and wrap tightly with foil all over. 4. Place the dish on the Deluxe Reversible Rack, close and secure the lid. 5. Lock lid; move slider towards PRESSURE. Adjust pressure release valve in the SEAL position. Close pressure-release valve. The cooking temperature will default to HIGH, which is accurate. Set the time for 17 minutes at LOW pressure. Select START/STOP and start cooking. 6. When cooking is complete, let pressure release quickly by turning it into VENT position. 7. Carefully unlock the lid. Serve.
Per Serving: Calories 374; Fat 31.7g; Sodium 287mg; Carbs 7g; Fiber 3g; Sugar 1g; Protein 18.7g

Jelly stuffed Muffins

Prep Time: 10 minutes | Cook Time: 7-8 minutes | Serves: 4

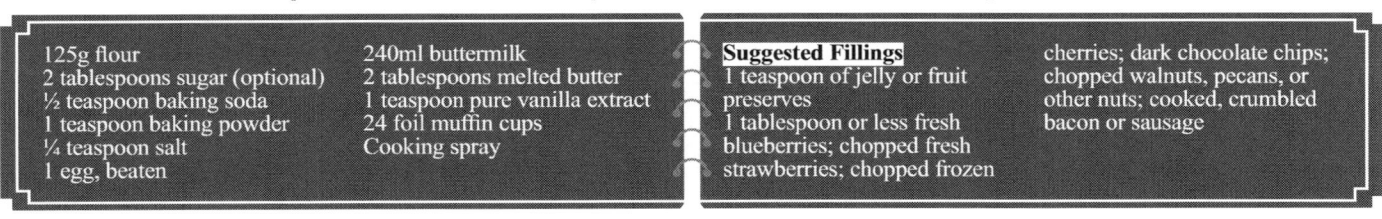

125g flour	240ml buttermilk	**Suggested Fillings**	cherries; dark chocolate chips;
2 tablespoons sugar (optional)	2 tablespoons melted butter	1 teaspoon of jelly or fruit	chopped walnuts, pecans, or
½ teaspoon baking soda	1 teaspoon pure vanilla extract	preserves	other nuts; cooked, crumbled
1 teaspoon baking powder	24 foil muffin cups	1 tablespoon or less fresh	bacon or sausage
¼ teaspoon salt	Cooking spray	blueberries; chopped fresh	
1 egg, beaten		strawberries; chopped frozen	

1. In a suitable bowl, stir flour, optional sugar, baking soda, baking powder, and salt. 2. In a suitable bowl, mix egg, buttermilk, butter, and vanilla. Mix well. 3. Pour egg mixture into dry recipe ingredients and stir to mix well but don't over beat. 4. Place the Cook & Crisp Basket in your Pressure Cooker Steam Fryer. 5. Double up the muffin cups and remove the paper liners from the top cups. Grease the foil cups with cooking spray. 6. Place 6 sets of muffin cups in "cook & crisp basket". Pour just enough batter into each cup to cover the bottom. Sprinkle with desired filling. Pour the prepared batter to cover the filling and fill the cups about ¾ full. 7. Put on the Smart Lid on top of the Ninja Foodi Steam Fryer. 8. Move the Lid Slider to the "Air Fry/Stovetop". Select the "Air Fry" mode for cooking. 9. Air Fry at 165°C for around 7 to 8 minutes. 10. Repeat to cook the remaining 6 pancake muffins.
Per serving: Calories: 219; Fat: 10g; Sodium: 891mg; Carbs: 22.9g; Fiber: 4g; Sugar 4g; Protein 13g

Healthy Blueberry Oat Mini Muffins

Prep time: 12 minutes | Cook time: 10 minutes | Serves: 7

- 40g rolled oats
- 30g whole wheat pastry flour or white whole wheat flour
- ½ tablespoon baking powder
- ½ teaspoon ground cardamom or ground cinnamon
- ⅛ teaspoon salt
- 2 large eggs
- 120g plain Greek yogurt
- 2 tablespoons pure maple syrup
- 2 teaspoons extra-virgin olive oil
- ½ teaspoon vanilla extract
- 75 g frozen blueberries

1. In a large bowl, stir together the oats, flour, baking powder, cardamom, and salt. 2. In a medium bowl, whisk together the eggs, yogurt, maple syrup, oil, and vanilla. 3. Add the egg mixture to oat mixture and stir just until combined. Gently fold in the blueberries. 4. Scoop the batter into each cup of the egg bite mold. 5. Pour 240ml water into the Ninja Foodi XL Pressure Cooker Steam Fryer with SmartLid cooking pot. Place the egg in Deluxe Reversible Rack and lower it into the pot. 6. Lock lid; move slider towards PRESSURE. Adjust pressure release valve in the SEAL position. Close pressure-release valve. The cooking temperature will default to HIGH, which is accurate. Set time to 10 minutes. Select START/STOP and start cooking. When cooking is complete, let pressure release naturally for about 10 minutes, then quickly release any remaining pressure by turning it into VENT position. 7. Lift the rack out of the pot and place on a cooling rack for 5 minutes. Invert the mold onto the cooling rack to release the muffins. 8. Serve the muffins warm or refrigerate or freeze.

Per Serving: Calories 278; Fat 20.9g; Sodium 145mg; Carbs 1.5g; Fiber 0.3g; Sugar 0.1g; Protein 20g

Cranberry Nutty Grits

Prep time: 10 minutes | Cook time: 10 minutes | Serves: 5

- 120g stone-ground grits or polenta
- 55g unsweetened dried cranberries
- Pinch salt
- 1 tablespoon unsalted butter or ghee
- 1 tablespoon half-and-half
- 25 g sliced almonds, toasted

1. In the Ninja Foodi XL Pressure Cooker Steam Fryer with SmartLid cooking pot, stir together the grits, cranberries, salt, and 360ml water. 2. Lock lid; move slider towards PRESSURE. Adjust pressure release valve in the SEAL position. Close pressure-release valve. The cooking temperature will default to HIGH, which is accurate. 3. Set QUICK RELEASE and time to 10 minutes. Select START/STOP and start cooking. 4. When cooking is complete, let pressure release quickly by turning it into VENT position. 5. unlock and remove the lid. 6. Add the butter and half-and-half. Stir until the mixture is creamy, adding more half-and-half if necessary. 7. Spoon into serving bowls and sprinkle with almonds.

Per Serving: Calories 107; Fat 10.9g; Sodium 471mg; Carbs 2.7g; Fiber 1.3g; Sugar 1g; Protein 1.2g

Delicious Mushroom Frittata

Prep time: 5 minutes | Cook time: 15 minutes | Serves: 2

- 4 beaten eggs
- 70g fresh mushrooms, chopped
- 60ml milk
- Salt and freshly ground black pepper to taste
- 100g sharp cheddar cheese, shredded and divided
- 240ml water

1. In a medium bowl, combine the eggs, mushrooms, milk, and salt and pepper, and 50 g cheese. Mix well. Divide mixture into jars evenly and sprinkle with remaining cheese. 2. Cover the jars with lids loosely. Pour the water into the Ninja Foodi XL Pressure Cooker Steam Fryer with SmartLid cooking pot and insert a Deluxe reversible rack. Place the jars on top of Deluxe reversible rack. 3. Lock lid; move slider towards PRESSURE. Adjust pressure release valve in the SEAL position. Close pressure-release valve. The cooking temperature will default to HIGH, which is accurate. Set the time for 3 minutes at HIGH pressure. Select START/STOP and start cooking. 4. When cooking is complete, let pressure release quickly by turning it into VENT position. Carefully unlock the lid. 5. Serve.

Per Serving: Calories 222; Fat 11g; Sodium 314mg; Carbs 6g; Fiber 4g; Sugar 1g; Protein 12g

Healthy Egg Muffins

Prep time: 5 minutes | Cook time: 15 minutes | Serves: 2

- 4 beaten eggs
- 4 bacon slices, cooked and crumbled
- 4 tablespoons cheddar cheese, shredded
- 1 green onion, chopped
- A pinch of salt
- 360ml water

1. In a medium bowl, whisk together eggs, bacon, cheese, onion and salt until combined. Divide the mixture into muffin cups. 2. Pour the water into the Ninja Foodi XL Pressure Cooker Steam Fryer with SmartLid cooking pot and insert the Cook & Crisp Basket. Place the muffin cups in the basket. 3. Lock lid; move slider towards PRESSURE. Adjust pressure release valve in the SEAL position. Close pressure-release valve. The cooking temperature will default to HIGH, which is accurate. Set the time for 8 minutes at HIGH pressure. Select START/STOP and start cooking. 4. When cooking is complete, let pressure release quickly by turning it into VENT position. Carefully unlock the lid. 5. Remove the Cook & Crisp Basket with muffins from the pot. Serve.

Per Serving: Calories 93; Fat 6.6g; Sodium 277mg; Carbs 1g; Fiber 0.2g; Sugar 0g; Protein 7.7g

Tomato and Spinach Healthy Breakfast

Prep time: 5 minutes | Cook time: 30 minutes | Serves: 6

360ml water	to the taste	90g baby spinach, chopped	25g parmesan, grated
12 beaten eggs	120ml milk	3 green onions, sliced	
Salt and ground black pepper	220g tomato, diced	4 tomatoes, sliced	

1. Prepare the Ninja Foodi XL Pressure Cooker Steam Fryer with SmartLid by adding the water to the cooking pot and placing the Deluxe Reversible Rack in it. 2. In a bowl, mix the eggs with salt, pepper and milk. Stir to combine. In a baking dish, mix diced tomato, spinach, and green onions. Pour the eggs mix over veggies, spread tomato slices on top. Sprinkle with parmesan. Place the dish on the Deluxe Reversible Rack. 3. Lock lid; move slider towards PRESSURE. Adjust pressure release valve in the SEAL position. Close pressure-release valve. The cooking temperature will default to HIGH, which is accurate. Set the time for 20 minutes at HIGH pressure. Select START/STOP and start cooking. 4. When cooking is complete, let pressure release quickly by turning it into VENT position. Carefully uncover the pot. 5. If you want a crisp top, slide under the broiler for a few minutes at the end.
Per Serving: Calories 191; Fat 6g; Sodium 298mg; Carbs 1.4g; Fiber 0.3g; Sugar 0.1g; Protein 31.2g

Baked Cheesy Hash Brown Bake

Prep time: 5 minutes | Cook time: 10 minutes | Serves: 4

6 slices bacon, chopped	8 beaten eggs	60ml milk	½ teaspoon ground black pepper
420g frozen hash browns	100g shredded cheddar cheese	½ teaspoon salt	

1. Move the slider towards "AIR FRY/STOVETOP" and set Ninja Foodi XL Pressure Cooker Steam Fryer with SmartLid to SEAR/SAUTÉ mode. Adjust the temperature to "Hi5" by using up arrow. Press START/STOP to begin cooking. Sauté the bacon until lightly crispy. 2. Add hash brown. Cook, stirring occasionally, for 2 minutes or until they start to thaw. Press the START/STOP button to stop the cooking program. In a medium bowl, whisk together the eggs, cheese, milk, salt and pepper. Pour the mixture over the hash browns. 3. Lock lid; move slider towards PRESSURE. Adjust pressure release valve in the SEAL position. Close pressure-release valve. The cooking temperature will default to HIGH, which is accurate. Set the time for 5 minutes at HIGH pressure. Select START/STOP and start cooking. 4. When cooking is complete, let pressure release quickly by turning it into VENT position. 5. Slice and serve.
Per Serving: Calories 230; Fat 15.9g; Sodium 300mg; Carbs 15.9g; Fiber 9.3g; Sugar 3g; Protein 10g

Mayo Egg Salad

Prep time: 5 minutes | Cook time: 15 minutes | Serves: 2

360ml water	4 large eggs	chopped	1 tablespoon mustard
6 russet potatoes, peeled and diced	240g mayonnaise	40g onion, chopped	Pinch of salt
	2 tablespoons fresh parsley,	1 tablespoon dill pickle juice	Pinch of ground black pepper

1. Pour the water into the Ninja Foodi XL Pressure Cooker Steam Fryer with SmartLid cooking pot and insert a Cook & Crisp Basket. Place the potatoes and eggs in the basket. 2. Lock lid; move slider towards PRESSURE. Adjust pressure release valve in the SEAL position. Close pressure-release valve. The cooking temperature will default to HIGH, which is accurate. Set the time for 5 minutes at HIGH pressure. Select START/STOP and start cooking. 3. When cooking is complete, let pressure release quickly by turning it into VENT position. Carefully unlock the lid. 4. Transfer the eggs to the bowl of cold water and cool for 2-3 minutes. In a medium bowl, combine the mayonnaise, parsley, onion, dill pickle juice, and mustard. Mix well. 5. Add salt and pepper. Peel and slice the eggs. Toss the potatoes and eggs in the bowl. Stir and serve.
Per Serving: Calories 271; Fat 14g; Sodium 288mg; Carbs 5g; Fiber 3g; Sugar 5g; Protein 11g

Eggs Dish

Prep time: 5 minutes | Cook time: 15 minutes | Serves: 6

240ml water	1 teaspoon mayo sauce	pepper	5g dill, chopped
8 eggs	1 tablespoon mustard	1 teaspoon minced garlic	
60g cream	1 teaspoon ground white	½ teaspoon sea salt	

1. Pour the water into the Ninja Foodi XL Pressure Cooker Steam Fryer with SmartLid cooking pot and insert a Cook & Crisp Basket. Place the eggs in the basket. 2. Lock lid; move slider towards PRESSURE. Adjust pressure release valve in the SEAL position. Close pressure-release valve. The cooking temperature will default to HIGH, which is accurate. Set the time for 5 minutes at HIGH pressure. Select START/STOP and start cooking. 3. When cooking is complete, let pressure release quickly by turning it into VENT position. Carefully unlock the lid. Transfer the eggs to the bowl of cold water and cool for 2-3 minutes. Peel the eggs, remove the egg yolks and mash them. 4. In a medium bowl, combine the cream, mayo sauce, mustard, pepper, garlic, salt and mashed egg yolks. Sprinkle the mixture with the dill. Mix well. Transfer the egg yolk mixture to the pastry bag. Fill the egg whites with the yolk mixture. 5. Serve.
Per Serving: Calories 142; Fat 10.2g; Sodium 269mg; Carbs 4.9g; Fiber 2.7g; Sugar 2g; Protein 8.8g

Ham Casserole

Prep time: 5 minutes | Cook time: 30 minutes | Serves: 4

6 beaten eggs	100g cheddar cheese, shredded	10g chives, chopped	240ml water
120g plain Greek yogurt	135g ham, diced	½ teaspoon black pepper	

1. In a medium bowl, whisk together eggs and yogurt until combined. Add the cheese, ham, chives, and pepper. Stir well. 2. Prepare the Ninja Foodi XL Pressure Cooker Steam Fryer with SmartLid by adding the water to the cooking pot and placing the Deluxe Reversible Rack in it. Pour the mixture into the heatproof bowl or cup. Place the bowl on the Deluxe Reversible Rack. 3. Lock lid; move slider towards PRESSURE. Adjust pressure release valve in the SEAL position. Close pressure-release valve. The cooking temperature will default to HIGH, which is accurate. Set the time to 20 minutes. Select START/STOP and start cooking. 4. When cooking is complete, let pressure release quickly by turning it into VENT position. Carefully unlock the lid. 5. Serve the dish warm.
Per Serving: Calories 221; Fat 9.4g; Sodium 321mg; Carbs 8.6g; Fiber 2g; Sugar 1g; Protein 14.2g

Cheesy Bacon Quiche

Prep time: 5 minutes | Cook time: 45 minutes | Serves: 2

240ml water	¼ teaspoon salt	70g diced ham	bacon
6 large eggs, beaten	⅛ teaspoon black pepper, ground	185g ground sausage, cooked	100g parmesan cheese
120ml almond or coconut milk		4 slices cooked and crumbled	2 large green onions, chopped

1. Pour the water into the Ninja Foodi XL Pressure Cooker Steam Fryer with SmartLid cooking pot and insert the Deluxe Reversible Rack. In a bowl, whisk together the eggs, milk, salt and pepper until combined. Add the ham, sausage, bacon, cheese and green onion and stir well. Cover the dish with foil and place on the Deluxe Reversible Rack. 2. Lock lid; move slider towards PRESSURE. Adjust pressure release valve in the SEAL position. Close pressure-release valve. The cooking temperature will default to HIGH, which is accurate. Set the time for 30 minutes. Select START/STOP and start cooking. 3. When cooking is complete, let pressure release naturally for 10 minutes, then quick-release any remaining pressure by turning it into VENT position. Remove the foil. 4. Serve. If you like a crisp top, you can sprinkle the dish with some additional cheese then slide under the broiler for a few minutes at the end.
Per Serving: Calories 224; Fat 12.3g; Sodium 458mg; Carbs 11.2g; Fiber 2g; Sugar 1g; Protein 14.2g

Tasty Tomato Spinach Quiche

Prep time: 5 minutes | Cook time: 40 minutes | Serves: 6

10-12 large eggs, beaten	Ground black pepper to taste	roughly chopped	3 tomato slices
120ml milk	75g baby spinach, diced	4 medium green onions, chopped	35g parmesan cheese, shredded
½ teaspoon salt	180g tomato, deseeded and		480ml water

1. In a large bowl, whisk together eggs, milk, salt, and pepper until combined. In a baking dish that can fit into the pot, combine the spinach, tomato and green onions. Add the egg mixture to the baking dish and stir well. Place 3 tomato slices on top and sprinkle with cheese. 2. Prepare the Ninja Foodi XL Pressure Cooker Steam Fryer with SmartLid cooking pot by adding the water to the pot and placing the Deluxe Reversible Rack in it. Put the baking dish on the rack. 3. Lock lid; move slider towards PRESSURE. Adjust pressure release valve in the SEAL position. Close pressure-release valve. The cooking temperature will default to HIGH, which is accurate. Set the time for 20 minutes. Select START/STOP and start cooking. 4. When cooking is complete, let pressure release naturally for 5 minutes, then quick-release any remaining pressure by turning it into VENT position. 5. Uncover the pot. Remove the dish from the pot. If desired, broil in the oven for a few minutes for a browned top. Serve.
Per Serving: Calories 242; Fat 13.1g; Sodium 269mg; Carbs 9.6g; Fiber 2g; Sugar 1g; Protein 14.2g

Fried PB&J Sandwich

Prep Time: 10 minutes | Cook Time: 6–8 minutes | Serves: 4

20g cornflakes, crushed	whole-grain, oversize bread	cm-thick slices	1 egg, beaten
25g shredded coconut	6 tablespoons peanut butter	6 tablespoons pineapple preserves	Oil for misting or cooking spray
8 slices oat nut bread or any	2 medium bananas, cut into 1		

1. Place the Cook & Crisp Basket in your Pressure Cooker Steam Fryer. 2. In a shallow dish, mix the coconut and cornflake crumbs. 3. For each sandwich, spread one bread slice with 1½ tablespoons of peanut butter. Top with banana slices. Spread another bread slice with 1½ tablespoons of preserves. 4. Using a pastry brush, brush top of sandwich with beaten egg. Sprinkle with about 1½ tablespoons of crumb coating, pressing it in to make it stick. Grease with oil. 5. Turn sandwich over and repeat to coat and grease the other side. 6. Put on the Smart Lid on top of the Ninja Foodi Steam Fryer. 7. Move the Lid Slider to the "Air Fry/Stovetop". Select the "Air Fry" mode for cooking. 8. Cook at 180°C for around 6 to 7 minutes or until coating is golden brown and crispy. If sandwich doesn't brown enough, spray with a little more oil and cook for another minutes. 9. Cut cooked sandwiches in half and serve warm.
Per serving: Calories: 372; Fat: 20g; Sodium: 891mg; Carbs: 29g; Fiber: 3g; Sugar 8g; Protein 7g

Pork Quiche Cups

Prep Time: 15 minutes | Cook Time: 20 minutes | Serves: 10

115g pork sausage	180ml milk	Cooking spray	grated
3 eggs	20 foil muffin cups	100g sharp Cheddar cheese,	

1. Divide sausage into 3 portions and shape each into a thin patty. 2. Place the Cook & Crisp Basket in your Pressure Cooker Steam Fryer. 3. Place patties in "cook & crisp basket". Put on the Smart Lid on top of the Ninja Foodi Steam Fryer. Move the Lid Slider to the "Air Fry/Stovetop". Select the "Air Fry" mode for cooking. Cook at 200°C for 6 minutes. 4. While sausage is cooking, prepare the egg mixture. A suitable measuring cup or bowl with a pouring lip works best. Mix the eggs and milk and mix until well blended. Set aside. 5. When sausage has cooked fully, remove patties from basket, drain well, and use a fork to crumble the meat into small pieces. 6. Double the foil cups into 10 sets. Remove paper liners from the top muffin cups and grease the foil cups with cooking spray. 7. Divide crumbled sausage among the 10 muffin cup sets. 8. Top each with grated cheese evenly among the cups. 9. Place 5 cups in "cook & crisp basket". 10. Pour egg mixture into each cup, filling until each cup is at least ⅔ full. 11. Put on the Smart Lid on top of the Ninja Foodi Steam Fryer. 12. Move the Lid Slider to the "Air Fry/Stovetop". Select the "Air Fry" mode for cooking. 13. Cook at 200°C for around 8 minutes and test for doneness. A knife inserted into the center shouldn't have any raw egg on it when removed. 14. If needed, cook 1 to 2 more minutes, until egg completely sets. 15. Repeat to cook the remaining quiches.
Per serving: Calories: 351; Fat: 7.9g; Sodium: 704mg; Carbs: 6g; Fiber: 3.6g; Sugar 6g; Protein 18g

Shakshuka

Prep time: 15 minutes | Cook time: 25 minutes | Serves: 4

2 tablespoons extra-virgin olive oil	black pepper	360g Marinara Sauce with Red Lentils or tomato-based pasta sauce	parsley
½ medium onion, chopped	½ tablespoon Italian seasoning		2 tablespoons freshly grated Parmesan cheese
½ teaspoon salt	2 teaspoons minced garlic	4 large eggs	
½ teaspoon freshly ground	100g Swiss chard (about 4 large stems and leaves)	1 tablespoon chopped fresh	

1. Separate stems from the leaves of the Swiss chard. Finely chop the stems. Stack the leaves, slice into thin strips, then chop. Set aside. 2. Move the slider towards "AIR FRY/STOVETOP" and Set Ninja Foodi XL Pressure Cooker Steam Fryer with SmartLid to SEAR/SAUTÉ mode. Adjust the temperature to "Hi5" by using up arrow. Press START/STOP to begin cooking. Once the pot is hot, pour in the olive oil. 3. Add the Swiss chard stems, pepper, onion, salt, and Italian seasoning to the pot, cook for 3 to 5 minutes or until the vegetables start to soften. 4. Add the Swiss chard leaves and garlic, and sauté for 2 more minutes. 5. Hit START/STOP to stop cooking. Add the pasta sauce and then let the pot cool for about 5 minutes. 6. Make 4 evenly spaced indentions in the sauce mixture. Carefully crack an egg in a custard cup, pour it into one of the indentions. Repeat with the remaining eggs. 7. Lock lid; move slider towards PRESSURE. Adjust pressure release valve in the SEAL position. Close pressure-release valve. The cooking temperature will default to HIGH, which is accurate. 8. Set time to 10 minutes. Select START/STOP and start cooking. 9. When cooking is complete, let pressure release quickly by turning it into VENT position. 10. Sprinkle with parsley and Parmesan. Serve immediately.
Per Serving: Calories 65; Fat 3.5g; Sodium 247mg; Carbs 4.9g; Fiber 0.3g; Sugar 0g; Protein 3.5g

Baked Egg

Prep time: 5 minutes | Cook time: 20 minutes | Serves: 4

1 teaspoon olive oil	420g frozen hash browns	8 beaten eggs	Salt to taste
6 slices of turkey bacon, cubed	100g cheddar cheese, shredded	120ml milk	

1. Move the slider towards "AIR FRY/STOVETOP" and set Ninja Foodi XL Pressure Cooker Steam Fryer with SmartLid to SEAR/SAUTÉ mode. Adjust the temperature to "Hi5" by using up arrow. 2. Press START/STOP to begin cooking and heat the oil. Add the slices of turkey bacon. Sauté for about 1-2 minutes until the bacon is browned. Press the START/STOP button to stop the cooking program. Layer the hash brown potatoes over the top of the bacon. 3. Sprinkle one half of the cheddar cheese over the potatoes. In a medium bowl, whisk together the eggs, milk and salt until well combined. Pour the mixture into the Ninja Foodi XL Pressure Cooker Steam Fryer with SmartLid cooking pot and sprinkle with the remaining half of the cheddar cheese. 4. Lock lid; move slider towards PRESSURE. Adjust pressure release valve in the SEAL position. Close pressure-release valve. The cooking temperature will default to HIGH, which is accurate. Set the time for 7 minutes at HIGH pressure. Select START/STOP and start cooking. 5. When cooking is complete, let pressure release quickly by turning it into VENT position. Carefully unlock the lid. 6. Taste and season more if necessary.
Per Serving: Calories 216; Fat 11g; Sodium 230mg; Carbs 5g; Fiber 3g; Sugar 1g; Protein 9g

Chapter 2 Vegetable and Sides Recipes

29	Maple Carrots with Dill	36	Szechuan Beans
29	Air-Fried Brown Mushrooms	36	Artichoke Stuffed Aubergine
29	Roasted Country-Style Vegetables	37	Roasted Red Hummus
29	Spicy Potatoes	37	Sesame Carrots
29	Roasted Broccoli	37	Lemony Brussels Sprout Salad
30	Swiss Chard and Vegetables in Cheesy Sauce	37	Crispy Parmesan Artichokes
30	Crispy Sweet Potatoes	38	Crispy Sweet Brussels Sprouts
30	Roasted Peppers	38	Green Beans Salad
30	Cheese Broccoli Pizza	38	Garlicky Roasted Cauliflower
31	The Baked Beans	38	Mushroom Cheese Loaf
31	Corn on The Cob	39	Pearl Couscous Salad
31	Air-Fried Brussels Sprouts	39	Garlicky Mashed Vegetables
31	Crusted Aubergine	39	Chow Relish
32	Bacon Red Cabbage with Cheese	39	Parmesan Green Bean Casserole
32	Delicious Mustard Potato Salad	40	Creamy Cauliflower Puree
32	Parmesan Cauliflower	40	Paprika Cabbage Steaks
32	Parsnips Meal	40	Gingered Potatoes
33	Garlic and Chive Fries	40	Creamy Corn
33	Potato Salad	41	Cranberry-citrus Sauce
33	Cheese Stuffed Peppers	41	Delicious Collard Greens
33	Cayenne Parsnip Burgers	41	Refreshing Steamed Broccoli
34	Colourful Ratatouille Stew	41	Turnips with Greens
34	Crusted Portobello Mushrooms	42	Buttery Egg Noodles
34	Broccoli Cranberry Salad	42	Szechuan-Style String Beans
34	Parmesan Potatoes	42	Creamy Corn with Crabmeat
35	Delicious Portobello Pot Roast	42	Mushroom 'Pot Roast'
35	Yellow Pea Curry	43	Green Rice
35	Colourful Burgundy Mushrooms	43	Colourful Vegetable Rice
36	Fried Beans	43	Savoury Beans
36	Lemony Broccoli Salad	43	Warm Lentils

Maple Carrots with Dill

Prep time: 10 minutes | Cook time: 5 minutes | Serves: 6

| 455g carrots, peeled and diced large | 1 tablespoon minced fresh dill
1 tablespoon pure maple syrup | 1 tablespoon ghee
½ teaspoon sea salt | 240ml water |

1. Add all ingredients to the cooking pot. 2. Lock lid; move slider towards PRESSURE. Adjust pressure release valve in the SEAL position. Close pressure-release valve. The cooking temperature will default to HIGH, which is accurate. Set time to 5 minutes. Select START/STOP and start cooking. When cooking is complete, let pressure release naturally. 3. Transfer to a serving dish and serve warm.
Per Serving: Calories 79; Fat 2g; Sodium 332mg; Carbs 12g; Fiber 2g; Sugar 4g; Protein 4g

Air-Fried Brown Mushrooms

Prep Time: 10 minutes | Cook Time: 9 minutes | Serves: 4

| 455g brown mushrooms, quartered | 2 tablespoons sesame oil
1 tablespoon tamari sauce | 1 garlic clove, pressed
Sea salt and black pepper, to | taste |

1. Place the Cook & Crisp Basket in your Pressure Cooker Steam Fryer. 2. Toss the mushrooms with the remaining ingredients. Toss until coated on all sides. 3. Arrange the mushrooms in the Ninja Foodi Pressure Steam Fryer basket. 4. Put on the Smart Lid on top of the Ninja Foodi Steam Fryer. 5. Move the Lid Slider to the "Air Fry/Stovetop". Select the "Air Fry" mode for cooking. 6. Cook your mushrooms at 200°C for about 7 minutes, shaking the basket halfway through the cooking time. 7. Serve.
Per serving: Calories: 349; Fat: 2.9g; Sodium: 511mg; Carbs: 12g; Fiber: 3g; Sugar 8g; Protein 7g

Roasted Country-Style Vegetables

Prep Time: 10 minutes | Cook Time: 20 minutes | Serves: 4

| 1 carrot, trimmed and sliced
1 parsnip, trimmed and sliced
1 celery stalk, trimmed and | sliced
1 onion, peeled and diced
2 tablespoons olive oil | Sea salt and black pepper, to taste
1 teaspoon red pepper flakes, | crushed |

1. Place the Cook & Crisp Basket in your Pressure Cooker Steam Fryer. 2. Toss all the recipe ingredients in the Ninja Foodi Pressure Steam Fryer basket. 3. Put on the Smart Lid on top of the Ninja Foodi Steam Fryer. 4. Move the Lid Slider to the "Air Fry/Stovetop". Select the "Air Fry" mode for cooking. 5. Cook your mushrooms at 195°C for about 15 minutes, shaking the basket halfway through the cooking time. 6. Serve.
Per serving: Calories: 281; Fat: 7.9g; Sodium: 704mg; Carbs: 6g; Fiber: 3.6g; Sugar 6g; Protein 18g

Spicy Potatoes

Prep Time: 10 minutes | Cook Time: 20 minutes | Serves: 4

| 455g potatoes, diced into bite-sized chunks | 1 tablespoon olive oil
Sea salt and black pepper, to | taste
1 teaspoon chili powder | |

1. Place the Cook & Crisp Basket in your Pressure Cooker Steam Fryer. 2. Toss the potatoes with the remaining recipe ingredients until well coated on all sides. 3. Arrange the potatoes in the Ninja Foodi Pressure Steam Fryer basket. 4. Put on the Smart Lid on top of the Ninja Foodi Steam Fryer. 5. Move the Lid Slider to the "Air Fry/Stovetop". Select the "Air Fry" mode for cooking. 6. Cook the potatoes at 200°C for about 13 minutes, shaking the basket halfway through the cooking time. 7. Serve.
Per serving: Calories: 289; Fat: 14g; Sodium: 791mg; Carbs: 18.9g; Fiber: 4.6g; Sugar 8g; Protein 6g

Roasted Broccoli

Prep Time: 10 minutes | Cook Time: 8 minutes | Serves: 3

| 340g broccoli florets
1½ tablespoons olive oil | 1 teaspoon garlic powder
½ teaspoon onion powder | ½ teaspoon mustard seeds
Sea salt and black pepper, to | taste
2 tablespoons pepitas, roasted |

1. Place the Cook & Crisp Basket in your Pressure Cooker Steam Fryer. 2. Toss the broccoli florets with the olive oil, garlic powder, onion powder, mustard seeds, salt, and black pepper. 3. Put on the Smart Lid on top of the Ninja Foodi Steam Fryer. 4. Move the Lid Slider to the "Air Fry/Stovetop". Select the "Air Fry" mode for cooking. 5. Cook the broccoli florets at 200°C for around 6 minutes, shaking the basket halfway through the cooking time. 6. Top with roasted pepitas and serve warm. Serve.
Per serving: Calories: 334; Fat: 7.9g; Sodium: 704mg; Carbs: 6g; Fiber: 3.6g; Sugar 6g; Protein 18g

Swiss Chard and Vegetables in Cheesy Sauce

Prep time: 15 minutes | Cook time: 15 minutes | Serves: 8

- 2 tablespoons olive oil
- 1 small onion, peeled and sliced
- 3 stalks celery, diced
- 2 medium carrots, peeled and sliced
- 4 cloves garlic, minced
- 1 head cauliflower, chopped into florets
- 455g Brussels sprouts, cleaned and halved
- 1 medium courgette, diced
- large
- 455g Swiss chard, cleaned, deveined, and chopped
- 240ml water
- 120g heavy cream
- 1 tablespoon flour
- 4 tablespoons butter
- 50g grated Parmesan cheese
- ⅛ teaspoon red pepper flakes

1. Move the slider towards "AIR FRY/STOVETOP" and set Ninja Foodi XL Pressure Cooker Steam Fryer with SmartLid to SEAR/SAUTÉ mode. Adjust the temperature to "Hi5" by using up arrow. Press START/STOP to begin cooking and heat oil. Add onion, celery, and carrots. Stir-fry 3–5 minutes until onions are translucent. Add garlic. Cook for an additional minute. 2. Add a layer of cauliflower, a layer of Brussels sprouts, a layer of courgette, and a layer of Swiss chard. Gently pour in 240ml water. 3. Lock lid; move slider towards PRESSURE. Adjust pressure release valve in the SEAL position. Close pressure-release valve. The cooking temperature will default to HIGH, which is accurate. Set time to 3 minutes. Select START/STOP and start cooking. 4. While vegetables are cooking, in a small bowl whisk together heavy cream and flour to create a slurry. Set aside. 5. When cooking is complete, let pressure release quickly by turning it into VENT position then unlock lid. Drain the vegetables, reserving liquid. 6. Add 2 tablespoons reserved cooking liquid, butter, Parmesan cheese, red pepper flakes, and heavy cream slurry to vegetables in the pot. Stir and let warm unlidded for 5 minutes until sauce thickens. Add more reserved cooking liquid if needed. 7. Transfer vegetables and sauce to a serving bowl and serve warm.

Per Serving: Calories 85; Fat 2.9g; Sodium 233mg; Carbs 9g; Fiber 4g; Sugar 2g; Protein 2.7g

Crispy Sweet Potatoes

Prep Time: 10 minutes | Cook Time: 40 minutes | Serves: 4

- 455g sweet potatoes, scrubbed and halved
- 3 tablespoons olive oil
- 1 teaspoon paprika
- Sea salt and black pepper, to taste

1. Place the Cook & Crisp Basket in your Pressure Cooker Steam Fryer. 2. Toss the halved sweet potatoes with the olive oil, paprika, salt, and black pepper. 3. Put on the Smart Lid on top of the Ninja Foodi Steam Fryer. 4. Move the Lid Slider to the "Air Fry/Stovetop". Select the "Air Fry" mode for cooking. 5. Cook the sweet potatoes at 195°C for around 35 minutes, shaking the basket halfway through the cooking time. 6. Taste and adjust the seasonings. Serve.

Per serving: Calories: 372; Fat: 20g; Sodium: 891mg; Carbs: 29g; Fiber: 3g; Sugar 8g; Protein 7g

Roasted Peppers

Prep Time: 10 minutes | Cook Time: 15 minutes | Serves: 3

- 455g peppers, seeded and halved
- 1 chili pepper, seeded
- 2 tablespoons olive oil
- Salt and black pepper, to taste
- 1 teaspoon granulated garlic

1. Place the Cook & Crisp Basket in your Pressure Cooker Steam Fryer. 2. Toss the peppers with the remaining ingredients; place them in the cook and crisp basket. 3. Put on the Smart Lid on top of the Ninja Foodi Steam Fryer. 4. Move the Lid Slider to the "Air Fry/Stovetop". Select the "Air Fry" mode for cooking. 5. Cook the peppers at 200°C for about 15 minutes, shaking the basket halfway through the cooking time. 6. Taste, adjust the seasonings and serve at room temperature. Serve.

Per serving: Calories: 270; Fat: 10.9g; Sodium: 454mg; Carbs: 10g; Fiber: 3.1g; Sugar 5.2g; Protein 10g

Cheese Broccoli Pizza

Prep Time: 10 minutes | Cook Time: 30 minutes | Serves: 1

- 265g broccoli rice, steamed
- 50g parmesan cheese, grated
- 1 egg
- 3 tablespoon low-carb Alfredo sauce
- 55g mozzarella cheese, grated

1. Place the Cook & Crisp Basket in your Pressure Cooker Steam Fryer. 2. Drain the broccoli rice and mix with the parmesan cheese and egg in a suitable bowl, mixing well. 3. Cut a piece of parchment paper the size of the base of the basket. Using a spoon, place four equal-sized amounts of the broccoli mixture on the paper. And press each part into the shape of a pizza crust. You may have to complete this part in two batches. Transfer the parchment to the Cook & Crisp Basket. 4. Put on the Smart Lid on top of the Ninja Foodi Steam Fryer. 5. Move the Lid Slider to the "Air Fry/Stovetop". Select the "Air Fry" mode for cooking. 6. Air Fry broccoli at 185°C. Cook for 5 minutes. When the crust is firm, flip over. Cook for an additional 2 minutes. 7. Pour the sauce and mozzarella cheese on top of the crusts. Cook for an additional 7 minutes until the sauce and cheese melt. 8. Serve hot.

Per serving: Calories: 295; Fat: 12.9g; Sodium: 414mg; Carbs: 11g; Fiber: 5g; Sugar 9g; Protein 11g

The Baked Beans

Prep time: 10 minutes | Cook time: 40 minutes | Serves: 6

455g dried pinto beans (not canned), rinsed and drained	1 large Vidalia (sweet) onion, diced	80g ketchup	1 teaspoon ground mustard powder
1.9L ham or chicken stock or water	1 tablespoon Worcestershire sauce	80g barbecue sauce	¼ teaspoon allspice (or cinnamon if you don't have allspice in your cupboard)
2 tablespoons salted butter	110g molasses	65g dark-brown sugar	
455g thick-cut bacon, diced	105g maple syrup	3 tablespoons tomato paste	
		1 tablespoon Dijon mustard	
		2 teaspoons liquid smoke	

1. Place the beans and the stock or water in the Ninja Foodi XL Pressure Cooker Steam Fryer with SmartLid cooking pot. Lock lid; move slider towards PRESSURE. Adjust pressure release valve in the SEAL position. Close pressure-release valve. The cooking temperature will default to HIGH, which is accurate. Set time to 25 minutes. Select START/STOP and start cooking. When cooking is complete, let pressure release naturally for about 25 minutes, then quickly release any remaining pressure by turning it into VENT position. Hit START/STOP to turn the pot off. 2. Carefully remove the liner pot and pour the beans into a colander, rinse with cool water, and set aside. Return the liner pot to the Ninja Foodi XL Pressure Cooker Steam Fryer—no need to clean it. 3. Move the slider towards "AIR FRY/STOVETOP" and set Ninja Foodi XL Pressure Cooker Steam Fryer with SmartLid to SEAR/SAUTÉ mode. Adjust the temperature to "Hi5" by using up arrow. Press START/STOP to begin cooking, and add the butter. Once melted, add the bacon and sauté, stirring occasionally, until nice and crispy, about 10 minutes. Set aside the cooked bacon in a paper towel–lined bowl, reserving the bacon grease in the pot. 4. Sauté the onion, stirring occasionally, in the bacon grease for 5 minutes, until beginning to soften. Add the Worcestershire sauce and scrape up any caked-on bacon grease. 5. Add the molasses, maple syrup, ketchup, barbecue sauce, brown sugar, tomato paste, Dijon mustard, liquid smoke, mustard powder, and allspice to the pot and stir until fully combined. 6. Gently stir the cooked beans and bacon into the sauce, tossing and coating until well combined. Serve with basically any savory dish!

Per Serving: Calories 85; Fat 3.1g; Sodium 278mg; Carbs 0.9g; Fiber 0.3g; Sugar 0.1g; Protein 12.9g

Corn on The Cob

Prep Time: 10 minutes | Cook Time: 10 minutes | Serves: 2

2 ears of corn, husked and halved	2 tablespoons Chinese chili oil	2 tablespoons fresh coriander, chopped
	Sea salt and red pepper, to taste	

1. Place the Cook & Crisp Basket in your Pressure Cooker Steam Fryer. 2. Toss the ears of corn with the oil, salt, and red pepper. Arrange the ears of corn in the Cook and crisp basket. 3. Put on the Smart Lid on top of the Ninja Foodi Steam Fryer. 4. Move the Lid Slider to the "Air Fry/Stovetop". Select the "Air Fry" mode for cooking. 5. Cook the ears of Corn at 200°C for about 6 minutes, tossing them halfway through the cooking time. 6. Garnish the ears of Corn with the fresh coriander. Serve.

Per serving: Calories: 382; Fat: 7.9g; Sodium: 704mg; Carbs: 6g; Fiber: 3.6g; Sugar 6g; Protein 38g

Air-Fried Brussels Sprouts

Prep Time: 10 minutes | Cook Time: 15 minutes | Serves: 3

340g Brussels sprouts, trimmed	1 teaspoon red pepper flakes, crushed	Salt and black pepper, to taste
1 tablespoon butter, melted		

1. Place the Cook & Crisp Basket in your Pressure Cooker Steam Fryer. 2. Toss the trimmed Brussels sprouts with the butter and spices until they are well coated on all sides; then, arrange the Brussels sprouts in the Ninja Foodi Pressure Steam Fryer basket. 3. Put on the Smart Lid on top of the Ninja Foodi Steam Fryer. 4. Move the Lid Slider to the "Air Fry/Stovetop". Select the "Air Fry" mode for cooking. 5. Cook the Brussels sprouts at 195°C for around 10 minutes, shaking the basket halfway through the cooking time. 6. Serve warm and enjoy!

Per serving: Calories: 184; Fat: 5g; Sodium: 441mg; Carbs: 17g; Fiber: 4.6g; Sugar 5g; Protein 9g

Crusted Aubergine

Prep Time: 10 minutes | Cook Time: 13 minutes | Serves: 3

Salt and black pepper, to taste	2 eggs	50g bread crumbs
60g plain flour	340g aubergine, sliced	

1. Place the Cook & Crisp Basket in your Pressure Cooker Steam Fryer. 2. In a shallow bowl, mix the salt, black pepper, and flour. Mix the eggs in the second bowl, and place the breadcrumbs in the third bowl. 3. Dip the aubergine slices in the flour mixture, then in the whisked eggs; finally, roll the aubergine slices over the breadcrumbs until they are well coated on all sides. 4. Arrange the aubergine in the Ninja Foodi Pressure Steam Fryer basket. 5. Put on the Smart Lid on top of the Ninja Foodi Steam Fryer. 6. Move the Lid Slider to the "Air Fry/Stovetop". Select the "Air Fry" mode for cooking. 7. Cook the aubergine at 200°C for about 13 minutes, shaking the basket halfway through the cooking time. 8. Serve.

Per serving: Calories: 219; Fat: 10g; Sodium: 891mg; Carbs: 22.9g; Fiber: 4g; Sugar 4g; Protein 13g

Bacon Red Cabbage with Cheese

Prep time: 10 minutes | Cook time: 20 minutes | Serves: 4

1 tablespoon olive oil	1 small apple, peeled, cored, and diced	240ml chicken stock	90g crumbled goat cheese
1 small onion, peeled and diced	445g chopped red cabbage	120ml apple cider vinegar	
3 slices bacon, diced		½ teaspoon sea salt	

1. Move the slider towards "AIR FRY/STOVETOP" and set Ninja Foodi XL Pressure Cooker Steam Fryer with SmartLid to SEAR/SAUTÉ mode. Adjust the temperature to "Hi5" by using up arrow. Press START/STOP to begin cooking. Heat olive oil. Add the onion and sauté for 3–5 minutes until translucent. Add bacon and stir-fry an additional 3 minutes until the bacon starts to crisp. Toss in apple and cabbage. Add stock and vinegar. 2. Lock lid; move slider towards PRESSURE. Adjust pressure release valve in the SEAL position. Close pressure-release valve. The cooking temperature will default to HIGH, which is accurate. Set time to 10 minutes. Select START/STOP and start cooking. When cooking is complete, let pressure release quickly by turning it into VENT position. 3. Using a slotted spoon, transfer ingredients to a serving plate. Let cool for 10 minutes. 4. Toss in salt and garnish with goat cheese. Serve warm.
Per Serving: Calories 26; Fat 0.6g; Sodium 123mg; Carbs 3.4g; Fiber 0g; Sugar 0g; Protein 1.4g

Delicious Mustard Potato Salad

Prep time: 10 minutes | Cook time: 5 minutes | Serves: 8

455g (about 5 medium) red potatoes, cut in 1 cm cubes	240ml water	80g peeled and chopped onion	½ teaspoon ground black pepper
120ml stock	24g mayonnaise	1 tablespoon dill relish	
3 large eggs	1 teaspoon apple cider vinegar	¼ teaspoon fine sea salt	
8–10 ice cubes	1 tablespoon yellow mustard	¼ teaspoon celery salt	
	60g chopped celery	½ teaspoon smoked paprika	

1. Place potatoes in the cooking pot. Add stock. Nestle the eggs in the potatoes. 2. Lock lid; move slider towards PRESSURE. Adjust pressure release valve in the SEAL position. Close pressure-release valve. The cooking temperature will default to HIGH, which is accurate. Set time to 5 minutes. Select START/STOP and start cooking. When cooking is complete, let pressure release quickly by turning it into VENT position. Unlock lid. 3. Transfer eggs to an iced water bath by placing 8–10 ice cubes in a medium bowl filled with about 240ml water leaving enough room to add eggs. Drain potatoes and set aside. 4. In a medium bowl, combine mayonnaise, vinegar, yellow mustard, celery, onion, dill relish, salt, celery salt, smoked paprika, and black pepper. Peel eggs and dice. Add to mayonnaise mixture. Add potatoes. Carefully toss. 5. Refrigerate lidded until ready to serve chilled.
Per Serving: Calories 382; Fat 0.6g; Sodium 711mg; Carbs 62.6g; Fiber 12g; Sugar 14g; Protein 62.5g

Parmesan Cauliflower

Prep Time: 10 minutes | Cook Time: 15 minutes | Serves: 4

455g cauliflower florets	1 teaspoon smoked paprika	taste
2 tablespoons olive oil	Sea salt and black pepper, to	100g parmesan cheese, grated

1. Place the Cook & Crisp Basket in your Pressure Cooker Steam Fryer. 2. Mix the cauliflower florets with the olive oil and spices. Mix until they are well coated on all sides. 3. Arrange the cauliflower florets in the Ninja Foodi Pressure Steam Fryer basket. 4. Put on the Smart Lid on top of the Ninja Foodi Steam Fryer. 5. Move the Lid Slider to the "Air Fry/Stovetop". Select the "Air Fry" mode for cooking. 6. Cook the cauliflower florets at 200°C for about 13 minutes, shaking the basket halfway through the cooking time. 7. Toss the warm cauliflower florets with cheese. Serve.
Per serving: Calories: 295; Fat: 10.9g; Sodium: 354mg; Carbs: 20.5g; Fiber: 4.1g; Sugar 8.2g; Protein 06g

Parsnips Meal

Prep Time: 10 minutes | Cook Time: 10 minutes | Serves: 4

455g parsnips, trimmed	1 teaspoon Herbs de province	Sea salt and black pepper, to
1 tablespoon olive oil	1 teaspoon cayenne pepper	taste

1. Place the Cook & Crisp Basket in your Pressure Cooker Steam Fryer. 2. Toss the parsnip with the olive oil and spices until they are well coated on all sides; then, arrange the parsnip in the Ninja Foodi Pressure Steam Fryer basket. 3. Put on the Smart Lid on top of the Ninja Foodi Steam Fryer. 4. Move the Lid Slider to the "Air Fry/Stovetop". Select the "Air Fry" mode for cooking. 5. Cook the parsnip at 195°C for around 10 minutes, shaking the basket halfway through the cooking time. 6. Serve.
Per serving: Calories: 282; Fat: 7.9g; Sodium: 704mg; Carbs: 6g; Fiber: 3.6g; Sugar 6g; Protein 18g

Garlic and Chive Fries

Prep time: 5 minutes | Cook time: 10 minutes | Serves: 4

120ml chicken stock	3 cloves garlic, minced	½ teaspoon ground black pepper	chives
530g cubed sweet potatoes	1 teaspoon paprika	1 tablespoon chopped fresh	
2 tablespoons ghee	1 teaspoon sea salt		

1. Place the Cook & Crisp Basket into your Ninja Foodi XL Pressure Cooker Steam Fryer with SmartLid cooking pot. Pour in chicken stock. Add potatoes to the Cook & Crisp Basket. 2. Lock lid; move slider towards PRESSURE. Adjust pressure release valve in the SEAL position. Close pressure-release valve. The cooking temperature will default to HIGH, which is accurate. Set time to 5 minutes. Select START/STOP and start cooking. When cooking is complete, let pressure release naturally for about 10 minutes, then quickly release any remaining pressure by turning it into VENT position. 3. Remove potatoes and Cook & Crisp Basket from the pot. Set potatoes aside. Discard stock. 4. Move the slider towards "AIR FRY/STOVETOP" and set Ninja Foodi XL Pressure Cooker Steam Fryer with SmartLid to SEAR/SAUTÉ mode. Adjust the temperature to "Hi5" by using up arrow. Press START/STOP to begin cooking. 5. Heat ghee. Add the potatoes and stir-fry for 3–5 minutes until browned. Add garlic and heat an additional minute. Transfer potatoes to a bowl and toss with paprika, salt, and pepper. 6. Garnish with chives and serve warm.
Per Serving: Calories 30; Fat 1.9g; Sodium 269mg; Carbs 2.4g; Fiber 1.9g; Sugar 0.9g; Protein 1.6g

Potato Salad

Prep time: 10 minutes | Cook time: 20 minutes | Serves: 6

5 large raw eggs in their shells	1 tablespoon apple cider vinegar	1½ teaspoons celery seed	into small pieces
480g mayonnaise	1 tablespoon Dijon mustard	1 bunch spring onions, thinly sliced	100g shredded Cheddar cheese
320g sweet relish	1 tablespoon yellow mustard	10g fresh dill, roughly chopped	
2 tablespoons Russian or Thousand Island salad dressing	½ teaspoon paprika	6 strips of cooked bacon, diced	

1. Pour 240ml water in the Ninja Foodi XL Pressure Cooker Steam Fryer with SmartLid cooking pot, followed by a Cook & Crisp Basket holding the potatoes and eggs. Lock lid; move slider towards PRESSURE. Adjust pressure release valve in the SEAL position. Close pressure-release valve. The cooking temperature will default to HIGH, which is accurate. Set time to 6 minutes. Select START/STOP and start cooking. When cooking is complete, let pressure release quickly by turning it into VENT position. 2. Meanwhile, make the dressing. In a mixing bowl, stir together the mayonnaise, relish, salad dressing, vinegar, mustards, paprika, celery seed, spring onions, and dill. Set aside in the fridge until ready to use. 3. Prepare an ice bath by filling a large bowl halfway with ice and water. 4. Once the cooking is finished, remove the Cook & Crisp Basket from the pot and immediately transfer the eggs to the ice bath and let them cool for 90 seconds. Drain the potatoes in a colander if you didn't use a basket. Allow the potatoes to cool for 10–20 minutes. Peel the eggs and coarsely chop them. 5. Once the potatoes have cooled down a bit, add them to a large serving bowl, topped with the dressing along with the egg, bacon, and cheese and gently toss until fully coated. 6. Place in the fridge to cool and set for 3–4 hours before serving.
Per Serving: Calories 256; Fat 12g; Sodium 311mg; Carbs 6g; Fiber 4g; Sugar 2g; Protein 14g

Cheese Stuffed Peppers

Prep Time: 10 minutes | Cook Time: 13 minutes | Serves: 3

3 peppers, seeded and halved	1 small onion, chopped	Sea salt and black pepper, to taste	240g tomato sauce
1 tablespoon olive oil	2 garlic cloves, minced		50g cheddar cheese, shredded

1. Place the Cook & Crisp Basket in your Pressure Cooker Steam Fryer. 2. Toss the peppers with the oil; place them in the cook and crisp basket. 3. Mix the onion, garlic, salt, black pepper, and tomato sauce. Spoon the sauce into the pepper halves. 4. Put on the Smart Lid on top of the Ninja Foodi Steam Fryer. 5. Move the Lid Slider to the "Air Fry/Stovetop". Select the "Air Fry" mode for cooking. 6. Cook the peppers at 200°C for about 10 minutes. Top the peppers with the cheese. Continue to cook for around 5 minutes more. 7. Serve.
Per serving: Calories: 289; Fat: 14g; Sodium: 791mg; Carbs: 18.9g; Fiber: 4.6g; Sugar 8g; Protein 6g

Cayenne Parsnip Burgers

Prep Time: 10 minutes | Cook Time: 20 minutes | Serves: 3

340g peeled parsnips, shredded	30g corn flour	1 teaspoon cayenne pepper	taste
30g plain flour	1 egg, beaten	Sea salt and black pepper, to	

1. Place the Cook & Crisp Basket in your Pressure Cooker Steam Fryer. 2. Mix all the recipe ingredients until everything is well mixed. Form the mixture into three patties. 3. Put on the Smart Lid on top of the Ninja Foodi Steam Fryer. 4. Move the Lid Slider to the "Air Fry/Stovetop". Select the "Air Fry" mode for cooking. 5. Cook the burgers at 195°C for about 15 minutes or until cooked through. 6. Serve.
Per serving: Calories: 184; Fat: 5g; Sodium: 441mg; Carbs: 17g; Fiber: 4.6g; Sugar 5g; Protein 9g

Colourful Ratatouille Stew

Prep time: 15 minutes | Cook time: 30 minutes | Serves: 6

- 60ml extra-virgin olive oil
- 1 large Vidalia (sweet) onion, coarsely chopped
- 1 green pepper, cut into medium dice
- 1 red pepper, cut into medium dice
- 6 cloves garlic, minced or pressed
- 1 large aubergine, skin on, sliced into 1 cm disks and then quartered
- 1 large courgette, skin on, cut into ½ cm disks and then quartered
- 1 medium yellow (summer) squash, skin on, cut into 1/2 cm disks and then quartered
- 1 (360g) can diced tomatoes, drained
- 2 teaspoons Italian seasoning
- 1½ teaspoons herbs de Provence
- 1 teaspoon salt
- 1 teaspoon black pepper
- ½ teaspoon dried thyme
- 120ml vegetable stock or dry red wine (like a cabernet)
- 1 tablespoon Worcestershire sauce
- 1 (150g) can of tomato paste
- Grated Parmesan cheese, for serving

1. Move the slider towards "AIR FRY/STOVETOP" and set Ninja Foodi XL Pressure Cooker Steam Fryer with SmartLid to SEAR/SAUTÉ mode. Adjust the temperature to "Hi5" by using up arrow. Press START/STOP to begin cooking. Pour the oil into the cooking pot. Heat about 3 minutes, then add the onion and peppers and sauté, stirring, for about 3 minutes, until they begin to soften. Add the garlic and sauté for another minute. 2. Add the other vegetables along with the Italian seasoning, herbs de Provence, salt, black pepper, dried thyme, vegetable stock or wine, and Worcestershire sauce. 3. Lock lid; move slider towards PRESSURE. Adjust pressure release valve in the SEAL position. Close pressure-release valve. The cooking temperature will default to HIGH, which is accurate. Set time to 2 minutes. Select START/STOP and start cooking. When cooking is complete, let pressure release quickly by turning it into VENT position. 4. Stir in the tomato paste. Let stand for about 10 minutes before serving. Don't worry if it looks a little soupy—it will thicken as it cools down and the vegetables continue to absorb the stock. 5. Serve with grated Parmesan cheese, if desired.

Per Serving: Calories 139; Fat 3g; Sodium 433mg; Carbs 2g; Fiber 0.2g; Sugar 0.8g; Protein 24.2g

Crusted Portobello Mushrooms

Prep Time: 10 minutes | Cook Time: 10 minutes | Serves: 3

- 60g flour
- 2 eggs
- 100g seasoned breadcrumbs
- 1 teaspoon smoked paprika
- Sea salt and black pepper, to taste
- 340g Portobello mushrooms, sliced

1. Place the Cook & Crisp Basket in your Pressure Cooker Steam Fryer. 2. Place the flour in a plate. Mix the eggs in a shallow bowl. In a third bowl, whisk the breadcrumbs, paprika, salt, and black pepper. 3. Dip your mushrooms in the flour, then dunk them in the whisked eggs, and finally toss them in the breadcrumb mixture. Toss until well coated on all sides. 4. Put on the Smart Lid on top of the Ninja Foodi Steam Fryer. 5. Move the Lid Slider to the "Air Fry/Stovetop". Select the "Air Fry" mode for cooking. 6. Cook the mushrooms at 200°C for about 7 minutes, turning them halfway through the cooking time. 7. Serve.

Per serving: Calories: 221; Fat: 12.9g; Sodium: 414mg; Carbs: 11g; Fiber: 5g; Sugar 9g; Protein 11g

Broccoli Cranberry Salad

Prep Time: 10 minutes | Cook Time: 8 minutes | Serves: 3

- 340g broccoli florets
- 30g raw sunflower seeds
- 1 clove garlic, peeled and minced
- 1 small red onion, sliced
- 30g dried cranberries
- 60ml extra-virgin olive oil
- 2 tablespoons fresh lemon juice
- 1 tablespoon Dijon mustard
- Sea salt and black pepper, to taste

1. Place the Cook & Crisp Basket in your Pressure Cooker Steam Fryer. 2. Place the broccoli florets in the greased "cook & crisp basket". 3. Put on the Smart Lid on top of the Ninja Foodi Steam Fryer. 4. Move the Lid Slider to the "Air Fry/Stovetop". Select the "Air Fry" mode for cooking. 5. Cook the broccoli florets at 200°C for around 6 minutes, shaking the basket halfway through the cooking time. 6. Toss the broccoli florets with the remaining ingredients. Serve at room temperature.

Per serving: Calories: 122; Fat: 7.9g; Sodium: 704mg; Carbs: 6g; Fiber: 3.6g; Sugar: 6g; Protein 18g

Parmesan Potatoes

Prep Time: 10 minutes | Cook Time: 20 minutes | Serves: 3

- 340g potatoes, diced
- 1 tablespoon olive oil
- 1 teaspoon smoked paprika
- 1 teaspoon red pepper flakes, crushed
- Sea salt and black pepper, to taste
- 50g parmesan cheese, grated

1. Place the Cook & Crisp Basket in your Pressure Cooker Steam Fryer. 2. Mix the potatoes with the olive oil and spices until well coated on all sides. 3. Arrange the potatoes in the Ninja Foodi Pressure Steam Fryer basket. 4. Put on the Smart Lid on top of the Ninja Foodi Steam Fryer. 5. Move the Lid Slider to the "Air Fry/Stovetop". Select the "Air Fry" mode for cooking. 6. Cook the potatoes at 200°C for about 15 minutes, shaking the basket halfway through the cooking time. 7. Top the warm potatoes with cheese and serve immediately. Enjoy!

Per serving: Calories: 361; Fat: 10.9g; Sodium: 454mg; Carbs: 10g; Fiber: 3.1g; Sugar 5.2g; Protein 10g

Delicious Portobello Pot Roast

Prep time: 15 minutes | Cook time: 30 minutes | Serves: 8

2 tablespoons extra-virgin olive oil	sauce	1½ teaspoons dried parsley flakes	caps, stems removed
2 medium yellow onions, sliced into thick wedges	900g baby bella mushrooms, 450 g left whole and 450 g sliced	1½ teaspoons seasoned salt	1 bunch asparagus, tough ends removed
6 cloves garlic, sliced	120ml dry red wine	2 teaspoons black pepper	2 tablespoons corn flour
6 tablespoons salted butter	240ml mushroom stock or vegetable stock	1 teaspoon dried thyme	1 mushroom gravy packet
2 tablespoons Worcestershire		1 teaspoon dried rosemary	
		675g portobello mushroom	

1. Move the slider towards "AIR FRY/STOVETOP" and set Ninja Foodi XL Pressure Cooker Steam Fryer with SmartLid to SEAR/SAUTÉ mode. Adjust the temperature to "Hi5" by using up arrow. Press START/STOP to begin cooking. Heat the oil for 3 minutes, add the onions, and sauté for 3 minutes, until slightly softened. Add the garlic and cook for 1 minute more. 2. Add the butter and Worcestershire sauce and, once the butter is melted, add all the baby bella mushrooms and sauté for 5 minutes, until they begin to brown and cook down. 3. Pour the wine and stock over everything and add the parsley flakes, seasoned salt, black pepper, thyme, and rosemary. Stir well and then lay the portobello mushrooms on top, stacking them. 4. Gently place the asparagus on top of the mushrooms. 5. Lock lid; move slider towards PRESSURE. Adjust pressure release valve in the SEAL position. Close pressure-release valve. The cooking temperature will default to HIGH, which is accurate. Set time to 3 minutes. Select START/STOP and start cooking. When cooking is complete, let pressure release quickly by turning it into VENT position. 6. Meanwhile, stir the corn flour into 2 tablespoons of cold water to form a slurry and set aside. 7. Remove the asparagus and set aside. Using a slotted spoon and tongs, carefully transfer all the mushrooms to a serving dish and rest the asparagus beside them. 8. On the pot, press START/STOP and move the slider towards "AIR FRY/STOVETOP", set Ninja Foodi XL Pressure Cooker Steam Fryer with SmartLid to SEAR/SAUTÉ mode. Adjust the temperature to "Hi5" by using up arrow. Press START/STOP to begin cooking and bring the sauce to a simmer. Add the gravy packet and the corn flour slurry, and immediately stir until combined. Allow to simmer for 30 seconds, then hit START/STOP to turn off the pot and allow to sit for a minute. 9. Ladle the sauce over the mushrooms and serve with crusty bread.

Per Serving: Calories 270; Fat 12g; Sodium 444mg; Carbs 6g; Fiber 3g; Sugar 1g; Protein 17g

Yellow Pea Curry

Prep time: 5 minutes | Cook time: 40 minutes | Serves: 6

2 tablespoons salted butter	ginger	385g yellow split peas or yellow lentils, rinsed	1 teaspoon granulated sugar
1 red onion, diced	2 (350g) cans unsweetened coconut milk	2 tablespoons curry powder	1 teaspoon turmeric
6 cloves garlic, minced or pressed	120ml vegetable stock, plus more if desired after cooking	2 tablespoons garam masala	⅛ teaspoon cayenne pepper
1 tablespoon minced or pressed		1 tablespoon seasoned salt	200g baby spinach
			240g heavy cream

1. Move the slider towards "AIR FRY/STOVETOP" and set Ninja Foodi XL Pressure Cooker Steam Fryer with SmartLid to SEAR/SAUTÉ mode. Adjust the temperature to "Hi5" by using up arrow. Press START/STOP to begin cooking, place the butter in the cooking pot. 2. Once the butter's melted, add the onion and sauté until translucent, about 3 minutes. Add the garlic and ginger and sauté for 2 minutes longer. 3. Pour in the coconut milk and stock and deglaze (scrape) the bottom of the pot until nice and smooth. Add in the split peas, curry powder, garam masala, seasoned salt, sugar, turmeric, and cayenne pepper. Stir to combine. 4. Top off with the spinach, but do not stir—just let it rest on top. 5. Lock lid; move slider towards PRESSURE. Adjust pressure release valve in the SEAL position. Close pressure-release valve. The cooking temperature will default to HIGH, which is accurate. Set time to 15 minutes. Select START/STOP and start cooking. 6. When cooking is complete, let pressure release naturally for about 10 minutes, then quickly release any remaining pressure by turning it into VENT position. Remove the lid and stir in the cream. 7. Serve over rice, with naan, or on a bun.

Per Serving: Calories 263; Fat 14g; Sodium 547mg; Carbs 6g; Fiber 4g; Sugar 2g; Protein 15g

Colourful Burgundy Mushrooms

Prep time: 5 minutes | Cook time: 30 minutes | Serves: 8

100g ghee	mushrooms	1 teaspoon dried thyme	pepper
3 cloves garlic, halved	360ml dry red wine	1 tablespoon Dijon mustard	720ml beef stock
400g whole white mushrooms	1 teaspoon Worcestershire sauce	1 teaspoon ground celery seed	2 slices bacon
400g whole baby bella		½ teaspoon ground black	

1. Move the slider towards "AIR FRY/STOVETOP" and set Ninja Foodi XL Pressure Cooker Steam Fryer with SmartLid to SEAR/SAUTÉ mode. Adjust the temperature to "Hi5" by using up arrow. Press START/STOP to begin cooking. Add ghee and melt. Add garlic and mushrooms and toss to coat with butter. Stir-fry for 3 minutes until mushrooms start to get tender. Add red wine, and simmer for 5 minutes. 2. Place remaining ingredients into Ninja Foodi XL Pressure Cooker Steam Fryer with SmartLid cooking pot. 3. Lock lid; move slider towards PRESSURE. Adjust pressure release valve in the SEAL position. Close pressure-release valve. The cooking temperature will default to HIGH, which is accurate. Set time to 20 minutes. Select START/STOP and start cooking. When cooking is complete, let pressure release naturally. Discard bacon and garlic. 4. Using a slotted spoon, remove mushrooms and transfer to a serving bowl. Serve warm.

Per Serving: Calories 92; Fat 9g; Sodium 104mg; Carbs 2g; Fiber 0.2g; Sugar 0.1g; Protein 5g

Fried Beans

Prep time: 5 minutes | Cook time: 95 minutes | Serves: 6

- 60ml vegetable oil
- 1 large Spanish (or yellow) onion, diced
- 3 cloves garlic, minced or pressed
- 100g canned green chilies, with their juices
- 1.2L water or garlic stock
- 385 g dried pinto beans (not canned), rinsed and drained
- 1½ teaspoons salt, divided
- 3 bay leaves
- 1 teaspoon seasoned salt
- 305g crumbled feta cheese

1. Move the slider towards "AIR FRY/STOVETOP" and set Ninja Foodi XL Pressure Cooker Steam Fryer with SmartLid to SEAR/SAUTÉ mode. Adjust the temperature to "Hi5" by using up arrow. Press START/STOP to begin cooking. Pour the oil into the Ninja Foodi XL Pressure Cooker Steam Fryer. Heat for 3 minutes, then add the onion, garlic, and green chilies. Give it all a good stir and then let it cook, stirring occasionally, until softened and very fragrant, about 5 minutes. 2. Add the water or stock and stir, scraping up any browned bits from the bottom of the pot. Add the pinto beans, 1 teaspoon of the salt, and the bay leaves. 3. Lock lid; move slider towards PRESSURE. Adjust pressure release valve in the SEAL position. Close pressure-release valve. The cooking temperature will default to HIGH, which is accurate. Set time to 35 minutes. Select START/STOP and start cooking. When cooking is complete, let pressure release naturally for 30 minutes, then quick-release any remaining pressure by turning it into VENT position. 4. When the lid comes off, discard the bay leaves. Don't worry if the beans appear a little watery. Leaving everything in the pot, use a potato masher to mash the beans to the desired consistency. The starchy innards of the beans will thicken the dish, and the more/harder the mashing, the less chunky and smoother the beans will be. 5. Stir in the remaining ½ teaspoon of salt, seasoned salt, and feta cheese and serve.

Per Serving: Calories 172; Fat 6.9g; Sodium 302mg; Carbs 0.5g; Fiber 0g; Sugar 0g; Protein 25.6g

Lemony Broccoli Salad

Prep Time: 10 minutes | Cook Time: 15 minutes | Serves: 2

- 265g fresh broccoli florets
- 2 tablespoon coconut oil, melted
- 40g sliced spring onion
- ½ medium lemon, juiced

1. Place the Cook & Crisp Basket in your Pressure Cooker Steam Fryer. 2. Fill the broccoli florets on the Cook & Crisp Basket. Pour the melted coconut oil over the broccoli and add in the sliced spring onion. Toss together. Put the basket in the Ninja Foodi Pressure Steam Fryer. 3. Put on the Smart Lid on top of the Ninja Foodi Steam Fryer. 4. Move the Lid Slider to the "Air Fry/Stovetop". Select the "Air Fry" mode for cooking. 5. Air Fry at 195°C for 7 minutes, stirring at the halfway point. 6. Place the broccoli in a suitable bowl and drizzle the lemon juice over it.

Per serving: Calories: 221; Fat: 19g; Sodium: 354mg; Carbs: 15g; Fiber: 5.1g; Sugar 8.2g; Protein 12g

Szechuan Beans

Prep Time: 10 minutes | Cook Time: 9 minutes | Serves: 4

- 455g fresh green beans, trimmed
- 1 tablespoon sesame oil
- ½ teaspoon garlic powder
- 1 tablespoon soy sauce
- Sea salt and Szechuan pepper, to taste
- 2 tablespoons sesame seeds, toasted

1. Place the Cook & Crisp Basket in your Pressure Cooker Steam Fryer. 2. Mix the green beans with the sesame oil and garlic powder; then, arrange them in the Ninja Foodi Pressure Steam Fryer basket. 3. Put on the Smart Lid on top of the Ninja Foodi Steam Fryer. 4. Move the Lid Slider to the "Air Fry/Stovetop". Select the "Air Fry" mode for cooking. 5. Cook the green beans at 195°C for around 7 minutes; make sure to check the green beans halfway through the cooking time. 6. Toss the green beans with the remaining recipe ingredients and stir to mix well. Enjoy!

Per serving: Calories: 334; Fat: 7.9g; Sodium: 704mg; Carbs: 6g; Fiber: 3.6g; Sugar 6g; Protein 18g

Artichoke Stuffed Aubergine

Prep Time: 10 minutes | Cook Time: 35 minutes | Serves: 2

- 1 large aubergine
- ¼ medium yellow onion, diced
- 2 tablespoons red pepper, diced
- 30g spinach
- 45g artichoke hearts, chopped
- Cooking spray

1. Place the Cook & Crisp Basket in your Pressure Cooker Steam Fryer. 2. Slice the aubergine lengthwise and scoop out the flesh with a spoon, leaving a shell about 1 cm thick. Chop it up and set aside. 3. Set a suitable frying pan over a suitable heat and spritz with cooking spray. Cook the onions for about 3 to 5 minutes to soften. Then add the pepper, spinach, artichokes, and the flesh of aubergine. Fry for a further 5 minutes, then remove from the heat. 4. Scoop this mixture in equal parts into the aubergine shells and place each one in the basket. 5. Put on the Smart Lid on top of the Ninja Foodi Steam Fryer. 6. Move the Lid Slider to the "Air Fry/Stovetop". Select the "Air Fry" mode for cooking. 7. Cook for 20 minutes at 160°C until the aubergine shells are soft. Serve warm.

Per serving: Calories: 122; Fat: 7.9g; Sodium: 704mg; Carbs: 6g; Fiber: 3.6g; Sugar 6g; Protein 18g

Roasted Red Hummus

Prep time: 10 minutes | Cook time: 50 minutes | Serves: 6

- 200g dried chickpeas
- 840ml vegetable stock
- 6 cloves garlic, minced or pressed
- 1 bay leaf
- Juice of 1 lemon
- 3 tablespoons tahini (sesame paste)
- 2 tablespoons extra-virgin olive oil, plus more for drizzling
- 1 teaspoon cumin
- 1 teaspoon seasoned salt
- 1 teaspoon garlic salt
- 1 (175g) jar roasted red peppers, divided and juice reserved
- Any other of your favorite seasonings, to taste

1. Place the chickpeas in a large pot or mixing bowl, add about 960ml of hot water, and cover. Allow to soak at room temperature for 8 hours. 2. After soaking, drain and rinse the chickpeas in a strainer. Place them in the Ninja Foodi XL Pressure Cooker Steam Fryer with SmartLid cooking pot along with the stock, garlic, and bay leaf. 3. Lock lid; move slider towards PRESSURE. Adjust pressure release valve in the SEAL position. Close pressure-release valve. The cooking temperature will default to HIGH, which is accurate. Set time to 20 minutes. Select START/STOP and start cooking. When cooking is complete, let pressure release naturally for about 5 minutes, then quickly release any remaining pressure by turning it into VENT position. 4. Discard the bay leaf and reserve 120ml of the cooking liquid before straining the chickpeas. 5. Then in a food processor or blender, combine the chickpeas, lemon juice, tahini, olive oil, cumin, seasoned salt, garlic salt, half of the roasted red peppers and a few drops of the juice from the jar, and the reserved cooking liquid. Pulse and blend until creamy, scraping down the sides halfway through. Add your choice of seasoning to taste. 6. Cool in the refrigerator for 2 hours. Meanwhile, roughly chop the remaining chills for garnish. 7. When you are ready to serve, use a spoon to chisel a small pit in the center of the hummus and fill with the remaining red chilies. At the table, drizzle some olive oil over the top.

Per Serving: Calories 270; Fat 14g; Sodium 200mg; Carbs 6g; Fiber 1.3g; Sugar 0.9g; Protein 18g

Sesame Carrots

Prep Time: 10 minutes | Cook Time: 20 minutes | Serves: 3

- 340g carrots, trimmed and cut into sticks
- 2 tablespoons butter, melted
- Salt and white pepper, to taste
- 1 tablespoon sesame seeds, toasted

1. Place the Cook & Crisp Basket in your Pressure Cooker Steam Fryer. 2. Toss the carrots with the butter, salt, and white pepper; then, arrange them in the Ninja Foodi Pressure Steam Fryer basket. 3. Put on the Smart Lid on top of the Ninja Foodi Steam Fryer. 4. Move the Lid Slider to the "Air Fry/Stovetop". Select the "Air Fry" mode for cooking. 5. Cook the carrots at 195°C for around 15 minutes; make sure to check the carrots halfway through the cooking time. 6. Top the carrots with the sesame seeds. Serve.

Per serving: Calories: 382; Fat: 7.9g; Sodium: 704mg; Carbs: 6g; Fiber: 3.6g; Sugar: 6g; Protein: 18g

Lemony Brussels Sprout Salad

Prep Time: 10 minutes | Cook Time: 12 minutes | Serves: 3

- 340g Brussels sprouts, trimmed
- 2 tablespoons olive oil
- Sea salt and black pepper, to taste
- ½ teaspoon dried dill weed
- 1 tablespoon fresh lemon juice
- 1 tablespoon rice vinegar

1. Place the Cook & Crisp Basket in your Pressure Cooker Steam Fryer. 2. Mix the Brussels sprouts with the oil and spices until they are well coated on all sides; then, arrange the Brussels sprouts in the Ninja Foodi Pressure Steam Fryer basket. 3. Put on the Smart Lid on top of the Ninja Foodi Steam Fryer. 4. Move the Lid Slider to the "Air Fry/Stovetop". Select the "Air Fry" mode for cooking. 5. Cook the Brussels sprouts at 195°C for around 10 minutes, shaking the basket halfway through the cooking time. 6. Mix the Brussels sprouts with lemon juice and vinegar. Enjoy!

Per serving: Calories: 184; Fat: 5g; Sodium: 441mg; Carbs: 17g; Fiber: 4.6g; Sugar: 5g; Protein: 9g

Crispy Parmesan Artichokes

Prep Time: 10 minutes | Cook Time: 35 minutes | Serves: 4

- 2 medium artichokes, with the centers removed
- 2 tablespoon coconut oil, melted
- 1 egg, beaten
- 50g parmesan cheese, grated
- 30g blanched, finely flour

1. Place the Cook & Crisp Basket in your Pressure Cooker Steam Fryer. 2. Place the artichokes in a suitable bowl with the coconut oil and stir well, then dip the artichokes into a suitable bowl of beaten egg. 3. In another bowl, mix the parmesan cheese and the flour. Mix with artichoke, making 4. sure to coat each piece well. Transfer the artichoke to the basket. 5. Put on the Smart Lid on top of the Ninja Foodi Steam Fryer. 6. Move the Lid Slider to the "Air Fry/Stovetop". Select the "Air Fry" mode for cooking. 7. Air Fry artichoke at 200°C. Cook for 10 minutes, shaking occasionally throughout the cooking time. Serve hot.

Per serving: Calories: 372; Fat: 20g; Sodium: 891mg; Carbs: 29g; Fiber: 3g; Sugar: 8g; Protein: 7g

Crispy Sweet Brussels Sprouts

Prep time: 5 minutes | Cook time: 30 minutes | Serves: 6

- 2 tablespoons salted butter
- 2 shallots, diced
- 900g – 1.2 kg Brussels sprouts, stems trimmed, halved
- 80ml balsamic vinegar
- 80g maple syrup
- 110g dried cranberries or raisins
- 10–20 almonds, crushed
- Balsamic glaze, for topping

1. Place the butter in the cooking pot and Move the slider towards "AIR FRY/STOVETOP" and set Ninja Foodi XL Pressure Cooker Steam Fryer with SmartLid to SEAR/SAUTÉ mode. Adjust the temperature to "Hi5" by using up arrow. Press START/STOP to begin cooking. Once the butter melted, add the shallots and sauté for 3 minutes, until slightly softened. 2. Add the Brussels sprouts, vinegar, maple syrup, cranberries, and almonds. Stir until everything is mixed together and the Brussels sprouts are well-coated in the sauce. 3. Lock lid; move slider towards PRESSURE. Adjust pressure release valve in the SEAL position. Close pressure-release valve. The cooking temperature will default to HIGH, which is accurate. Set time to 1 minutes. Select START/STOP and start cooking. When cooking is complete, let pressure release quickly by turning it into VENT position. 4. To crisp the sprouts: Lock lid; move slider towards STEAMCRISP. Select STEAM & BAKE, set temperature to 200°C, and set time to 15 minutes. Press START/STOP to begin cooking until they reach the desired crispiness. 5. Place the Brussels sprouts in a serving dish, along with their sauce, and drizzle with some balsamic glaze, if desired.

Per Serving: Calories 318; Fat 16.5g; Sodium 245mg; Carbs 1.5g; Fiber 0.5g; Sugar 0.5g; Protein 40.7g

Green Beans Salad

Prep Time: 10 minutes | Cook Time: 10 minutes | Serves: 3

- 340g fresh green beans, washed and trimmed
- 2 tablespoons olive oil
- 80g green onions, sliced
- 60g baby spinach
- 1 tablespoon fresh basil, chopped
- 1 green pepper, sliced
- 2 tablespoons fresh lemon juice
- Sea salt and black pepper, to taste

1. Place the Cook & Crisp Basket in your Pressure Cooker Steam Fryer. 2. Toss the green beans with 1 tablespoon of the olive oil. Arrange the green beans in the Ninja Foodi Pressure Steam Fryer basket. 3. Put on the Smart Lid on top of the Ninja Foodi Steam Fryer. 4. Move the Lid Slider to the "Air Fry/Stovetop". Select the "Air Fry" mode for cooking. 5. Cook the green beans at 190°C for around 7 minutes; make sure to check the green beans halfway through the cooking time. 6. Add the green beans to a salad bowl; add in the remaining recipe ingredients and stir to mix well. Enjoy!

Per serving: Calories: 312; Fat: 19g; Sodium: 354mg; Carbs: 15g; Fiber: 5.1g; Sugar: 8.2g; Protein 12g

Garlicky Roasted Cauliflower

Prep Time: 10 minutes | Cook Time: 20 minutes | Serves: 2

- 1 medium head cauliflower
- 2 tablespoon salted butter, melted
- 1 medium lemon
- 1 teaspoon dried parsley
- ½ teaspoon garlic powder

1. Place the Cook & Crisp Basket in your Pressure Cooker Steam Fryer. 2. Having removed the leaves from the cauliflower head, brush it with the melted butter. Grate the rind of the lemon over it and then drizzle some juice. Finally add the parsley and garlic powder on top. 3. Transfer the cauliflower to the basket of the Pressure Cooker Steam Fryer. 4. Put on the Smart Lid on top of the Ninja Foodi Steam Fryer. 5. Move the Lid Slider to the "Air Fry/Stovetop". Select the "Air Fry" mode for cooking. 6. Cook for fifteen minutes at 175°C, checking regularly to ensure it doesn't overcook. The cauliflower is ready when it is hot and fork tender. 7. Take care when removing it from the fryer, cut up and serve.

Per serving: Calories: 219; Fat: 10g; Sodium: 891mg; Carbs: 22.9g; Fiber: 4g; Sugar 4g; Protein 13g

Mushroom Cheese Loaf

Prep Time: 10 minutes | Cook Time: 20 minutes | Serves: 2

- 200g mushrooms, chopped
- 50g cheddar cheese, shredded
- 90g flour
- 2 tablespoons butter, melted
- 2 eggs
- Black pepper and salt, if desired

1. Place the deluxe reversible rack in your Pressure Cooker Steam Fryer. 2. In a food processor, pulse the mushrooms, cheese, flour, melted butter, and eggs, along with some black pepper and salt if desired, until a uniform consistency is achieved. 3. Transfer into a silicone loaf pan, spreading and levelling with a palette knife. 4. Set the loaf pan on the rack. Put on the Smart Lid on top of the Ninja Foodi Steam Fryer. Move the Lid Slider to the "Air Fry/Stovetop". Select the "Air Fry" mode for cooking. Adjust the cooking temperature to 190°C and cook for 15 minutes. 5. Take care when removing the pan from the Pressure Cooker Steam Fryer. 6. and leave it to cool. Then slice and serve.

Per serving: Calories: 334; Fat: 7.9g; Sodium: 704mg; Carbs: 6g; Fiber: 3.6g; Sugar 6g; Protein 18g

Pearl Couscous Salad

Prep time: 15 minutes | Cook time: 10 minutes | Serves: 6

- 3 tablespoons olive oil, divided
- 170g pearl couscous
- 240ml water
- 240ml fresh orange juice
- 1 small cucumber, seeded and diced
- 1 small yellow pepper, seeded and diced
- 2 small Roma tomatoes, seeded and diced
- 30g slivered almonds
- 10g chopped fresh mint leaves
- 2 tablespoons lemon juice
- 1 teaspoon lemon zest
- 60g feta cheese
- ¼ teaspoon fine sea salt
- 1 teaspoon smoked paprika
- 1 teaspoon garlic powder

1. Move the slider towards "AIR FRY/STOVETOP" and set Ninja Foodi XL Pressure Cooker Steam Fryer with SmartLid to SEAR/SAUTÉ mode. Adjust the temperature to "Hi5" by using up arrow. Press START/STOP to begin cooking. Heat 1 tablespoon olive oil, add couscous, and stir-fry for 2–4 minutes until couscous is slightly browned. Add water and orange juice. 2. Lock lid; move slider towards PRESSURE. Adjust pressure release valve in the SEAL position. Close pressure-release valve. The cooking temperature will default to HIGH, which is accurate. Set time to 5 minutes. Select START/STOP and start cooking. When cooking is complete, let pressure release naturally for about 5 minutes, then quickly release any remaining pressure by turning it into VENT position. Drain any liquid. 3. Combine remaining ingredients in a medium bowl. Set aside. Once couscous has cooled, toss it into bowl ingredients. Cover and refrigerate overnight until ready to serve chilled.
Per Serving: Calories 222; Fat 11g; Sodium 245mg; Carbs 6g; Fiber 4g; Sugar 1g; Protein 12g

Garlicky Mashed Vegetables

Prep time: 15 minutes | Cook time: 5 minutes | Serves: 4

- 2 medium turnips, peeled and diced
- 2 medium parsnips, peeled and diced
- 1 large Yukon gold potato, peeled and diced
- 3 cloves garlic, peeled and halved
- 1 medium shallot, peeled and quartered
- 120ml chicken stock
- 240ml water
- 60ml unsweetened almond milk
- 2 tablespoons ghee
- ½ teaspoon sea salt
- ½ teaspoon ground black pepper

1. Add the turnips, parsnips, potato, garlic, shallot, stock, and water to the cooking pot. 2. Lock lid; move slider towards PRESSURE. Adjust pressure release valve in the SEAL position. Close pressure-release valve. The cooking temperature will default to HIGH, which is accurate. Set time to 5 minutes. Select START/STOP and start cooking. When cooking is complete, let pressure release quickly by turning it into VENT position. 3. Transfer vegetables to a medium bowl. Add milk, ghee, salt, and pepper. Using a hand-held mixer or immersion blender, purée mixture until smooth. Add additional stock 1 tablespoon at a time from the pot if mixture is too thick. 4. Serve warm.
Per Serving: Calories 263; Fat 6g; Sodium 200mg; Carbs 28.3g; Fiber 11g; Sugar 10g; Protein 13g

Chow Relish

Prep time: 15 minutes | Cook time: 20 minutes | Serves: 8

- 2 large green peppers, seeded and diced small
- 1 large red pepper, seeded and diced small
- 2 large green tomatoes, diced small
- 180g finely diced cabbage
- 1 large sweet onion, peeled and diced small
- 1 tablespoon ground mustard
- 2 teaspoons red pepper flakes
- 2 teaspoons celery seed
- 2 teaspoons ground ginger
- 1 teaspoon ground turmeric
- 1 tablespoon sea salt
- 100g granulated sugar
- 110g packed dark brown sugar
- 240ml apple cider vinegar
- 240ml water

1. Place all ingredients into Ninja Foodi XL Pressure Cooker Steam Fryer with SmartLid cooking pot. 2. Lock lid; move slider towards PRESSURE. Adjust pressure release valve in the SEAL position. Close pressure-release valve. The cooking temperature will default to HIGH, which is accurate. Set time to 20 minutes. Select START/STOP and start cooking. When cooking is complete, let pressure release naturally. 3. Use a slotted spoon to transfer relish to a serving dish. Serve warmed or chilled.
Per Serving: Calories 234; Fat 11.7g; Sodium 411mg; Carbs 6.6g; Fiber 3.7g; Sugar 2g; Protein 24.3g

Parmesan Green Bean Casserole

Prep Time: 10 minutes | Cook Time: 10 minutes | Serves: 2

- 1 tablespoon butter, melted
- 100g green beans
- 150g cheddar cheese, shredded
- 175g parmesan cheese, shredded
- 60g heavy cream

1. Place the Cook & Crisp Basket in your Pressure Cooker Steam Fryer. 2. Cover the Cook & Crisp Basket with melted butter. Throw in the green beans, cheddar cheese, and any seasoning as desired, then give it a stir. Add the parmesan on top and finally the heavy cream. 3. Put on the Smart Lid on top of the Ninja Foodi Steam Fryer. 4. Move the Lid Slider to the "Air Fry/Stovetop". Select the "Air Fry" mode for cooking. 5. Adjust the cooking temperature to 200°C. 6. Cook for 6 minutes. Allow to cool before serving.
Per serving: Calories: 184; Fat: 5g; Sodium: 441mg; Carbs: 17g; Fiber: 4.6g; Sugar 5g; Protein 9g

Creamy Cauliflower Puree

Prep time: 5 minutes | Cook time: 15 minutes | Serves: 6

- 240ml chicken or vegetable stock
- 1 head cauliflower, stalk and green leaves removed, cut into large chunks
- 120ml milk or heavy cream,
- 2 tablespoons salted butter
- Seasoned salt and black pepper to taste
- Chopped chives, for garnish

1. Place the Deluxe reversible rack in the Ninja Foodi XL Pressure Cooker Steam Fryer with SmartLid cooking pot, pour in the stock, and place the cauliflower on top. 2 Lock lid; move slider towards PRESSURE. Adjust pressure release valve in the SEAL position. Close pressure-release valve. The cooking temperature will default to HIGH, which is accurate. Set time to 4 minutes. Select START/STOP and start cooking. When cooking is complete, let pressure release quickly by turning it into VENT position. 3. Place the cauliflower to a food processor or blender. Pour in about a third of the stock from the pot. Pulse and then blend to form a smooth puree. 4. Add the milk, butter, seasoned salt, and pepper to the blender. Pulse and blend again until totally smooth and creamy before serving with some chives, perhaps.
Per Serving: Calories 238; Fat 10.9g; Sodium 111mg; Carbs 6.8g; Fiber 3.5g; Sugar 2g; Protein 26.7g

Paprika Cabbage Steaks

Prep Time: 10 minutes | Cook Time: 5 minutes | Serves: 2

- 1 small head cabbage
- 1 teaspoon butter, butter
- 1 teaspoon paprika
- 1 teaspoon olive oil

1. Place the Cook & Crisp Basket in your Pressure Cooker Steam Fryer. 2. Halve the cabbage. 3. In a suitable bowl, mix the melted butter, paprika, and olive oil. Massage into the cabbage slices, making sure to coat it well. Season as desired with black pepper and salt or any other seasonings of your choosing. 4. Put the cabbage in the Cook & Crisp Basket. Put on the Smart Lid on top of the Ninja Foodi Steam Fryer. Move the Lid Slider to the "Air Fry/Stovetop". Select the "Air Fry" mode for cooking. 5. Adjust the cooking temperature to 200°C. 6. and cook for 3 minutes. Flip it. Cook for on the other side for another 2 minutes. Enjoy!
Per serving: Calories: 314; Fat: 7.9g; Sodium: 704mg; Carbs: 6g; Fiber: 3.6g; Sugar 6g; Protein 18g

Gingered Potatoes

Prep time: 10 minutes | Cook time: 10 minutes | Serves: 6

- 1.1kg sweet potatoes, peeled and diced large
- 480ml water
- 1 tablespoon minced fresh ginger
- ½ teaspoon sea salt
- 1 tablespoon pure maple syrup
- 1 tablespoon butter
- 60ml milk

1. Add potatoes and water to the cooking pot. 2. Lock lid; move slider towards PRESSURE. Adjust pressure release valve in the SEAL position. Close pressure-release valve. The cooking temperature will default to HIGH, which is accurate. Set time to 10 minutes. Select START/STOP and start cooking. When cooking is complete, let pressure release naturally. 3. Drain water from the pot. Add remaining ingredients to the potatoes. Using an immersion blender directly in the pot, cream the potatoes until desired consistency. 4. Serve warm.
Per Serving: Calories 187; Fat 12.4g; Sodium 110mg; Carbs 8.9g; Fiber 2g; Sugar 1g; Protein 4.7g

Creamy Corn

Prep time: 15 minutes | Cook time: 7 minutes | Serves: 6

- 6 large ears of corn or 8 medium, husked
- 120ml water
- ½ teaspoon sea salt
- ½ teaspoon ground black pepper
- 100g cream cheese, cubed and room temperature
- 4 tablespoons ghee, cubed and room temperature
- 1 teaspoon sugar
- 240g heavy cream
- 1 tablespoon flour

1. Cut off the corn kernels from the cob, really scraping the cobs to release that milky substance. Place the kernels, water, salt, pepper, cream cheese, ghee, and sugar in the cooking pot. 2. Lock lid; move slider towards PRESSURE. Adjust pressure release valve in the SEAL position. Close pressure-release valve. The cooking temperature will default to HIGH, which is accurate. Set time to 2 minutes. Select START/STOP and start cooking. 3. In a small bowl, whisk together the heavy cream and flour to create a slurry. 4. When cooking is complete, let pressure release quickly by turning it into VENT position and then unlock lid. Add the slurry to the corn in the pot and stir. 5. Transfer to a medium bowl and serve warm.
Per Serving: Calories 273; Fat 23g; Sodium 111mg; Carbs 8g; Fiber 2g; Sugar 1g; Protein 8g

Cranberry-citrus Sauce

Prep time: 5 minutes | Cook time: 1 minutes | Serves: 8

400g fresh cranberries	Juice from 1 orange	160g pure maple syrup	Pinch of salt
130g canned crushed pineapple	2 teaspoons orange zest	¼ teaspoon cinnamon	2 tablespoons sugar

1. Add all ingredients to Ninja Foodi XL Pressure Cooker Steam Fryer with SmartLid cooking pot. 2. Lock lid; move slider towards PRESSURE. Adjust pressure release valve in the SEAL position. Close pressure-release valve. The cooking temperature will default to HIGH, which is accurate. Set time to 1 minutes. Select START/STOP and start cooking. When cooking is complete, let pressure release quickly by turning it into VENT position. 3. Stir ingredients in the pot and smash any unpopped cranberries with the back of a wooden spoon. 4. Transfer sauce to a serving dish and serve warm.

Per Serving: Calories 95; Fat 6g; Sodium 132mg; Carbs 6g; Fiber 1.8g; Sugar 0.6g; Protein 3g

Delicious Collard Greens

Prep time: 10 minutes | Cook time: 10 minutes | Serves: 6

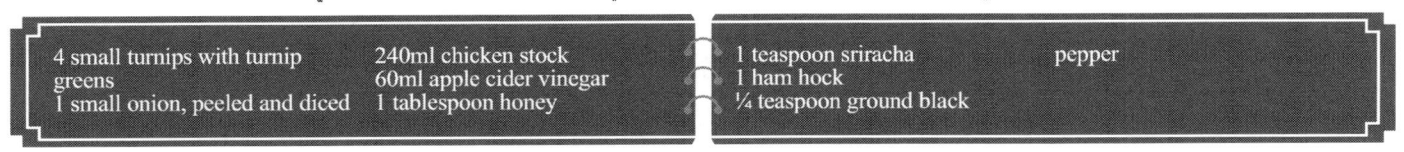

900g collard greens, washed, spines removed, and chopped	240ml chicken stock	1 slice bacon	pepper
1 small onion, peeled and diced	60ml apple cider vinegar	½ teaspoon sea salt	
	1 teaspoon sriracha	¼ teaspoon ground black	

1. Place all ingredients in cooking pot. 2. Lock lid; move slider towards PRESSURE. Adjust pressure release valve in the SEAL position. Close pressure-release valve. The cooking temperature will default to HIGH, which is accurate. Set time to 10 minutes. Select START/STOP and start cooking. When cooking is complete, let pressure release naturally. Discard bacon. 3. Using a slotted spoon, transfer collard greens to a dish and serve warm.

Per Serving: Calories 88; Fat 6g; Sodium 102mg; Carbs 9g; Fiber 2.3g; Sugar 1.2g; Protein 1g

Refreshing Steamed Broccoli

Prep time: 5 minutes | Cook time: 0 minutes | Serves: 4

240ml water	chopped	½ teaspoon sea salt
1 medium head broccoli,	1 teaspoon lemon juice	1 teaspoons ghee

1. Pour water into cooking pot. Insert the Cook & Crisp Basket and arrange broccoli on the basket in an even layer. 2. Lock lid; move slider towards PRESSURE. Adjust pressure release valve in the SEAL position. Close pressure-release valve. The cooking temperature will default to HIGH, which is accurate. Set QUICK RELEASE and time to 0 minutes. Select START/STOP and start cooking. The broccoli will steam in the time it takes the pressure to build. When cooking is complete, let pressure release quickly by turning it into VENT position. and then unlock lid. 3. Use retriever tongs to remove Cook & Crisp Basket. Transfer broccoli to a serving dish and toss with lemon juice, salt, and ghee. Serve warm.

Per Serving: Calories 280; Fat 12g; Sodium 678mg; Carbs 6g; Fiber 4g; Sugar 2g; Protein 14g

Turnips with Greens

Prep time: 10 minutes | Cook time: 10 minutes | Serves: 4

4 small turnips with turnip greens	240ml chicken stock	1 teaspoon sriracha	pepper
1 small onion, peeled and diced	60ml apple cider vinegar	1 ham hock	
	1 tablespoon honey	¼ teaspoon ground black	

1. Wash turnips. Peel and dice. Wash turnip greens. Cut out stems and spines. Dice leaves. 2. Place all ingredients in Ninja Foodi XL Pressure Cooker Steam Fryer with SmartLid cooking pot. 3. Lock lid; move slider towards PRESSURE. Adjust pressure release valve in the SEAL position. Close pressure-release valve. The cooking temperature will default to HIGH, which is accurate. Set time to 10 minutes. Select START/STOP and start cooking. When cooking is complete, let pressure release naturally and then unlock lid. Remove ham hock, pull meat off of the bone, and dice. Add meat back to pot. Discard bone. 4. Using a slotted spoon, transfer turnip greens, turnips, and ham to a serving dish. Serve warm.

Per Serving: Calories 177; Fat 4.1g; Sodium 568mg; Carbs 4.4g; Fiber 1g; Sugar 1g; Protein 29.3g

Buttery Egg Noodles

Prep time: 2 minutes | Cook time: 4 minutes | Serves: 6

1 (300g) bag egg noodles	25g grated Parmesan cheese	¼ teaspoon ground black pepper	10g chopped fresh parsley
3 tablespoons butter	½ teaspoon sea salt		

1. Place noodles in an even layer in Ninja Foodi XL Pressure Cooker Steam Fryer with SmartLid cooking pot. Pour enough water to come about ½ cm over pasta. 2. Lock lid; move slider towards PRESSURE. Adjust pressure release valve in the SEAL position. Close pressure-release valve. The cooking temperature will default to HIGH, which is accurate. Set time to 4 minutes. Select START/STOP and start cooking. 3. When cooking is complete, let pressure release naturally for about 10 minutes, then quickly release any remaining pressure by turning it into VENT position. 4. Drain any residual water. Toss pasta with butter, Parmesan cheese, salt, pepper, and parsley. Serve immediately.
Per Serving: Calories 246; Fat 10.4g; Sodium 368mg; Carbs 8.6g; Fiber 4g; Sugar 4g; Protein 8.4g

Szechuan-Style String Beans

Prep time: 5 minutes | Cook time: 15 minutes | Serves: 6

675g green beans, ends trimmed	chopped	1 tablespoon rice vinegar	¼ teaspoon crushed red pepper flakes
60ml vegetable or garlic stock	3 cloves garlic, minced or pressed	1 tablespoon paprika	
60ml low-sodium soy sauce	2 tablespoons sesame oil	2 teaspoons garlic powder	
2 tablespoons almonds,	2 tablespoons sriracha	1 teaspoon onion powder	
		¼ teaspoon cayenne pepper	

1. Put all the ingredients in the Ninja Foodi XL Pressure Cooker Steam Fryer with SmartLid cooking pot and stir well. 2. Lock lid; move slider towards PRESSURE. Adjust pressure release valve in the SEAL position. Close pressure-release valve. The cooking temperature will default to HIGH, which is accurate. Set time to 3 minutes. Select START/STOP and start cooking. When cooking is complete, let pressure release quickly by turning it into VENT position. 3. When the lid comes off, you're ready to serve.
Per Serving: Calories 280; Fat 11g; Sodium 511mg; Carbs 6g; Fiber 4g; Sugar 2g; Protein 17g

Creamy Corn with Crabmeat

Prep time: 3 minutes | Cook time: 15 minutes | Serves: 6

240ml water	1 (130g) package Boursin spread	50g grated Parmesan cheese	1 teaspoon black pepper
750g frozen corn	120g heavy cream	3 tablespoons salted butter	
225g crabmeat		1½ teaspoons granulated sugar	

1. Pour the water in the Ninja Foodi XL Pressure Cooker Steam Fryer with SmartLid cooking pot then place the corn in a Cook & Crisp Basket and lower into the pot. 2. Lock lid; move slider towards PRESSURE. Adjust pressure release valve in the SEAL position. Close pressure-release valve. The cooking temperature will default to HIGH, which is accurate. Set time to 1 minutes. Select START/STOP and start cooking. When cooking is complete, let pressure release quickly by turning it into VENT position. Dump the corn from the basket back into the pot. 3. Add all the other ingredients and stir until the Boursin (or cream cheese) has melted completely before serving.
Per Serving: Calories 244; Fat 11g; Sodium 410mg; Carbs 6g; Fiber 4g; Sugar 2g; Protein 17g

Mushroom 'Pot Roast'

Prep time: 15 minutes | Cook time: 1 hour 10 minutes | Serves: 8

455g portobello mushrooms, cut into 5 cm pieces	1 rib of celery, chopped	720ml vegetable stock, divided	2 tablespoons corn flour
2 large carrots, peeled and diced	185g frozen pearl onions	120ml dry red wine	Salt and freshly-cracked black pepper
3 large parsnips, diced large	4 cloves garlic, peeled and minced	3 tablespoons tomato paste	Egg noodles with butter, optional side
	3 sprigs fresh thyme	2 tablespoons vegetarian Worcestershire sauce	

1. Add mushrooms, carrots, parsnips, celery, onions, garlic, thyme, 600ml vegetable stock, wine and Worcestershire to the Ninja Foodi XL Pressure Cooker Steam Fryer with SmartLid cooking pot; gently toss to combine. 2. Lock lid; move slider towards AIR FRY/STOVETOP. Select STEAM, and set time to 30 minutes. Press START/STOP to begin cooking. Cook for 30 minutes more. 3. Whisk together the remaining 120ml vegetable stock and corn flour until well-combined. Add to the pot roast and gently toss to combine. 4. Continue on Steam for an additional 5 minutes, until the sauce thickens. 5. Serve hot and enjoy with buttered egg noodles!
Per Serving: Calories 78; Fat 0.2g; Sodium 331mg; Carbs 14.8g; Fiber 2.7g; Sugar 3g; Protein 2.4g

Green Rice

Prep time: 5 minutes | Cook time: 35 minutes | Serves: 5

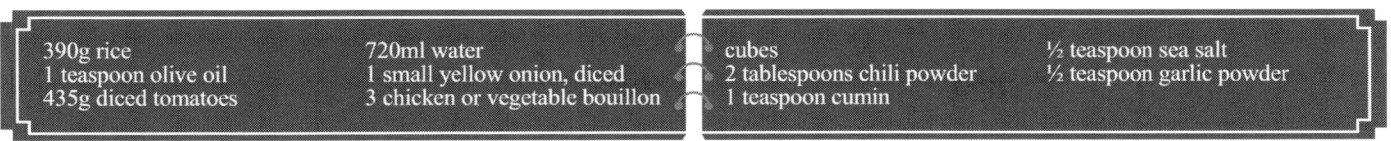

390g rice	720ml water	cubes	½ teaspoon sea salt
1 teaspoon olive oil	1 small yellow onion, diced	2 tablespoons chili powder	½ teaspoon garlic powder
435g diced tomatoes	3 chicken or vegetable bouillon	1 teaspoon cumin	

1. Combine rice, water, and diced tomatoes in the Ninja Foodi XL Pressure Cooker Steam Fryer with SmartLid cooking pot. 2. Fold in the onion, bouillon cubes and spices into the rice and stir well to help the spices dissolve in the water. Lock lid; move slider towards AIR FRY/STOVETOP. Select STEAM, and set time to 15 minutes. 3. Press START/STOP to begin cooking. When cook time reaches zero, the unit will beep and "End" will flash 3 times on the display. 4. Keep warm until serving with your favorite lean meats, enchiladas, or tacos! Alternatively, you can use the rice to fill burritos for an authentic South Western meal.
Per Serving: Calories 468; Fat 11.6g; Sodium 502mg; Carbs 74.6g; Fiber 4g; Sugar 2g; Protein 15.5g

Colourful Vegetable Rice

Prep time: 10 minutes | Cook time: 30 minutes | Serves: 4

370g Jasmine rice	½ small onion, finely chopped	small	1-½ tablespoons Mirin
720ml vegetable stock	35g green beans, chopped	3 tablespoons soy sauce, extra	½ teaspoon sea salt
1 small carrot, finely chopped	small	for drizzling	3 spring onions, finely chopped
20g white cabbage, shredded	8 button mushrooms, chopped	2 tablespoons sake	250g firm tofu, cubed, optional

1. Add rice to the bowl and rinse until water runs clear; drain. Place washed rice in Ninja Foodi XL Pressure Cooker Steam Fryer with SmartLid cooking pot. 2. Add soy sauce, sake, mirin, salt and water. 3. Top with carrots, cabbage, onion, green beans, and mushrooms and tofu; do not stir. 4. Lock lid; move slider towards AIR FRY/STOVETOP. Select STEAM, and set time to 15 minutes. Press START/STOP to begin cooking. When cook time reaches zero, the unit will beep and "End" will flash 3 times on the display. 5. Gently fluff the rice with a fork and serve hot topped with spring onions and extra soy sauce!
Per Serving: Calories 385; Fat 0.1g; Sodium 973mg; Carbs 86g; Fiber 5.7g; Sugar 6g; Protein 8.5g

Savoury Beans

Prep time: 10 minutes | Cook time: 1 hour 30 minutes | Serves: 4

385g dried beans, like pinto, navy or black beans	1 bay leaf	960ml water	Black pepper, optional
	1 small ham hock	Chopped onion, optional	Sea salt, optional

1. Add beans to the pot and cover with water; soak overnight. 2. Drain and rinse the beans the following morning, then put them in the Ninja Foodi XL Pressure Cooker Steam Fryer with SmartLid cooking pot, and add 960ml water, along with 1 bay leaf and a ham hock or bouillon cube. 3. Lock lid; move slider towards AIR FRY/STOVETOP. Select STEAM, and set time to 30 minutes. Press START/STOP to begin cooking. Then cook for 30 minutes more. Check that beans are still covered with water after the cycle; if needed, add a little more water and STEAM for an additional 30 minutes. 4. Remove the bay leaf and ham hock. Cut ham hock and add to bowls. 5. Serve beans hot, as a soup with chopped onion, sea salt, and pepper—or drain and use in your favorite recipes.
Per Serving: Calories 279; Fat 14.5g; Sodium 233mg; Carbs 3.4g; Fiber 1.7g; Sugar 1.6g; Protein 32.4g

Warm Lentils

Prep time: 8 minutes | Cook time: 1hour 10 minutes | Serves: 4

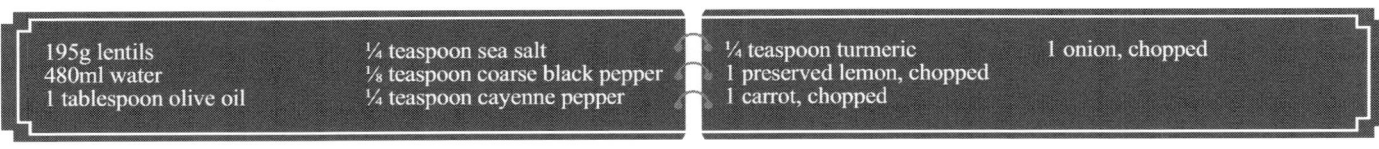

195g lentils	¼ teaspoon sea salt	¼ teaspoon turmeric	1 onion, chopped
480ml water	⅛ teaspoon coarse black pepper	1 preserved lemon, chopped	
1 tablespoon olive oil	¼ teaspoon cayenne pepper	1 carrot, chopped	

1. Pour washed lentils into Ninja Foodi XL Pressure Cooker Steam Fryer with SmartLid cooking pot. 2. Move the slider towards "AIR FRY/STOVETOP" and set Ninja Foodi XL Pressure Cooker Steam Fryer with SmartLid to SEAR/SAUTÉ mode. Adjust the temperature to "Hi5" by using up arrow. Press START/STOP to begin cooking. 3. Add oil and cook onion until soft. Add the lentils and other ingredients to the pressure cooker, top with 480ml water; stir to combine. 4. Lock lid; move slider towards AIR FRY/STOVETOP. Select STEAM, and set time to 20 minutes. Press START/STOP to begin cooking. 5. Transfer the lentils to a bowl and serve. Try with a dollop of plain yogurt and a zest of lime for a special touch.
Per Serving: Calories 79; Fat 2g; Sodium 332mg; Carbs 12g; Fiber 2g; Sugar 4g; Protein 4g

Chapter 3 Poultry Mains Recipes

45	Korean Wings	52	Delicious Arroz Con Pollo
45	Spicy Buffalo Chicken Wings	52	Chicken with Mushrooms
45	Spicy Chicken Alfredo	53	Spicy Teriyaki Chicken
45	Crispy Honey Chicken Wings	53	Paprika Chicken Cutlets
46	Turkey with Mustard Glaze	53	Hawaiian Roll Sliders
46	Mexican Burgers	53	Mediterranean Chicken Fillets
46	Crispy Fried Chicken	54	Chicken Egg Roll
46	Fajita Rollups	54	Mayo Chicken Salad
47	Indian Chicken Marsala	54	Chicken Taquitos
47	Spicy Buffalo Wings	54	Chicken with Pineapple
47	Delicious Teriyaki Chicken	55	Delicious Sesame Chicken
48	Chicken with Broccoli Stir-Fry	55	Chicken Pepper Fajitas
48	Chicken Mushroom Kabobs	55	Air-Fried Turkey Wings
48	Chicken Tenders	55	Limey Duck Breast
48	KFC Chicken	56	Fried Chicken
49	Chicken Fritters	56	Salsa Chicken
49	Chicken Wing Stir-Fry	56	Chicken Thighs with Salsa
49	Chicken Parmesan	56	Artichoke Hearts and Chicken
49	Jerk-Spiced Chicken Wings	57	Stuffed Turkey Breast with Gravy
50	Crusted Chicken Fingers	57	Thai Chicken Rice
50	Air Fried Turkey Breast	57	Chicken with Marinara Sauce
50	Air-Fried Chicken Breasts	58	Lemon Chicken with Herbed Potatoes
50	Spiced Chicken Thighs	58	Shredded Greek-Style Chicken
50	Air-Fried Chicken Legs	58	Smoky Barbecue Chicken
51	Turkey with Gravy	58	Lo Mein
51	Thanksgiving Turkey	59	Pesto Turkey Meatballs with Pasta
51	Asian-Spiced Duck	59	Refreshing Chicken Tacos
51	Chicken BBQ Burgers	59	Burrito Bowls with Chicken And Beans
52	Tuscan Chicken	59	Chile Verde

Korean Wings

Prep Time: 10 minutes | Cook Time: 45 minutes | Serves: 4

Wings:
- 1 teaspoon pepper
- 1 teaspoon salt
- 900g chicken wings

Sauce:
- 2 packets Splenda
- 1 tablespoon minced garlic
- 1 tablespoon minced ginger
- 1 tablespoon sesame oil
- 1 teaspoon agave nectar
- 1 tablespoon mayo
- 2 tablespoon gochujang

Finishing:
- 30g chopped green onions
- 2 teaspoon sesame seeds

1. Place the Cook & Crisp Basket in your Pressure Cooker Steam Fryer. 2. Line the Cook & Crisp Basket with foil. 3. Season the chicken wings with black pepper and salt and place in the Cook & Crisp Basket. 4. Put on the Smart Lid on top of the Ninja Foodi Steam Fryer. 5. Move the Lid Slider to the "Air Fry/Stovetop". Select the "Air Fry" mode for cooking. 6. Adjust the cooking temperature to 200°C. 7. Air fry the seasoned chicken wings for around 20 minutes, turning at 10 minutes. 8. As chicken wings air fries, mix all the sauce components. 9. Once a thermometer says that the chicken has reached 70°C, take out wings and place into a suitable bowl. 10. Add half of the prepared sauce mixture over wings, tossing well to coat. 11. Put coated wings back into Pressure Cooker Steam Fryer for around 5 minutes or till they reach 75°C. 12. Remove and sprinkle with green onions and sesame seeds. Dip into extra sauce.

Per serving: Calories: 489; Fat: 11g; Sodium: 501mg; Carbs: 8.9g; Fiber: 4.6g; Sugar 8g; Protein 26g

Spicy Buffalo Chicken Wings

Prep Time: 10 minutes | Cook Time: 25 minutes | Serves: 6-8

- 1 teaspoon salt
- 1-2 tablespoon brown sugar
- 1 tablespoon Worcestershire sauce
- 115g vegan butter
- 120g cayenne pepper sauce
- 1.8kg chicken wings

1. Place the Cook & Crisp Basket in your Pressure Cooker Steam Fryer. 2. Mix salt, brown sugar, Worcestershire sauce, butter, and hot sauce and set to the side. 3. Dry wings and add to "cook & crisp basket". 4. Put on the Smart Lid on top of the Ninja Foodi Steam Fryer. 5. Move the Lid Slider to the "Air Fry/Stovetop". Select the "Air Fry" mode for cooking. 6. Cook 25 minutes at 195°C, tossing halfway through. 7. When timer sounds, shake wings and bump up the temperature to 200°C. Cook for another 5 minutes. 8. Take out wings and place into a big bowl. Add sauce and toss well. 9. Serve alongside celery sticks!

Per serving: Calories: 221; Fat: 7.9g; Sodium: 704mg; Carbs: 6g; Fiber: 3.6g; Sugar 6g; Protein 18g

Spicy Chicken Alfredo

Prep time: 10 minutes | Cook time: 20 minutes | Serves: 2

- 1 tablespoon olive oil
- 1 (125-150g) boneless, skinless chicken breast, cut into 2.5 cm pieces
- ¼ teaspoon salt
- ¼ teaspoon black pepper
- 240ml chicken stock
- 240g heavy cream
- 100g fettuccine noodles, broken in half
- 100g grated Parmesan cheese

1. Move the slider towards "AIR FRY/STOVETOP" and set Ninja Foodi XL Pressure Cooker Steam Fryer with SmartLid to SEAR/SAUTÉ mode. Adjust the temperature to "Hi5" by using up arrow. Press START/STOP to begin cooking and pour in the olive oil. 2. Season the chicken with the salt and pepper. Once the oil is shimmering, add the chicken and cook until golden brown, 3 to 4 minutes. Press START/STOP to turn off the pot and transfer the chicken to a plate. 3. Add the stock to the pot and scrape up any bits from the bottom of the pot. 4. Add the heavy cream and fettuccine to the pot and stir, then top with the chicken. 5. Lock lid; move slider towards PRESSURE. Adjust pressure release valve in the SEAL position. Close pressure-release valve. The cooking temperature will default to HIGH, which is accurate. Set time to 6 minutes. Select START/STOP and start cooking. When cooking is complete, let pressure release quickly by turning it into VENT position. 6. Open the lid. Stir the pasta and chicken, and slowly add the Parmesan cheese until melted. Serve warm.

Per Serving: Calories 494; Fat 24.3g; Sodium 257mg; Carbs 43.8g; Fiber 8.3g; Sugar 3.7g; Protein 28.8g

Crispy Honey Chicken Wings

Prep Time: 10 minutes | Cook Time: 35 minutes | Serves: 8

- 30ml water
- ½ teaspoon salt
- 4 tablespoon minced garlic
- 30g vegan butter
- 85g raw honey
- 85g almond flour
- 16 chicken wings

1. Place the Cook & Crisp Basket in your Pressure Cooker Steam Fryer. 2. Grease your Ninja Foodi "cook & crisp basket" with olive oil. 3. Coat chicken wings with almond flour and add coated wings to basket. 4. Put on the Smart Lid on top of the Ninja Foodi Steam Fryer. 5. Move the Lid Slider to the "Air Fry/Stovetop". Select the "Air Fry" mode for cooking. 6. Cook 25 minutes at 195°C. 7. Then cook 5 to 10 minutes at 200°C till skin becomes crispy and dry. 8. As chicken cooks, melt butter in a suitable saucepan and add garlic. Sauté garlic 5 minutes. Add salt and honey, simmering 20 minutes. 9. Add a bit of water after 15 minutes to ensure sauce does not harden. 10. Take out chicken wings from Pressure Cooker Steam Fryer and coat in sauce. Enjoy!

Per serving: Calories: 289; Fat: 14g; Sodium: 791mg; Carbs: 18.9g; Fiber: 4.6g; Sugar 8g; Protein 26g

Turkey with Mustard Glaze

Prep Time: 10 minutes | Cook Time: 30 minutes | Serves: 5-7

- 1 tablespoon vegan butter
- 1 tablespoon stone-brown mustard
- 80g pure maple syrup
- 1 teaspoon crushed pepper
- 2 teaspoon salt
- ½ teaspoon dried rosemary
- 2 minced garlic cloves
- 60ml olive oil
- 1.1kg turkey breast loin

1. Place the Cook & Crisp Basket in your Pressure Cooker Steam Fryer. 2. Mix pepper, salt, rosemary, garlic, and olive oil together. Spread herb mixture over turkey breast. Cover and chill 2 hours or overnight to marinade. 3. Make sure to remove from fridge about half an hour before cooking. 4. Place loin into the basket. Put on the Smart Lid on top of the Ninja Foodi Steam Fryer. Move the Lid Slider to the "Air Fry/Stovetop". Select the "Air Fry" mode for cooking. 5. Adjust the cooking temperature to 200°C. Cook for 20 minutes. 6. While turkey cooks, melt butter in the microwave. Then add brown mustard and maple syrup. 7. Spoon on butter mixture over turkey. Cook another 10 minutes. 8. Remove turkey from the Pressure Cooker Steam Fryer and let rest 5 to 10 minutes before attempting to slice. 9. Slice against the grain and enjoy!
Per serving: Calories: 372; Fat: 20g; Sodium: 891mg; Carbs: 29g; Fiber: 3g; Sugar 8g; Protein 27g

Mexican Burgers

Prep Time: 10 minutes | Cook Time: 20 minutes | Serves: 6-8

- 1 jalapeno pepper
- 1 teaspoon cayenne pepper
- 1 tablespoon mustard powder
- 1 tablespoon oregano
- 1 tablespoon thyme
- 3 tablespoon smoked paprika
- 1 beaten egg
- 1 small head of cauliflower
- 4 chicken breasts

1. Place the Cook & Crisp Basket in your Pressure Cooker Steam Fryer. 2. Add seasonings to a blender. Slice cauliflower into florets and add to blender. 3. Pulse till mixture resembles that of breadcrumbs. 4. Take out ¾ of cauliflower mixture and add to a suitable bowl. Set to the side. In another bowl, beat your egg and set to the side. 5. Remove skin and bones from chicken breasts and add to blender with remaining cauliflower mixture. Season with pepper and salt. 6. Take out mixture and form into burger shapes. Roll each patty in cauliflower crumbs, then the egg, and back into crumbs again. 7. Put on the Smart Lid on top of the Ninja Foodi Steam Fryer. 8. Move the Lid Slider to the "Air Fry/Stovetop". Select the "Air Fry" mode for cooking. 9. Adjust the cooking temperature to 175°C. 10. Place coated patties into the Ninja Foodi Pressure Steam Fryer, cooking 20 minutes. 11. Flip over at 10-minute mark. They are done when crispy!
Per serving: Calories: 184; Fat: 5g; Sodium: 441mg; Carbs: 17g; Fiber: 4.6g; Sugar 5g; Protein 29g

Crispy Fried Chicken

Prep Time: 10 minutes | Cook Time: 20 minutes | Serves: 4

- 1 teaspoon cayenne pepper
- 2 tablespoon mustard powder
- 2 tablespoon oregano
- 2 tablespoon thyme
- 3 tablespoon coconut milk
- 1 beaten egg
- 25g cauliflower
- 20g gluten-free oats
- 8 chicken drumsticks

1. Place the Cook & Crisp Basket in your Pressure Cooker Steam Fryer. 2. Lay out chicken and season with pepper and salt on all sides. 3. Add all other ingredients to a blender, blending till a smooth-like breadcrumb mixture is created. Place in a suitable bowl and add a beaten egg to another bowl. 4. Dip chicken into breadcrumbs, then into egg, and breadcrumbs once more. 5. Place coated drumsticks into basket. Put on the Smart Lid on top of the Ninja Foodi Steam Fryer. Move the Lid Slider to the "Air Fry/Stovetop". Select the "Air Fry" mode for cooking. 6. Adjust the cooking temperature to 175°C. 7. Cook for 20 minutes. Bump up the temperature to 200°C. Cook for another 5 minutes till crispy.
Per serving: Calories: 489; Fat: 11g; Sodium: 501mg; Carbs: 8.9g; Fiber: 4.6g; Sugar 8g; Protein 26g

Fajita Rollups

Prep Time: 10 minutes | Cook Time: 12 minutes | Serves: 6-8

- ½ teaspoon oregano
- ½ teaspoon cayenne pepper
- 1 teaspoon cumin
- 1 teaspoon garlic powder
- 2 teaspoons paprika
- ½ sliced red onion
- ½ yellow pepper, sliced into strips
- ½ green pepper, sliced into strips
- ½ red pepper, sliced into strips
- 3 chicken breasts

1. Place the Cook & Crisp Basket in your Pressure Cooker Steam Fryer. 2. Mix oregano, cayenne pepper, garlic powder, cumin and paprika along with a pinch or two of pepper and salt. Set to the side. 3. Slice chicken breasts lengthwise into 2 slices. 4. Between two pieces of parchment paper, add breast slices and pound till they are ½ cm thick. With seasoning, liberally season both sides of chicken slices. 5. Put 2 strips of each color of pepper and a few onion slices onto chicken pieces. 6. Roll up tightly and secure with toothpicks. 7. Repeat with remaining ingredients and sprinkle and rub mixture that is left over the chicken rolls. 8. Grease your Ninja Foodi Pressure Steam Fryer basket and place 3 rollups into the fryer. 9. Put on the Smart Lid on top of the Ninja Foodi Steam Fryer. 10. Move the Lid Slider to the "Air Fry/Stovetop". Select the "Air Fry" mode for cooking. 11. Cook 12 minutes at 200°C. 12. Repeat with remaining rollups. 13. Serve with salad!
Per serving: Calories: 372; Fat: 20g; Sodium: 891mg; Carbs: 29g; Fiber: 3g; Sugar 8g; Protein 7g

Indian Chicken Marsala

Prep time: 10 minutes | Cook time: 28 minutes | Serves: 2

1 tablespoon olive oil	chicken breasts	120ml water, plus 2 tablespoons, divided	120ml marsala wine
30g plain flour, divided	¼ teaspoon salt	70g sliced mushrooms	2 tablespoons heavy cream
2 (125–150g) boneless, skinless	⅛ teaspoon black pepper		

1. Move the slider towards "AIR FRY/STOVETOP" and set Ninja Foodi XL Pressure Cooker Steam Fryer with SmartLid to SEAR/SAUTÉ mode. Adjust the temperature to "Hi5" by using up arrow. Press START/STOP to begin cooking and pour in the olive oil. 2. Set aside 1 tablespoon of flour for use later. Put the rest of the flour in a shallow dish. Season the chicken breasts with the salt and pepper, then dredge them in the flour. Once the oil is shimmering, add the chicken and cook until golden brown, 3 to 4 minutes per side. Press START/STOP to turn off the pot and transfer the chicken to a plate. 3. Pour the water into the Ninja Foodi XL Pressure Cooker Steam Fryer and scrape up any bits from the bottom of the pot. 4. Return the chicken to the pot and top with the mushrooms and wine. 5. Lock lid; move slider towards PRESSURE. Adjust pressure release valve in the SEAL position. Close pressure-release valve. The cooking temperature will default to HIGH, which is accurate. Set time to 8 minutes. Select START/STOP and start cooking. When cooking is complete, let the pressure release naturally for about 5 minutes, then quickly release any remaining pressure by turning it into VENT position. 6. Transfer the chicken breasts to a clean plate. 7. Move the slider towards "AIR FRY/STOVETOP" and set Ninja Foodi XL Pressure Cooker Steam Fryer with SmartLid to SEAR/SAUTÉ mode. Adjust the temperature to "Hi5" by using up arrow. Press START/STOP to begin cooking. 8. In a small bowl, whisk together the reserved 1 tablespoon of flour and the remaining 2 tablespoons of water until completely dissolved. Pour the flour slurry into the pot while whisking the sauce. 9. Allow to cook for 2 to 3 minutes, stirring occasionally, until the sauce has thickened. Stir in the heavy cream. Press START/STOP to turn off. 10. Serve the chicken breasts warm, topped with the mushroom sauce.
Per Serving: Calories 279; Fat 11.6g; Sodium 741mg; Carbs 9.3g; Fiber 2g; Sugar 2g; Protein 16.2g

Spicy Buffalo Wings

Prep time: 5 minutes | Cook time: 20 minutes | Serves: 2

900g chicken wings (10 to 12 wings)	1 teaspoon garlic powder	¼ teaspoon black pepper	120g Buffalo sauce
	¼ teaspoon salt	4 tablespoons butter	

1. Place a Deluxe reversible rack in the bottom of the Ninja Foodi XL Pressure Cooker Steam Fryer with SmartLid cooking pot, then pour in 180ml water. 2. Season the wings with the garlic powder, salt, and pepper, and place on top of the Deluxe reversible rack. 3. Lock lid; move slider towards PRESSURE. Adjust pressure release valve in the SEAL position. Close pressure-release valve. The cooking temperature will default to HIGH, which is accurate. Set time to 10 minutes. Select START/STOP and start cooking. When cooking is complete, let pressure release quickly by turning it into VENT position. 4. Open the lid and carefully transfer the wings to a plate. Press START/STOP to turn off the Ninja Foodi XL Pressure Cooker Steam Fryer and wipe out the cooking pot. 5. Move the slider towards "AIR FRY/STOVETOP" and set Ninja Foodi XL Pressure Cooker Steam Fryer with SmartLid to SEAR/SAUTÉ mode. Adjust the temperature to "Hi5" by using up arrow. Press START/STOP to begin cooking add butter to the cooking pot. Once melted, whisk in the hot sauce. 6. Return the wings to the pot and toss until coated with sauce. Serve warm.
Per Serving: Calories 404; Fat 10.3g; Sodium 347mg; Carbs 37.2g; Fiber 1.7g; Sugar 0.7g; Protein 39g

Delicious Teriyaki Chicken

Prep time: 10 minutes | Cook time: 25 minutes | Serves: 2

1 tablespoon sesame oil	¼ teaspoon salt	2 teaspoons minced garlic	1 tablespoon corn flour
3 (100–125 g) boneless, skinless chicken thighs	⅛ teaspoon black pepper	60ml soy sauce	
	120ml water, divided	55g packed light brown sugar	

1. Move the slider towards "AIR FRY/STOVETOP" and set Ninja Foodi XL Pressure Cooker Steam Fryer with SmartLid to SEAR/SAUTÉ mode. Adjust the temperature to "Hi5" by using up arrow. Press START/STOP to begin cooking and pour in the sesame oil. 2. Season the chicken thighs with the salt and pepper. Once the oil is shimmering, put the thighs into the Ninja Foodi XL Pressure Cooker Steam Fryer with SmartLid cooking pot and allow them to sear for 2 minutes on each side. Press START/STOP to turn off the Ninja Foodi XL Pressure Cooker Steam Fryer. Transfer the thighs to a plate. 3. Pour 60ml of water into the Ninja Foodi XL Pressure Cooker Steam Fryer and scrape up any brown bits from the bottom of the pot. 4. Add the garlic, soy sauce, and brown sugar and stir. Return the chicken thighs to the pot and stir to coat. 5. Lock lid; move slider towards PRESSURE. Adjust pressure release valve in the SEAL position. Close pressure-release valve. The cooking temperature will default to HIGH, which is accurate. Set time to 8 minutes. Select START/STOP and start cooking. When cooking is complete, let pressure release naturally for about 5 minutes, then quickly release any remaining pressure by turning it into VENT position. 6. Open the lid. Transfer the chicken thighs to a clean plate. Then set Ninja Foodi XL Pressure Cooker Steam Fryer with SmartLid to SEAR/SAUTÉ mode. Adjust the temperature to "Hi5" by using up arrow. Press START/STOP to begin cooking. 7. In a small bowl, whisk together the corn flour and remaining 60ml of water until completely dissolved. Pour the corn flour slurry into the pot while whisking the sauce. Allow to cook for 2 to 3 minutes, stirring occasionally, until the sauce has thickened. Press START/STOP to turn off the pot. 8. Serve the chicken thighs warm, topped with the thickened sauce.
Per Serving: Calories 279; Fat 12.3g; Sodium 520mg; Carbs 10.4g; Fiber 2g; Sugar 2g; Protein 15.2g

Chicken with Broccoli Stir-Fry

Prep time: 10 minutes | Cook time: 20 minutes | Serves: 2

2 (125–150 g) boneless, skinless chicken breasts, cut into 2.5 cm pieces	1 tablespoon packed light brown sugar 60ml soy sauce	1 teaspoon sesame oil 240ml water, divided 1 tablespoon corn flour	90g frozen broccoli florets Sesame seeds, for garnish

1. Combine the chicken, brown sugar, soy sauce, sesame oil, and 180ml of water in the Ninja Foodi XL Pressure Cooker Steam Fryer with SmartLid cooking pot and stir. 2. Lock lid; move slider towards PRESSURE. Adjust pressure release valve in the SEAL position. Close pressure-release valve. The cooking temperature will default to HIGH, which is accurate. Set time to 4 minutes. Select START/STOP and start cooking. When cooking is complete, let pressure release quickly by turning it into VENT position. 3. Open the lid. Press START/STOP to turn off the pot, then move the slider towards "AIR FRY/STOVETOP" and set Ninja Foodi XL Pressure Cooker Steam Fryer with SmartLid to SEAR/SAUTÉ mode. Adjust the temperature to "Hi5" by using up arrow. Select START/STOP and start cooking. 4. In a small bowl, whisk together the corn flour and remaining 60ml of water until completely dissolved. Pour the corn flour slurry into the pot while whisking the sauce. 5. Add the broccoli and stir until the broccoli cooks through and the sauce thickens, 2 to 3 minutes. Press START/STOP to turn off the Ninja Foodi XL Pressure Cooker Steam Fryer. 6. Serve warm, garnished with sesame seeds if you like.
Per Serving: Calories 283; Fat 12.3g; Sodium 432mg; Carbs 11.5g; Fiber 3g; Sugar 3g; Protein 16.5g

Chicken Mushroom Kabobs

Prep Time: 10 minutes | Cook Time: 20 minutes | Serves: 4

2 diced chicken breasts 3 peppers	6 mushrooms Sesame seeds	80ml low-sodium soy sauce 110g raw honey	Olive oil Salt and pepper, to taste

1. Place the Cook & Crisp Basket in your Pressure Cooker Steam Fryer. 2. Chop up chicken into cubes, seasoning with a few sprays of olive oil, pepper, and salt. 3. Dice up peppers and cut mushrooms in half. 4. Mix soy sauce and honey till well mixed. Add sesame seeds and stir. 5. Skewer chicken, peppers, and mushrooms onto wooden skewers. 6. Coat kabobs with honey-soy sauce. 7. Place coated kabobs in "cook & crisp basket". Put on the Smart Lid on top of the Ninja Foodi Steam Fryer. Move the Lid Slider to the "Air Fry/Stovetop". Select the "Air Fry" mode for cooking. 8. Adjust the cooking temperature to 200°C. Cook for 15 to 20 minutes.
Per serving: Calories: 219; Fat: 10g; Sodium: 891mg; Carbs: 22.9g; Fiber: 4g; Sugar: 4g; Protein 13g

Chicken Tenders

Prep Time: 10 minutes | Cook Time: 15 minutes | Serves: 4-6

55g coconut flour 1 tablespoon spicy brown	mustard 2 beaten eggs	455g of chicken tenders

1. Place the Cook & Crisp Basket in your Pressure Cooker Steam Fryer. 2. Season tenders with pepper and salt. 3. Place a thin layer of mustard onto tenders and then dredge in flour and dip in egg. 4. Place tenders in the Cook & Crisp Basket. Put on the Smart Lid on top of the Ninja Foodi Steam Fryer. Move the Lid Slider to the "Air Fry/Stovetop". Select the "Air Fry" mode for cooking. 5. Cook for 10 to 15 minutes at 200°C till crispy.
Per serving: Calories: 478; Fat: 12.9g; Sodium: 414mg; Carbs: 11g; Fiber: 5g; Sugar: 9g; Protein: 11g

KFC Chicken

Prep Time: 10 minutes | Cook Time: 20 minutes | Serves: 6

1 teaspoon chili flakes 1 teaspoon curcumin 1 teaspoon white pepper 1 teaspoon ginger powder 1 teaspoon garlic powder	1 teaspoon paprika 1 teaspoon powdered mustard 1 teaspoon pepper 1 tablespoon celery salt ⅓ teaspoon oregano	½ tablespoon basil ½ teaspoon thyme 2 garlic cloves 1 egg 6 boneless, skinless chicken	thighs 2 tablespoons unsweetened almond milk 35g whey protein isolate powder

1. Place the Cook & Crisp Basket in your Pressure Cooker Steam Fryer. 2. Wash and pat dry chicken thighs. Slice into small chunks. 3. Mash cloves and add them along with all spices in a blender. Blend until smooth and pour over chicken, adding milk and egg. Mix thoroughly. 4. Cover chicken and chill for around 1 hour. Add whey protein to a suitable bowl and dredge coated chicken pieces. Shake excess powder. Place coated chicken in the Cook & Crisp Basket. 5. Put on the Smart Lid on top of the Ninja Foodi Steam Fryer. Move the Lid Slider to the "Air Fry/Stovetop". Select the "Air Fry" mode for cooking. Adjust the cooking temperature to 200°C. 6. Cook for 20 minutes till crispy, making sure to turn halfway through cooking.
Per serving: Calories: 184; Fat: 5g; Sodium: 441mg; Carbs: 17g; Fiber: 4.6g; Sugar: 5g; Protein 9g

Chicken Fritters

Prep Time: 10 minutes | Cook Time: 20 minutes | Serves: 16-18 fritters

Chicken Fritters:	150g shredded mozzarella cheese	2 eggs	¼ teaspoon salt
½ teaspoon salt	35g coconut flour	675g chicken breasts	½ tablespoon lemon juice
⅛ teaspoon pepper	80g vegan mayo	Garlic Dip:	1 pressed garlic cloves
1 ½ tablespoon fresh dill		⅛ teaspoon pepper	80g vegan mayo

1. Place the Cook & Crisp Basket in your Pressure Cooker Steam Fryer. 2. Slice chicken breasts into ⅓ pieces and place in a suitable bowl. Add all remaining fritter ingredients to the bowl and stir well. Cover and chill 2 hours or overnight. 3. Spray "cook & crisp basket" with a bit of olive oil. 4. Add marinated chicken to basket. Put on the Smart Lid on top of the Ninja Foodi Steam Fryer. Move the Lid Slider to the "Air Fry/Stovetop". Select the "Air Fry" mode for cooking. 5. Adjust the cooking temperature to 175°C. 6. Cook for 20 minutes, making sure to turn halfway through cooking process. 7. To make the dipping sauce, mix all the dip ingredients until smooth.
Per serving: Calories: 334; Fat: 12.9g; Sodium: 414mg; Carbs: 11g; Fiber: 5g; Sugar 9g; Protein 31g

Chicken Wing Stir-Fry

Prep Time: 10 minutes | Cook Time: 25 minutes | Serves: 14-20 wings

80g corn flour	1 egg white	Stir-fry:	2 tablespoons avocado oil
¼ teaspoon pepper	14-20 chicken wing pieces	¼ teaspoon pepper	2 trimmed spring onions
½ teaspoon salt		1 teaspoon sea salt	2 jalapeno peppers

1. Place the Cook & Crisp Basket in your Pressure Cooker Steam Fryer. 2. Coat the Cook & Crisp Basket with oil. 3. Mix pepper, salt, and egg white till foamy. 4. Pat wings dry and add to the bowl of egg white mixture. Coat well. Let marinate at least 20 minutes. 5. Place coated wings in a big bowl and add corn flour. Dredge wings well. Shake off and add to "cook & crisp basket". 6. Put on the Smart Lid on top of the Ninja Foodi Steam Fryer. 7. Move the Lid Slider to the "Air Fry/Stovetop". Select the "Air Fry" mode for cooking. 8. Cook 25 minutes at 195°C. When timer sounds, bump up the temperature to 200°C. Cook for an additional 5 minutes till browned. 9. For stir fry, remove seeds from jalapenos and chop up spring onions. Add both to bowl and set to the side. Heat a wok with oil and add pepper, salt, spring onions, and jalapenos. Cook 1 minute. 10. Add air fried chicken to frying pan and toss with stir-fried veggies. Cook 1 minute and devour!
Per serving: Calories: 489; Fat: 11g; Sodium: 501mg; Carbs: 8.9g; Fiber: 4.6g; Sugar 8g; Protein 26g

Chicken Parmesan

Prep Time: 10 minutes | Cook Time: 9 minutes | Serves: 4

120g keto marinara	2 tablespoon grated parmesan cheese	seasoned breadcrumbs
6 tablespoon mozzarella cheese	6 tablespoon gluten-free	2 (200g) chicken breasts
1 tablespoon melted ghee		Olive oil

1. Place the Cook & Crisp Basket in your Pressure Cooker Steam Fryer. 2. Grease the "cook & crisp basket" with olive oil. 3. Mix parmesan cheese and breadcrumbs together. 4. Brush melted ghee onto the chicken and dip into breadcrumb mixture. 5. Place the coated chicken in the basket and top with olive oil. 6. Put on the Smart Lid on top of the Ninja Foodi Steam Fryer. 7. Move the Lid Slider to the "Air Fry/Stovetop". Select the "Air Fry" mode for cooking. 8. Adjust the cooking temperature to 180°C. 9. Cook 2 breasts for around 6 minutes and top each breast with a tablespoon of sauce and 1 ½ tablespoons of mozzarella cheese. Cook another 3 minutes to melt cheese. 10. Keep cooked pieces warm as you repeat the process with remaining breasts.
Per serving: Calories: 584; Fat: 15g; Sodium: 441mg; Carbs: 17g; Fiber: 4.6g; Sugar 5g; Protein 29g

Jerk-Spiced Chicken Wings

Prep Time: 10 minutes | Cook Time: 16 minutes | Serves: 8

1 teaspoon salt	2 tablespoon brown sugar	1 tablespoon allspice	2 tablespoons olive oil
120ml red wine vinegar	1 tablespoon chopped thyme	1 Habanero pepper, chopped	1.8kg of chicken wings
5 tablespoon lime juice	1 teaspoon white pepper	6 chopped garlic cloves	
4 chopped spring onions	1 teaspoon cayenne pepper	2 tablespoon low-sodium soy sauce	
1 tablespoon grated ginger	1 teaspoon cinnamon		

1. Place the Cook & Crisp Basket in your Pressure Cooker Steam Fryer. 2. Mix all the recipe ingredients except wings in a suitable bowl. 3. Pour the prepared marinade into a gallon bag and add chicken wings. Chill 2 to 24 hours to marinate. 4. Place all the chicken wings into a strainer to drain excess liquids. 5. Pour half of the wings into your Ninja Foodi Pressure Steam Fryer. 6. Put on the Smart Lid on top of the Ninja Foodi Steam Fryer. 7. Move the Lid Slider to the "Air Fry/Stovetop". Select the "Air Fry" mode for cooking. 8. Adjust the cooking temperature to 200°C. 9. Cook for 14 to 16 minutes, making sure to shake halfway through the cooking process. 10. Remove and repeat the process with remaining wings.
Per serving: Calories: 483; Fat: 7.9g; Sodium: 704mg; Carbs: 6g; Fiber: 3.6g; Sugar 6g; Protein 21g

Crusted Chicken Fingers

Prep Time: 10 minutes | Cook Time: 10 minutes | Serves: 4

- 675g chicken tenders
- 1 tablespoon olive oil
- 1 egg, whisked
- 1 teaspoon fresh parsley, minced
- 1 teaspoon garlic, minced
- Sea salt and black pepper, to taste
- 100g breadcrumbs

1. Place the Cook & Crisp Basket in your Pressure Cooker Steam Fryer. 2. Pat the chicken dry with kitchen towels. 3. In a suitable bowl, mix the oil, egg, parsley, garlic, salt, and black pepper. 4. Dip the prepared chicken tenders into the egg mixture. Then, roll the chicken over the breadcrumbs. 5. Put on the Smart Lid on top of the Ninja Foodi Steam Fryer. 6. Move the Lid Slider to the "Air Fry/Stovetop". Select the "Air Fry" mode for cooking. 7. Cook the chicken tenders at 180°C for around 10 minutes, shaking the "cook & crisp basket" halfway through the cooking time. 8. Serve.
Per serving: Calories: 302; Fat: 7g; Sodium: 224mg; Carbs: 6g; Fiber: 6g; Sugar 2g; Protein 22g

Air Fried Turkey Breast

Prep Time: 10 minutes | Cook Time: 60 minutes | Serves: 6-8

- Pepper and salt
- 1 oven-ready turkey breast
- Turkey seasonings of choice

1. Place the Cook & Crisp Basket in your Pressure Cooker Steam Fryer. 2. Season turkey with pepper, salt, and other desired seasonings. 3. Place turkey in "cook & crisp basket". 4. Put on the Smart Lid on top of the Ninja Foodi Steam Fryer. 5. Move the Lid Slider to the "Air Fry/Stovetop". Select the "Air Fry" mode for cooking. 6. Adjust the cooking temperature to 175°C. 7. Cook 60 minutes. The meat should be at 75°C when done. 8. Allow to rest 10 to 15 minutes before slicing. Enjoy!
Per serving: Calories: 237; Fat: 10.9g; Sodium: 354mg; Carbs: 20.5g; Fiber: 4.1g; Sugar 8.2g; Protein 26g

Air-Fried Chicken Breasts

Prep Time: 10 minutes | Cook Time: 12 minutes | Serves: 4

- 455g chicken breasts raw, boneless and skinless
- 1 tablespoon butter, room temperature
- 1 teaspoon garlic powder
- Salt and black pepper, to taste
- 1 teaspoon dried parsley flakes
- 1 teaspoon smoked paprika
- ½ teaspoon dried oregano

1. Place the Cook & Crisp Basket in your Pressure Cooker Steam Fryer. 2. Pat the chicken dry with kitchen towels. Toss the chicken breasts with the remaining ingredients. 3. Put on the Smart Lid on top of the Ninja Foodi Steam Fryer. 4. Move the Lid Slider to the "Air Fry/Stovetop". Select the "Air Fry" mode for cooking. 5. Cook the prepared chicken at 195°C for around 12 minutes, turning them over halfway through the cooking time. Serve.
Per serving: Calories: 227; Fat:13.4g; Carbs: 0.2g; Proteins: 23.4g; Sugars: 0.2g; Fiber: 1g

Spiced Chicken Thighs

Prep Time: 10 minutes | Cook Time: 22 minutes | Serves: 4

- 455g chicken thighs, bone-in
- Sea salt and black pepper, to taste
- 2 tablespoons olive oil
- 1 teaspoon stone-mustard
- 60ml hot sauce

1. Place the Cook & Crisp Basket in your Pressure Cooker Steam Fryer. 2. Pat the chicken dry with kitchen towels. Toss the chicken with the remaining ingredients. 3. Put on the Smart Lid on top of the Ninja Foodi Steam Fryer. 4. Move the Lid Slider to the "Air Fry/Stovetop". Select the "Air Fry" mode for cooking. 5. Cook the prepared chicken at 195°C for around 22 minutes, turning them over halfway through the cooking time. 6. Serve.
Per serving: Calories: 317; Fat:25.4g; Carbs: 1.5g; Proteins: 19.1g; Sugars: 0.6g; Fiber: 1g

Air-Fried Chicken Legs

Prep Time: 10 minutes | Cook Time: 30 minutes | Serves: 4

- 4 chicken legs, bone-in
- 2 tablespoons sesame oil
- Salt and black pepper, to taste
- ½ teaspoon mustard seeds
- 1 teaspoon cayenne pepper
- ½ teaspoon onion powder
- ½ teaspoon garlic powder

1. Place the Cook & Crisp Basket in your Pressure Cooker Steam Fryer. 2. Pat the chicken dry with paper towels. Toss the bone-in chicken legs with the remaining ingredients. 3. Put on the Smart Lid on top of the Ninja Foodi Steam Fryer. 4. Move the Lid Slider to the "Air Fry/Stovetop". Select the "Air Fry" mode for cooking. 5. Cook the prepared chicken at 195°C for around 30 minutes, turning them over halfway through the cooking time. 6. Serve.
Per serving: Calories: 387; Fat:18.1g; Carbs: 1.9g; Proteins: 51.1g; Sugars: 0.6g; Fiber: 0.4g

Turkey with Gravy

Prep time: 25 minutes | Cook time: 60 minutes | Serves: 4

1 (2kg) bone-in turkey breast	240ml low-sodium chicken stock	melted
4 teaspoons poultry seasoning	2 tablespoons unsalted butter,	2 tablespoons plain flour
¾ teaspoon fine sea salt		2 tablespoons heavy cream

1. Prepare the turkey: Pat the turkey breast dry. Mix together the poultry seasoning and salt. Rub about half of the mixture on the skin and in the cavity on the underside of the breast; reserve the rest. 2. Pour the chicken stock into the cooking pot. Place a Deluxe reversible rack in the pot. Lock lid; move slider towards PRESSURE. Adjust pressure release valve in the SEAL position. Close pressure-release valve. The cooking temperature will default to HIGH, which is accurate. Set time to 8 minutes. Select START/STOP and start cooking. When cooking is complete, let pressure release naturally for about 8 minutes, then quickly release any remaining pressure by turning it into VENT position. Unlock and remove the lid. 3. Mix the remaining seasoning mixture with the butter. When the turkey is ready, remove it from the pot and place it, skin-side up, on a rack set over a rimmed baking sheet. Brush the turkey skin with the seasoned butter. 4. Lock lid; move slider to STEAMCRISP. Select STEAM & CRISP, set temperature to 200°C, and set time to 15 minutes. Press START/STOP to begin cooking. Roast the turkey for 10 to 15 minutes, until the skin is browned and the interior temperature reaches at least 70°C. 5. While the turkey roasts, remove the Deluxe reversible rack from the cooking pot. Remove about 120ml of the cooking liquid and leave the rest in the pot. Move the slider towards "AIR FRY/STOVETOP" and set Ninja Foodi XL Pressure Cooker Steam Fryer with SmartLid to SEAR/SAUTÉ mode. Adjust the temperature to "3" by using up arrow. Press START/STOP to begin cooking. In a small bowl, stir together the flour and the 120ml cooking liquid. When the liquid in the pot is simmering, gradually stir in the flour mixture. Cook for 3 to 5 minutes, until the gravy comes to a boil and is thickened. For a creamier gravy, stir in the optional cream. 6. When the turkey is done, remove it from the oven and let it rest for about 10 minutes before slicing.
Per Serving: Calories 286; Fat 12.5g; Sodium 711mg; Carbs 11.6g; Fiber 3g; Sugar 1.3g; Protein 16.3g

Thanksgiving Turkey

Prep Time: 10 minutes | Cook Time: 1 hour | Serves: 4

1 tablespoon butter	1 teaspoon cayenne pepper	455g turkey breast, bone-in
Salt and black pepper, to taste	1 teaspoon Italian herb mix	

1. Place the Cook & Crisp Basket in your Pressure Cooker Steam Fryer. 2. In a suitable mixing bowl, mix the butter, salt, black pepper, cayenne pepper, and herb mix. 3. Rub the mixture all over the turkey breast. 4. Put on the Smart Lid on top of the Ninja Foodi Steam Fryer. 5. Move the Lid Slider to the "Air Fry/Stovetop". Select the "Air Fry" mode for cooking. 6. Cook the turkey breast at 175°C for around 1 hour, turning them over every 20 minutes. 7. Serve.
Per serving: Calories: 210; Fat:10.1g; Carbs: 1.3g; Proteins: 25.1g; Sugars: 0.6g; Fiber: 0.4g

Asian-Spiced Duck

Prep Time: 10 minutes | Cook Time: 30 minutes | Serves: 3

455g duck breast	1 tablespoon Five-spice powder	taste
1 tablespoon Hoisin sauce	Sea salt and black pepper, to	¼ teaspoon cinnamon

1. Place the Cook & Crisp Basket in your Pressure Cooker Steam Fryer. 2. Toss the duck breast with the remaining ingredients. 3. Put on the Smart Lid on top of the Ninja Foodi Steam Fryer. 4. Move the Lid Slider to the "Air Fry/Stovetop". Select the "Air Fry" mode for cooking. 5. Cook the duck breast at 165°C for around 15 minutes, turning them over halfway through the cooking time. 6. Turn the heat to 175°C; continue to cook for about 15 minutes or until cooked through. 7. Serve.
Per serving: Calories: 345; Fat:23.2g; Carbs: 5.7g; Proteins: 27.1g; Sugars: 2.3g; Fiber: 0.8g

Chicken BBQ Burgers

Prep Time: 10 minutes | Cook Time: 17 minutes | Serves: 3

340g chicken, ground	25g Parmesan cheese, grated	2 tablespoons onion, minced	1 tablespoon BBQ sauce
10g tortilla chips, crushed	1 egg, beaten	2 garlic cloves, minced	

1. Place the Cook & Crisp Basket in your Pressure Cooker Steam Fryer. 2. Mix all the recipe ingredients until everything is well mixed. Form the mixture into three patties. 3. Put on the Smart Lid on top of the Ninja Foodi Steam Fryer. 4. Move the Lid Slider to the "Air Fry/Stovetop". Select the "Air Fry" mode for cooking. 5. Cook the burgers at 195°C for about 17 minutes or until cooked through; make sure to turn them over halfway through the cooking time. 6. Serve.
Per serving: Calories: 373; Fat:23.8g; Carbs: 7g; Proteins: 27g; Sugars: 0.7g; Fiber: 0.9g

Tuscan Chicken

Prep time: 10 minutes | Cook time: 23 minutes | Serves: 4

900g boneless, skinless chicken breasts	4 garlic cloves, minced	18g heavy cream	60g chopped fresh spinach
1 tablespoon Italian seasoning	2 tablespoons olive oil	75g grated Parmesan cheese	
½ teaspoon fine sea salt	180ml low-sodium chicken stock	30g oil-packed sun-dried tomatoes, drained	

1. Cut the chicken breasts in half lengthwise. One at a time, place the chicken breasts between two pieces of plastic wrap. On top of a protected surface, like a cutting board on the counter, use a pan or rolling pin to pound the meat to about 1 cm thick. Season the chicken with the Italian seasoning, salt, and garlic, pressing the seasonings into the chicken with your fingertips. 2. Move the slider towards "AIR FRY/STOVETOP" and set Ninja Foodi XL Pressure Cooker Steam Fryer with SmartLid to SEAR/SAUTÉ mode. Adjust the temperature to "Hi5" by using up arrow. Press START/STOP to begin cooking. Add the oil to the cooking pot. When the oil is hot, add the chicken and brown for 2 minutes on each side. Remove the chicken and add the stock, stirring to loosen any chicken pieces that may have stuck to the bottom. Return the chicken to the pot. 3. Lock lid; move slider towards PRESSURE. Adjust pressure release valve in the SEAL position. Close pressure-release valve. The cooking temperature will default to HIGH, which is accurate. Set time to 3 minutes. Select START/STOP and start cooking. When cooking is complete, let pressure release quickly by turning it into VENT position. 4. Unlock and remove the lid. Use tongs to transfer the chicken pieces to a plate. Move the slider towards "AIR FRY/STOVETOP" and set Ninja Foodi XL Pressure Cooker Steam Fryer with SmartLid to SEAR/SAUTÉ mode. Adjust the temperature to "Hi5" by using up arrow. Press START/STOP to begin cooking and whisk the cream into the stock, stirring to combine. Bring to a simmer and cook, stirring occasionally, for 5 minutes. 5. Add the cheese and sun-dried tomatoes and stir until the cheese melts. Add the spinach and stir just until the spinach wilts.

Per Serving: Calories 282; Fat 12.6g; Sodium 269mg; Carbs 11.5g; Fiber 2g; Sugar 2g; Protein 17.3g

Delicious Arroz Con Pollo

Prep time: 10 minutes | Cook time: 36 minutes | Serves: 4

4 tablespoons olive oil, divided	pepper	370g long-grain white rice	tomatoes
3 boneless, skinless chicken breasts, cut into small pieces	180g finely chopped onion	2 teaspoons ground cumin	510g frozen peas and carrots
2 teaspoons fine sea salt	150g chopped green pepper	720ml low-sodium chicken stock	65g green olives, plus 1 tablespoon of their brine
¼ teaspoon ground black	150g chopped red pepper	1 (350g) can fire-roasted	
	3 garlic cloves, minced		

1. Move the slider towards "AIR FRY/STOVETOP" and set Ninja Foodi XL Pressure Cooker Steam Fryer with SmartLid to SEAR/SAUTÉ mode. Adjust the temperature to "Hi5" by using up arrow. Press START/STOP to begin cooking. Add 2 tablespoons of the oil to the cooking pot. When the oil is hot, season the chicken with the salt and pepper and add it to the pot. Cook for 3 minutes on each side, or until golden brown. Transfer the chicken to a plate. 2. Move the slider towards "AIR FRY/STOVETOP" and set Ninja Foodi XL Pressure Cooker Steam Fryer with SmartLid to SEAR/SAUTÉ mode. Adjust the temperature to "Hi5" by using up arrow. Press START/STOP to begin cooking. Add the remaining 2 tablespoons of oil to the pot, and then add the onion, green and red peppers, and garlic. Cook the vegetables for 3 minutes. Add the rice and stir to coat the grains. Add the cumin, stock, tomatoes with their juices, frozen peas and carrots, and olives and brine. Return the chicken to the pot. 3. Lock lid; move slider towards PRESSURE. Adjust pressure release valve in the SEAL position. Close pressure-release valve. The cooking temperature will default to HIGH, which is accurate. Set time to 10 minutes. Select START/STOP and start cooking. When cooking is complete, let pressure release naturally for about 10 minutes, then quickly release any remaining pressure by turning it into VENT position. 4. Unlock and remove the lid. Fluff the rice with a fork before serving.

Per Serving: Calories 268; Fat 12.3g; Sodium 358mg; Carbs 11g; Fiber 3g; Sugar 2g; Protein 16.2g

Chicken with Mushrooms

Prep time: 15 minutes | Cook time: 45 minutes | Serves: 4

30g plain flour	1 teaspoon ground black pepper	200g mushrooms, sliced	stock
4 bone-in, skinless chicken thighs or breasts	4 tablespoons olive oil, divided	1 small onion, chopped	240g tomato sauce
1 teaspoon fine sea salt	2 bacon slices, cut into 2.5 cm pieces	2 garlic cloves, minced	1 (250g) can condensed cream of mushroom soup
		240ml low-sodium chicken	

1. Put the flour in a wide, shallow bowl. Season the chicken with the salt and pepper. Use 2 tablespoons of oil to coat each piece of chicken, then roll it in the flour to coat. 2. Move the slider towards "AIR FRY/STOVETOP" and set Ninja Foodi XL Pressure Cooker Steam Fryer with SmartLid to SEAR/SAUTÉ mode. Adjust the temperature to "Hi5" by using up arrow. Press START/STOP to begin cooking. Add the remaining 2 tablespoons of oil to the pot. When the oil is hot, add the chicken and cook until browned, about 3 minutes on each side. Add the bacon, mushrooms, onion, and garlic and sauté for 5 minutes. Add the stock and stir to loosen any ingredients that may have stuck to the bottom of the pot. Add the tomato sauce and cook, stirring, for 1 minute. 3. Lock lid; move slider towards PRESSURE. Adjust pressure release valve in the SEAL position. Close pressure-release valve. The cooking temperature will default to HIGH, which is accurate. Set time to 20 minutes. Select START/STOP and start cooking. When cooking is complete, let pressure release naturally for about 5 minutes, then quickly release any remaining pressure by turning it into VENT position. 4. Unlock and remove the lid and stir in the cream of mushroom soup until heated through.

Per Serving: Calories 265; Fat 12.6g; Sodium 365mg; Carbs 12.2g; Fiber 4g; Sugar 3g; Protein 16.5g

Spicy Teriyaki Chicken

Prep time: 15 minutes | Cook time: 30 minutes | Serves: 4

4 to 6 bone-in, skin-on chicken thighs	2 tablespoons olive oil	teriyaki sauce, divided (see tip to make your own)	cut into 2.5 cm chunks
½ teaspoon salt	60ml low-sodium chicken stock	1 large red pepper, seeded and	1 (200g) can unsweetened pineapple chunks, drained
	60ml plus 2 tablespoons		

1. Season the chicken thighs on both sides with the salt. Move the slider towards "AIR FRY/STOVETOP" and set Ninja Foodi XL Pressure Cooker Steam Fryer with SmartLid to SEAR/SAUTÉ mode. Adjust the temperature to "Hi5" by using up arrow. Press START/STOP to begin cooking. Add the oil to the pot and heat until it shimmers and flows like water. Add the chicken thighs, skin-side down, and let them cook, undisturbed, for about 4 minutes, until the skin is golden brown. Transfer the thighs to a plate. 2. Pour out the fat. Add the stock and scrape the bottom of the pan to release the browned bits. Add 2 tablespoons of teriyaki sauce and stir to combine. Add the pepper chunks and chicken thighs, skin-side up. 3. Lock lid; move slider towards PRESSURE. Adjust pressure release valve in the SEAL position. Close pressure-release valve. The cooking temperature will default to HIGH, which is accurate. Set time to 8 minutes. Select START/STOP and start cooking. When cooking is complete, let pressure release naturally for about 5 minutes, then quickly release any remaining pressure by turning it into VENT position. 4. Lock lid; move slider to STEAMCRISP. Select STEAM & CRISP, set temperature to 200°C, and set time to 5 minutes. Press START/STOP to begin cooking. Remove the chicken thighs from the pan and place them on a rack set over a rimmed baking sheet. Brush with the remaining 60 g of teriyaki sauce. Crisp the chicken thighs for 3 to 5 minutes, until browned. 5. While the chicken broils, add the pineapple chunks to the pot. Select Sauté again and adjust the heat to Medium. Bring to a simmer to thicken the sauce and warm the pineapple through. 6. When the chicken is done, top it with the peppers and pineapple, and drizzle with the sauce.
Per Serving: Calories 283; Fat 12.3g; Sodium 444mg; Carbs 11.5g; Fiber 2g; Sugar 2g; Protein 16.7g

Paprika Chicken Cutlets

Prep Time: 10 minutes | Cook Time: 12 minutes | Serves: 4

455g chicken breasts, boneless, skinless, cut into 4 pieces	1 tablespoon butter, melted	Salt and black pepper, to taste
	1 teaspoon smoked paprika	1 teaspoon garlic powder

1. Place the Cook & Crisp Basket in your Pressure Cooker Steam Fryer. 2. Flatten the chicken breasts to ½ cm thickness. 3. Toss the chicken breasts with the remaining ingredients. 4. Put on the Smart Lid on top of the Ninja Foodi Steam Fryer. 5. Move the Lid Slider to the "Air Fry/Stovetop". Select the "Air Fry" mode for cooking. 6. Cook the prepared chicken at 195°C for around 12 minutes, turning them over halfway through the cooking time. 7. Serve.
Per serving: Calories: 229; Fat:13.8g; Carbs: 1.9g; Proteins: 24.1g; Sugars: 0.6g; Fiber: 0.4g

Hawaiian Roll Sliders

Prep Time: 10 minutes | Cook Time: 17 minutes | Serves: 3

340g chicken,	minced	½ teaspoon cumin	2 tablespoons olive oil
1 teaspoon garlic, minced	2 tablespoons fresh coriander, minced	½ teaspoon paprika	6 Hawaiian rolls
1 small onion, minced		Sea salt and black pepper, to taste	
2 tablespoons fresh parsley,	½ teaspoon mustard seeds		

1. Place the Cook & Crisp Basket in your Pressure Cooker Steam Fryer. 2. Mix all the recipe ingredients, except for the Hawaiian rolls, until everything is well mixed. Shape the mixture into six patties. 3. Put on the Smart Lid on top of the Ninja Foodi Steam Fryer. 4. Move the Lid Slider to the "Air Fry/Stovetop". Select the "Air Fry" mode for cooking. 5. Cook the burgers at 195°C for about 17 minutes or until cooked through; make sure to turn them over halfway through the cooking time. 6. Serve your burgers over Hawaiian rolls and garnish with toppings of choice. Serve.
Per serving: Calories: 490; Fat:21.8g; Carbs: 46.7g; Proteins: 28g; Sugars: 7g; Fiber: 2.7g

Mediterranean Chicken Fillets

Prep Time: 10 minutes | Cook Time: 12 minutes | Serves: 4

675g chicken fillets	1 tablespoon Greek seasoning mix	crushed
1 tablespoon olive oil		Sea salt and black pepper, to taste
1 teaspoon garlic, minced	½ teaspoon red pepper flakes,	

1. Place the Cook & Crisp Basket in your Pressure Cooker Steam Fryer. 2. Pat the chicken dry with paper towels. Toss the chicken with the remaining ingredients. 3. Put on the Smart Lid on top of the Ninja Foodi Steam Fryer. 4. Move the Lid Slider to the "Air Fry/Stovetop". Select the "Air Fry" mode for cooking. 5. Cook the chicken fillets at 195°C for around 12 minutes, turning them over halfway through the cooking time. 6. Serve.
Per serving: Calories: 227; Fat:13.4g; Carbs: 0.2g; Proteins: 23.4g; Sugars: 0.2g; Fiber: 1g

Chicken Egg Roll

Prep time: 10 minutes | Cook time: 14 minutes | Serves: 4

3 tablespoons soy sauce 1 tablespoon rice vinegar, white wine vinegar, or lime juice 1 teaspoon granulated sugar 355g shredded cabbage or	coleslaw mix 1 large carrot, shredded 35g chopped mushrooms 3 spring onions, chopped 2 teaspoons minced garlic	1 teaspoon grated fresh ginger 1 tablespoon toasted sesame oil 300g chicken tenders or chicken breast, cut into 2.5 cm strips	4 to 6 flour tortillas or other wraps, warmed

1. Combine the soy sauce, vinegar, and sugar in the cooking pot. Add the cabbage, carrot, mushrooms, spring onions, garlic, ginger, and sesame oil and stir. Lay the chicken tenders on top. 2. Lock lid; move slider towards PRESSURE. Adjust pressure release valve in the SEAL position. Close pressure-release valve. The cooking temperature will default to HIGH, which is accurate. Set time to 2 minutes. Select START/STOP and start cooking. When cooking is complete, let pressure release quickly by turning it into VENT position. 3. Unlock and remove the lid. Use tongs to transfer the chicken to a plate. When the chicken is cool enough to handle, shred it with two forks or cut it into bite-size pieces. Stir the chicken back into the vegetables. Move the slider towards "AIR FRY/STOVETOP" and set Ninja Foodi XL Pressure Cooker Steam Fryer with SmartLid to SEAR/SAUTÉ mode. Adjust the temperature to "Hi5" by using up arrow. Press START/STOP to begin cooking. Bring the mixture to a boil for a minute or so, just to reduce the liquid by about half and finish cooking the chicken if necessary. 4. Using a slotted spoon, scoop out the filling onto the wraps, leaving most of the liquid behind so the wraps don't get soggy. Fold the wraps around the filling, tucking in the edges.
Per Serving: Calories 286; Fat 12.6g; Sodium 399mg; Carbs 11.4g; Fiber 5g; Sugar 6g; Protein 16.6g

Mayo Chicken Salad

Prep Time: 10 minutes | Cook Time: 12 minutes | Serves: 3

455g chicken breast 2 tablespoons spring onions, chopped	1 carrot, shredded 120g mayonnaise 1 tablespoon mustard	Sea salt and black pepper, to taste Oil

1. Place the Cook & Crisp Basket in your Pressure Cooker Steam Fryer. 2. Pat the chicken dry with kitchen towels. Brush the oil on the Cook & Crisp Basket and place the chicken in it. 3. Put on the Smart Lid on top of the Ninja Foodi Steam Fryer. 4. Move the Lid Slider to the "Air Fry/Stovetop". Select the "Air Fry" mode for cooking. 5. Cook the prepared chicken at 195°C for around 12 minutes, turning them over halfway through the cooking time. 6. Chop the chicken breasts and transfer it to a salad bowl; add in the remaining recipe ingredients and toss to mix well. Serve.
Per serving: Calories: 373; Fat:23.8g; Carbs: 7g; Proteins: 27g; Sugars: 0.7g; Fiber: 0.9g

Chicken Taquitos

Prep Time: 10 minutes | Cook Time: 18 minutes | Serves: 5

340g chicken breasts, boneless and skinless	Salt and black pepper, to taste ½ teaspoon red chili powder	5 small corn tortillas 125g feta cheese, crumbled

1. Place the Cook & Crisp Basket in your Pressure Cooker Steam Fryer. 2. Pat the chicken dry with kitchen towels. Toss the boneless chicken breasts with the salt, pepper, and red chili powder. 3. Put on the Smart Lid on top of the Ninja Foodi Steam Fryer. 4. Move the Lid Slider to the "Air Fry/Stovetop". Select the "Air Fry" mode for cooking. 5. Cook the prepared chicken at 195°C for around 12 minutes, turning them over halfway through the cooking time. 6. Place the shredded chicken and cheese on one end of each tortilla. Roll them up tightly and transfer them to an oiled "cook & crisp basket". 7. Air fry your taquitos at 180°C for around 6 minutes. 8. Serve.
Per serving: Calories: 256; Fat:13g; Carbs: 14.2g; Proteins: 20.4g; Sugars: 2.7g; Fiber: 1.7g

Chicken with Pineapple

Prep Time: 10 minutes | Cook Time: 35 minutes | Serves: 4

455g chicken legs, boneless Salt and black pepper, to taste	2 tablespoons tamari sauce 1 tablespoon hot sauce	175g pineapple, peeled and diced	1 tablespoon fresh coriander, chopped

1. Place the Cook & Crisp Basket in your Pressure Cooker Steam Fryer. 2. Pat the chicken dry with paper towels. Toss the chicken legs with the salt, black pepper, tamari sauce, and hot sauce. 3. Put on the Smart Lid on top of the Ninja Foodi Steam Fryer. 4. Move the Lid Slider to the "Air Fry/Stovetop". Select the "Air Fry" mode for cooking. 5. Cook the prepared chicken at 195°C for around 30 minutes, turning them over halfway through the cooking time. 6. Top the chicken with the pineapple and continue to cook for around 5 minutes more. Serve warm, garnished with the fresh coriander. 7. Serve.
Per serving: Calories: 267; Fat:18.1g; Carbs: 6.5g; Proteins: 19g; Sugars: 4.6g; Fiber: 0.8g

Delicious Sesame Chicken

Prep time: 5 minutes | Cook time: 15 minutes | Serves: 4

- 2 tablespoons corn flour, divided
- ¼ teaspoon fine sea salt
- 455g chicken tenders, cut into 2.5 cm pieces
- 2 tablespoons toasted sesame oil, divided
- 60ml soy sauce
- 2 tablespoons ketchup
- ¼ teaspoon red pepper flakes
- 85g honey
- 2 tablespoons water
- 2 teaspoons sesame seeds

1. In a small bowl, combine 1 tablespoon of corn flour with the salt. Toss the chicken pieces in the corn flour mixture until it is coated evenly. Move the slider towards "AIR FRY/STOVETOP" and set Ninja Foodi XL Pressure Cooker Steam Fryer with SmartLid to SEAR/SAUTÉ mode. Adjust the temperature to "Hi5" by using up arrow. Press START/STOP to begin cooking. Add 1 tablespoon of sesame oil. When the oil is hot, add the chicken and cook for about 4 minutes, turning occasionally, or until golden brown. 2. In another small bowl, combine the soy sauce, ketchup, and red pepper flakes and stir until well combined. Pour this sauce over the chicken. 3. Lock lid; move slider towards PRESSURE. Adjust pressure release valve in the SEAL position. Close pressure-release valve. The cooking temperature will default to HIGH, which is accurate. Set time to 3 minutes. Select START/STOP and start cooking. When cooking is complete, let pressure release quickly by turning it into VENT position. 4. Unlock and remove the lid. Add the remaining 1 tablespoon of sesame oil and the honey and stir quickly to combine. Move the slider towards "AIR FRY/STOVETOP" and set Ninja Foodi XL Pressure Cooker Steam Fryer with SmartLid to SEAR/SAUTÉ mode. Adjust the temperature to "Hi5" by using up arrow. Press START/STOP to begin cooking. 5. In a clean small bowl, whisk the remaining 1 tablespoon of corn flour into the water until it is smooth. Stir this slurry into the chicken, stirring constantly for 2 minutes, or until sauce reaches the desired consistency. 6. Sprinkle with the sesame seeds.

Per Serving: Calories 287; Fat 12.4g; Sodium 333mg; Carbs 11.6g; Fiber 7g; Sugar 2g; Protein 16.5g

Chicken Pepper Fajitas

Prep Time: 10 minutes | Cook Time: 30 minutes | Serves: 4

- 455g chicken legs, boneless, skinless, cut into pieces
- 2 tablespoons rapeseed oil
- 1 red pepper, sliced
- 1 yellow pepper, sliced
- 1 jalapeno pepper, sliced
- 1 onion, sliced
- ½ teaspoon onion powder
- ½ teaspoon garlic powder
- Sea salt and black pepper, to taste

1. Place the Cook & Crisp Basket in your Pressure Cooker Steam Fryer. 2. Pat the chicken dry with paper towels. Toss the chicken legs with 1 tablespoon of the rapeseed oil. 3. Put on the Smart Lid on top of the Ninja Foodi Steam Fryer. 4. Move the Lid Slider to the "Air Fry/Stovetop". Select the "Air Fry" mode for cooking. 5. Cook the prepared chicken at 195°C for around 15 minutes, shaking the "cook & crisp basket" halfway through the cooking time. 6. Add the remaining recipe ingredients to the Ninja Foodi Pressure Steam Fryer "cook & crisp basket" and turn the heat to 200°C. Let it cook for around 15 minutes more or until cooked through. 7. Serve.

Per serving: Calories: 330; Fat:25.1g; Carbs: 6.1g; Proteins: 19.6g; Sugars: 1.4g; Fiber: 1g

Air-Fried Turkey Wings

Prep Time: 10 minutes | Cook Time: 40 minutes | Serves: 5

- 900g turkey wings, bone-in
- 2 garlic cloves, minced
- 1 small onion, chopped
- 1 tablespoon Dijon mustard
- 120ml red wine
- Sea salt and black pepper, to taste
- 1 teaspoon poultry seasoning

1. Place the Cook & Crisp Basket in your Pressure Cooker Steam Fryer. 2. Place the turkey wings, garlic, onion, mustard, and wine in a ceramic bowl. Cover the bowl and let the turkey marinate in your refrigerator overnight. 3. Discard the marinade and toss the turkey wings with the salt, black pepper, and poultry seasoning. 4. Put on the Smart Lid on top of the Ninja Foodi Steam Fryer. 5. Move the Lid Slider to the "Air Fry/Stovetop". Select the "Air Fry" mode for cooking. 6. Cook the turkey wings at 200°C for around 40 minutes, turning them over halfway through the cooking time. 7. Serve.

Per serving: Calories: 377; Fat:22.5g; Carbs: 3.2g; Proteins: 37.4g; Sugars: 1.3g; Fiber: 0.6g

Limey Duck Breast

Prep Time: 10 minutes | Cook Time: 30 minutes | Serves: 4

- 2 tablespoons fresh lime juice
- 675g duck breast
- 2 tablespoons olive oil
- 1 teaspoon cayenne pepper
- Salt and black pepper, to taste

1. Place the Cook & Crisp Basket in your Pressure Cooker Steam Fryer. 2. Toss the duck breast with the remaining ingredients. 3. Put on the Smart Lid on top of the Ninja Foodi Steam Fryer. 4. Move the Lid Slider to the "Air Fry/Stovetop". Select the "Air Fry" mode for cooking. 5. Cook the duck breast at 165°C for around 15 minutes, turning them over halfway through the cooking time. 6. Turn the heat to 175°C; continue to cook for about 15 minutes or until cooked through. 7. Let the duck breasts rest for around 10 minutes before serving.

Per serving: Calories: 295; Fat:16.4g; Carbs: 2.2g; Proteins: 31.4g; Sugars: 0.1g; Fiber: 0.1g

Fried Chicken

Prep Time: 10 minutes | Cook Time: 12 minutes | Serves: 4

455g chicken fillets	1 tablespoon fresh coriander, minced	Sea salt and black pepper, to taste	1 teaspoon celery seeds
1 egg	1 tablespoon fresh parsley, minced	¼ teaspoon cumin	
1 tablespoon olive oil		¼ teaspoon mustard seeds	
70g crackers, crushed			

1. Place the Cook & Crisp Basket in your Pressure Cooker Steam Fryer. 2. Mix the egg in a shallow bowl. 3. Mix the remaining recipe ingredients in a separate shallow bowl. 4. Dip the dry chicken breasts into the egg mixture. Then, roll the chicken breasts over the cracker crumb mixture. 5. Put on the Smart Lid on top of the Ninja Foodi Steam Fryer. 6. Move the Lid Slider to the "Air Fry/Stovetop". Select the "Air Fry" mode for cooking. 7. Cook the prepared chicken at 195°C for around 12 minutes, turning them over halfway through the cooking time. 8. Serve.
Per serving: Calories: 318; Fat:23.3g; Carbs: 2.1g; Proteins: 23.7g; Sugars: 0.8g; Fiber: 0.3g

Salsa Chicken

Prep time: 5 minutes | Cook time: 5 minutes | Serves: 4

675g boneless, skinless chicken breasts, cut into 2.5 cm cubes	1 (400g) jar salsa	120ml chicken stock

1. Add chicken, salsa, and stock to the Ninja Foodi XL Pressure Cooker Steam Fryer with SmartLid cooking pot. 2. Lock lid; move slider towards PRESSURE. Adjust pressure release valve in the SEAL position. Close pressure-release valve. The cooking temperature will default to HIGH, which is accurate. Set time to 5 minutes. Select START/STOP and start cooking. 3. When cooking is complete, let pressure release naturally for about 10 minutes, then quickly release any remaining pressure by turning it into VENT position. Check chicken using a meat thermometer to ensure the internal temperature is at least 165°F/75°C. 4. Transfer chicken and salsa to a serving dish and serve warm.
Per Serving: Calories 180; Fat 11.8g; Sodium 248mg; Carbs 2.9g; Fiber 1g; Sugar 1g; Protein 16.3g

Chicken Thighs with Salsa

Prep time: 5 minutes | Cook time: 7 minutes | Serves: 8

80g diced peeled pineapple	diced	10g chopped fresh coriander	chicken thighs
80g diced peeled mango	40g peeled and finely diced red onion	10g chopped fresh mint leaves	1 teaspoon salt
120ml fresh lime juice		1 teaspoon salt	½ teaspoon ground black pepper
1 tablespoon lime zest	1 medium avocado, peeled, pitted, and diced	**Chicken**	
1 Roma tomato, seeded and		1.3kg boneless, skinless	240ml water

1. In a large bowl, combine pineapple, mango, lime juice, lime zest, tomato, onion, avocado, coriander, mint, and salt. Refrigerate salsa covered at least 1 hour or up to overnight. 2. Pat chicken thighs dry with a paper towel. Season with salt and pepper. 3. Add water to the Ninja Foodi XL Pressure Cooker Steam Fryer with SmartLid cooking pot and insert Deluxe Reversible Rack. Arrange thighs evenly in rack. 4. Lock lid; move slider towards PRESSURE. Adjust pressure release valve in the SEAL position. Close pressure-release valve. The cooking temperature will default to HIGH, which is accurate. Set time to 7 minutes. Select START/STOP and start cooking. 5. When cooking is complete, let pressure release quickly by turning it into VENT position. Carefully unlock lid. Check chicken using a meat thermometer to ensure the internal temperature is at least 75°C. 6. Transfer chicken to eight plates. Garnish with salsa and serve.
Per Serving: Calories 306; Fat 11g; Sodium 288mg; Carbs 10.7g; Fiber 2g; Sugar 2g; Protein 16.5g

Artichoke Hearts and Chicken

Prep time: 5 minutes | Cook time: 7 minutes | Serves: 8

1 teaspoon sea salt	pepper	120ml water	15g chopped fresh parsley
1 teaspoon smoked paprika	1.3kg boneless, skinless chicken thighs	2 (160g) jars marinated artichoke hearts, undrained	
½ teaspoon ground black			

1. In a medium bowl, combine salt, smoked paprika, and pepper. Add chicken and toss. Refrigerate covered at least 30 minutes or up to overnight. 2. Add chicken, water, and artichoke hearts with juice to the Ninja Foodi XL Pressure Cooker Steam Fryer with SmartLid cooking pot. 3. Lock lid; move slider towards PRESSURE. Adjust pressure release valve in the SEAL position. Close pressure-release valve. The cooking temperature will default to HIGH, which is accurate. Set time to 7 minutes. Select START/STOP and start cooking. 4. When cooking is complete, let pressure release quickly by turning it into VENT position. Check chicken using a meat thermometer to ensure the internal temperature is at least 75°C. 5. Using a slotted spoon, transfer chicken and artichokes to serving dish. Garnish with parsley and serve.
Per Serving: Calories 262; Fat 11.5g; Sodium 311mg; Carbs 9.7g; Fiber 2g; Sugar 2g; Protein 15.2g

Stuffed Turkey Breast with Gravy

Prep time: 25 minutes | Cook time: 60 minutes | Serves: 4

5 tablespoons unsalted butter	660ml store-bought chicken stock, or homemade	breast roast	2½ tablespoons plain flour
1 small yellow onion, chopped	1 (1.1kg) boneless, skin-on turkey breast half or tied turkey	Salt and freshly ground black pepper	
2 celery ribs, chopped		1 tablespoon olive oil	
800g dry sage stuffing mix			

1. Smear 1 tablespoon of the butter in the Cook & Crisp Basket. 2. Put 1 tablespoon of the butter in the pot, move the slider towards "AIR FRY/STOVETOP" and set Ninja Foodi XL Pressure Cooker Steam Fryer with SmartLid to SEAR/SAUTÉ mode. Adjust the temperature to "Hi5" by using up arrow. Press START/STOP to begin cooking. When the butter has melted, add the onion and celery and cook, stirring frequently, until tender, 4 minutes. Press START/STOP. Pour the vegetables into a bowl, add the stuffing mix and 300ml of the stock, and stir to moisten. Pour into the Cook & Crisp Basket and cover tightly with foil. set aside. 3. Season the turkey breast all over with salt and pepper and drizzle with the oil. Select SAUTÉ like before. When the pot is hot, place the turkey breast skin-side down in the pot and cook until golden brown, 3 minutes. Press START/STOP. Remove the turkey breast from the pot. 4. Add the remaining 360ml stock to the pot and scrape up any browned bits on the bottom. 5. Place a Deluxe reversible rack with handles into the pot and place the turkey breast skin-side up on the Deluxe reversible rack. Place the stuffing in the Cook & Crisp Basket on top of the turkey breast. 6. Lock lid; move slider towards PRESSURE. Adjust pressure release valve in the SEAL position. Close pressure-release valve. The cooking temperature will default to HIGH, which is accurate. Set time to 35 minutes. Select START/STOP and start cooking. When cooking is complete, let pressure release naturally for about 10 minutes, then quickly release any remaining pressure by turning it into VENT position. Remove the stuffing from the pot. 7. Insert an instant-read thermometer into the thickest part of the breast; it should read 70°C. If it doesn't, cover the pot with a regular pot lid, select SEAR/SAUTÉ again and simmer briefly until 70°C is reached. Press START/STOP. Transfer the turkey breast to a cutting board and cover loosely with foil; leave the cooking liquid in the pot. 8. In a medium bowl, combine the remaining 3 tablespoons butter with the flour and stir until smooth. Select SEAR/SAUTÉ gradually whisk the flour mixture into the cooking liquid and cook until bubbly, 3 minutes. Season with salt and pepper. Press START/STOP. 9. Slice the turkey roast crosswise. Serve with the gravy and stuffing.
Per Serving: Calories 282; Fat 11.3g; Sodium 113mg; Carbs 10.3g; Fiber 3g; Sugar 4g; Protein 16.2g

Thai Chicken Rice

Prep time: 7 minutes | Cook time: 25 minutes | Serves: 4

2 tablespoons toasted sesame oil	3 tablespoons soy sauce	1 teaspoon freshly squeezed lime juice	480ml low-sodium chicken stock
900g boneless, skinless chicken breast	1½ teaspoons fish sauce	1 teaspoon hot sauce	
120ml Thai sweet chili sauce	1½ teaspoons minced fresh ginger	1 tablespoon peanut butter	
	1 garlic clove, minced	245g long-grain white rice	

1. Move the slider towards "AIR FRY/STOVETOP" and set Ninja Foodi XL Pressure Cooker Steam Fryer with SmartLid to SEAR/SAUTÉ mode. Adjust the temperature to "Hi5" by using up arrow. Press START/STOP to begin cooking. Add the oil to the cooking pot. When the oil is hot, add the chicken and brown, about 3 minutes per side. Transfer the chicken to a plate. 2. In a medium bowl, whisk the sweet chili sauce, soy sauce, fish sauce, ginger, garlic, lime juice, hot sauce, and peanut butter until well combined. 3. Add the rice to the pot. Place the chicken breasts on top of the rice. Pour the sauce over the chicken and rice. Pour in the stock. 4. Lock lid; move slider towards PRESSURE. Adjust pressure release valve in the SEAL position. Close pressure-release valve. The cooking temperature will default to HIGH, which is accurate. Set time to 10 minutes. Select START/STOP and start cooking. When cooking is complete, let pressure release naturally. 5. Unlock and remove the lid. Transfer the chicken to a clean plate. Using a hand mixer or two forks, shred the chicken. Stir the rice, divide it between four serving bowls, and top with the chicken.
Per Serving: Calories 267; Fat 12.3g; Sodium 432mg; Carbs 11.6g; Fiber 2g; Sugar 3g; Protein 16.4g

Chicken with Marinara Sauce

Prep time: 10 minutes | Cook time: 28 minutes | Serves: 2

1 tablespoon olive oil	2 teaspoons Italian seasoning	120ml water	cheese
2 (125-150g) boneless, skinless chicken breasts	¼ teaspoon salt	240g marinara sauce	
	⅛ teaspoon black pepper	110g shredded mozzarella	

1. Move the slider towards "AIR FRY/STOVETOP" and set Ninja Foodi XL Pressure Cooker Steam Fryer with SmartLid to SEAR/SAUTÉ mode. Adjust the temperature to "Hi5" by using up arrow. Press START/STOP to begin cooking. and pour in the olive oil. 2. Season the chicken breasts with the Italian seasoning, salt, and pepper. Once the oil is shimmering, add the chicken and cook until golden brown, 3 to 4 minutes per side. Press START/STOP to turn off the pot and transfer the chicken to a plate. 3. Pour the water into the pot and scrape up any bits from the bottom of the pot. 4. Transfer the chicken breasts to the pot and top with the marinara sauce. 5. Lock lid; move slider towards PRESSURE. Adjust pressure release valve in the SEAL position. Close pressure-release valve. The cooking temperature will default to HIGH, which is accurate. Set time to 8 minutes. Select START/STOP and start cooking. When cooking is complete, let pressure release naturally for about 5 minutes, then quickly release any remaining pressure by turning it into VENT position. 6. Scatter the cheese over the top, put the lid back on, and let stand until the cheese is melted, 2 to 3 minutes. Serve warm.
Per Serving: Calories 218; Fat 6.8g; Sodium 268mg; Carbs 2.3g; Fiber 0.3g; Sugar 0.7g; Protein 34.6g

Lemon Chicken with Herbed Potatoes

Prep time: 5 minutes | Cook time: 25 minutes | Serves: 4

- 900g chicken thighs
- 1 teaspoon fine sea salt
- ½ teaspoon ground black pepper
- 2 tablespoons olive oil
- 180ml low-sodium chicken stock
- 60ml freshly squeezed lemon juice
- 2 to 3 tablespoons Dijon mustard
- 2 tablespoons Italian seasoning
- 2 to 1.3kg red potatoes, quartered

1. Season the chicken with the salt and pepper. 2. Move the slider towards "AIR FRY/STOVETOP" and set Ninja Foodi XL Pressure Cooker Steam Fryer with SmartLid to SEAR/SAUTÉ mode. Adjust the temperature to "Hi5" by using up arrow. Press START/STOP to begin cooking. Add the oil to the cooking pot. Add the chicken and brown for 3 minutes on each side. 3. In a medium mixing bowl, combine the chicken stock, lemon juice, mustard, and Italian seasoning and mix well. Pour over the chicken. Add the potatoes. 4. Lock lid; move slider towards PRESSURE. Adjust pressure release valve in the SEAL position. Close pressure-release valve. The cooking temperature will default to HIGH, which is accurate. Set time to 15 minutes. Select START/STOP and start cooking. 5. When cooking is complete, let pressure release quickly by turning it into VENT position. Carefully open it and serve hot.

Per Serving: Calories 284; Fat 12.5g; Sodium 412mg; Carbs 11.2g; Fiber 3g; Sugar 3g; Protein 16.5g

Shredded Greek-Style Chicken

Prep time: 5 minutes | Cook time: 15 minutes | Serves: 8

- 900g boneless, skinless chicken breasts
- 240g plain Greek yogurt
- 80g diced red onion
- 3 tablespoons freshly squeezed lemon juice
- 3 tablespoons red wine vinegar
- 2 tablespoons olive oil
- 2 tablespoons Greek seasoning
- 2 tablespoons dried dill
- 1 or 2 garlic cloves, minced
- 1 teaspoon dried oregano

1. In the cooking pot, combine the chicken, yogurt, onion, lemon juice, vinegar, olive oil, Greek seasoning, dried dill, garlic, and oregano. 2. Lock lid; move slider towards PRESSURE. Adjust pressure release valve in the SEAL position. Close pressure-release valve. The cooking temperature will default to HIGH, which is accurate. Set time to 15 minutes. Select START/STOP and start cooking. When cooking is complete, let pressure release quickly by turning it into VENT position. 3. Remove the chicken from the pot, place it in a medium bowl, and shred it using two forks. Return the chicken to the juices and serve warm.

Per Serving: Calories 230; Fat 14.3g; Sodium 258mg; Carbs 0.8g; Fiber 0.2g; Sugar 0.2g; Protein 22.3g

Smoky Barbecue Chicken

Prep time: 5 minutes | Cook time: 15 minutes | Serves: 8

- 900g boneless, skinless chicken breasts
- 1 small red onion, diced
- 240g Sweet and Smoky Barbecue Sauce or store-bought
- 2 tablespoons olive oil

1. In the Ninja Foodi XL Pressure Cooker Steam Fryer with SmartLid cooking pot combine the chicken, onion, barbecue sauce, and oil. 2. Lock lid; move slider towards PRESSURE. Adjust pressure release valve in the SEAL position. Close pressure-release valve. The cooking temperature will default to HIGH, which is accurate. Set time to 15 minutes. Select START/STOP and start cooking. 3. When cooking is complete, let pressure release quickly by turning it into VENT position. 4. Remove the chicken from the pot, place it in a medium bowl, and shred it using two forks. Return the chicken to the juices and serve warm.

Per Serving: Calories 243; Fat 13.3g; Sodium 269mg; Carbs 5.5g; Fiber 1.2g; Sugar 2g; Protein 24.4g

Lo Mein

Prep time: 10 minutes | Cook time: 30 minutes | Serves: 4

- 1 tablespoon toasted sesame oil
- 675g boneless, skinless chicken breast, cut into bite-size pieces
- 1 garlic clove, minced
- 200g dried linguine, broken in half
- 145g snow peas
- 90g broccoli florets
- 1 carrot, peeled and thinly sliced
- 360ml low-sodium chicken stock
- 1 tablespoon soy sauce
- 1 tablespoon fish sauce
- 1 tablespoon Shaoxing rice wine
- 1 teaspoon grated fresh ginger
- 1 tablespoon brown sugar

1. Move the slider towards "AIR FRY/STOVETOP" and set Ninja Foodi XL Pressure Cooker Steam Fryer with SmartLid to SEAR/SAUTÉ mode. Adjust the temperature to "Hi5" by using up arrow. Press START/STOP to begin cooking. Add the sesame oil. When the oil is hot, add the chicken and garlic and cook until the garlic is light brown and chicken is opaque, about 5 minutes. Fan the noodles across the bottom of the pot. Add the snow peas, broccoli, and carrot on top of the noodles. 2. In a medium bowl, combine the stock, soy sauce, fish sauce, rice wine, ginger, and brown sugar. Stir until the sugar is dissolved. Pour the sauce over the vegetables in the pot. 3. Lock lid; move slider towards PRESSURE. Adjust pressure release valve in the SEAL position. Close pressure-release valve. The cooking temperature will default to HIGH, which is accurate. Set time to 5 minutes. Select START/STOP and start cooking. When cooking is complete, let pressure release quickly by turning it into VENT position. 4. Unlock and remove the lid. Stir the noodles, breaking up any clumps, until the liquid is absorbed.

Per Serving: Calories 287; Fat 12.5g; Sodium 364mg; Carbs 11.5g; Fiber 3g; Sugar 2g; Protein 16.2g

Pesto Turkey Meatballs with Pasta

Prep time: 15 minutes | Cook time: 20 minutes | Serves: 4

- 455g Italian turkey sausage, casings removed and discarded
- 25g dry Italian breadcrumbs
- 1 large egg
- 300g dry gemelli pasta, medium shells, or rotini
- 720ml store-bought chicken stock, or homemade
- 230g fresh prepared basil pesto
- Salt and freshly ground black pepper
- 20g fresh basil leaves, torn into small pieces

1. In a medium bowl, mix the sausage meat, breadcrumbs, and egg. Divide the mixture into 20 portions, about 1 heaping tablespoon each. Set aside. 2. Place the pasta, stock, pesto, 240ml water, ½ teaspoon salt, and several grinds of pepper in the pot and stir to combine. Place the meatballs on top of the pasta mixture. Lock lid; move slider towards PRESSURE. Adjust pressure release valve in the SEAL position. Close pressure-release valve. The cooking temperature will default to HIGH, which is accurate. Adjust to low pressure and set time to 5 minutes. Select START/STOP and start cooking. When cooking is complete, let pressure release quickly by turning it into VENT position. 3. Gently stir the fresh basil into the pasta mixture and season with salt and pepper, taking care not to break up the meatballs.

Per Serving: Calories 288; Fat 12.2g; Sodium 339mg; Carbs 11.6g; Fiber 3g; Sugar 2g; Protein 16.5g

Refreshing Chicken Tacos

Prep time: 5 minutes | Cook time: 25 minutes | Serves: 2

- 145g salsa
- 120ml chicken stock
- 1 tablespoon olive oil
- ½ teaspoon salt
- 2 (125–150 g) boneless, skinless chicken breasts
- 4 (20 cm) corn tortillas
- Optional toppings: shredded cheddar cheese, sliced onion, sliced avocado, chopped fresh coriander

1. Combine the salsa, stock, olive oil, and salt in the Ninja Foodi XL Pressure Cooker Steam Fryer. 2. Lock lid; move slider towards PRESSURE. Adjust pressure release valve in the SEAL position. Close pressure-release valve. The cooking temperature will default to HIGH, which is accurate. Set time to 15 minutes. Select START/STOP and start cooking. 3. When cooking is complete, let pressure release naturally for about 5 minutes, then quickly release any remaining pressure by turning it into VENT position. Open the lid and transfer the chicken to a plate or cutting board. 4. Shred the chicken with two forks, then return the meat to the salsa mixture and stir it in. 5. Serve the chicken warm on corn tortillas with your favorite toppings.

Per Serving: Calories 286; Fat 12.7g; Sodium 444mg; Carbs 11.5g; Fiber 3g; Sugar 3g; Protein 16.4g

Burrito Bowls with Chicken And Beans

Prep time: 10 minutes | Cook time: 15 minutes | Serves: 2

- 1 (125-150g) boneless, skinless chicken breast, cut into 2.5 cm pieces
- 1 tablespoon taco seasoning
- 90g long-grain rice
- 120g canned black beans, drained and rinsed
- 240ml water
- 215g salsa
- Optional toppings: shredded cheddar cheese, sliced tomatoes, chopped fresh coriander

1. Combine the chicken, taco seasoning, rice, beans, and water to the Ninja Foodi XL Pressure Cooker Steam Fryer with SmartLid cooking pot and stir. 2. Top with the salsa, but do not stir. 3. Lock lid; move slider towards PRESSURE. Adjust pressure release valve in the SEAL position. Close pressure-release valve. The cooking temperature will default to HIGH, which is accurate. Set time to 10 minutes. Select START/STOP and start cooking. 4. When cooking is complete, let pressure release quickly by turning it into VENT position. 5. Open the lid. Stir the mixture. If using shredded cheese, add it now and put the lid back on until the cheese is melted, 2 to 3 minutes. 6. Serve warm, with cheese, tomatoes and coriander, if using.

Per Serving: Calories 494; Fat 24.3g; Sodium 257mg; Carbs 43.8g; Fiber 8.3g; Sugar 3.7g; Protein 28.8g

Chile Verde

Prep time: 5 minutes | Cook time: 30 minutes | Serves: 4

- 1.3kg bone-in, skin-on chicken drumsticks and/or thighs
- 1 (375g) jar salsa verde (green chili salsa)
- 1 (675g) can roasted poblano peppers, drained
- 1 (175g) jar chopped green chiles, drained
- 1 tablespoon chopped jalapeño
- 1 onion, chopped
- 4 teaspoons minced garlic
- 1 tablespoon ground cumin
- 1 teaspoon fine sea salt

1. Combine the chicken, salsa verde, poblano peppers, green chiles, jalapeño, onion, garlic, cumin, and salt in the cooking pot. Stir to mix well. 2. Lock lid; move slider towards PRESSURE. Adjust pressure release valve in the SEAL position. Close pressure-release valve. The cooking temperature will default to HIGH, which is accurate. Set time to 15 minutes. Select START/STOP and start cooking. When cooking is complete, let pressure release quickly by turning it into VENT position. 3. Unlock and remove the lid. Use tongs to transfer the chicken to a plate. When the chicken is cool enough to handle, remove and discard the bones and skin. Shred the chicken with two forks or cut it into bite-size pieces. Return the chicken to the sauce and stir.

Per Serving: Calories 287; Fat 12.3g; Sodium 254mg; Carbs 10.6g; Fiber 3g; Sugar 3g; Protein 16.2g

Chapter 4 Meat Mains Recipes

61	Muffin Burgers	69	Mushroom Burgers
61	Pork Cutlets	69	California-style Pot Roast
61	Honey Bratwurst with Brussels Sprouts	70	Italian Sauce
61	Dijon Glazed Pork Loin	70	Delicious Beef Stroganoff
61	Sriracha Glazed Ribs	70	Smoky Beef Tacos
62	Swedish Beef Meatloaf	71	Beef Taco Pasta
62	Beef Steak Nuggets	71	Barbecue Spicy Meatloaf
62	Madeira Glazed Ham	71	Meatballs with Creamy Pan Sauce
62	Citrus-Glazed Pork Chops	72	Pulled Pork Barbecue
63	Beef Carne Asada	72	Beer–Braised Short Ribs
63	Easy Pork Chops	72	Cheesy Philly Steaks
63	Indian Lamb Steaks	73	Bratwurst with Sauerkraut
63	Meatloaf	73	Herby Pork Chops with Squash
64	Beefy Poppers	73	Pork Chops with Beans
64	German Roulade	74	Pork Ragu with Gnocchi
64	Air-Fried Bacon Slices	74	Short Rib Bibimbap
64	Bacon Cups	74	Chinese Braised Pork with Aubergine
65	Crusted Lamb Chops	75	Vietnamese Beef Soup
65	Beef Meat Loaf	75	Tuscan Beef Stew
65	Taco Seasoned Meatballs	75	Spicy Lamb Tagine
65	Steak Bulgogi	76	Fig-Glazed Ham with Potatoes
66	Salisbury Steak with Mushroom Gravy	76	Moroccan Meat Soup with Chickpeas and Lentils
66	Pork Bun Thit Nuong		
66	Air Fried Bacon Slices	76	Cinnamon-Spiced Beef Noodle Soup
66	Italian Pork Loin	77	Persian Beef and Kidney Bean Stew
67	BBQ Baby Ribs	77	Delicious Pork Vindaloo
67	Spicy Bacon Pieces	77	Delicious Lamb Gyros
67	Meatball Lettuce Wraps	78	Beef and Tomatillo Stew
67	Beef Reuben Fritters	78	Sweet Barbecue Spareribs
68	Stuffed Venison Tenderloin	78	Pakistani Spiced Beef Stew
68	Hamburgers	79	Delicious Moroccan Meatballs
68	Sweet and Sour Beef Brisket	79	Cumin-Spiced Beef and Potato Stew
69	Herbed Lamb Chops		

Muffin Burgers

Prep Time: 10 minutes | Cook Time: 15 minutes | Serves: 4

455g pork	1 teaspoon dried oregano	taste	1 tablespoon olive oil
1 egg	½ teaspoon dried basil	1 small red onion, chopped	4 English muffins
50g seasoned breadcrumbs	Sea salt and black pepper, to	1 teaspoon garlic, minced	

1. Place the Cook & Crisp Basket in your Pressure Cooker Steam Fryer. 2. In a suitable mixing bowl, mix the pork, egg, breadcrumbs, spices, onion, garlic, and olive oil. 3. Form the mixture into four patties. 4. Put on the Smart Lid on top of the Ninja Foodi Steam Fryer. 5. Move the Lid Slider to the "Air Fry/Stovetop". Select the "Air Fry" mode for cooking. 6. Cook the burgers at 195°C for about 15 minutes or until cooked through; make sure to turn them over halfway through the cooking time. 7. Serve your burgers with English muffins and enjoy!
Per serving: Calories: 479; Fat:48.1g; Carbs: 2.3g; Fiber: 0.1g; Sugars: 1.6g; Proteins: 8.6g

Pork Cutlets

Prep Time: 10 minutes | Cook Time: 15 minutes | Serves: 4

675g pork cutlets	to taste	½ teaspoon cayenne pepper
Seasoned salt and black pepper,	35g tortilla chips, crushed	2 tablespoons olive oil

1. Toss the pork cutlets with the remaining ingredients; brush the Cook & Crisp Basket with oil. 2. Place the Cook & Crisp Basket in your Pressure Cooker Steam Fryer. 3. Put on the Smart Lid on top of the Ninja Foodi Steam Fryer. 4. Move the Lid Slider to the "Air Fry/Stovetop". Select the "Air Fry" mode for cooking. 5. Cook the pork cutlets at 200°C for around 15 minutes, turning them over halfway through the cooking time. 6. Serve.
Per serving: Calories: 480; Fat:25.1g; Carbs: 18.2g; Fiber: 1.4g; Sugars: 0.9g; Proteins: 43.7g

Honey Bratwurst with Brussels Sprouts

Prep Time: 10 minutes | Cook Time: 15 minutes | Serves: 4

455g bratwurst	1 large onion, cut into wedges	1 tablespoon mustard
455g Brussels sprouts	1 teaspoon garlic, minced	2 tablespoons honey

1. Toss all the recipe ingredients in a greased Cook & Crisp Basket. 2. Place the Cook & Crisp Basket in your Pressure Cooker Steam Fryer. 3. Put on the Smart Lid on top of the Ninja Foodi Steam Fryer. 4. Move the Lid Slider to the "Air Fry/Stovetop". Select the "Air Fry" mode for cooking. 5. Air fry the sausage at 195°C for approximately 15 minutes, tossing the basket halfway through the cooking time. 6. Serve.
Per serving: Calories: 438; Fat:30.3g; Carbs: 25g; Fiber: 5.1g; Sugars: 12g; Proteins: 18.7g

Dijon Glazed Pork Loin

Prep Time: 10 minutes | Cook Time: 55 minutes | Serves: 4

675g pork top loin	2 cloves garlic, crushed	½ teaspoon red pepper flakes, crushed
1 tablespoon olive oil	1 tablespoon parsley	Salt and black pepper, to taste
1 tablespoon Dijon mustard	1 tablespoon coriander	

1. Toss all the recipe ingredients in a greased Cook & Crisp Basket. 2. Place the Cook & Crisp Basket in your Pressure Cooker Steam Fryer. 3. Put on the Smart Lid on top of the Ninja Foodi Steam Fryer. 4. Move the Lid Slider to the "Air Fry/Stovetop". Select the "Air Fry" mode for cooking. 5. Cook the pork at 180°C for around 55 minutes, turning it over halfway through the cooking time. 6. Serve warm and enjoy!
Per serving: Calories: 302; Fat:15.3g; Carbs: 1g; Fiber: 0.3g; Sugars: 0g; Proteins: 36.9g

Sriracha Glazed Ribs

Prep Time: 10 minutes | Cook Time: 35 minutes | Serves: 5

900g Country-style ribs	2 tablespoons bourbon	1 teaspoon stone-ground mustard
60g Sriracha sauce	1 tablespoon honey	

1. Toss all the recipe ingredients in a greased Cook & Crisp Basket. 2. Place the Cook & Crisp Basket in your Pressure Cooker Steam Fryer. 3. Put on the Smart Lid on top of the Ninja Foodi Steam Fryer. 4. Move the Lid Slider to the "Air Fry/Stovetop". Select the "Air Fry" mode for cooking. 5. Cook the pork ribs at 175°C for around 35 minutes, turning them over halfway through the cooking time. 6. Serve.
Per serving: Calories: 371; Fat:21.6g; Carbs: 4.4g; Fiber: 0.3g; Sugars: 3.9g; Proteins: 35.4g

Swedish Beef Meatloaf

Prep Time: 10 minutes | Cook Time: 45 minutes | Serves: 8

675g (85% lean)	2 tablespoons dry mustard	**Sauce:**	80ml beef stock
115g pork	2 cloves garlic, minced	115g unsalted butter	⅛ teaspoon nutmeg
1 large egg (omit for egg-free)	2 teaspoons fine sea salt	50g shredded Swiss or mild cheddar cheese	Halved cherry tomatoes, for serving (optional)
80g minced onions	1 teaspoon black pepper, more for garnish	50g cream cheese, softened	
60g tomato sauce			

1. Place the Cook & Crisp Basket in your Pressure Cooker Steam Fryer. 2. In a suitable bowl, mix the beef, pork, egg, onions, tomato sauce, dry mustard, garlic, salt, and pepper. Using your hands, mix until well mixed. 3. Place the meatloaf mixture in the Cook & Crisp Basket. 4. Put on the Smart Lid on top of the Ninja Foodi Steam Fryer. 5. Move the Lid Slider to the "Air Fry/Stovetop". Select the "Air Fry" mode for cooking. 6. Adjust the cooking temperature to 200°C. 7. Cook for around 35 minutes, or until cooked through and the internal temperature reaches 60°C. Check the meatloaf after 25 minutes; if it's too brown on the top, you can cover it loosely with foil to prevent burning. 8. While the meatloaf cooks, make the sauce: Add the butter in a suitable saucepan over medium-high heat until it sizzles and brown flecks appear, with constant stirring to keep the butter from burning. Turn the heat to low and mix in the Swiss cheese, cream cheese, stock, and nutmeg. Cook on a simmer for at least 10 minutes. The longer it simmers, the more the flavors open up. 9. When the meatloaf is done, transfer it to a serving tray and pour the sauce over it. Garnish with black pepper and serve with cherry tomatoes, if desired. Allow the meatloaf to rest for around 10 minutes before slicing so it doesn't crumble apart. 10. Store leftovers in an airtight container, then put in the fridge for around 3 days or in the freezer for up to a month. Reheat at 175°C for around 4 minutes in your Pressure Cooker Steam Fryer, or until heated through.
Per serving: Calories 426; Fat: 8.6g; Sodium 588mg; Carbs: 67g; Fiber: 16.4g; Sugars 2.4g; Protein 23.2g

Beef Steak Nuggets

Prep Time: 10 minutes | Cook Time: 35 minutes | Serves: 4

1 large egg	**For the Breading**	**For the Dip**	½ teaspoon dip mix and ranch dressing
455g diced beef steak	55g pork panko	¼ lemon juice	1 teaspoon chipotle paste
Cooking oil	½ teaspoon seasoned salt	60g sour cream	
	50g shaved parmesan cheese	60g mayonnaise	

1. Place the Cook & Crisp Basket in your Pressure Cooker Steam Fryer. 2. Using a suitable sized mixing bowl, add in all the dip ingredients and incorporate then refrigerate until ready to use. 3. Using a separate mixing bowl, add in the parmesan cheese, pork panko, salt then incorporate and set aside. 4. Break the egg into a suitable bowl and mix then dredge the diced beef steak in the egg mixture then the pork panko mix and transfer unto a paper lined plate. 5. Transfer the plate into a freezer and allow to set for around 30 minutes then Grease the "cook & crisp basket" with cooking oil. 6. Put on the Smart Lid on top of the Ninja Foodi Steam Fryer. 7. Move the Lid Slider to the "Air Fry/Stovetop". Select the "Air Fry" mode for cooking. 8. Heat the fryer up to 160°C then fry the steak nuggets for around 3 to 5 minutes until browned. 9. Season the fried nuggets with little salt then serve along with the dip and enjoy as desired.
Per serving: Calories 562; Fat: 2.1g; Sodium 238mg; Carbs: 108.8g; Fiber: 19g; Sugars 5.3g; Protein 28.6g

Madeira Glazed Ham

Prep Time: 10 minutes | Cook Time: 1 hour | Serves: 5

900g cooked ham	80g maple syrup	60ml Madeira wine
1 apple, cored and chopped	2 garlic cloves, crushed	

1. Place the Cook & Crisp Basket in your Pressure Cooker Steam Fryer. 2. In a suitable mixing bowl, mix all the remaining recipe ingredients to make the glaze. 3. Wrap the ham in a piece of aluminum foil and lower it onto the Cook & Crisp Basket. Reduce the temperature to 190°C. Put on the Smart Lid on top of the Ninja Foodi Steam Fryer. Move the Lid Slider to the "Air Fry/Stovetop". Select the "Air Fry" mode for cooking. Cook for the ham for about 30 minutes. 4. Remove the foil, turn the temperature to 200°C, and continue to cook an additional 15 minutes, coating the ham with the glaze every 5 minutes. 5. Serve.
Per serving: Calories: 359; Fat:15.6g; Carbs: 23g; Fiber: 3.3g; Sugars: 13.4g; Proteins: 30.3g

Citrus-Glazed Pork Chops

Prep Time: 10 minutes | Cook Time: 15 minutes | Serves: 3

455g rib pork chops	2 tablespoons orange juice, freshly squeezed	1 teaspoon rosemary, chopped
1½ tablespoons butter, melted		Sea salt and cayenne pepper, to taste

1. Toss all the recipe ingredients in a greased Cook & Crisp Basket. 2. Place the Cook & Crisp Basket in your Pressure Cooker Steam Fryer. 3. Put on the Smart Lid on top of the Ninja Foodi Steam Fryer. 4. Move the Lid Slider to the "Air Fry/Stovetop". Select the "Air Fry" mode for cooking. 5. Cook the pork chops at 200°C for around 15 minutes, turning them over halfway through the cooking time. 6. Serve.
Per serving: Calories: 372; Fat:22.5g; Carbs: 1.3g; Fiber: 0.2g; Sugars: 1g; Proteins: 38.6g

Beef Carne Asada

Prep Time: 5 minutes | Cook Time: 8 minutes | Serves: 8

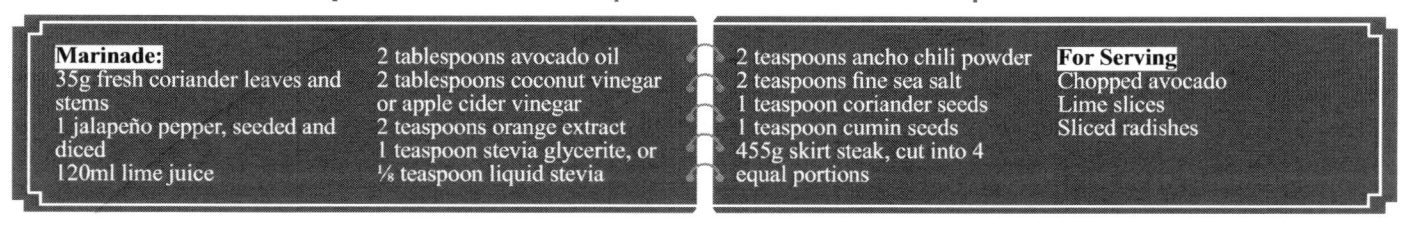

Marinade:
- 35g fresh coriander leaves and stems
- 1 jalapeño pepper, seeded and diced
- 120ml lime juice
- 2 tablespoons avocado oil
- 2 tablespoons coconut vinegar or apple cider vinegar
- 2 teaspoons orange extract
- 1 teaspoon stevia glycerite, or ⅛ teaspoon liquid stevia
- 2 teaspoons ancho chili powder
- 2 teaspoons fine sea salt
- 1 teaspoon coriander seeds
- 1 teaspoon cumin seeds
- 455g skirt steak, cut into 4 equal portions

For Serving
- Chopped avocado
- Lime slices
- Sliced radishes

1. Place the Cook & Crisp Basket in your Pressure Cooker Steam Fryer. 2. Make the marinade: Place all the recipe ingredients for the marinade in a blender and puree until smooth. 3. Place the steak in a shallow dish and pour the marinade in it, making sure the meat is covered completely. Cover and place in the fridge for around 2 hours or overnight. 4. Grease the Ninja Foodi Pressure Steam Fryer basket with avocado oil. 5. Transfer the steak from the marinade and place it in the "cook & crisp basket" in one layer. 6. Put on the Smart Lid on top of the Ninja Foodi Steam Fryer. 7. Move the Lid Slider to the "Air Fry/Stovetop". Select the "Air Fry" mode for cooking. 8. Adjust the cooking temperature to 200°C. 9. Cook for around 8 minutes, or until the internal temperature is 60°C; do not overcook or it will become tough. 10. Remove the steak from the basket and place it on a cutting board, rest for around 10 minutes before slicing it against the grain. Garnish with coriander, if need, and serve with chopped avocado, lime slices, sliced radishes, if desired. 11. Store leftovers in the airtight container and put in the fridge for around 3 days or in the freezer for up to a month. Reheat them at 175°C for around 4 minutes in your Pressure Cooker Steam Fryer, or until heated through.
Per serving: Calories 336; Fat: 9.9g; Sodium 1672mg; Carbs: 42.6g; Fiber: 1.7g; Sugars 2.1g; Protein 12.3g

Easy Pork Chops

Prep Time: 15 minutes | Cook Time: 15 minutes | Serves: 4

- 120ml water
- 1 teaspoon sugar
- 4 pork chops
- Melted butter
- Salt, to taste

1. Place the Cook & Crisp Basket in your Pressure Cooker Steam Fryer. 2. Mix the water, sugar and salt into a suitable mixing bowl. 3. Add the pork chops into the water mixture and brine. 4. Pat dry the pork chops then coat with the melted butter. 5. Place the coated chops into the "cook & crisp basket". 6. Put on the Smart Lid on top of the Ninja Foodi Steam Fryer. 7. Move the Lid Slider to the "Air Fry/Stovetop". Select the "Air Fry" mode for cooking. 8. Air fry for around 15 minutes at 195°C. 9. Once done, serve and enjoy as desired.
Per serving: Calories 557; Fat: 10g; Sodium 2706mg; Carbs: 87.6g; Fiber: 17.8g; Sugars 5.6g; Protein 29.2g

Indian Lamb Steaks

Prep Time: 40 minutes | Cook Time: 7 minutes | Serves: 4

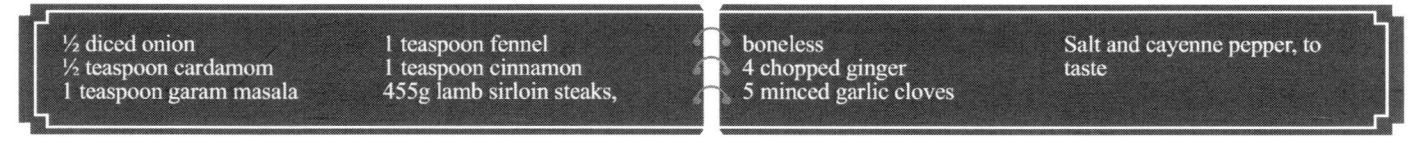

- ½ diced onion
- ½ teaspoon cardamom
- 1 teaspoon garam masala
- 1 teaspoon fennel
- 1 teaspoon cinnamon
- 455g lamb sirloin steaks, boneless
- 4 chopped ginger
- 5 minced garlic cloves
- Salt and cayenne pepper, to taste

1. Place the Cook & Crisp Basket in your Pressure Cooker Steam Fryer. 2. Using a high speed blender, add in all the recipe ingredients (except the lamb steaks) and pulse until blended. 3. Make small incisions on the body of the lamb steaks then place into a suitable Ziploc bag. 4. Pour the blender marinade into the Ziploc bag and allow the steaks to marinate for an hour. 5. Transfer the marinated steaks into the basket. Put on the Smart Lid on top of the Ninja Foodi Steam Fryer. Move the Lid Slider to the "Air Fry/Stovetop". Select the "Air Fry" mode for cooking. Air Fry for around 8 minutes at 165°C. 6. Flip the lamb steaks and cook for another 7 minutes. 7. Serve hot and enjoy as desired.
Per serving: Calories 100; Fat: 1.1g; Sodium 741mg; Carbs: 19.4g; Fiber: 5.2g; Sugars 6.2g; Protein 4.3g

Meatloaf

Prep Time: 10 minutes | Cook Time: 10 minutes | Serves: 10

- 60g ketchup
- 40g diced onion
- 25g coconut flour
- ½ teaspoon sea salt
- ½ teaspoon black pepper
- ½ teaspoon dried tarragon
- 45g blanched almond flour
- 455g beef
- 1 minced garlic clove
- 1 teaspoon Italian seasoning
- 1 tablespoon Worcestershire sauce
- 2 beaten eggs

1. Place the Cook & Crisp Basket in your Pressure Cooker Steam Fryer. 2. Using a suitable mixing bowl, add in all the recipe ingredients and incorporate until a batter is formed. 3. Mold 10 even loaves from the patties then transfer into the refrigerator to firm up for about 15 minutes. 4. Transfer the firm loaves into the Cook & Crisp Basket. Put on the Smart Lid on top of the Ninja Foodi Steam Fryer. Move the Lid Slider to the "Air Fry/Stovetop". Select the "Air Fry" mode for cooking. Air Fry at 180°C for around 10 minutes. 5. If cooking in batches, keep the cooked ones warm until done cooking. 6. Serve hot and enjoy as desired.
Per serving: Calories 390; Fat: 15.3g; Sodium 1086mg; Carbs: 50g; Fiber: 17.3g; Sugars 6.6g; Protein 18.2g

Beefy Poppers

Prep Time: 15 minutes | Cook Time: 15 minutes | Serves: 8 poppers

8 medium jalapeño peppers, stemmed, halved, and seeded	900g beef (85% lean)	8 slices thin-cut bacon	Avocado oil
1 (200g) package cream cheese	1 teaspoon fine sea salt	Fresh coriander leaves, for garnish	
	½ teaspoon black pepper		

1. Place the Cook & Crisp Basket in your Pressure Cooker Steam Fryer. 2. Grease the Ninja Foodi Pressure Steam Fryer basket with avocado oil. 3. Stuff each jalapeño half with a few tablespoons of cream cheese. Place the halves back again to form 8 jalapeños. 4. Season the beef with the black pepper and salt and mix with your hands to incorporate. Flatten about 115 g of beef in the palm of your hand and place a stuffed jalapeño in the center. Fold the beef around the jalapeño, forming an egg shape. Wrap the beef-covered jalapeño with a slice of bacon and secure it with a toothpick. 5. Place the jalapeños in the "cook & crisp basket", leaving space between them. 6. Put on the Smart Lid on top of the Ninja Foodi Steam Fryer. Move the Lid Slider to the "Air Fry/Stovetop". Select the "Air Fry" mode for cooking. 7. Adjust the cooking temperature to 200°C. 8. Cook for around 15 minutes, or until the beef is cooked through and the bacon is crispy. Garnish with coriander before serving. 9. Store leftovers in an airtight container in the fridge for around 3 days or in the freezer for up to a month. 10. Reheat in your Pressure Cooker Steam Fryer at 175°C for around 4 minutes, or until heated through and the bacon is crispy.
Per serving: Calories 396; Fat: 8.6g; Sodium 596mg; Carbs: 65.9g; Fiber: 3.4g; Sugars 3.8g; Protein 12.1g

German Roulade

Prep Time: 10 minutes | Cook Time: 18 minutes | Serves: 4

For the Sauce	1 teaspoon chopped parsley	**For the Meat**	1 teaspoon black pepper
40g chopped dill pickles	320g diced onion	60g Dijon mustard	4 bacon slices
120g sour cream	3 tablespoons avocado oil	10g chopped parsley	
1 tablespoon tomato paste	Black pepper and salt, to taste	455g flank steak	

1. Place the Cook & Crisp Basket in your Pressure Cooker Steam Fryer. Brush the basket with oil. 2. Using a suitable mixing bowl, add in the pepper, salt, diced onions and incorporate together. 3. Put on the Smart Lid on top of the Ninja Foodi Steam Fryer. 4. Move the Lid Slider to the "Air Fry/Stovetop". Select the "Air Fry" mode for cooking. 5. Air fry the seasoned onions for around 6 minutes at 200°C. 6. Once fried, mix half of the onion with the chopped parsley, pickles, tomato paste, sour cream and add in a tablespoon of water you desire to thin out the sauce. 7. Cover the meat with the mustard then add on the slices of bacon, chopped parsley remaining fried onion and season with the pepper. 8. Tightly roll up the steak, holding it firm at the end then transfer into the Cook & Crisp Basket. 9. Air fry the meat wrap for around 10 minutes at 200°C, flipping the wrap halfway through. 10. Serve and enjoy with the sauce mixture.
Per serving: Calories 254; Fat: 10.3g; Sodium 514mg; Carbs: 32.8g; Fiber: 3.3g; Sugars 5g; Protein 7.9g

Air-Fried Bacon Slices

Prep Time: 4 minutes | Cook Time: 10 minutes | Serves: 10

10 bacon slices	Beef seasoning

1. Place the Cook & Crisp Basket in your Pressure Cooker Steam Fryer. 2. Generously coat the bacon slices with the seasonings. 3. Place the seasoned slices into the Cook & Crisp Basket. 4. Put on the Smart Lid on top of the Ninja Foodi Steam Fryer. 5. Move the Lid Slider to the "Air Fry/Stovetop". Select the "Air Fry" mode for cooking. 6. Cook for around 10 minutes at 200°C until crispy to taste. 7. Serve and enjoy as desired.
Per serving: Calories 460; Fat: 10.1g; Sodium 332mg; Carbs: 73.9g; Fiber: 20.3g; Sugars 14.5g; Protein 21.7g

Bacon Cups

Prep Time: 10 minutes | Cook Time: 15 minutes | Serves: 8

40g minced onions	10g chopped fresh spinach	2 tablespoons heavy whipping cream	slices
35g diced red peppers	30g shaved mozzarella cheese		6 large eggs
35g diced green peppers	50g shaved cheddar cheese	3 crumbled and cooked bacon	Black pepper and salt, to taste

1. Place the Cook & Crisp Basket in your Pressure Cooker Steam Fryer. 2. Break the eggs into a suitable mixing bowl then add in the pepper, salt, whipping cream and mix until mixed. 3. Add in the cheeses, onions, red peppers, spinach, green peppers, bacon and mix until incorporated. 4. Pour the mixture into 8 silicone molds and sprinkle the top with the remaining veggies then place the molds in the Ninja Foodi Pressure Steam Fryer. 5. Put on the Smart Lid on top of the Ninja Foodi Steam Fryer. 6. Move the Lid Slider to the "Air Fry/Stovetop". Select the "Air Fry" mode for cooking. 7. Air Fry at 150°C for 15 minutes then check to confirm if the eggs have set and done as desired. 8. Serve warm and enjoy as desired.
Per serving: Calories 276; Fat: 11.8g; Sodium 888mg; Carbs: 33.1g; Fiber: 6.2g; Sugars 2.6g; Protein 14.4g

Crusted Lamb Chops

Prep Time: 10 minutes | Cook Time: 5 minutes | Serves: 2

1 large egg	1 tablespoon chopped fresh rosemary leaves	4 (2.5 cm thick) lamb chops	Sprigs of fresh thyme
2 cloves garlic, minced	1 teaspoon chopped fresh thyme leaves	Avocado oil	Lavender flowers
50g powdered Parmesan cheese	½ teaspoon black pepper	**For Garnish**	Lemon slices
1 tablespoon chopped fresh oregano leaves		Sprigs of fresh oregano	
		Sprigs of fresh rosemary	

1. Place the Cook & Crisp Basket in your Pressure Cooker Steam Fryer. 2. Grease the Ninja Foodi Pressure Steam Fryer basket with avocado oil. 3. Beat the egg in a shallow bowl, add the garlic, and stir well to mix. In another shallow bowl, mix the Parmesan, herbs, and pepper. 4. One at a time, dip the lamb chops into the egg mixture, shake off the excess egg, and then dredge them in the Parmesan mixture. Use your hands to coat the chops well in the Parmesan mixture and form a nice crust on all sides; if necessary, dip the chops again in both the egg and the Parmesan mixture. 5. Place the lamb chops in the "cook & crisp basket", leaving space between them. Put on the Smart Lid on top of the Ninja Foodi Steam Fryer. Move the Lid Slider to the "Air Fry/Stovetop". Select the "Air Fry" mode for cooking. 6. Adjust the cooking temperature to 200°C. 7. Cook for around 5 minutes, or until the internal temperature reaches 60°C for medium doneness. Allow to rest for around 10 minutes before serving. 8. Garnish with sprigs of oregano, rosemary, and thyme, and lavender flowers, if desired. Serve with lemon slices, if desired. 9. Best served fresh. Store the leftovers in an airtight container, then put in the fridge for up to 4 days. 10. Serve chilled over a salad, or reheat at 175°C for around 4 minutes in your Pressure Cooker Steam Fryer, or until heated through.
Per serving: Calories 373; Fat: 3.1g; Sodium 687mg; Carbs: 69.2g; Fiber: 9.6g; Sugars 3.4g; Protein 17.8g

Beef Meat Loaf

Prep Time: 10 minutes | Cook Time: 15 minutes | Serves: 4

⅛ teaspoon cardamom	160g diced onion	1 tablespoon minced ginger	2 teaspoons garam masala
5g chopped coriander	1 teaspoon turmeric	1 tablespoon minced garlic	salt and cayenne pepper to taste
½ teaspoon cinnamon	455g lean beef	2 large eggs	

1. Place the Cook & Crisp Basket in your Pressure Cooker Steam Fryer. 2. Using a suitable mixing bowl, add in all the recipe ingredients and mix until incorporated. 3. Transfer the meat batter into the "cook & crisp basket". 4. Put on the Smart Lid on top of the Ninja Foodi Steam Fryer. 5. Move the Lid Slider to the "Air Fry/Stovetop". Select the "Air Fry" mode for cooking. 6. Air fry for around 15 minutes at 180°C. 7. Slice the fried meat loaf, serve and enjoy as desired.
Per serving: Calories 353; Fat: 28.2g; Sodium 472mg; Carbs: 14.9g; Fiber: 9.9g; Sugars 1.2g; Protein 14.6g

Taco Seasoned Meatballs

Prep Time: 10 minutes | Cook Time: 10 minutes | Serves: 4

40g diced onions	455g lean beef	**For the Sauce**	145g salsa
10g chopped coriander	1 tablespoon minced garlic	60g heavy cream	Hot sauce
25g shredded cheese	2 tablespoons taco seasoning		
1 large eggs	Salt and black pepper, to taste		

1. Place the Cook & Crisp Basket in your Pressure Cooker Steam Fryer. 2. Add all the recipe ingredients into a suitable mixing bowl then incorporate until a paste like texture is achieved. 3. Scoop bits from the mixture and mold out 15 even sized meatballs. 4. Arrange the meatballs in the "cook & crisp basket". 5. Put on the Smart Lid on top of the Ninja Foodi Steam Fryer. 6. Move the Lid Slider to the "Air Fry/Stovetop". Select the "Air Fry" mode for cooking. 7. Air fry for around 10 minutes at 200°C. 8. In the meantime, mix all the sauce ingredients together. 9. Serve the meatballs and enjoy along with the creamy sauce.
Per serving: Calories 448; Fat: 32.9g; Sodium 71mg; Carbs: 28.1g; Fiber: 9.4g; Sugars 6.3g; Protein 14.6g

Steak Bulgogi

Prep Time: 10 minutes | Cook Time: 12 minutes | Serves: 6

½ teaspoon black pepper	2 tablespoons coconut oil	2 teaspoons minced garlic cloves	3 chopped green spring onions
100g diced carrots	2 tablespoons brown sugar	3 tablespoons soy sauce	
675g sliced sirloin steak	2 tablespoons sesame seeds		

1. Place the Cook & Crisp Basket in your Pressure Cooker Steam Fryer. 2. Using a suitable Ziploc bag, add in the green spring onions, carrots and sirloin steak. 3. Pour in the pepper, garlic, sesame seeds, coconut oil, brown sugar, soy sauce and massage into the steak. 4. Set the Ziploc bag aside to marinate for an hour. 5. Transfer the veggies and marinated beef into the "cook & crisp basket". 6. Put on the Smart Lid on top of the Ninja Foodi Steam Fryer. 7. Move the Lid Slider to the "Air Fry/Stovetop". Select the "Air Fry" mode for cooking. 8. Air fry for around 6 minutes at 200°C. 9. Shake the basket and flip the beef over then air fry for an extra 6 minutes. 10. Serve and enjoy as desired.
Per serving: Calories 253; Fat: 13.9g; Sodium 21mg; Carbs: 27g; Fiber: 9.3g; Sugars 3.8g; Protein 8.3g

Salisbury Steak with Mushroom Gravy

Prep Time: 10 minutes | Cook Time: 33 minutes | Serves: 2

Mushroom Onion Gravy	60ml beef stock	2 tablespoons tomato paste	¼ teaspoon black pepper, more
75g sliced button mushrooms	**Steaks:**	1 tablespoon dry mustard	for garnish if desired
40g sliced onions	225g beef (85% lean)	1 clove garlic, minced, or ¼	Chopped fresh thyme leaves,
55g unsalted butter, melted	40g minced onions, or ½	teaspoon garlic powder	for garnish (optional)
½ teaspoon fine sea salt	teaspoon onion powder	½ teaspoon fine sea salt	

1. Place the Cook & Crisp Basket in your Pressure Cooker Steam Fryer. 2. Make the gravy: Place the mushrooms and onions in the Cook & Crisp Basket. Pour the melted butter over them and stir to coat, then season with the salt. Place the Cook & Crisp Basket in your Pressure Cooker Steam Fryer. 3. Put on the Smart Lid on top of the Ninja Foodi Steam Fryer. Move the Lid Slider to the "Air Fry/Stovetop". Select the "Air Fry" mode for cooking. 4. Adjust the cooking temperature to 200°C. 5. Cook for around 5 minutes, stir, then cook for another 3 minutes, or until the onions are soft and the mushrooms are browning. Add the stock. Cook for another 10 minutes. 6. While the gravy is cooking, prepare the steaks: In a suitable bowl, mix the beef, onions, tomato paste, dry mustard, garlic, salt, and pepper until well mixed. Form the mixture into 2 oval-shaped patties. 7. Place the patties on top of the mushroom gravy. Cook for around 10 minutes, gently flip the patties, then cook for another 2 to 5 minutes, until the beef is cooked through or the internal temperature reaches 60°C. 8. Remove the steaks to a serving platter and pour the gravy over them. Garnish with black pepper and chopped fresh thyme, if desired. Store leftovers in an airtight container and put in the fridge for around 3 days or in the freezer for up to a month. 9. Reheat at 175°C for around 4 minutes in your Pressure Cooker Steam Fryer, or until heated through.
Per serving: Calories 371; Fat: 4.9g; Sodium 1207mg; Carbs: 57.5g; Fiber: 25g; Sugars 7g; Protein 25.6g

Pork Bun Thit Nuong

Prep Time: 40 minutes | Cook Time: 10 minutes | Serves: 4

For the Pork	1 tablespoon minced garlic	lemongrass paste	**To Garnish**
40g diced onions	cloves	2 tablespoons sugar	35g crushed roasted peanuts
½ teaspoon black pepper	455g pork shoulder, sliced thin	2 teaspoons soy sauce	2 tablespoons coriander,
1 tablespoon fish sauce	1 tablespoon minced	2 tablespoons avocado oil	chopped

1. Using a suitable mixing bowl, add in the black pepper, sugar, onions, avocado oil, soy sauce, fish sauce, garlic and lemongrass then mix together. 2. Cut the sliced pork shoulders crisscross ways into 4 pieces then add into the marinade and allow to marinate for around 2 hours. 3. Transfer the marinated pork into the "cook & crisp basket". 4. Put on the Smart Lid on top of the Ninja Foodi Steam Fryer. Move the Lid Slider to the "Air Fry/Stovetop". Select the "Air Fry" mode for cooking. 5. Cook for around 5 minutes at 200°C. 6. Flip the pork shoulders over. 7. Cook for an extra 5 minutes then transfer into serving platters. 8. Top with the coriander, roasted peanuts, serve and enjoy as desired.
Per serving: Calories 589; Fat: 18.2g; Sodium 513mg; Carbs: 85.6g; Fiber: 24.5g; Sugars 13.2g; Protein 26g

Air Fried Bacon Slices

Prep Time: 2 minutes | Cook Time: 10 minutes | Serves: 2

6 bacon slices	

1. Place the Cook & Crisp Basket in your Pressure Cooker Steam Fryer. 2. Prepare the basket with a parchment paper then add in the bacon slices. 3. Put on the Smart Lid on top of the Ninja Foodi Steam Fryer. 4. Move the Lid Slider to the "Air Fry/Stovetop". Select the "Air Fry" mode for cooking. 5. Air fryer at 195°C for 10 minutes then open and check for desired doneness. 6. Once done and ready, serve and enjoy with any dipping sauce of choice.
Per serving: Calories 589; Fat: 22.7g; Sodium 266mg; Carbs: 76.5g; Fiber: 23.9g; Sugars 5.1g; Protein 25.5g

Italian Pork Loin

Prep Time: 5 minutes | Cook Time: 40 minutes | Serves: 8

60ml Italian vinaigrette	1 teaspoon thyme	4 minced garlic cloves	Black pepper and salt, to taste
½ teaspoon Italian Seasoning	1 teaspoon rosemary	1.8kg boneless pork loin	

1. Place the Cook & Crisp Basket in your Pressure Cooker Steam Fryer. 2. Generously coat the pork loin with the Italian vinaigrette then sprinkle with the remaining seasoning. 3. Transfer the seasoned pork loin into a Ziploc bag and place in a refrigerator for around 2 hours to marinate. 4. Transfer the marinated pork loin into the "cook & crisp basket" lined with parchment paper. 5. Put on the Smart Lid on top of the Ninja Foodi Steam Fryer. 6. Move the Lid Slider to the "Air Fry/Stovetop". Select the "Air Fry" mode for cooking. 7. Air fry the pork loin at 180°C for around 25 minutes. 8. Open the Pressure Cooker Steam Fryer and flip the pork over then fry for an extra 15 minutes. 9. Allow the pork to cool off then slices into pieces, glaze with extra vinaigrette, serve and enjoy as desired.
Per serving: Calories 687; Fat: 17.1g; Sodium 495mg; Carbs: 112.7g; Fiber: 27.3g; Sugars 12.9g; Protein 26g

BBQ Baby Ribs

Prep Time: 30 minutes | Cook Time: 30 minutes | Serves: 4

120g BBQ sauce 1 baby back rack ribs	1 tablespoon liquid smoke 3 tablespoons pork rub	Black pepper and salt, to taste

1. Place the Cook & Crisp Basket in your Pressure Cooker Steam Fryer. 2. Take the membrane off from the ribs back then slice the rib in half. 3. Drizzle the two sides of the rib with the liquid smoke then generously season with salt, pepper and pork rub. 4. Set the ribs aside to marinate for an hour then transfer into the basket. 5. Put on the Smart Lid on top of the Ninja Foodi Steam Fryer. 6. Move the Lid Slider to the "Air Fry/Stovetop". Select the "Air Fry" mode for cooking. 7. Air fry at 180°C for around 15 minutes then flip over and fry for an extra 15 minutes. 8. Allow the ribs to cool for a few minutes then top with the sauce, serve and enjoy.
Per serving: Calories 280; Fat: 4.6g; Sodium 271mg; Carbs: 52.7g; Fiber: 7.4g; Sugars 6.3g; Protein 8g

Spicy Bacon Pieces

Prep Time: 5 minutes | Cook Time: 10 minutes | Serves: 3

60g hot sauce	50g parmesan, grated	6 uncooked bacon strips

1. Place the Cook & Crisp Basket in your Pressure Cooker Steam Fryer. 2. Slice the bacon strips into 6 pieces then transfer into a suitable mixing bowl. 3. Pour the hot sauce into the mixing bowl and ensure the bacon pieces are well coated. 4. Dredge the coated bacon pieces in the grated parmesan until well covered. 5. Transfer the covered pieces into the "cook & crisp basket". 6. Put on the Smart Lid on top of the Ninja Foodi Steam Fryer. 7. Move the Lid Slider to the "Air Fry/Stovetop". Select the "Air Fry" mode for cooking. 8. Air fry for around 10 minutes at 175°C. 9. Serve and enjoy as desired.
Per serving: Calories 483; Fat: 6g; Sodium 184mg; Carbs: 77.2g; Fiber: 31.2g; Sugars 6g; Protein 30.4g

Meatball Lettuce Wraps

Prep Time: 10 minutes | Cook Time: 10 minutes | Serves: 4

455g beef (85% lean) 145g salsa, more for serving if desired 40g chopped onions	35g diced green or red peppers 1 large egg, beaten 1 teaspoon fine sea salt ½ teaspoon chili powder	½ teaspoon cumin 1 clove garlic, minced Avocado oil	**For Serving (optional)** 8 leaves Boston lettuce Pico De Gallo or salsa Lime slices

1. Place the Cook & Crisp Basket in your Pressure Cooker Steam Fryer. 2. Grease the Ninja Foodi Pressure Steam Fryer basket with avocado oil. 3. In a suitable bowl, mix all the recipe ingredients until well mixed. 4. Make the meat mixture into eight 2.5 cm balls. Put the meatballs in the "cook & crisp basket", leaving a little space between them. Put on the Smart Lid on top of the Ninja Foodi Steam Fryer. 5. Move the Lid Slider to the "Air Fry/Stovetop". Select the "Air Fry" mode for cooking. 6. Adjust the cooking temperature to 175°C. 7. Cook for around 10 minutes, or until cooked through and no longer pink inside and the internal temperature reaches 60°C. 8. Serve each meatball on a lettuce leaf, topped with Pico De Gallo or salsa, if desired. Serve with lime slices if desired. 9. Store the leftovers in an airtight container and then put in the fridge for around 3 days or in the freezer for up to a month. Reheat at 175°C for around 4 minutes in your Pressure Cooker Steam Fryer, or until heated through.
Per serving: Calories 499; Fat: 9.4g; Sodium 422mg; Carbs: 83.4g; Fiber: 17.2g; Sugars 1.6g; Protein 26.9g

Beef Reuben Fritters

Prep Time: 10 minutes | Cook Time: 16 minutes | Serves: 12

470g finely diced cooked corned beef 1 (200g) package cream cheese, softened	50g finely shredded Swiss cheese 35g sauerkraut 100g parmesan	Chopped fresh thyme, for garnish Thousand Island Dipping Sauce, for serving	Cornichons, for serving (optional)

1. Place the Cook & Crisp Basket in your Pressure Cooker Steam Fryer. 2. Grease the Ninja Foodi Pressure Steam Fryer basket with avocado oil. 3. In a suitable bowl, mix the corned beef, cream cheese, Swiss cheese, and sauerkraut until well mixed. Form the corned beef mixture into twelve 11 cm balls. 4. Place the parmesan in a shallow bowl. Roll the corned beef balls in the parmesan and use your hands to form it into a thick crust around each ball. 5. Place 6 balls in the "cook & crisp basket", spaced about 1 cm apart. Put on the Smart Lid on top of the Ninja Foodi Steam Fryer. Move the Lid Slider to the "Air Fry/Stovetop". Select the "Air Fry" mode for cooking. 6. Adjust the cooking temperature to 200°C. 7. Cook for around 8 minutes, or until golden brown and crispy. Allow them to cool a bit before lifting them out of the Pressure Cooker Steam Fryer (the fritters are very soft when the cheese is melted; they're easier to handle once the cheese has hardened a bit). Repeat with the remaining fritters. 8. Garnish with chopped fresh thyme and serve with the dipping sauce and cornichons, if desired. Store the leftovers in an airtight container and then put in the fridge for around 3 days or in the freezer for up to a month. 9. Reheat them at 175°C for around 4 minutes in your Pressure Cooker Steam Fryer, or until heated through.
Per serving: Calories 339; Fat: 14g; Sodium 556mg; Carbs: 44.6g; Fiber: 6.4g; Sugars 3.8g; Protein 10.5g

Stuffed Venison Tenderloin

Prep Time: 10 minutes | Cook Time: 10 minutes | Serves: 4

675g venison or beef tenderloin, pounded to ½ cm thick	1 teaspoon black pepper	2 cloves garlic, minced	Halved cherry tomatoes
	50g creamy goat cheese	Avocado oil	Extra-virgin olive oil
	50g crumbled feta cheese	**For Garnish**	Sprigs of fresh rosemary
3 teaspoons fine sea salt	40g finely chopped onions	Prepared yellow mustard	Lavender flowers

1. Place the Cook & Crisp Basket in your Pressure Cooker Steam Fryer. 2. Grease the Ninja Foodi Pressure Steam Fryer basket with avocado oil. 3. Season the tenderloin on all sides with the black pepper and salt. 4. In a suitable-sized mixing bowl, mix the goat cheese, feta, onions, and garlic. Place the mixture in the center of the tenderloin. Starting at the end closest to you, tightly roll the tenderloin like a jelly roll. Tie the rolled tenderloin tightly with kitchen twine. 5. Place the meat in the "cook & crisp basket". Put on the Smart Lid on top of the Ninja Foodi Steam Fryer. Move the Lid Slider to the "Air Fry/Stovetop". Select the "Air Fry" mode for cooking. 6. Adjust the cooking temperature to 200°C. 7. Cook for around 5 minutes. Flip the meat over. Cook for 5 minutes more, or until the internal temperature reaches 55°C for medium-rare. 8. To serve, smear a line of prepared yellow mustard on a platter, then place the meat next to it and add halved cherry tomatoes on the side, if desired. Drizzle with olive oil and garnish with rosemary sprigs and lavender flowers, if desired. 9. Best served fresh. Store leftovers in an airtight container and put in the fridge for around 3 days. Reheat them at 175°C for around 4 minutes in your Pressure Cooker Steam Fryer, or until heated through.
Per serving: Calories 231; Fat: 2.1g; Sodium 816mg; Carbs: 38.1g; Fiber: 14.4g; Sugars 4.5g; Protein 16.6g

Hamburgers

Prep Time: 6 minutes | Cook Time: 10 minutes | Serves: 2

½ teaspoon fine sea salt	¼ teaspoon smoked paprika	2 Hamburger Buns	Avocado oil
¼ teaspoon black pepper	2 (115g) hamburger patties, 1 cm thick	2 tablespoons mayonnaise	
¼ teaspoon garlic powder		6 red onion slices	
¼ teaspoon onion powder	120g crumbled blue cheese	2 lettuce leaves	

1. Place the Cook & Crisp Basket in your Pressure Cooker Steam Fryer. 2. Grease the Ninja Foodi Pressure Steam Fryer basket with avocado oil. 3. In a suitable bowl, mix the salt, pepper, and seasonings. Season the patties well on both sides with the seasoning mixture. 4. Place the patties in the "cook & crisp basket". Put on the Smart Lid on top of the Ninja Foodi Steam Fryer. Move the Lid Slider to the "Air Fry/Stovetop". Select the "Air Fry" mode for cooking. Adjust the cooking temperature to 180°C. Cook for around 7 minutes, or until the internal temperature reaches 60°C for a suitable-done burger. Place the blue cheese on top of the patties. Cook for another minute to melt the cheese. Remove the burgers and allow to rest for around 5 minutes. 5. Slice the buns in half and smear 2 halves with a tablespoon of mayo each. Place the buns in the "cook & crisp basket" cut side up. Put on the Smart Lid on top of the Ninja Foodi Steam Fryer. Move the Lid Slider to the "Air Fry/Stovetop". Select the "Air Fry" mode for cooking. Toast the buns at 200°C for around 1 to 2 minutes, until golden brown. 6. Remove the buns from the Ninja Foodi Pressure Steam Fryer and place them on a serving plate. Put the burgers on the buns and top each burger with 3 red onion slices and a lettuce leaf. 7. Best served fresh. Store leftover patties in an airtight container and put in the fridge for around 3 days or in the freezer for up to a month. 8. Reheat it at 175°C for around 4 minutes in your Pressure Cooker Steam Fryer, or until heated through.
Per serving: Calories 283; Fat: 3.6g; Sodium 381mg; Carbs: 55.4g; Fiber: 8.1g; Sugars 3.1g; Protein 8.7g

Sweet and Sour Beef Brisket

Prep time: 20 minutes | Cook time: 2 ½ hours | Serves: 6

1.3kg beef brisket, fat cap trimmed to ½ cm	pepper	235g crushed tomatoes with basil and garlic	sugar
1 tablespoon olive oil, plus more for drizzling the meat	1 large onion, sliced through the root end	120ml store-bought beef stock, or homemade	2 tablespoons red wine vinegar
	1 tablespoon chopped fresh rosemary		3 large carrots, peeled and left whole
Salt and freshly ground black		2 tablespoons packed brown	

1. Move the slider towards "AIR FRY/STOVETOP" and set Ninja Foodi XL Pressure Cooker Steam Fryer with SmartLid to SEAR/SAUTÉ mode. Adjust the temperature to "Hi5" by using up arrow. Press START/STOP to begin cooking. Drizzle the meaty side of the brisket with oil and season liberally all over with salt and pepper. When the pot is hot, add the brisket meaty-side down and cook until browned on that side, 4 minutes. Transfer to a plate. 2. Add the oil to the pot. When the oil is hot, add the onion and rosemary and cook, stirring frequently, until the onion begins to brown, 5 minutes. Press START/STOP. Add the tomatoes, stock, brown sugar, and vinegar and stir to combine. 3. Return the brisket to the pot fat-side up with any accumulated juices on the plate. Place the carrots on top of the brisket. 4. Lock lid; move slider towards PRESSURE. Adjust pressure release valve in the SEAL position. Close pressure-release valve. The cooking temperature will default to HIGH, which is accurate. Set time to 1 ½ hours. Select START/STOP and start cooking. When the cooking time is up, let the pressure come down naturally for about 25 minutes and then quickly release the remaining pressure. 5. Transfer the brisket and carrots to a cutting board and cover loosely with foil. 6. Move the slider towards "AIR FRY/STOVETOP" and set Ninja Foodi XL Pressure Cooker Steam Fryer with SmartLid to SEAR/SAUTÉ mode. Adjust the temperature to "Hi5" by using up arrow. Press START/STOP to begin cooking. Simmer the cooking liquid until it is reduced by about half, about 10 minutes. 7. Liquid fat will pool around the edges of the pot while it's simmering; use a ladle to skim this off and discard. Season with salt and pepper. Press START/STOP. 8. Thinly slice the brisket against the grain and cut the carrots into bite-size pieces, and serve with the sauce.
Per Serving: Calories 156; Fat 10.6g; Sodium 236mg; Carbs 6.5g; Fiber 3.1g; Sugar 2.4g; Protein 6.5g

Herbed Lamb Chops

Prep Time: 5 minutes | Cook Time: 5 minutes | Serves: 2

Marinade: 2 teaspoons grated lime zest 120ml lime juice 60ml avocado oil	10g chopped fresh mint leaves 4 cloves garlic, chopped 2 teaspoons fine sea salt ½ teaspoon black pepper	4 (2.5 cm-thick) lamb chops (optional) Sprigs of fresh mint, for garnish (optional) Lime slices, for serving

1. Place the Cook & Crisp Basket in your Pressure Cooker Steam Fryer. 2. Make the marinade: Place all the recipe ingredients for the marinade in a food processor and puree until mostly smooth with a few small chunks. Transfer half of the marinade to a shallow dish and set the other half aside for serving. Add the lamb to the shallow dish, cover, and put in the refrigerator to marinate for at least 2 hours or overnight. 3. Grease the Ninja Foodi Pressure Steam Fryer basket with avocado oil. 4. Transfer the chops from the marinade and place them in the "cook & crisp basket". 5. Put on the Smart Lid on top of the Ninja Foodi Steam Fryer. 6. Move the Lid Slider to the "Air Fry/Stovetop". Select the "Air Fry" mode for cooking. 7. Adjust the cooking temperature to 200°C. 8. Cook for around 5 minutes, or until the internal temperature reaches 60°C for medium doneness. 9. Allow the chops to rest for around 10 minutes before serving with the rest of the marinade as a sauce. Garnish with fresh mint leaves and serve with lime slices, if desired. Best served fresh.
Per serving: Calories 128; Fat: 1.7g; Sodium 771mg; Carbs: 22.1g; Fiber: 4.5g; Sugars 3.9g; Protein 7.1g

Mushroom Burgers

Prep Time: 5 minutes | Cook Time: 16 minutes | Serves: 2

2 large portobello mushrooms 1 teaspoon fine sea salt ¼ teaspoon garlic powder ¼ teaspoon black pepper	¼ teaspoon onion powder ¼ teaspoon smoked paprika 2(115g) hamburger patties, 1 cm thick	2 slices Swiss cheese for serving Condiments of choice, such as Ranch Dressing, prepared yellow mustard, or mayonnaise,

1. Place the Cook & Crisp Basket in your Pressure Cooker Steam Fryer. 2. Clean the portobello mushrooms and then remove the stems. Grease the mushrooms on all sides with avocado oil and season them with ½ teaspoon of the salt. Place the mushrooms in the Ninja Foodi Pressure Steam Fryer basket. Put on the Smart Lid on top of the Ninja Foodi Steam Fryer. Move the Lid Slider to the "Air Fry/Stovetop". Select the "Air Fry" mode for cooking. Adjust the cooking temperature to 180°C. 3. Cook for around 7 to 8 minutes, until fork-tender and soft to the touch. 4. While the mushrooms cook, in a suitable bowl mix the remaining ½ teaspoon of salt, the garlic powder, pepper, onion powder, and paprika. Sprinkle the hamburger patties with the seasoning mixture. 5. When the mushrooms are done cooking, remove them from the Pressure Cooker Steam Fryer and place them on a serving platter with the cap side down. 6. Place the hamburger patties in the Pressure Cooker Steam Fryer. Put on the Smart Lid on top of the Ninja Foodi Steam Fryer. Move the Lid Slider to the "Air Fry/Stovetop". Select the "Air Fry" mode for cooking. Cook at 180°C for around 7 minutes, or until the internal temperature reaches 60°C for a suitable-done burger. Place a slice of Swiss cheese on each patty. Cook for another minute to melt the cheese. 7. Place the burgers on top of the mushrooms and drizzle with condiments of your choice. Best served fresh.
Per serving: Calories 244; Fat: 9.1g; Sodium 199mg; Carbs: 34.3g; Fiber: 8.7g; Sugars 15.7g; Protein 8.3g

California-style Pot Roast

Prep time: 30 minutes | Cook time: 2½ hours | Serves: 4

1 (1.3kg) cross-rib chuck roast, cut into 3 large pieces Salt and freshly ground black pepper	2 tablespoons olive oil 1 large yellow onion, sliced through the root end 120ml Zinfandel wine	10ml store-bought beef stock, or homemade 2 large carrots, cut into 4 cm lengths	900g large Yukon Gold potatoes (about 5), peeled 30g crumbled Gorgonzola dolce cheese, at room temperature

1. Move the slider towards "AIR FRY/STOVETOP" and set Ninja Foodi XL Pressure Cooker Steam Fryer with SmartLid to SEAR/SAUTÉ mode. Adjust the temperature to "Hi5" by using up arrow. Press START/STOP to begin cooking. Season the meat liberally with salt and pepper and drizzle with the oil. When the pot is hot, add the roast and cook until browned on one side, 4 minutes. Transfer to a plate. 2. Add the onion to the pot and cook, stirring frequently, until tender, 4 minutes. Add the wine and simmer, scraping up the browned bits on the bottom of the pot, for 1 minute. Press START/STOP. 3. Return the roast to the pot browned-side down with any accumulated juices on the plate. Add the stock and arrange the carrots on top. Place a Cook & Crisp Basket on top of the beef and set the potatoes in the basket. 4. Lock lid; move slider towards PRESSURE. Adjust pressure release valve in the SEAL position. Close pressure-release valve. The cooking temperature will default to HIGH, which is accurate. Set time to 1 ½ hours. Select START/STOP and start cooking. When the cooking time is up, let the pressure come down naturally for about 15 minutes and then quickly release the remaining pressure. 5. Transfer all but one of the potatoes to a serving bowl; the one in the pot will thicken the sauce. Mash the potatoes in the bowl with the cheese until smooth. Season with salt and pepper, cover, and set aside. Transfer most of the carrots and the meat to a serving platter; cover with foil. 6. Move the slider towards "AIR FRY/STOVETOP" and Set Ninja Foodi XL Pressure Cooker Steam Fryer with SmartLid to SEAR/SAUTÉ mode. Adjust the temperature to "Hi5" by using up arrow. Press START/STOP to begin cooking. Simmer the cooking liquid until it is reduced by about half, 10 minutes. 7. Using a ladle, skim off the liquid fat that pools around the edges of the pot and discard. Blend the sauce with an immersion blender or potato masher to break up the vegetables. Season with salt and pepper. Press START/STOP. 8. Slice or shred the roast into thick slices and serve with the carrots, mashed potatoes, and sauce.
Per Serving: Calories 358; Fat 37.3g; Sodium 745mg; Carbs 14.9g; Fiber 3.6g; Sugar 4.5g; Protein 14.9g

Italian Sauce

Prep time: 15 minutes | Cook time: 35 minutes | Serves: 6

- 1 tablespoon olive oil
- 455g 95% lean ground chuck
- 1 medium yellow onion, chopped
- 3 tablespoons tomato paste
- 3 medium garlic cloves, chopped
- 2 teaspoons Italian seasoning
- 1 (700g) can San Marzano-style tomatoes, chopped, with juice
- 120ml store-bought beef stock, or homemade
- Salt and freshly ground black pepper

1. Put the oil in the pot, move the slider towards "AIR FRY/STOVETOP" and set Ninja Foodi XL Pressure Cooker Steam Fryer with SmartLid to SEAR/SAUTÉ mode. Adjust the temperature to "Hi5" by using up arrow. Press START/STOP to begin cooking. When the oil is hot, add the beef mince and onion and cook, stirring frequently, until the meat is cooked and the onion is tender, 8 minutes. Leave some of the beef in large chunks for the best texture. 2. Push the meat and onion mixture to one side of the pot. Add the tomato paste, garlic, and Italian seasoning to the other side of the pot and cook until fragrant, 1 minute. Press START/STOP. 3. Lock lid; move slider towards PRESSURE. Adjust pressure release valve in the SEAL position. Close pressure-release valve. The cooking temperature will default to HIGH, which is accurate. Set time to 10 minutes. Select START/STOP and start cooking. 4. When cooking is complete, let pressure release quickly by turning it into VENT position. Season the sauce with salt and pepper and serve.

Per Serving: Calories 127; Fat 7.3g; Sodium 269mg; Carbs 5.8g; Fiber 4.3g; Sugar 3.5g; Protein 5.8g

Delicious Beef Stroganoff

Prep time: 15 minutes | Cook time: 50 minutes | Serves: 4

- 900g beef tenderloin steak, sirloin steak, or boneless short ribs, fat trimmed
- Salt and freshly ground black pepper
- 2 tablespoons olive oil
- 1 medium onion, finely chopped
- 240ml plus 2 tablespoons store-bought beef stock, or homemade
- 10g dried porcini or mixed wild mushrooms, rinsed to remove any grit
- 1 tablespoon Worcestershire sauce
- 2 tablespoons plain flour
- 120g cultured sour cream
- **Optional Garnish**
- 10g chopped fresh dill

1. Move the slider towards "AIR FRY/STOVETOP" and set Ninja Foodi XL Pressure Cooker Steam Fryer with SmartLid to SEAR/SAUTÉ mode. Adjust the temperature to "Hi5" by using up arrow. Press START/STOP to begin cooking. Season the steaks with salt and pepper and drizzle with 1 tablespoon of the oil. When the pot is hot, add the steak in batches and cook until browned on both sides, 6 minutes per batch. Transfer the meat to a cutting board. Press START/STOP. 2. Select SAUTÉ. Put the remaining 1 tablespoon oil in the pot, add the onion, and cook until tender, 3 minutes. While the onion cooks, use a fork and knife to cut the seared steaks into 2.5 cm pieces, returning the meat to the pot as you work. Press START/STOP. 3. Add 240ml of the stock, the dried mushrooms, and the Worcestershire sauce to the pot and scrape up the browned bits on the bottom of the pot. 4. Lock lid; move slider towards PRESSURE. Adjust pressure release valve in the SEAL position. Close pressure-release valve. The cooking temperature will default to HIGH, which is accurate. Set time to for 10 minutes if using tenderloin, 20 minutes if using sirloin or boneless short ribs. Select START/STOP and start cooking. 5. When the cooking is complete, let the pressure release naturally for 10 minutes and then quickly release the remaining pressure by turning it to VENT position. Place the flour in a small bowl and gradually whisk in the remaining 2 tablespoons stock. 6. Add the mixture to the pot, select SEAR/SAUTÉ mode again. Simmer, stirring very gently, until the sauce has thickened, 1 minute. Press START/STOP. Remove the pot from the appliance. Stir in the sour cream and season with salt and pepper. Stir in the dill, if desired. 7. Serve with noodles or rice, if desired.

Per Serving: Calories 442; Fat 33g; Sodium 411mg; Carbs 32.3g; Fiber 0.5g; Sugar 1.9g; Protein 32.3g

Smoky Beef Tacos

Prep time: 15 minutes | Cook time: 2 ½ hours | Serves: 4

- 1kg beef chuck roast, cut into 6 large pieces
- Salt and freshly ground black pepper
- 80ml store-bought beef stock, or homemade
- 1 (250g) can Ro-Tel tomatoes, with juice
- 3 medium garlic cloves, chopped
- 1 chipotle pepper in adobo, chopped
- 1 tablespoon ground cumin
- 8 (15 cm) flour tortillas, warmed
- **Optional Garnishes**
- Guacamole
- Shredded cheddar cheese
- Shredded romaine lettuce

1. Move the slider towards "AIR FRY/STOVETOP" and set Ninja Foodi XL Pressure Cooker Steam Fryer with SmartLid to SEAR/SAUTÉ mode. Adjust the temperature to "Hi5" by using up arrow. Press START/STOP to begin cooking and add the oil. Sprinkle the beef liberally with salt and pepper. When the pot is hot, add the meat and cook until browned all over, about 8 minutes. Transfer to a plate. Press START/STOP. 2. Add the stock and cook, scraping up any browned bits on the bottom of the pot. Add the tomatoes, garlic, chipotle pepper, and cumin and stir to combine. Return the meat and any accumulated juices to the pot and turn the meat in the tomato mixture to coat. 3. Lock lid; move slider towards PRESSURE. Adjust pressure release valve in the SEAL position. Close pressure-release valve. The cooking temperature will default to HIGH, which is accurate. Set time to 35 minutes. Select START/STOP and start cooking. 4. When the cooking is complete, let the pressure release naturally for about 20 minutes and then quickly release the remaining pressure by turning it to VENT position. 5. Transfer the meat to a cutting board and shred or chop it, discarding the fat and connective tissue. Put the beef in a large serving bowl. Use a slotted spoon to retrieve the tomatoes and garlic from the cooking liquid; add them to the beef. Cover. 6. If you'd like to serve the beef with the cooking liquid, select SEAR/SAUTÉ mode again. Simmer the cooking liquid until it is reduced by about half, about 10 minutes. Liquid fat will pool around the edges of the pot while it's simmering; use a ladle to skim this off and discard it. Press START/STOP. 7. If you don't want to take this extra step, just spoon a few tablespoons of the liquid over the beef to moisten it and discard the remaining liquid. Serve the beef with the tortillas and optional garnishes.

Per Serving: Calories 104; Fat 6.3g; Sodium 154mg; Carbs 1.8g; Fiber 3.7g; Sugar 6g; Protein 1.8g

Beef Taco Pasta

Prep time: 10 minutes | Cook time: 25 minutes | Serves: 4

1 tablespoon olive oil	1 (35g) packet taco seasoning	60g tomato paste	**Optional garnish**
455g 95% lean beef mince	300g (dried/uncooked) short, chunky twisted pasta such as campanelle or gigli	1 large red pepper, chopped	250g grated feta or pepper Jack cheese
1 medium yellow onion, chopped		Salt and freshly ground black pepper	

1. Put the oil in the pot, move the slider towards "AIR FRY/STOVETOP" and set Ninja Foodi XL Pressure Cooker Steam Fryer with SmartLid to SEAR/SAUTÉ mode. Adjust the temperature to "Hi5" by using up arrow. Press START/STOP to begin cooking. When the oil is hot, add the beef, onion, and 1 tablespoon of the taco seasoning and cook, breaking the meat into 1.5 cm chunks and stirring frequently, until the onion is tender (the beef will finish cooking under pressure), 6 minutes. Press START/STOP. 2. Add the pasta and stir to coat with the onions and beef. In a medium bowl or large measuring cup, whisk together 920ml water, the tomato paste, and the remaining taco seasoning. Pour the mixture over the pasta in the pot and stir gently to combine. Place the pepper on top of the pasta mixture. 3. Lock lid; move slider towards PRESSURE. Adjust pressure release valve in the SEAL position. Close pressure-release valve. The cooking temperature will default to HIGH, which is accurate. Set LOW pressure and time to 5 minutes. Select START/STOP and start cooking. 4. When cooking is complete, let pressure release quickly by turning it into VENT position. Gently stir the pasta with a rubber spatula, scraping any browned bits on the bottom of the pot. Season with salt and pepper. The sauce will thicken upon standing. 5. Serve sprinkled with the optional cheese, if desired.
Per Serving: Calories 404; Fat 25.8g; Sodium 358mg; Carbs 3.7g; Fiber 1.3g; Sugar 0.5g; Protein 37.5g

Barbecue Spicy Meatloaf

Prep time: 10 minutes | Cook time: 55 minutes | Serves: 6

675g minced meatloaf mix (beef and pork)	6 tablespoons dry Italian breadcrumbs	40g finely chopped shallots	pepper
240g thick barbecue sauce	1 large carrot, grated	1 large egg, beaten	
		Salt and freshly ground black	

1. In a large bowl, combine the meat, 60g of the barbecue sauce, the breadcrumbs, carrot, shallots, egg, and ½ teaspoon each salt and pepper. Place a 35 cm-long piece of foil on a work surface. 2. Put another 10 cm piece of foil on top of the first to create a cross. Place the meatloaf mixture in the center of the sheets of foil and form it into a loaf that is about 18 cm in length. Use the side of your hand to create a 1 cm-deep trench in the center of the loaf). Bring the edges of the foil up, folding them into a little pan with 7 to 9-cm-high sides. 3. Pour 360ml water into the pot. Place the meatloaf in its foil pan on a Deluxe reversible rack with handles. 4. Pour the remaining barbecue sauce over the top of the meatloaf, and carefully lower it into the pot on the Deluxe reversible rack. 5. Lock lid; move slider towards PRESSURE. Adjust pressure release valve in the SEAL position. Close pressure-release valve. The cooking temperature will default to HIGH, which is accurate. Set time to 25 minutes. Select START/STOP and start cooking. 6. When cooking is complete, let pressure release quickly by turning it into VENT position. Carefully lift the meatloaf from the pot. Drain the drippings from the foil pan and discard. Cut the meatloaf into thick slices and serve.
Per Serving: Calories 153; Fat 2.8g; Sodium 28mg; Carbs 26g; Fiber 1g; Sugar 1g; Protein 6g

Meatballs with Creamy Pan Sauce

Prep time: 22 minutes | Cook time: 40 minutes | Serves: 4

1 slice dark rye sandwich bread, torn into pieces, crusts discarded	or homemade	pepper	**Optional Garnish**
60g plus 2 tablespoons cream cheese, at room temperature	675g meatloaf mix (or 340g each pork and lean beef mince)	1 tablespoon olive oil	Lingonberry jam or cranberry sauce
360ml store-bought beef stock,	10g chopped fresh dill, or 2½ teaspoons dried dill	½ medium yellow onion, finely chopped	
	Salt and freshly ground black	30g plain flour	
		Cooking spray	

1. Preheat the grill and adjust an oven rack so it is 10 cm from the element. Line a baking sheet with foil and spray with cooking spray. 2. In a large bowl, combine the bread, 2 tablespoons of the cream cheese, and 2 tablespoons of the stock and mix well until the bread is softened to mush. Add the meat, dill, 1 teaspoon salt, and several grinds of pepper. Mix until well combined. Roll into 28 meatballs (about 1½ tablespoons each) and place them on the prepared baking sheet. Grill until browned on one side, about 5 minutes. 3. Meanwhile, put the oil in the pot, move the slider towards "AIR FRY/STOVETOP" and set Ninja Foodi XL Pressure Cooker Steam Fryer with SmartLid to SEAR/SAUTÉ mode. Adjust the temperature to "Hi5" by using up arrow. Press START/STOP to begin cooking. When the oil is hot, add the onion, and cook, stirring frequently, until well browned, 6 minutes. Press START/STOP. 4. Transfer the meatballs to the pot, discarding any drippings on the baking sheet. Add the remaining stock to the pot. 5. Lock lid; move slider towards PRESSURE. Adjust pressure release valve in the SEAL position. Close pressure-release valve. The cooking temperature will default to HIGH, which is accurate. Set time to 5 minutes. Select START/STOP and start cooking. 6. When cooking is complete, let pressure release quickly by turning it into VENT position. Use a slotted spoon to transfer the meatballs to a serving dish. Cover with foil. 7. Place the flour in a small bowl and slowly whisk in 60ml water until smooth. Select SAUTÉ. Add the flour mixture and remaining cream cheese to the pot. Simmer, whisking constantly, until the sauce is smooth and bubbly, 2 minutes. Press START/STOP. 8. Season with salt and pepper. Pour the sauce over the meatballs and serve with lingonberry jam or cranberry sauce, if desired.
Per Serving: Calories 723; Fat 58.8g; Sodium 1982mg; Carbs 26.5g; Fiber 0.5g; Sugar 3.3g; Protein 22.2g

Pulled Pork Barbecue

Prep time: 10 minutes | Cook time: 1 ½ hours | Serves: 6

- 1 (1.8kg) boneless pork shoulder
- 3 tablespoons packed brown sugar
- 1 tablespoon seasoning salt (such as Johnny's Fine Foods)
- 1½ teaspoons smoked paprika
- 240g ketchup
- 120ml cider vinegar

1. Trim any excess fat off the outside of the pork and cut the meat into four large pieces. In a small bowl, combine the brown sugar, seasoning salt, and paprika. Rub evenly all over the meat. 2. Combine the ketchup, vinegar, and 120ml water in the pot. Add the meat and turn to coat in the sauce. 3. Lock lid; move slider towards PRESSURE. Adjust pressure release valve in the SEAL position. Close pressure-release valve. The cooking temperature will default to HIGH, which is accurate. Set time to 40 minutes. Select START/STOP and start cooking. When cooking is complete, let pressure release naturally for about 15 minutes, then quickly release any remaining pressure by turning it into VENT position. 4. Put the pork to a cutting board and shred with two forks, discarding any large chunks of fat. Place in a serving bowl and cover with foil. 5. While you're shredding the meat, move the slider towards "AIR FRY/STOVETOP" and Set Ninja Foodi XL Pressure Cooker Steam Fryer with SmartLid to SEAR/SAUTÉ mode. Adjust the temperature to "Hi5" by using up arrow. Press START/STOP to begin cooking and bring the sauce to a simmer. Skim the liquid fat off the top of the sauce and discard. Press START/STOP. 6. Ladle some of the sauce over the pork and serve with the remaining sauce on the side.

Per Serving: Calories 62; Fat 13.3g; Sodium 1572mg; Carbs 15.5g; Fiber 0.12g; Sugar 0.5g; Protein 0.5g

Beer-Braised Short Ribs

Prep time: 45 minutes | Cook time: 1 hour 55 minutes | Serves: 4

- 1.5–1.8kg meaty English-cut short ribs, fat trimmed
- Salt and freshly ground black pepper
- 2 tablespoons olive oil
- 1 medium onion, sliced through the root end
- 4 medium garlic cloves, thinly sliced
- 3 tablespoons tomato paste
- 1 (300g) bottle good-quality root beer
- 120ml store-bought beef stock, or homemade
- 2 tablespoons cider vinegar

1. Move the slider towards "AIR FRY/STOVETOP" and set Ninja Foodi XL Pressure Cooker Steam Fryer with SmartLid to SEAR/SAUTÉ mode. Adjust the temperature to "Hi5" by using up arrow. Press START/STOP to begin cooking. Season the short ribs all over with salt and several grinds of pepper. Drizzle the meaty sides of the ribs with 1 tablespoon of the oil. When the pot is hot, brown the short ribs in batches, meaty-side down, until well browned, about 5 minutes per batch. Transfer the browned short ribs to a plate. Press START/STOP. Pour off the drippings in the pan and return the pot to the appliance. 2. Select SEAR/SAUTÉ mode. Add the remaining 1 tablespoon oil and the onion to the pot and cook until tender, 4 minutes. Add the garlic and tomato paste and cook until fragrant, 30 seconds. Add the root beer and bring to a simmer, scraping up the browned bits on the bottom of the pot. Add the stock and vinegar and stir to combine. Return the short ribs and accumulated juices to the pot, standing the ribs on their skinny sides so they are partially submerged in the cooking liquid. 3. Lock lid; move slider towards PRESSURE. Adjust pressure release valve in the SEAL position. Close pressure-release valve. The cooking temperature will default to HIGH, which is accurate. Set time to 40 minutes. Select START/STOP and start cooking. 4. When cooking is complete, let pressure release naturally for about 15 minutes, then quickly release any remaining pressure by turning it into VENT position. Carefully transfer the ribs to a large serving bowl and cover with foil. A few may fall off their bones; just discard the bones and know that the meat is going to be very tender. 5. Select SEAR/SAUTÉ mode again. Liquid fat will pool around the edges of the pot while it's simmering; use a ladle to skim off the fat and discard it. You may get as much as 1 to 1½ cups fat; short ribs are a fatty cut of beef. 6. Simmer the sauce until reduced by half, about 10 minutes. Pour the sauce over the ribs and serve.

Per Serving: Calories 1052; Fat 50g; Sodium 438mg; Carbs 7g; Fiber 0g; Sugar 7g; Protein 132g

Cheesy Philly Steaks

Prep time: 12 minutes | Cook time: 30 minutes | Serves: 4

- 675g flat iron steak, top sirloin steak, or flank steak, cut to fit into the pot
- 1 tablespoon olive oil
- 4 teaspoons steak seasoning or garlic seasoning blend
- 240ml store-bought beef stock, or homemade
- 1 large red pepper, cut into 2.5 cm-wide strips
- 2 tablespoons soy sauce
- 4 crusty hoagie or sub sandwich rolls, split lengthwise
- 4 slices provolone or American cheese

1. Move the slider towards "AIR FRY/STOVETOP" and set Ninja Foodi XL Pressure Cooker Steam Fryer with SmartLid to SEAR/SAUTÉ mode. Adjust the temperature to "Hi5" by using up arrow. Press START/STOP to begin cooking. Brush the steak with the oil and rub the steak seasoning into the meat. When the pot is hot, add the steaks in batches and cook until well browned, about 4 minutes per side. Press START/STOP. 2. Transfer the steaks to a cutting board and slice against the grain into ½ 1 cm-thick slices. Return the meat and accumulated juices on the cutting board to the pot. Add the stock, peppers, and soy sauce. 3. Lock lid; move slider towards PRESSURE. Adjust pressure release valve in the SEAL position. Close pressure-release valve. The cooking temperature will default to HIGH, which is accurate. Set time to 5 minutes. Select START/STOP and start cooking. 4. When cooking is complete, let pressure release naturally for about 10 minutes, then quickly release any remaining pressure by turning it into VENT position. 5. Toast the rolls, if desired. With a slotted spoon, remove the beef and vegetables from the pot; reserve the cooking liquid for another use. Mound the beef and peppers on the rolls. 6. Top with slices of cheese and serve.

Per Serving: Calories 492; Fat 17.8g; Sodium 1051mg; Carbs 33.2g; Fiber 0.12g; Sugar 7.3g; Protein 47.5g

Bratwurst with Sauerkraut

Prep time: 10 minutes | Cook time: 40 minutes | Serves: 4

1 tablespoon olive oil	1 (300g) bottle dry, hard apple cider	1 large Honeycrisp or Fuji apple, peeled, cored, and cut into 2.5 cm-thick wedges	kielbasa sausages, left whole
1 medium yellow onion, thinly sliced through the root end	1 (400g) package refrigerated sauerkraut, drained		Mustard, for serving
1 teaspoon caraway seeds		455g smoked bratwurst or	

1. Move the slider towards "AIR FRY/STOVETOP" and set Ninja Foodi XL Pressure Cooker Steam Fryer with SmartLid to SEAR/SAUTÉ mode. Adjust the temperature to "Hi5" by using up arrow. Press START/STOP to begin cooking. When the oil is hot, add the onion and caraway seeds and cook until beginning to brown, 6 minutes. Add the cider and cook for 1 minute, scraping up the browned bits on the bottom of pot. Press START/STOP. 2. Add the sauerkraut and apple to the pot and stir to combine. Nestle the sausages into the sauerkraut mixture. Lock lid; move slider towards PRESSURE. Adjust pressure release valve in the SEAL position. Close pressure-release valve. The cooking temperature will default to HIGH, which is accurate. Set time to 6 minutes. Select START/STOP and start cooking. 3. When the cooking time is up, let the pressure come down naturally for 10 minutes and then quick-release the remaining pressure. 4. Serve hot, with mustard on the side, if desired.
Per Serving: Calories 134; Fat 2.8g; Sodium 64mg; Carbs 26g; Fiber 4g; Sugar 8g; Protein 3g

Herby Pork Chops with Squash

Prep time: 20 minutes | Cook time: 1 hour 5 minutes | Serves: 4

3 tablespoons olive oil	3 medium garlic cloves, chopped	120ml dry white wine	into 2.5 cm cubes
4 (150–200g) center-cut bone-in pork rib chops, 2.5 cm thick	1 tablespoon plus 1½ teaspoons finely chopped mixed fresh poultry herbs	120ml store-bought chicken stock, or homemade	1 tablespoon corn flour
Salt and freshly ground black pepper		1 medium (900g) butternut squash, peeled, seeded, and cut	

1. Put 2 tablespoons of the oil in the pot, move the slider towards "AIR FRY/STOVETOP" and Set Ninja Foodi XL Pressure Cooker Steam Fryer with SmartLid to SEAR/SAUTÉ mode. Adjust the temperature to "Hi5" by using up arrow. Press START/STOP to begin cooking. Season the chops all over with salt and pepper. When the oil is hot, add two of the chops and cook until browned on one side, about 3 minutes. Transfer to a plate and repeat with the remaining chops. 2. Add the garlic and 1 tablespoon of the herbs and cook, stirring constantly, until fragrant, 30 seconds. Add the wine and simmer, scraping up the browned bits from the bottom of the pot, for 2 minutes. Press START/STOP. Return the chops and any accumulated juices to the pot and add the stock. 3. Set the Cook & Crisp Basket over the chops. In a large bowl, combine the squash, the remaining 1 tablespoon oil, and the remaining 1½ teaspoons herbs. Season liberally with salt and pepper and place in the Cook & Crisp Basket. 4. Lock lid; move slider towards PRESSURE. Adjust pressure release valve in the SEAL position. Close pressure-release valve. The cooking temperature will default to HIGH, which is accurate. Set time to 10 minutes. Select START/STOP and start cooking. 5. When cooking is complete, let pressure release naturally for about 15 minutes, then quickly release any remaining pressure by turning it into VENT position. Transfer the squash to a serving bowl. Transfer the chops to a serving plate. 6. Remove 120ml of the cooking liquid from the pot and discard. Select SEAR/SAUTÉ mode again. When the liquid comes to a simmer, use a ladle to skim off most of the liquid fat that pools around the edges of the pot. In a small bowl, mix the corn flour with 1 tablespoon cold water. Add the corn flour mixture to the pot, stir, and simmer until thickened, 1 minute. Press START/STOP. 7. Spoon the sauce over the chops and serve with the squash.
Per Serving: Calories 429; Fat 32.4g; Sodium 325mg; Carbs 5g; Fiber 1g; Sugar 3g; Protein 28g

Pork Chops with Beans

Prep time: 20 minutes | Cook time: 50 minutes | Serves: 4

195g dried cannellini beans, picked over and rinsed	4 (200g) center-cut bone-in pork chops (1 to 2.5 cm thick)	chopped	tomatoes, drained and chopped
Salt and freshly ground black pepper	2 tablespoons olive oil	180ml store-bought chicken stock, or homemade	1 teaspoon dried sage
	1 medium yellow onion,	15g oil-packed sun-dried	Finely grated zest and juice of ½ lemon

1. Place the beans in a large bowl, cover with cold water and 1 teaspoon salt, and soak at room temperature for 8 to 9 hours. Alternatively, quick-soak the beans: Combine them with several cups of water and 1 teaspoon salt, and boil them on the stove for 1 minute. Let them soak off the heat for 1 hour. Drain. 2. Move the slider towards "AIR FRY/STOVETOP" and set Ninja Foodi XL Pressure Cooker Steam Fryer with SmartLid to SEAR/SAUTÉ mode. Adjust the temperature to "Hi5" by using up arrow. Press START/STOP to begin cooking. Drizzle the chops with 1 tablespoon of the oil and season all over with salt and pepper. When the pot is hot, brown the chops in batches, about 4 minutes for the first batch, 2 minutes for the second batch. Transfer to a plate. 3. Add the remaining 1 tablespoon oil to the pot. Add the onion and sauté, scraping up the browned bits on the bottom of the pot, until tender, 4 minutes. Press START/STOP. 4. Add the drained beans, stock, sun-dried tomatoes, sage, and ½ teaspoon salt and stir to combine. Place the pork chops on top of the bean mixture. 5. Lock lid; move slider towards PRESSURE. Adjust pressure release valve in the SEAL position. Close pressure-release valve. The cooking temperature will default to HIGH, which is accurate. Set time to 5 minutes. Select START/STOP and start cooking. 6. When cooking is complete, let pressure release naturally for about 15 minutes, then quickly release any remaining pressure by turning it into VENT position. Stir in the lemon zest and juice. 7. Using a slotted spoon, transfer the chops and beans to plates. Drizzle some of the cooking liquid over the top.
Per Serving: Calories 173; Fat 13.6g; Sodium 281mg; Carbs 3g; Fiber 1g; Sugar 1g; Protein 10g

Pork Ragu with Gnocchi
Prep time: 25 minutes | Cook time: 1 hour 15 minutes | Serves: 8

1.3kg boneless country-style pork ribs	2 tablespoons olive oil	chopped	1 (700g) can San Marzano-style tomatoes, chopped, with juices
Salt and freshly ground black pepper	1 medium yellow onion, chopped	2 teaspoons Italian seasoning	
	4 medium garlic cloves,	60ml store-bought chicken stock, or homemade or water	1 (440g) package fresh gnocchi

1. Move the slider towards "AIR FRY/STOVETOP" and set Ninja Foodi XL Pressure Cooker Steam Fryer with SmartLid to SEAR/SAUTÉ mode. Adjust the temperature to "Hi5" by using up arrow. Press START/STOP to begin cooking. When the pot is hot, season the pork all over with salt and pepper and drizzle with 1 tablespoon of the oil. Working in two batches, sear the pork until browned on two sides, 5 minutes each batch. Transfer to a plate. 2. Pour the remaining 1 tablespoon oil into the pot. Add the onion and cook until tender, 4 minutes. Add the garlic and 1½ teaspoons of the Italian seasoning and cook until fragrant, 45 seconds. Add the stock or water and scrape up the browned bits on the bottom of the pot. Press START/STOP. 3. Return the pork and any accumulated juices to the pot and add the tomatoes. Lock lid; move slider towards PRESSURE. Adjust pressure release valve in the SEAL position. Close pressure-release valve. The cooking temperature will default to HIGH, which is accurate. Set time to 20 minutes. Select START/STOP and start cooking. 4. Meanwhile, cook the gnocchi according to the package instructions. 5. When cooking is complete, let the pressure release naturally for about 10 minutes and then quickly release the remaining pressure. Place the meat to a cutting board and shred or chop it, discarding any large bits of fat. While you're shredding the meat, select SAUTÉ and bring the sauce to a simmer. 6. Liquid fat will pool around the edges of the pot while it's simmering; use a ladle to skim this off and discard. Add the remaining ½ teaspoon Italian seasoning and the shredded meat to the pot and simmer for 1 minute. Season with salt and pepper. Press START/STOP. 7. Serve half the sauce with the gnocchi.
Per Serving: Calories 314; Fat 13.3g; Sodium 699mg; Carbs 10g; Fiber 1.9g; Sugar 0.7g; Protein 37.g

Short Rib Bibimbap
Prep time: 10 minutes | Cook time: 35 minutes | Serves: 4

1.3kg flanken-style short ribs	280g short-grain white rice, rinsed well and drained in a sieve	4 large eggs	**Optional Garnish**
1 (300g) bottle Korean kalbi marinade sauce		150g napa cabbage kimchi	Gochujang (Korean red chile paste)
		Cooking spray	

1. Place the short ribs in a large nonreactive bowl or a large zip-top bag and add the marinade. Cover or seal and refrigerate for at least 1 hour and up to 24 hours. 2. Place the ribs and the marinade in the Ninja Foodi XL Pressure Cooker Steam Fryer, arranging the ribs on their edges and curving them into the pot so they all fit. Place the Deluxe reversible rack over the ribs. In an 18 cm round metal baking pan, combine the rice with 360ml cold water. Cover the pan tightly with foil. Place the baking pan on the Deluxe reversible rack above the ribs. 3. Lock lid; move slider towards PRESSURE. Adjust pressure release valve in the SEAL position. Close pressure-release valve. The cooking temperature will default to HIGH, which is accurate. Set time to 10 minutes. Press START/STOP to cooking. When cooking is complete, let pressure release naturally. 4. Lift the rice in the baking pan out of the pot, fluff with a fork, and set aside. Transfer the ribs to a large plate or cutting board, cut into manageable pieces with clean kitchen scissors, and spoon a few tablespoons of the cooking liquid over them. Cover with foil. 5. Spray a large nonstick frying pan with cooking spray and place over medium-high heat. Break the eggs into the pan and cook until the whites are set, about 3 minutes. 6. Divide the rice among four bowls. Top the rice with the ribs, eggs, and kimchi. Serve with gochujang, if desired.
Per Serving: Calories 134; Fat 9.8g; Sodium 394mg; Carbs 2g; Fiber 0g; Sugar 1g; Protein 9g

Chinese Braised Pork with Aubergine
Prep time: 10 minutes | Cook time: 30 minutes | Serves: 4

1 medium (455g) Japanese aubergine, cut crosswise into 4 cm thick slices, or globe aubergine cut into 5 cm chunks	60ml canned chicken stock, or homemade	675g thin-cut boneless pork chops, frozen for 15 minutes	**Optional Garnish**
	3 tablespoons soy sauce	1 tablespoon rapeseed oil	145g chopped dry-roasted peanuts
Salt and freshly ground black pepper	1 tablespoon balsamic or red wine vinegar	1 tablespoon finely chopped fresh ginger	
	1 tablespoon sambal oelek	1 tablespoon corn flour	

1. If using globe aubergine, toss the cubes with ¾ teaspoon salt and set aside in a colander for 20 minutes to draw out the bitter juices. Pat the aubergine dry with paper towels. 2. In a medium bowl, combine the stock, soy sauce, vinegar, and sambal oelek; set aside. Trim the fat from the chops and discard. Chop the pork into roughly 1 cm pieces. Season with salt and pepper. 3. Move the slider towards "AIR FRY/STOVETOP" and set Ninja Foodi XL Pressure Cooker Steam Fryer with SmartLid to SEAR/SAUTÉ mode. Adjust the temperature to "Hi5" by using up arrow. Press START/STOP to begin cooking. When the oil is hot, add the pork and ginger and cook, stirring frequently, until the pork is opaque and white all over, 3 minutes. Press START/STOP. 4. Add the stock mixture and stir. Add the aubergine to the pot, but do not stir it into the sauce. 5. Lock lid; move slider to PRESSURE. Make sure the pressure release valve is in the SEAL position. The cooking temperature will default to HIGH, which is accurate. Set time to 3 minutes. Press START/STOP to cooking. 6. When the cooking is complete, quickly release the pressure by turning it into VENT position. Using a slotted spoon, gently transfer the aubergine and most of the pork to a large serving bowl; set aside. In a small bowl, mix the corn flour and 1 tablespoon cold water. Add the corn flour mixture to the pot, select SEAR/SAUTÉ mode again. Simmer until thickened and bubbly, 1 minute. 7. Press START/STOP. Pour the sauce over the pork and aubergine, stir gently to combine, and serve immediately, garnished with peanuts, if desired.
Per Serving: Calories 509; Fat 40.6g; Sodium 525mg; Carbs 8g; Fiber 2g; Sugar 5g; Protein 28g

Vietnamese Beef Soup

Prep time: 30 minutes | Cook time: 1 hour 50 minutes | Serves: 4

1 tablespoon grapeseed or other neutral oil	8 cm piece fresh ginger (about 50g), peeled and sliced into 6 coins	60ml fish sauce	4 medium carrots (about 455g), peeled and cut into 2.5 to 4-cm chunks
3 tablespoons tomato paste	3 stalks lemon grass, trimmed to the bottom 15 cm, dry outer layers removed, bruised and halved	2 tablespoons white sugar	1 tablespoon lime juice, plus lime wedges to serve
5 medium garlic cloves, smashed and peeled		2 teaspoons chili powder	
4-star anise pods		Salt and ground black pepper	Fresh mint and/or coriander, to serve
2 cinnamon sticks		1.1kg boneless beef chuck roast, trimmed and cut into 2.5 cm chunks	

1. Move the slider towards "AIR FRY/STOVETOP" and set Ninja Foodi XL Pressure Cooker Steam Fryer with SmartLid to SEAR/SAUTÉ mode. Adjust the temperature to "Hi5" by using up arrow. Press START/STOP to begin cooking. 2. Heat the oil until shimmering, then add the tomato paste and garlic and cook, stirring often, until the paste is slightly darker, 2 to 3 minutes. Add the star anise, cinnamon sticks, ginger and lemon grass, then cook, stirring, until fragrant, about 30 seconds. Stir in 1.2L water, the fish sauce, sugar, chili powder and 1 teaspoon pepper, scraping up any browned bits. Add the beef and carrots, then distribute in an even layer. 3. Lock lid; move slider to PRESSURE. Make sure the pressure release valve is in the SEAL position The cooking temperature will default to HIGH, which is accurate. Set time to 15 minutes. Press START/STOP to cooking. 4. When pressure cooking is complete, let the pressure release naturally for about 15 minutes, then quickly release the remaining steam by turning it into VENT position. Then carefully open the pot. 5. Using a large spoon, skim off and discard the fat from the surface of the stock. Remove and discard the star anise, cinnamon sticks, ginger and lemon grass. Stir in the lime juice, then taste and adjust the seasoning with salt. 6. Ladle into bowls and top with mint and/or coriander, then serve with lime wedges.
Per Serving: Calories 293; Fat 13.8g; Sodium 855mg; Carbs 28g; Fiber 8g; Sugar 11g; Protein 19g

Tuscan Beef Stew

Prep time: 10 minutes | Cook time: 35 minutes | Serves: 6

2 tablespoons extra-virgin olive oil	12 medium garlic cloves, smashed and peeled	2 sprigs fresh rosemary, plus 1½ teaspoons minced	cm chunks
1 large yellow onion, halved and thinly sliced	480ml dry red wine	1.8kg boneless beef chuck roast, trimmed and cut into 4	Salt and coarsely ground black pepper
	3 tablespoons tomato paste		3 tablespoons plain flour

1. Move the slider towards "AIR FRY/STOVETOP" and set Ninja Foodi XL Pressure Cooker Steam Fryer with SmartLid to SEAR/SAUTÉ mode. Adjust the temperature to "Hi5" by using up arrow. Press START/STOP to begin cooking. 2. Add the oil and heat until shimmering. Add the onion and garlic, then cook, stirring occasionally, until the onion is lightly browned, 7 to 9 minutes. Add the wine and cook, scraping up any browned bits, until reduced to about 120ml, about 15 minutes. Stir in the tomato paste, rosemary sprigs and 1 tablespoon pepper. Stir in the beef and 2 teaspoons salt, then distribute in an even layer. 3. Lock lid; move slider to PRESSURE. Make sure the pressure release valve is in the SEAL position The cooking temperature will default to HIGH, which is accurate. Set time to 25 minutes. Press START/STOP to cooking. 4. When pressure cooking is complete, let the pressure release naturally for about 15 minutes, then quickly release the remaining steam by turning it into VENT position. Then carefully open the lid. 5. Using a large spoon, skim off and discard the fat from the surface of the cooking liquid. In a small bowl, whisk the flour with 6 tablespoons of the cooking liquid until smooth, then whisk into the pot. Select SEAR/SAUTÉ mode again. Bring to a simmer, stirring, and cook until lightly thickened, 6 to 8 minutes. 6. Press START/STOP to turn off the pot, then stir in the minced rosemary and 1 to 1½ tablespoons pepper. Taste and season with salt.
Per Serving: Calories 217; Fat 21.8g; Sodium 207mg; Carbs 7g; Fiber 4g; Sugar 3g; Protein 2g

Spicy Lamb Tagine

Prep time: 20 minutes | Cook time: 1 hour 15 minutes | Serves: 4

1.1kg blade lamb steaks, meat cut off the bones into 4 cm chunks, bones reserved	1 medium yellow onion, sliced through root end	2 large carrots, peeled and cut into 2.5 cm pieces	1 tablespoon white wine vinegar
2 tablespoons olive oil	4 teaspoons ras el hanout seasoning	35g dates, pitted and roughly chopped	**Optional Garnishes** Cooked couscous
Salt and freshly ground black pepper	360ml store-bought beef stock, or homemade	15g oil-packed sun-dried tomatoes, chopped	Harissa

1. Move the slider towards "AIR FRY/STOVETOP" and set Ninja Foodi XL Pressure Cooker Steam Fryer with SmartLid to SEAR/SAUTÉ mode. Adjust the temperature to "Hi5" by using up arrow. Press START/STOP to begin cooking. Toss the lamb meat with the oil and season all over with salt and several grinds of pepper. When the pot is hot, add half the meat and cook, stirring occasionally, until browned, 8 minutes. 2. Add the remaining lamb, the onion, and ras el hanout to the pot and cook, stirring occasionally, until the onion softens, 5 minutes. Add the stock, carrots, dates, and sun-dried tomatoes. Place the bones in the pot on top of the other ingredients. Press START/STOP. 3. Lock lid; move slider to PRESSURE. Make sure the pressure release valve is in the SEAL position The cooking temperature will default to HIGH, which is accurate. Set time to 25 minutes. Press START/STOP to cooking. When the cooking time is up, let the pressure come down naturally for about 15 minutes and then quickly release any remaining pressure. Discard the bones. 4. Select SEAR/SAUTÉ mode again. Add the vinegar to the pot and stir to combine. When the liquid comes to a simmer, use a ladle to spoon off most of the liquid fat that pools around the edges of the pot. Press START/STOP. 5. Season with salt and pepper. If desired, serve over couscous with dabs of harissa.
Per Serving: Calories 288; Fat 23.3g; Sodium 308mg; Carbs 6g; Fiber 1g; Sugar 5g; Protein 14g

Fig-Glazed Ham with Potatoes

Prep time: 15 minutes | Cook time: 1½ hours | Serves: 6

1 (1.3kg) smoked boneless ham	105g packed brown sugar	2 tablespoons chopped fresh dill	pepper
160g fig jam or orange marmalade	1½ to 900g small Yukon Gold potatoes (13 to 20 cm in diameter)	2 to 3 tablespoons olive oil	
125g grainy mustard		Salt and freshly ground black	

1. Place 120ml of water in the pot. Set a Deluxe reversible rack with handles in the pot and place the ham cut-side down on the Deluxe reversible rack. In a small bowl, mix the jam, mustard, and brown sugar until smooth. Spread over the ham. Place the potatoes on top of and around the sides of the ham. 2. Lock lid; move slider towards PRESSURE. Adjust pressure release valve in the SEAL position. Close pressure-release valve. The cooking temperature will default to HIGH, which is accurate. Cook on Low pressure for 45 minutes. Press START/STOP to cooking. When the cooking is complete, let the pressure release naturally. An instant-read thermometer should read 60°C. 3. Put the potatoes to a serving bowl and toss with the dill, olive oil, and salt and pepper. Cover with foil and set aside. Transfer the ham to a cutting board or serving platter and tent with foil. 4. Move the slider towards "AIR FRY/STOVETOP" and set Ninja Foodi XL Pressure Cooker Steam Fryer with SmartLid to SEAR/SAUTÉ mode. Adjust the temperature to "Hi5" by using up arrow. Press START/STOP to begin cooking. Simmer the cooking liquid until it is reduced by about half, 10 minutes. Press SATRT/STOP. 5. Slice the ham, drizzle with some of the cooking liquid, and serve with the potatoes.
Per Serving: Calories 227; Fat 9.8g; Sodium 525mg; Carbs 7g; Fiber 2g; Sugar 4g; Protein 28g

Moroccan Meat Soup with Chickpeas and Lentils

Prep time: 10 minutes | Cook time: 1 hour 10 minutes | Serves: 4

Salt and ground black pepper	6 medium garlic cloves, smashed and peeled	tomatoes, crushed by hand	30g lightly packed fresh coriander, flat-leaf parsley or a mixture, chopped, plus more to serve
2 tablespoons extra-virgin olive oil, plus more to serve	3 tablespoons finely chopped fresh ginger	900g boneless lamb shoulder or beef chuck roast, trimmed and cut into 1 to 2.5 cm chunks	
6 medium celery stalks, sliced 1 cm to 2 cm thick	¾ teaspoon ground cinnamon	65g lentils du Puy	
1 medium yellow onion, roughly chopped	½ teaspoon sweet paprika	390g can chickpeas, drained and rinsed	
	360g can whole peeled		

1. Move the slider towards "AIR FRY/STOVETOP" and set Ninja Foodi XL Pressure Cooker Steam Fryer with SmartLid to SEAR/SAUTÉ mode. Adjust the temperature to "Hi5" by using up arrow. Press START/STOP to begin cooking. 2. Add the oil and heat until shimmering. Add the celery, onion, garlic, ginger and 2½ teaspoons salt. Cook, stirring occasionally, until the vegetables are softened, about 5 minutes. Add the cinnamon, paprika and 1½ teaspoons pepper, then cook, stirring, until fragrant, about 10 seconds. Stir in the tomatoes with their juices and 960 g water, scraping up browned bits. Add the lamb or beef and lentils and stir to combine, then distribute in an even layer. 3. Lock lid; move slider to PRESSURE. Make sure the pressure release valve is in the SEAL position The cooking temperature will default to HIGH, which is accurate. Set time to 15 minutes. Press START/STOP to cooking. 4. When pressure cooking is complete, let the pressure release naturally for about 15 minutes, then quickly release the remaining steam by turning it into VENT position. Then carefully open the lid. Stir in the chickpeas. 5. Taste and season with salt and pepper, then stir in the parsley and/or coriander. Serve sprinkled with additional herbs and drizzled with oil.
Per Serving: Calories 25; Fat 0.1g; Sodium 546mg; Carbs 3g; Fiber 1g; Sugar 0g; Protein 3g

Cinnamon-Spiced Beef Noodle Soup

Prep time: 15 minutes | Cook time: 50 minutes | Serves: 4

6 cinnamon sticks	and green parts separated, green parts thinly sliced	1 bunch coriander	200g dried wheat noodles, cooked, drained and briefly rinsed
2 teaspoons aniseed	10 cm piece fresh ginger (75g), peeled, thinly sliced and smashed	1.1kg beef shanks (each about 2.5 cm thick), trimmed	
120ml soy sauce		125g container baby spinach	
120ml sake		Ground white pepper	
1 bunch spring onions, white			

1. Move the slider towards "AIR FRY/STOVETOP" and set Ninja Foodi XL Pressure Cooker Steam Fryer with SmartLid to SEAR/SAUTÉ mode. Adjust the temperature to "Hi5" by using up arrow. Press START/STOP to begin cooking. 2. Add the cinnamon sticks and aniseed, then toast, stirring often, until fragrant, 2 to 3 minutes. Add 1.2 L water, the soy sauce, sake, scallion whites and ginger. Set aside 10 g loosely packed coriander sprigs and add the remainder to the pot. Bring to a simmer, then add the beef, arranging the pieces in an even layer; they should be mostly submerged. Press START/STOP. 3. Lock lid; move slider to PRESSURE. Make sure the pressure release valve is in the SEAL position The cooking temperature will default to HIGH, which is accurate. Set time to 45 minutes. Press START/STOP to cooking. 4. When pressure cooking is complete, quickly release the steam by turning it into VENT position. Using a slotted spoon, transfer the shanks to a large plate and let cool slightly. Pour the stock through a fine mesh strainer set over a large bowl. Discard the solids and return the stock to the pot. Cut the meat into 1 cm chunks, discarding the fat and bones, then return the meat to the stock. 5. Select SEAR/SAUTÉ mode again and bring to a simmer. Stir in the spinach and cook just until wilted, about 1 minute. Press START/STOP to turn off the pot. Taste and season with white pepper. Divide the noodles among serving bowls and ladle the soup over. 6. Top with scallion greens, the reserved coriander and additional white pepper.
Per Serving: Calories 151; Fat 7.5g; Sodium 621mg; Carbs 20g; Fiber 5g; Sugar 2g; Protein 5g

Persian Beefand Kidney Bean Stew

Prep time: 5 minutes | Cook time: 1 ¼ hours | Serves: 4

Leaves and tender stems from 1 bunch coriander (80g lightly packed) Leaves and tender stems from ½ bunch flat-leaf parsley (35g lightly packed)	1 bunch spring onions, sliced, white and green parts reserved separately 60ml extra-virgin olive oil 2 tablespoons grated lime zest, plus 60ml lime juice, plus lime	wedges to serve 2 teaspoons ground turmeric 2½ to 1.3kg boneless beef chuck roast, trimmed and cut into 1½ to 5 cm chunks Salt and ground black pepper	Two 360g cans kidney beans or small red beans, drained but not rinsed, liquid reserved

1. In a food processor, combine the coriander, parsley and scallion greens. Pulse until finely chopped, about 10 pulses; transfer to a small bowl and set aside. Move the slider towards "AIR FRY/STOVETOP" and set Ninja Foodi XL Pressure Cooker Steam Fryer with SmartLid to SEAR/SAUTÉ mode. Adjust the temperature to "Hi5" by using up arrow. Press START/STOP to begin cooking. 2. Add the oil and heat until shimmering. Add the scallion whites and cook, stirring, until golden brown, 3 to 5 minutes. Stir in half the chopped herbs and cook, stirring, until wilted and the color is no longer vibrant green, about 2 minutes. If slow cooking, cover and refrigerate the remaining herb mixture. 3. Add the lime zest and juice, turmeric, beef, 1 teaspoon salt and 120ml of the reserved bean liquid if pressure cooking or 240ml if slow cooking. Stir, loosening any bits stuck to the bottom of the pot, then distribute in an even layer. 4. Press START/STOP, lock lid; move slider to PRESSURE. Make sure the pressure release valve is in the SEAL position The cooking temperature will default to HIGH, which is accurate. Set time to 25 minutes. Press START/STOP to cooking. 5. When pressure cooking is complete, let the pressure release naturally for about 15 minutes, then quickly release the remaining steam by turning it into VENT position. Then carefully open the lid. 6. Stir in the beans and remaining chopped herbs, then taste and season with salt and pepper. Serve with lime wedges.
Per Serving: Calories 56; Fat 2.2g; Sodium 177mg; Carbs 5g; Fiber 1g; Sugar 1g; Protein 5g

Delicious Pork Vindaloo

Prep time: 10 minutes | Cook time: 50 minutes | Serves: 4

1 tablespoon rapeseed oil 1 medium yellow onion, halved and sliced through the root end 900g boneless pork shoulder, cut into 5 cm cubes	4 teaspoons garam masala spice blend or curry powder 60ml store-bought chicken stock, or homemade, or water 1 (250g) can tomatoes with	green chilies 2 tablespoons red wine vinegar Salt and freshly ground black pepper 1 tablespoon corn flour	10g chopped fresh coriander **Optional** 1 serrano chili, chopped

1. Move the slider towards "AIR FRY/STOVETOP" and set Ninja Foodi XL Pressure Cooker Steam Fryer with SmartLid to SEAR/SAUTÉ mode. Adjust the temperature to "Hi5" by using up arrow. Press START/STOP to begin cooking. Add the onion and a small handful (6 or 7 pieces) of pork and cook, stirring frequently, until there are some browned bits on the bottom of the pot, 5 minutes. Press START/STOP. Add the garam masala and stir to combine. Add the stock and scrape up the browned bits on the bottom of the pot. 2. Add the tomatoes and vinegar to the pot. Season the remaining pork all over with salt and pepper. Add the pork to the pot and stir to coat it with the sauce. 3. Lock lid; move slider to PRESSURE. Make sure the pressure release valve is in the SEAL position. The cooking temperature will default to HIGH, which is accurate. Set time to 30 minutes. Press START/STOP to cooking. 4. When the cooking is complete, quickly release the pressure. In a bowl, mix the corn flour with 1½ tablespoons water. Select SEAR/SAUTÉ mode again. Add the corn flour mixture to the pot, stir gently, and simmer until bubbly, 1 minute. Fold in the coriander and season with salt and pepper. 5. Stir in the serrano, if desired, and serve.
Per Serving: Calories 200; Fat 15.6g; Sodium 165mg; Carbs 5g; Fiber 1g; Sugar 2g; Protein 10g

Delicious Lamb Gyros

Prep time: 20 minutes | Cook time: 40 minutes | Serves: 4

900g boneless leg of lamb 2 tablespoons olive oil 4 medium garlic cloves, finely chopped 2 teaspoons dried oregano	Salt and freshly ground black pepper 240ml store-bought beef stock, or homemade 4 pita breads or flatbreads	240g plain full-fat Greek yogurt 80g seeded and finely chopped cucumber	**Optional Garnishes** Chopped tomatoes Chopped romaine lettuce Thinly sliced red onions

1. With a boning knife, trim the fat and any silvery connective tissue from the meat. Slice the meat into ¼ - to ½ -cm-thick slices. Cut the slices into strips about 4 cm wide. In a nonreactive bowl or zip-top bag, combine the lamb strips, oil, 1 tablespoon of the garlic, the oregano, ¾ teaspoon salt, and several grinds of pepper. Cover or seal and refrigerate for at least 2 hours or up to 24 hours. 2. Place the meat and any marinade clinging to it in the pot. Add the stock and stir to combine. 3. Lock lid; move slider to Pressure. Make sure the pressure release valve is in the SEAL position. The cooking temperature will default to HIGH, which is accurate. Set time to 10 minutes. Press START/STOP to cooking. When the cooking is complete, let the pressure release naturally for about 10 minutes and then quickly release the remaining pressure. 4. Toast the pita breads or flatbreads in a toaster or toaster oven until warm and pliable. In a small bowl, combine the yogurt, cucumber, and remaining garlic. Use tongs to transfer the lamb to the pita breads; leave the cooking liquid in the pot. 5. Top the sandwiches with the yogurt mixture and garnishes, if desired.
Per Serving: Calories 314; Fat 25g; Sodium 138mg; Carbs 2g; Fiber 0g; Sugar 1g; Protein 17g

Beef and Tomatillo Stew

Prep time: 5 minutes | Cook time: 35 minutes | Serves: 4

1 tablespoon grapeseed or other neutral oil	smashed and peeled	1 teaspoon dried oregano	455g Yukon Gold potatoes, cut into 4 cm chunks
1 medium yellow onion, cut into 2.5 cm chunks	1 jalapeño chili, stemmed, seeded and roughly chopped	½ teaspoon ground cumin	8 small tomatillos (about 300g), husked, cored and quartered
5 medium garlic cloves,	3 bay leaves	1.1kg boneless beef chuck roast, trimmed and cut into 4 cm chunks	Fresh coriander, to serve
	Salt and ground black pepper		

1. Move the slider towards "AIR FRY/STOVETOP" and set Ninja Foodi XL Pressure Cooker Steam Fryer with SmartLid to SEAR/SAUTÉ mode. Adjust the temperature to "Hi5" by using up arrow. Press START/STOP to begin cooking. 2. Add the oil and heat until shimmering, then stir in the garlic, onion, jalapeño, bay and 1 teaspoon salt. Cook, stirring frequently, until the onion is soft and golden brown around the edges, for about 5 to 7 minutes. Add the cumin, 1 teaspoon pepper and the oregano, then cook, stirring, until fragrant, for about 30 seconds. Stir in 2 tablespoons water, scraping up any browned bits. Add the beef and potatoes; stir to combine, then distribute in an even layer. 3. Lock lid; move slider to PRESSURE. Make sure the pressure release valve is in the SEAL position. The cooking temperature will default to HIGH, which is accurate. Set time to 25 minutes. Press START/STOP to cooking. 4. When pressure cooking is complete, let the pressure release naturally for about 15 minutes, then quickly release the remaining steam by turning it into VENT position. Then carefully open the lid. 5. Using a slotted spoon, transfer the meat and potatoes to a medium bowl and set aside. Add the tomatillos to the pot and select SEAR/SAUTÉ mode again. Bring the mixture to a boil and cook, stirring occasionally and crushing the tomatillos, until the cooking liquid has thickened and the tomatillos are fully softened, about 15 minutes. 6. Stir in ½ teaspoon salt, then return the meat and potatoes to the pot. Return to a simmer and cook, stirring just once or twice, until heated through, 1 to 2 minutes. Press START/STOP to turn off the pot. 7. Taste and sprinkle with salt and pepper, then serve topped with coriander.
Per Serving: Calories 80; Fat 6g; Sodium 444mg; Carbs 6g; Fiber 1g; Sugar 4g; Protein 1g

Sweet Barbecue Spareribs

Prep time: 10 minutes | Cook time: 1 hour | Serves: 4

2 racks baby back ribs (1.2kg about 4 ribs each), cut into 12 to 15 cm portions	2 tablespoons chili powder	stock, or homemade	2 tablespoons toasted sesame oil
	240g ketchup	110g honey	
	120ml store-bought chicken	3 tablespoons grainy mustard	1 tablespoon red wine vinegar

1. Rub the ribs all over with the chili powder. In the pot, combine the ketchup, stock, honey, mustard, sesame oil, and vinegar and whisk until the honey has dissolved. Dunk the ribs in the sauce to coat them and then arrange them standing upright against the sides of the pot. 2. Lock lid; move slider to PRESSURE. Make sure the pressure release valve is in the SEAL position. The cooking temperature will default to HIGH, which is accurate. And set time to 25 minutes. Press START/STOP to cooking. 3. Preheat the grill and adjust an oven rack so that it is 10 cm below the element. Line a baking sheet with foil. 4. When the cooking time is up, let the pressure come down naturally for 15 minutes and then quick-release the remaining pressure. Transfer the ribs with tongs to the prepared baking sheet meat-side up; they will be very tender, so be gentle when transferring them out of the pot. 5. Stir the cooking liquid and spoon a generous amount over the ribs. Broil the ribs until browned in places, 5 minutes.
Per Serving: Calories 248; Fat 21.1g; Sodium 429mg; Carbs 2g; Fiber 0g; Sugar 1g; Protein 12g

Pakistani Spiced Beef Stew

Prep time: 5 minutes | Cook time: 35 minutes | Serves: 4

4 tablespoons salted butter	50g), peeled and cut into 6 coins	1½ teaspoons ground coriander	2 tablespoons plain flour
2 medium yellow onions, halved and sliced 1.5 cm thick	2 cinnamon sticks	1 teaspoon curry powder	2 tablespoons lemon juice, plus lemon wedges to serve
4 medium garlic cloves, smashed and peeled	Salt and ground black pepper	½ teaspoon garam masala	Chopped fresh coriander, to serve
8 cm piece fresh ginger (about	2 teaspoons sweet paprika	1.1 kg boneless beef chuck roast, trimmed and cut into 4 cm chunks	
	1½ teaspoons fennel seeds		

1. Move the slider towards "AIR FRY/STOVETOP" and set Ninja Foodi XL Pressure Cooker Steam Fryer with SmartLid to SEAR/SAUTÉ mode. Adjust the temperature to "Hi5" by using up arrow. Press START/STOP to begin cooking. 2. Add the butter and melt, then cook, stirring, until it is golden brown and has a nutty aroma, 2 to 3 minutes. Add the onions, garlic, ginger, cinnamon and ½ teaspoon salt. Cook, stirring, until the onions are soft and golden brown at the edges, 10 to 12 minutes. 3. Stir in the paprika, fennel seeds, coriander, curry powder, garam masala, 2 teaspoons salt and 1½ teaspoons pepper, then cook until fragrant, about 30 seconds. Add 240ml water and scrape up any browned bits. Add the beef and stir to combine, then distribute in an even layer. 4. Lock lid; move slider to PRESSURE. Make sure the pressure release valve is in the SEAL position. The cooking temperature will default to HIGH, which is accurate. Set time to 25 minutes. Press START/STOP to cooking. 5. When pressure cooking is complete, let the pressure release naturally for 15 minutes, then quickly release the remaining steam by turning it into VENT position. Then carefully open the lid. 6. Using a large spoon, skim and discard the fat from the surface of cooking liquid. Remove and discard the cinnamon sticks and ginger coins. In a small bowl, whisk the flour with 6 tablespoons of the cooking liquid until smooth, then stir into the pot. 7. Select SEAR/SAUTÉ mode again. Bring the stew to a simmer, stirring often, and cook until lightly thickened, 2 to 3 minutes. Press START/STOP to turn off the pot. Stir in the lemon juice, then taste and sprinkle with salt and pepper.
Per Serving: Calories 104; Fat 2.5g; Sodium 29mg; Carbs 18g; Fiber 4g; Sugar 2g; Protein 3g

Delicious Moroccan Meatballs

Prep time: 20 minutes | Cook time: 1 hour | Serves: 4

675g lamb or beef mince	80g finely chopped sweet onion	4 teaspoons ras el hanout Moroccan spice blend	1 (375g) can fire-roasted diced tomatoes with garlic
240ml plus 3 tablespoons store-bought chicken stock, or homemade	35g dry plain breadcrumbs	Salt and freshly ground black pepper	**Optional Side Dish**
	4 tablespoons pomegranate molasses		130 g instant couscous

1. In a large bowl, combine the lamb, 3 tablespoons of the stock, the onion, breadcrumbs, 1 tablespoon of the pomegranate molasses, the spice blend, ¾ teaspoon salt, and ½ teaspoon pepper. Mix until well combined and then roll into 32 meatballs, about 1 heaping tablespoon each. 2. Combine the 240ml remaining stock, the tomatoes, and the remaining 3 tablespoons pomegranate molasses in the pot and stir to combine. Add the meatballs. 3. Lock lid; move slider to PRESSURE. Make sure the pressure release valve is in the SEAL position The cooking temperature will default to HIGH, which is accurate. Set time to 10 minutes. Press START/STOP to cooking. 4. When the cooking is complete, let the pressure release naturally for about 10 minutes and then quickly release the remaining pressure by turning it into VENT position. Use a slotted spoon to transfer the meatballs to a serving dish. Using a ladle, skim off the liquid fat that pools around the edges of the pot and discard. Pour the cooking liquid over the meatballs and serve. 5. If you'd like to serve the meatballs with couscous, place the couscous in a medium serving bowl. Pour 1½ cups of the defatted cooking liquid over the couscous, cover, and let stand for 5 minutes. 6. Fluff with a fork and serve with the meatballs.
Per Serving: Calories 138; Fat 10.6g; Sodium 102mg; Carbs 1g; Fiber 0g; Sugar 1g; Protein 9g

Cumin-Spiced Beef and Potato Stew

Prep time: 5 minutes | Cook time: 35 minutes | Serves: 6

1 tablespoon grapeseed or other neutral oil	2 tablespoons tomato paste	cm chunks	3 tablespoons lime juice
1 large yellow onion, finely chopped	1 tablespoon ground cumin	700g can whole peeled tomatoes, crushed by hand	20g finely chopped fresh coriander
10 medium garlic cloves, smashed and peeled	1 jalapeño chili, stemmed, seeded and minced	Salt and ground black pepper	Sour cream, to serve
	1.1 kg boneless beef chuck roast, trimmed and cut into 2	300g sweet potatoes, peeled and cut into 1.5 cm chunks	Pickled jalapeños, to serve

1. Move the slider towards "AIR FRY/STOVETOP" and set Ninja Foodi XL Pressure Cooker Steam Fryer with SmartLid to SEAR/SAUTÉ mode. Adjust the temperature to "Hi5" by using up arrow. Press START/STOP to begin cooking. 2. Add the oil and heat, then add the onion and cook, stirring often, until softened, for about 5 minutes. Stir in the garlic, tomato paste, cumin and jalapeño, then cook until fragrant, about 30 seconds. Add the beef, tomatoes with their juices and 1½ teaspoons salt; stir to combine, then distribute in an even layer. 3. Lock lid; move slider to PRESSURE. Make sure the pressure release valve is in the SEAL position The cooking temperature will default to HIGH, which is accurate. Set time to 30 minutes. Press START/STOP to cooking. 4. When pressure cooking is complete, let the pressure release naturally for about 15 minutes, then quickly release the remaining steam by turning it into VENT position. Then carefully open the lid. 5. Select SEAR/SAUTÉ mode again and add the sweet potatoes. Cook, stirring occasionally, until a skewer inserted into the potatoes meets no resistance, 10 to 15 minutes. Press START/STOP to turn off the pot. 6. Stir in the lime juice and coriander, then taste and season with salt and pepper. Serve with sour cream and pickled jalapeños (if desired).
Per Serving: Calories 23; Fat 1.3g; Sodium 40mg; Carbs 2g; Fiber 1g; Sugar 1g; Protein 1g

Chapter 5 Soup, Stew, and Chili Recipes

81	Chicken with Dumplings	84	Chicken and Vegetable Stock
81	Clam Corn Chowder	84	Delicious Minestrone
81	Corn Chowder with Potatoes	84	Beefy Minestrone Soup
82	Traditional Beef Chili	85	Healthy White Chicken Chili
82	Tortellini Soup with pesto	85	Kale Sausage Soup
82	Regular Chicken Stock	85	Chicken Soup
82	Regular Vegetable Stock	85	Spicy Curried Cauliflower Soup
83	Potato Soup with cheese	86	Delicious Moroccan Carrot Soup
83	Bean Ham Soup	86	Pot Pie Soup
83	Clam Chowder	86	Healthy Three Bean Chili
83	Tomato Soup with basil		

Chicken with Dumplings

Prep time: 10 minutes | Cook time: 16 minutes | Serves: 6

- 125g plain flour
- 2 teaspoons baking powder
- 1¼ teaspoons salt, divided
- 360ml whole milk, divided
- 6 tablespoons olive oil, divided
- 4 medium carrots, diced
- 900g boneless, skinless chicken thighs, cut into 2.5 cm pieces
- 2 medium stalks celery, diced
- 1 medium yellow onion, peeled and diced
- 105g sliced mushrooms
- 2 cloves garlic, minced
- 960ml chicken stock
- 2 (260g) cans cream of mushroom soup
- ½ teaspoon red pepper flakes
- ½ teaspoon black pepper

1. In a medium bowl, whisk together flour, baking powder, and 1 teaspoon salt. 2. Make a well in center of dry mixture and pour in 120ml milk and 2 tablespoons olive oil. 3. Mix together with a fork until combined. This is your dumpling dough. Set aside. 4. Move the slider towards "AIR FRY/STOVETOP" and set Ninja Foodi XL Pressure Cooker Steam Fryer with SmartLid to SEAR/SAUTÉ mode. Adjust the temperature to "Hi5" by using up arrow. Press START/STOP to begin cooking. Pour in remaining 4 tablespoons olive oil. 5. Add in carrots, chicken, celery, onion, and mushrooms. Cover and cook 5 minutes until soft. Stir occasionally while it is cooking. 6. Remove lid and stir in minced garlic. Cook an additional 30 seconds. 7. Pour in chicken stock and deglaze pot. 8. Turn pot off and whisk in cream of mushroom soup, remaining 240ml milk, red pepper flakes, black pepper, and remaining ¼ teaspoon salt. 9. Rip dumpling dough into 2.5 cm pieces and toss on top of soup so they evenly over top of the soup. A few might sink down. 10. Lock lid; move slider towards PRESSURE. Adjust pressure release valve in the SEAL position. Close pressure-release valve. The cooking temperature will default to HIGH, which is accurate. Set time to 10 minutes. Select START/STOP and start cooking. 11. When cooking is complete, let pressure release naturally. Serve.

Per Serving: Calories 529; Fat 24g; Sodium 1165mg; Carbs 34g; Fiber 3g; Sugar 9g; Protein 45g

Clam Corn Chowder

Prep time: 10 minutes | Cook time: 15 minutes | Serves: 6

- 2 tablespoons (28g) grass-fed butter
- 1 large yellow onion, finely diced
- 4 fresh cloves garlic, finely chopped
- 2 tablespoons (15g) gluten-free plain flour
- 2 large celery ribs, sliced about (6mm) thick
- 1 large carrot, peeled and diced
- 1 large russet potato, peeled and diced
- 280g fresh or frozen corn kernels
- 15g chopped fresh flat-leaf parsley
- 240ml clam juice
- 240ml fish, chicken or vegetable stock
- 1 teaspoon sea salt
- 1 teaspoon dried thyme
- 1 teaspoon dried dill
- 1 teaspoon dried basil
- ½ teaspoon freshly ground black pepper
- ½ teaspoon dried oregano
- Zest of 1 lemon
- 370g canned clams, drained
- 240ml milk
- 175g heavy cream

1. Move the slider towards "AIR FRY/STOVETOP" and set Ninja Foodi XL Pressure Cooker Steam Fryer with SmartLid to SEAR/SAUTÉ mode. Adjust the temperature to "Hi5" by using up arrow. Press START/STOP to begin cooking. Place the butter in. Once the butter has melted, add the onion and sauté for 4 minutes, stirring occasionally. 2. Add the garlic and sauté for 1 minute, stirring occasionally. Add the flour and stir for 1 more minute. Add the celery, carrot, potato, corn, parsley, clam juice, stock, salt, thyme, dill, basil, pepper, oregano, lemon zest and clams, then give the mixture a quick stir. 3. Lock lid; move slider towards PRESSURE. Adjust pressure release valve in the SEAL position. Close pressure-release valve. The cooking temperature will default to HIGH, which is accurate. Set time to 9 minutes. Select START/STOP and start cooking. 4. When cooking is complete, let pressure release quickly by turning it into VENT position. 5. Move the slider towards "AIR FRY/STOVETOP" and set Ninja Foodi XL Pressure Cooker Steam Fryer with SmartLid to SEAR/SAUTÉ mode. Adjust the temperature to "Hi5" by using up arrow. Press START/STOP to begin cooking, add the milk and cream, then stir until they are fully mixed in. 6. Allow to come to a simmer and cook for about 5 minutes, or until the chowder slightly thickens. Taste for seasoning and adjust the salt to taste. Allow to rest for 10 minutes. 7. Serve immediately.

Per Serving: Calories 232; Fat 11.2g; Sodium 554mg; Carbs 10.6g; Fiber 3g; Sugar 1g; Protein 13.2g

Corn Chowder with Potatoes

Prep time: 15 minutes | Cook time: 20 minutes | Serves: 8

- 455g bacon, cut into 1 cm strips
- 2 medium stalks celery, diced
- 1 medium yellow onion, peeled and chopped
- 1 medium carrot, diced
- 2 cloves garlic, minced
- 960ml vegetable stock
- 675g baby yellow potatoes, quartered
- 1 (375g) can corn
- 1 (370g) can creamed corn
- 2 teaspoons salt
- ¼ teaspoon black pepper
- ¼ teaspoon cayenne pepper
- 240ml whole milk
- 4 medium green onions, sliced

1. Move the slider towards "AIR FRY/STOVETOP" and set Ninja Foodi XL Pressure Cooker Steam Fryer with SmartLid to SEAR/SAUTÉ mode. Adjust the temperature to "Hi5" by using up arrow. Press START/STOP to begin cooking. Add sliced bacon into cooking pot. Cook, stirring occasionally, for 7 minutes. 2. Remove bacon and place in between two paper towels. Set aside. 3. Remove bacon grease, reserving 2 tablespoons bacon grease inside cooking pot. Add celery, onion, and carrots. Cook, stirring occasionally, 7 minutes. 4. Add in garlic and cook an additional 30 seconds. 5. Pour in stock and deglaze the pot. Turn pot off. 6. Mix in corn, creamed corn, salt, black pepper, and cayenne. 7. Lock lid; move slider towards PRESSURE. Adjust pressure release valve in the SEAL position. Close pressure-release valve. The cooking temperature will default to HIGH, which is accurate. Set time to 3 minutes. Select START/STOP and start cooking. When cooking is complete, let pressure release quickly by turning it into VENT position. 8. Unlock lid and remove it. 9. Slowly whisk in milk. Serve topped with cooked bacon and green onions.

Per Serving: Calories 392; Fat 24g; Sodium 1170mg; Carbs 33g; Fiber 4g; Sugar 9g; Protein 12g

Traditional Beef Chili

Prep time: 10 minutes | Cook time: 55 minutes | Serves: 6

1 tablespoon olive oil	and diced	3 cloves garlic, minced	3 teaspoons chili powder
1 medium yellow onion, peeled and diced	900g beef mince	2 (375g) cans tomato sauce	½ teaspoon cayenne pepper
2 medium jalapeños, seeded	1 teaspoon salt	2 (390g) cans kidney beans, drained and rinsed	¼ teaspoon red pepper flakes
	1 teaspoon black pepper		

1. Move the slider towards "AIR FRY/STOVETOP" and set Ninja Foodi XL Pressure Cooker Steam Fryer with SmartLid to SEAR/SAUTÉ mode. Adjust the temperature to "Hi5" by using up arrow. Press START/STOP to begin cooking. Add oil. 2. Pour in onion, jalapeños, and beef mince. Sprinkle with salt and pepper. Stir and cook until onions are soft and meat is no longer pink, about 8 minutes. 3. Add in garlic and cook an additional 30 seconds. Turn Ninja Foodi XL Pressure Cooker Steam Fryer with SmartLid cooking pot off. Drain fat from the pot. 4. Mix in tomato sauce, kidney beans, chili powder, cayenne pepper, and red pepper flakes. Make sure to scrape the bottom of the pot for any stuck-on food. 5. Lock lid; move slider towards PRESSURE. Adjust pressure release valve in the SEAL position. Close pressure-release valve. The cooking temperature will default to HIGH, which is accurate. Set the time for 45 minutes. Select START/STOP and start cooking. 6. When cooking is complete, let pressure release naturally and unlock lid. Serve.
Per Serving: Calories 502; Fat 26g; Sodium 1382mg; Carbs 29g; Fiber 8g; Sugar 6g; Protein 38g

Tortellini Soup with pesto

Prep time: 5 minutes | Cook time: 1 minutes | Serves: 6

2.7L chicken stock	8 medium green onions, sliced	1½ teaspoons salt	½ teaspoon dried oregano
325g frozen tortellini	50g frozen chopped spinach	¾ teaspoon black pepper	120g basil pesto

1. Combine stock, tortellini, green onions, spinach, salt, pepper, and oregano in Ninja Foodi XL Pressure Cooker Steam Fryer with SmartLid cooking pot. 2. Lock lid; move slider towards PRESSURE. Adjust pressure release valve in the SEAL position. Close pressure-release valve. The cooking temperature will default to HIGH, which is accurate. Set the time for 1 minutes. Select START/STOP and start cooking. 3. When cooking is complete, let pressure release quickly by turning it into VENT position. 4. Unlock lid and remove it. 5. Ladle soup into bowls and top with pesto.
Per Serving: Calories 294; Fat 13g; Sodium 1105mg; Carbs 32g; Fiber 4g; Sugar 2g; Protein 14g

Regular Chicken Stock

Prep time: 5 minutes | Cook time: 30 minutes | Serves: 12

Leftover bones and skin from 1 (1.8kg) chicken	roughly chopped	2 medium stalks celery, roughly chopped	2 teaspoons salt
1 medium onion, peeled and	2 medium carrots, roughly chopped	1 bay leaf	2.9L water

1. Place chicken bones and skin in Ninja Foodi XL Pressure Cooker Steam Fryer with SmartLid cooking pot. 2. Place onion, carrots, and celery on top of chicken bones. 3. Add in bay leaf, salt, and water. Mix. 4. Lock lid; move slider towards PRESSURE. Adjust pressure release valve in the SEAL position. Close pressure-release valve. The cooking temperature will default to HIGH, which is accurate. Set the time for 30 minutes. Select START/STOP and start cooking. When cooking is complete, let pressure release naturally and unlock lid. 5. Strain Chicken Stock through a mesh strainer into a large bowl. 6. Ladle Chicken Stock into jars for refrigerator storage or freezer bags for freezer storage. Store in refrigerator up to one week or in freezer for up to three months.
Per Serving: Calories 27; Fat 0g; Sodium 477mg; Carbs 2g; Fiber 1g; Sugar 1g; Protein 4g

Regular Vegetable Stock

Prep time: 5 minutes | Cook time: 30 minutes | Serves: 12

2 medium stalks celery, roughly chopped	chopped	4 cloves garlic, roughly chopped	2 teaspoons salt
2 large carrots, roughly	1 medium yellow onion, peeled and roughly chopped	1 tablespoon tomato paste	⅛ teaspoon black pepper
			2.9L water

1. Place celery, carrots, onion, garlic, tomato paste, salt, and pepper in Ninja Foodi XL Pressure Cooker Steam Fryer with SmartLid cooking pot. 2. Pour water into pot. Mix until tomato paste is evenly distributed. 3. Lock lid; move slider towards PRESSURE. Adjust pressure release valve in the SEAL position. Close pressure-release valve. The cooking temperature will default to HIGH, which is accurate. Set the time for 30 minutes. Select START/STOP and start cooking. When cooking is complete, let pressure release naturally. 4. Strain Vegetable Stock through a mesh strainer into a large bowl. 5. Ladle Vegetable Stock into jars for refrigerator storage or freezer bags for freezer storage. Store in the refrigerator up to one week or in the freezer up to three months.
Per Serving: Calories 12; Fat 0g; Sodium 451mg; Carbs 3g; Fiber 1g; Sugar 3g; Protein 0g

Potato Soup with cheese

Prep time: 10 minutes | Cook time: 20 minutes | Serves: 8

- 1.3kg red potatoes, quartered
- 960ml vegetable stock
- 960ml water
- 2 teaspoons salt
- ½ teaspoon garlic powder
- ½ teaspoon onion powder
- ½ teaspoon dried oregano
- ¼ teaspoon black pepper
- 2 (375g) cans Cheddar cheese sauce

1. Combine potatoes, stock, water, salt, garlic powder, onion powder, oregano, and pepper in Ninja Foodi XL Pressure Cooker Steam Fryer with SmartLid cooking pot. 2. Lock lid; move slider towards PRESSURE. Adjust pressure release valve in the SEAL position. Close pressure-release valve. The cooking temperature will default to HIGH, which is accurate. Set the time for 10 minutes. Select START/STOP and start cooking. When cooking is complete, let pressure release quickly by turning it into VENT position and unlock lid. 3. Blend soup using an immersion blender until smooth. 4. Mix in Cheddar cheese sauce. Move the slider towards "AIR FRY/STOVETOP" and set Ninja Foodi XL Pressure Cooker Steam Fryer with SmartLid to SEAR/SAUTÉ mode. Adjust the temperature to "Hi5" by using up arrow. Press START/STOP to begin cooking. 5. Let cook, stirring occasionally, 10 minutes. Serve.
Per Serving: Calories 342; Fat 15g; Sodium 968mg; Carbs 36g; Fiber 4g; Sugar 11g; Protein 14g

Bean Ham Soup

Prep time: 10 minutes | Cook time: 7 minutes | Serves: 6

- 455g great northern beans
- 2 tablespoons olive oil
- 1 small yellow onion, peeled and chopped
- 6 cloves garlic, minced
- 1 (400g) ham steak, cubed with bone reserved
- 1.4L chicken stock
- 2 medium carrots, diced
- 1 teaspoon dried parsley
- ½ teaspoon black pepper
- 1 bay leaf

1. Soak beans overnight. 2. Move the slider towards "AIR FRY/STOVETOP" and set Ninja Foodi XL Pressure Cooker Steam Fryer with SmartLid to SEAR/SAUTÉ mode. Adjust the temperature to "Hi5" by using up arrow. Press START/STOP to begin cooking. Put oil and onion into cooking pot. Cook onion 2 minutes until soft. 3. Add in garlic and cook 30 seconds. Turn off. 4. Add beans, ham and ham bone, stock, carrots, parsley, pepper, and bay leaf to cooking pot. 5. Lock lid; move slider towards PRESSURE. Adjust pressure release valve in the SEAL position. Close pressure-release valve. The cooking temperature will default to HIGH, which is accurate. Set the time for 4 minutes. Select START/STOP and start cooking. 6. When cooking is complete, let pressure release quickly by turning it into VENT position. 7. Unlock lid and remove it. 8. Remove bay leaf and ham bone. Serve.
Per Serving: Calories 435; Fat 9g; Sodium 1068mg; Carbs 53g; Fiber 14g; Sugar 5g; Protein 37g

Clam Chowder

Prep time: 10 minutes | Cook time: 13 minutes | Serves: 4

- 2 tablespoons olive oil
- 1 medium yellow onion, peeled and chopped
- 3 cloves garlic, minced
- 240ml chicken stock
- 3 small russet potatoes, peeled and cubed
- 1 (200ml) bottle clam juice
- 2 teaspoons salt
- ½ teaspoon black pepper
- 480ml milk
- 2 (160g) cans minced clams

1. Move the slider towards "AIR FRY/STOVETOP" and set Ninja Foodi XL Pressure Cooker Steam Fryer with SmartLid to SEAR/SAUTÉ mode. Adjust the temperature to "Hi5" by using up arrow. Press START/STOP to begin cooking. Cook onion 2 minutes until soft. 2. Add in garlic and cook 30 seconds. Turn pot off. 3. Add stock, potatoes, clam juice, salt, and pepper to cooking pot. 4. Lock lid; move slider towards PRESSURE. Adjust pressure release valve in the SEAL position. Close pressure-release valve. The cooking temperature will default to HIGH, which is accurate. Set the time for 10 minutes. Select START/STOP and start cooking. 5. When cooking is complete, let pressure release quickly by turning it into VENT position. 6. Unlock lid and remove it. 7. Whisk in half-and-half to the chowder. Mix in clams. 8. Serve.
Per Serving: Calories 420; Fat 30g; Sodium 1737mg; Carbs 31g; Fiber 2g; Sugar 6g; Protein 9g

Tomato Soup with basil

Prep time: 5 minutes | Cook time: 9 minutes | Serves: 4

- 2 tablespoons olive oil
- 1 medium yellow onion, peeled and chopped
- 2 cloves garlic, minced
- 4 (360g) cans diced tomatoes
- 480ml vegetable stock
- 10g fresh basil, chopped
- 2 tablespoons granulated sugar
- 1 teaspoon salt
- 240g heavy whipping cream

1. Move the slider towards "AIR FRY/STOVETOP" and set Ninja Foodi XL Pressure Cooker Steam Fryer with SmartLid to SEAR/SAUTÉ mode. Adjust the temperature to "Hi5" by using up arrow. Press START/STOP to begin cooking. Put oil and onion into cooking pot. Cook onion 2 minutes until soft. 2. Add in garlic and cook 30 seconds. Turn off. 3. Add tomatoes, vegetable stock, basil, sugar, and salt to pot and stir to combine. 4. Lock lid; move slider towards PRESSURE. Adjust pressure release valve in the SEAL position. Close pressure-release valve. The cooking temperature will default to HIGH, which is accurate. Set QUICK RELEASE and time to 7 minutes. Select START/STOP and start cooking. 5. When cooking is complete, let pressure release quickly by turning it into VENT position. 6. Blend soup with an immersion blender. 7. Once blended, whisk in heavy whipping cream and serve.
Per Serving: Calories 341; Fat 29g; Sodium 822mg; Carbs 20g; Fiber 3g; Sugar 15g; Protein 4g

Chicken and Vegetable Stock

Prep time: 10 minutes | Cook time: 20 minutes | Serves: 6

4 thick-cut bacon slices cut into cubes	1.3kg Yukon gold potatoes, peeled	½ teaspoon black pepper	100g shredded sharp Cheddar cheese
960ml chicken stock	1 teaspoon salt	100g cream cheese, melted	2 medium green onions, sliced
		570ml milk	

1. Move the slider towards "AIR FRY/STOVETOP" and set Ninja Foodi XL Pressure Cooker Steam Fryer with SmartLid to SEAR/SAUTÉ mode. Adjust the temperature to "Hi5" by using up arrow. Press START/STOP to begin cooking and cook bacon pieces until crisp. Press START/STOP button. 2. Drain bacon fat and place cooked bacon in-between two paper towels. Set aside. 3. Pour in stock and deglaze pot. 4. Place whole potatoes, salt, and pepper into cooking pot. Lock lid; move slider towards PRESSURE. Adjust pressure release valve in the SEAL position. Close pressure-release valve. The cooking temperature will default to HIGH, which is accurate. Set the time for 10 minutes. Select START/STOP and start cooking. When cooking is complete, let pressure release quickly by turning it into VENT position and unlock the lid. 5. Using an immersion blender or potato masher, blend up potatoes and stock until only a few chunks are left. 6. Turn Ninja Foodi XL Pressure Cooker Steam Fryer back on and select Sauté setting. Whisk in cream cheese and milk. Let cook an additional 10 minutes, stirring occasionally. 7. Mix in half of the cooked bacon. 8. Serve topped with cheese, green onions, and remaining bacon.
Per Serving: Calories 578; Fat 36g; Sodium 823mg; Carbs 49g; Fiber 5g; Sugar 6g; Protein 17g

Delicious Minestrone

Prep time: 10 minutes | Cook time: 13 minutes | Serves: 6

2 tablespoons olive oil	480ml water	2 teaspoons salt	drained and rinsed
1 medium yellow onion, peeled and chopped	3 medium russet potatoes, peeled and cubed	1 teaspoon dried oregano	1 (390g) can red kidney beans, drained and rinsed
2 cloves garlic, minced	2 medium carrots, diced	½ teaspoon black pepper	50g medium shell-shaped pasta
960ml vegetable stock	100g chopped green beans	80 g chopped kale	
		1 (390g) can cannelloni beans,	

1. Move the slider towards "AIR FRY/STOVETOP" and set Ninja Foodi XL Pressure Cooker Steam Fryer with SmartLid to SEAR/SAUTÉ mode. Adjust the temperature to "Hi5" by using up arrow. Press START/STOP to begin cooking. Put oil and onion into pot. Cook onion 2 minutes until soft. 2. Add in garlic and cook 30 seconds. Turn Pot off. 3. Add stock, water, potatoes, carrots, green beans, salt, oregano, and pepper to pot and mix. 4. Lock lid; move slider towards PRESSURE. Adjust pressure release valve in the SEAL position. Close pressure-release valve. The cooking temperature will default to HIGH, which is accurate. Set QUICK RELEASE and time to 2 minutes. Select START/STOP and start cooking. When cooking is complete, let pressure release quickly by turning it into VENT position. 5. Move the slider towards "AIR FRY/STOVETOP" and set Ninja Foodi XL Pressure Cooker Steam Fryer with SmartLid to SEAR/SAUTÉ mode. Adjust the temperature to "Hi5" by using up arrow. Press START/STOP to begin cooking. Mix in kale, cannelloni beans, kidney beans, and pasta. Let cook 8 minutes. 6. Turn off and serve.
Per Serving: Calories 278; Fat 6g; Sodium 1044mg; Carbs 47g; Fiber 9g; Sugar 9g; Protein 11g

Beefy Minestrone Soup

Prep time: 15 minutes | Cook time: 15 minutes | Serves: 6

2 tablespoons (30ml) avocado oil or extra-virgin olive oil	3 carrots, sliced and diced	drained and rinsed	1 teaspoon salt, plus more to taste
1 yellow onion, diced	3 celery ribs, diced	1 tablespoon (6g) Italian seasoning	10g chopped fresh basil
2 cloves garlic, minced	1 (410g) can diced tomatoes	1.2L chicken stock	30g shredded Parmesan cheese, for garnish
455g beef mince	3 tablespoons (48g) tomato paste	2 tablespoons (30ml) red wine vinegar	
1 medium courgette, diced	1 (425g) can cannellini beans,		

1. Move the slider towards "AIR FRY/STOVETOP" and set Ninja Foodi XL Pressure Cooker Steam Fryer with SmartLid to SEAR/SAUTÉ mode. Adjust the temperature to "Hi5" by using up arrow. Press START/STOP to begin cooking. 2. Once hot, add the oil to the pot, then the onion and garlic. Cook for 2 to 3 minutes, then add the beef mince. Continue to cook for another 5 to 6 minutes, or until the beef mince is mostly cooked. Select START/STOP. 3. Add the courgette, carrots, celery, diced tomatoes, tomato paste, beans, Italian seasoning, stock, vinegar and salt. Lock lid; move slider towards PRESSURE. Adjust pressure release valve in the SEAL position. Close pressure-release valve. The cooking temperature will default to HIGH, which is accurate. Set time to 6 minutes. Select START/STOP and start cooking.
4. When cooking is complete, let pressure release quickly by turning it into VENT position. Serve hot and garnish with fresh basil and Parmesan cheese.
Per Serving: Calories 252; Fat 11.3g; Sodium 321mg; Carbs 10.2g; Fiber 3g; Sugar 1g; Protein 12.2g

Healthy White Chicken Chili

Prep time: 10 minutes | Cook time: 30 minutes | Serves: 6

960ml chicken stock	1 (400g) can creamed corn	and chopped	1 teaspoon dried oregano
3 (360g) cans cannellini beans	2 (100g) cans mild diced green	2 cloves garlic, minced	½ teaspoon black pepper
455g boneless, skinless chicken breasts	chilies	1 tablespoon chili powder	½ teaspoon crushed red pepper
	1 medium yellow onion, peeled	1 teaspoon salt	240g full-fat sour cream

1. Combine stock, beans, chicken, corn, green chilies, onion, garlic, chili powder, salt, oregano, black pepper, and crushed red pepper inside Ninja Foodi XL Pressure Cooker Steam Fryer with SmartLid cooking pot. 2. Lock lid; move slider towards PRESSURE. Adjust pressure release valve in the SEAL position. Close pressure-release valve. The cooking temperature will default to HIGH, which is accurate. 3. Set the time for 30 minutes. Select START/STOP and start cooking. 4. When cooking is complete, let pressure release naturally for 10 minutes, then quick-release any remaining pressure by turning it into VENT position. 5. Remove chicken from pot and shred using two forks. Place chicken back into cooking pot. Mix in sour cream. 6. Serve hot.
Per Serving: Calories 403; Fat 10g; Sodium 1119mg; Carbs 49g; Fiber 10g; Sugar 13g; Protein 33g

Kale Sausage Soup

Prep time: 10 minutes | Cook time: 18 minutes | Serves: 8

1 tablespoon olive oil	960ml water	1 small yellow onion, peeled and chopped	⅛ teaspoon black pepper
455g hot Italian sausage, casings removed	6 medium russet potatoes, peeled and cubed	3 cloves garlic, minced	240g heavy whipping cream
960ml chicken stock	85g kale, stems removed	½ teaspoon salt	1 tablespoon flour

1. Move the slider towards "AIR FRY/STOVETOP" and set Ninja Foodi XL Pressure Cooker Steam Fryer with SmartLid to SEAR/SAUTÉ mode. Adjust the temperature to "Hi5" by using up arrow. Press START/STOP to begin cooking. Put oil and sausage into cooking pot. Cook sausage 8 minutes until brown, breaking it up into pieces while cooking. Turn Ninja Foodi XL Pressure Cooker Steam Fryer off. 2. Add stock, water, potatoes, kale, onion, garlic, salt, and pepper and stir to combine. 3. Lock lid; move slider towards PRESSURE. Adjust pressure release valve in the SEAL position. Close pressure-release valve. The cooking temperature will default to HIGH, which is accurate. Set the time for 10 minutes. Select START/STOP and start cooking. When cooking is complete, let pressure release quickly by turning it into VENT position. 4. Whisk in heavy cream and flour. Serve.
Per Serving: Calories 350; Fat 21g; Sodium 426mg; Carbs 31g; Fiber 3g; Sugar 3g; Protein 11g

Chicken Soup

Prep time: 5 minutes | Cook time: 25 minutes | Serves: 6

1.4L chicken stock	1 (380g) can corn, drained	chilies	5g coriander, roughly chopped
1 (150g) can tomato paste	1 (360g) can black beans, rinsed and drained	1 teaspoon salt	
455g boneless, skinless chicken breasts	2 (175g) cans mild diced green	¼ teaspoon black pepper	
		65g tortilla chips	

1. Pour stock into Ninja Foodi XL Pressure Cooker Steam Fryer with SmartLid cooking pot. Whisk tomato paste into stock. 2. Add in chicken breasts, corn, beans, green chilies, salt, and pepper. Stir to combine. 3. Lock lid; move slider towards PRESSURE. Adjust pressure release valve in the SEAL position. Close pressure-release valve. 4. The cooking temperature will default to HIGH, which is accurate. Set time to 15 minutes. Select START/STOP and start cooking. 5. When cooking is complete, let pressure release naturally for 10 minutes, then quick-release any remaining pressure by turning it into VENT position. Unlock lid and remove it. 6. Remove chicken. Shred chicken using two forks and then place it back into Ninja Foodi XL Pressure Cooker Steam Fryer with SmartLid cooking pot. 7. Serve soup topped with tortilla chips and coriander.
Per Serving: Calories 289; Fat 6g; Sodium 920mg; Carbs 32g; Fiber 6g; Sugar 10g; Protein 30g

Spicy Curried Cauliflower Soup

Prep time: 10 minutes | Cook time: 25 minutes | Serves: 4

2 teaspoons (10ml) olive oil	1 tablespoon (15g) red curry paste	1 large head cauliflower, broken into florets, core discarded	1 teaspoon coarse salt
1 medium onion, chopped	710ml chicken stock	400ml can coconut milk	
3 cloves garlic, minced			

1. Move the slider towards "AIR FRY/STOVETOP" and set Ninja Foodi XL Pressure Cooker Steam Fryer with SmartLid to SEAR/SAUTÉ mode. Adjust the temperature to "Hi5" by using up arrow. Press START/STOP to begin cooking. 2. Add the olive oil, then the onion. Cook, stirring occasionally, until the onion is soft, about 5 minutes. Add the garlic and red curry paste. Cook for about another minute, stirring frequently. 3. Press START/STOP to turn off. Add the chicken stock, taking care to scrape up any browned bits from the bottom of the pot. Add the cauliflower florets. 4. Lock lid; move slider towards PRESSURE. Adjust pressure release valve in the SEAL position. Close pressure-release valve. The cooking temperature will default to HIGH, which is accurate. Set time to 20 minutes. Select START/STOP and start cooking. 5. When cooking is complete, let pressure release naturally for 10 minutes, then quick-release any remaining pressure by turning it into VENT position. 6. Carefully remove the lid. Stir in the coconut milk and salt. Using an immersion blender, puree the soup until smooth. 7. Serve immediately.
Per Serving: Calories 242; Fat 12.2g; Sodium 222mg; Carbs 10.5g; Fiber 1.6g; Sugar 2g; Protein 11.6g

Delicious Moroccan Carrot Soup

Prep time: 10 minutes | Cook time: 15 minutes | Serves: 6

1 yellow onion, diced	pepper	455g carrots, peeled and roughly chopped	175ml canned coconut milk
2 cloves garlic, minced	Salt	475ml vegetable stock	Chopped green onion, for topping
½ teaspoon ground cinnamon	Freshly ground black pepper	240ml water	Pomegranate seeds, for topping
½ teaspoon ground cumin	1 teaspoon grated fresh ginger	1 teaspoon honey	
¼ to ½ teaspoon cayenne	Juice of ½ lemon		

1. In the Ninja Foodi XL Pressure Cooker Steam Fryer with SmartLid cooking pot, combine the onion, garlic, cinnamon, cumin, cayenne, salt and black pepper to taste, ginger, lemon juice, carrots, stock and water. Stir to combine. 2. Lock lid; move slider towards PRESSURE. Adjust pressure release valve in the SEAL position. Close pressure-release valve. The cooking temperature will default to HIGH, which is accurate. Set time to 12 minutes. Select START/STOP and start cooking. 3. When cooking is complete, let pressure release quickly by turning it into VENT position. Remove the lid. Stir in the honey and coconut milk. Puree the soup until smooth and creamy, using an immersion blender. Adjust the salt, black pepper and cayenne to taste. 4. Serve with green onion and pomegranate seeds on top, if desired.
Per Serving: Calories 223; Fat 10.2g; Sodium 211mg; Carbs 9.4g; Fiber 2g; Sugar 2g; Protein 14.3g

Pot Pie Soup

Prep time: 10 minutes | Cook time: 5 minutes | Serves: 4

2 tablespoons olive oil	960ml chicken stock	2 teaspoons salt	1 bay leaf
1 medium yellow onion, peeled and chopped	140g diced cooked chicken	½ teaspoon black pepper	240g heavy whipping cream
2 cloves garlic, minced	1 (300g) bag frozen mixed vegetables	½ teaspoon dried parsley	40g plain flour
		¼ teaspoon dried sage	

1. Move the slider towards "AIR FRY/STOVETOP" and set Ninja Foodi XL Pressure Cooker Steam Fryer with SmartLid to SEAR/SAUTÉ mode. Adjust the temperature to "Hi5" by using up arrow. Press START/STOP to begin cooking. Put oil and onion into pot. Cook onion 2 minutes until soft. 2. Add in garlic and cook 30 seconds. Turn pot off. 3. Add stock, chicken, mixed vegetables, salt, pepper, parsley, sage, and bay leaf. 4. Lock lid; move slider towards PRESSURE. Adjust pressure release valve in the SEAL position. Close pressure-release valve. The cooking temperature will default to HIGH, which is accurate. Set the time for 2 minutes. Select START/STOP and start cooking. When cooking is complete, let pressure release quickly by turning it into VENT position and unlock lid. 5. In a small bowl, whisk together cream and flour. Whisk cream mixture into soup. 6. Remove bay leaf and serve.
Per Serving: Calories 472; Fat 31g; Sodium 1321mg; Carbs 29g; Fiber 4g; Sugar 8g; Protein 21g

Healthy Three Bean Chili

Prep time: 5 minutes | Cook time: 16 minutes | Serves: 4

2 tablespoons olive oil	4 cloves garlic, minced	drained and rinsed	1 tablespoon chili powder
1 medium yellow onion, peeled and chopped	240ml water	2 (390g) cans cannelloni beans, drained and rinsed	1 teaspoon dried oregano
1 medium green pepper, seeded and chopped	2 (390g) cans red kidney beans, drained and rinsed	1 (375g) can tomato sauce	½ teaspoon cayenne pepper
	2 (390g) cans black beans,	1 (150g) can tomato paste	

1. Move the slider towards "AIR FRY/STOVETOP" and set Ninja Foodi XL Pressure Cooker Steam Fryer with SmartLid to SEAR/SAUTÉ mode. Adjust the temperature to "Hi5" by using up arrow. Press START/STOP to begin cooking. Add oil to pot. Add in onion and pepper and cook 5 minutes until soft. 2. Add in garlic and cook an additional 30 seconds until fragrant. 3. Pour in water and deglazed bottom of pot. Turn pot off. 4. Add in kidney beans, black beans, cannelloni beans, tomato sauce, tomato paste, chili powder, oregano, and cayenne pepper. Mix well. 5. Lock lid; move slider towards PRESSURE. Adjust pressure release valve in the SEAL position. Close pressure-release valve. The cooking temperature will default to HIGH, which is accurate. Set the time for 10 minutes. Select START/STOP and start cooking. 6. When cooking is complete, let pressure release quickly by turning it into VENT position and unlock lid. 7. Serve.
Per Serving: Calories 625; Fat 11g; Sodium 1355mg; Carbs 102g; Fiber 28g; Sugar 11g; Protein 36g

Chapter 6 Fish and Seafood Recipes

Page	Recipe
88	Grilled Salmon with Capers
88	Cod with Grapes
88	Asian Style Sea Bass
88	Salmon with Courgette
89	Fish Capers Cakes
89	Crispy Fish Sticks
89	Fish Fingers
89	Vegetable with Salmon Fillets
90	Breaded Salmon
90	Parmesan Tilapia
90	Red Salmon Croquettes
90	Cajun Lemon Salmon
90	Crab Legs
91	Salmon Cakes
91	Grilled Salmon
91	Salmon Potato Patties
91	Fried Prawns
92	Mustard Coconut Prawns
92	Prawns Scampi
92	Miso Salmon Fillets
92	Delicious Umami Calamari
93	Delicious Louisiana Grouper
93	Creamy Scallops
93	Garlicky Salmon Fillets
93	Parmesan Cod
94	Regular Pad Thai
94	Mussels in White Wine
94	Bacon Wrapped Scallops
94	Cod with Spring Onions
95	Salmon with Chives Sauce
95	Country Boil
95	Mediterranean Spicy Cod
95	Lemon Salmon with Dill
96	Delicious Lobster Risotto
96	Mahi-Mahi with a Lemon-Caper Sauce
96	Steamed Prawns with Asparagus
96	Steaming Clams
97	Creamy Crab
97	Cod with Olives and Fennel
97	Fish Chowder
97	Steamed Crab
98	Curried Coconut Prawns
98	Fish Stew
98	Lobster with Butter Sauce
98	Prawns Scampi with Cheese
99	Prawns with tangy Risotto
99	Tilapia with Tomatoes
99	Delicious Seafood Gumbo

Grilled Salmon with Capers

Prep Time: 10 minutes | Cook Time: 8 minutes | Serves: 2

1 teaspoon capers, chopped	1 tablespoon olive oil	**Dressing:**	2 tablespoons plain yogurt
2 sprigs dill, chopped	4 slices lemon	5 capers, chopped	Pinch of lemon zest
1 lemon zest	275g salmon fillet	1 sprig dill, chopped	Salt and black pepper to taste

1. Place the Cook & Crisp Basket in your Pressure Cooker Steam Fryer. 2. Mix dill, capers, lemon zest, olive oil and salt in a suitable bowl. Cover the salmon with this mixture. Put on the Smart Lid on top of the Ninja Foodi Steam Fryer. 3. Move the Lid Slider to the "Air Fry/Stovetop". Select the "Air Fry" mode for cooking. 4. Adjust the cooking temperature to 200°C. Cook salmon for around 8 minutes. Mix the dressing ingredients in another bowl. 5. When salmon is cooked, place on serving plate and drizzle dressing over it. Place lemon slices at the side of the plate and serve.
Per serving: Calories 669; Fat: 53.8g; Sodium 905mg; Carbs: 41.7g; Fiber: 8.6g; Sugars 12.3g; Protein 14g

Cod with Grapes

Prep Time: 10 minutes | Cook Time: 15 minutes | Serves: 2

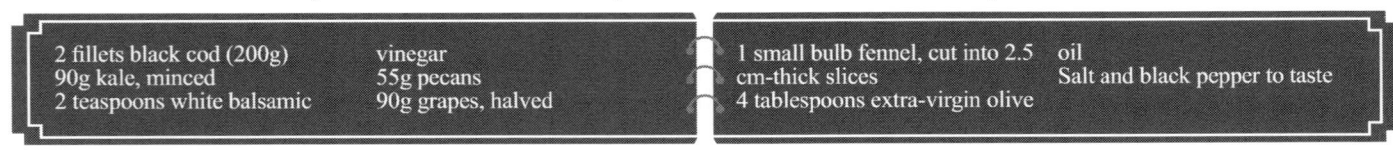

2 fillets black cod (200g)	vinegar	1 small bulb fennel, cut into 2.5 cm-thick slices	oil
90g kale, minced	55g pecans		Salt and black pepper to taste
2 teaspoons white balsamic	90g grapes, halved	4 tablespoons extra-virgin olive	

1. Place the Cook & Crisp Basket in your Pressure Cooker Steam Fryer. 2. Use black pepper and salt to season your fish fillets. Drizzle with 1 teaspoon of olive oil. Place the fish in the Cook & Crisp Basket with the skin side down. 3. Put on the Smart Lid on top of the Ninja Foodi Steam Fryer. Move the Lid Slider to the "Air Fry/Stovetop". Select the "Air Fry" mode for cooking. Adjust the cooking temperature to 200°C. Cook for around 10 minutes. 4. Take the fish out and cover loosely with aluminum foil. Mix fennel, pecans, and grapes. Pour 2 tablespoons of olive oil and season with black pepper and salt. 5. Add to the Ninja Foodi Pressure Steam Fryer basket. Put on the Smart Lid on top of the Ninja Foodi Steam Fryer. 6. Move the Lid Slider to the "Air Fry/Stovetop". Select the "Air Fry" mode for cooking. Cook for an additional 5 minutes. 7. In a suitable bowl mix minced kale and cooked grapes, fennel and pecans. Cover ingredients with balsamic vinegar and remaining 1 tablespoon of olive oil. 8. Toss gently. Serve fish with sauce and enjoy!
Per serving: Calories 194; Fat: 2.6g; Sodium 1257mg; Carbs: 35.4g; Fiber: 3.7g; Sugars 3.1g; Protein 9.4g

Asian Style Sea Bass

Prep Time: 10 minutes | Cook Time: 20 minutes | Serves: 2

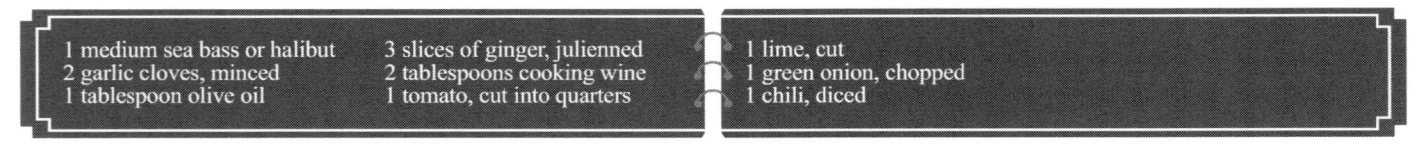

1 medium sea bass or halibut	3 slices of ginger, julienned	1 lime, cut	
2 garlic cloves, minced	2 tablespoons cooking wine	1 green onion, chopped	
1 tablespoon olive oil	1 tomato, cut into quarters	1 chili, diced	

1. Place the Cook & Crisp Basket in your Pressure Cooker Steam Fryer. 2. Prepare ginger, garlic oil mixture: sauté ginger and garlic with oil until golden brown in a suitable saucepan over medium-heat on top of the stove. Prepare fish: clean, rinse, and pat dry. Cut in half to fit into basket. 3. Place the fish inside of "cook & crisp basket" then drizzle it with cooking wine. Layer tomato and lime slices on top of fish. Cover with garlic ginger oil mixture. Top with green onion and slices of chili. Cover with aluminum foil. 4. Put on the Smart Lid on top of the Ninja Foodi Steam Fryer. Move the Lid Slider to the "Air Fry/Stovetop". Select the "Air Fry" mode for cooking. Adjust the cooking temperature to 180°C. 5. Cook for around 20 minutes.
Per serving: Calories 105; Fat: 2.4g; Sodium 812mg; Carbs: 12.2g; Fiber: 2.4g; Sugars 2.4g; Protein 9.5g

Salmon with Courgette

Prep Time: 10 minutes | Cook Time: 10 minutes | Serves: 2

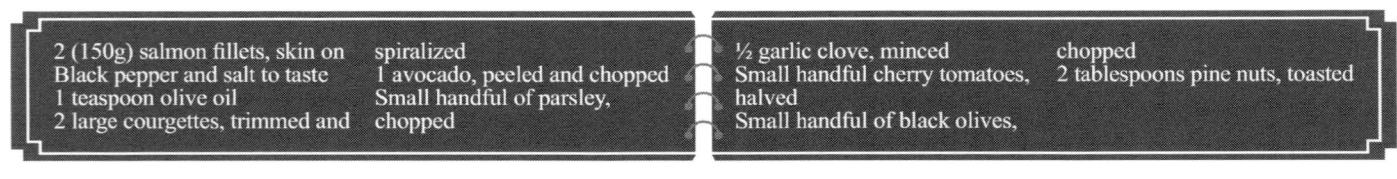

2 (150g) salmon fillets, skin on	spiralized	½ garlic clove, minced	chopped
Black pepper and salt to taste	1 avocado, peeled and chopped	Small handful cherry tomatoes, halved	2 tablespoons pine nuts, toasted
1 teaspoon olive oil	Small handful of parsley, chopped	Small handful of black olives,	
2 large courgettes, trimmed and			

1. Place the Cook & Crisp Basket in your Pressure Cooker Steam Fryer. 2. Brush salmon with olive oil and season with black pepper and salt. Place salmon in the Cook & Crisp Basket. Put on the Smart Lid on top of the Ninja Foodi Steam Fryer. 3. Move the Lid Slider to the "Air Fry/Stovetop". Select the "Air Fry" mode for cooking. Adjust the cooking temperature to 175°C. Cook for around 10 minutes. 4. Blend the avocado, garlic, and parsley in a food processor until smooth. Toss in a suitable bowl with courgette, olives, and tomatoes. 5. Divide vegetables between two plates, top each portion with salmon fillet, sprinkle with pine nuts, and serve.
Per serving: Calories 609; Fat: 19.5g; Sodium 132mg; Carbs: 49g; Fiber: 6g; Sugars 13.3g; Protein 57.5g

Fish Capers Cakes

Prep Time: 10 minutes | Cook Time: 8 minutes | Serves: 4

- 350g of potatoes, boiled and mashed
- 250g cooked salmon, flaked
- 1 teaspoon olive oil
- 20g almond flour
- 1 handful parsley, fresh, chopped
- 1 handful of capers
- 1 teaspoon lemon zest

1. Place the Cook & Crisp Basket in your Pressure Cooker Steam Fryer. 2. Brush salmon with olive oil. Place the potatoes, flaked salmon, lemon zest, parsley, and capers in a suitable bowl and mix well. 3. Make 4 large cakes out of the mixture. Dust fish cakes with flour. Place them in the fridge for an hour. Add salmon cakes to the Cook & Crisp Basket. 4. Put on the Smart Lid on top of the Ninja Foodi Steam Fryer. Move the Lid Slider to the "Air Fry/Stovetop". Select the "Air Fry" mode for cooking. Adjust the cooking temperature to 175°C. 5. Cook for around 8 minutes. Serve warm.

Per serving: Calories 303; Fat: 10.4g; Sodium 703mg; Carbs: 9.2g; Fiber: 0g; Sugars 8.7g; Protein 40.6g

Crispy Fish Sticks

Prep Time: 10 minutes | Cook Time: 13 minutes | Serves: 4

- 3 eggs
- 200g breadcrumbs
- 455g. codfish
- 90g almond flour
- 3 tablespoons skim milk
- Salt and black pepper to taste

1. Place the Cook & Crisp Basket in your Pressure Cooker Steam Fryer. 2. Mix milk and egg in a suitable mixing bowl. In another bowl, add breadcrumbs, and in a third bowl mix flour. Slice the fish into strips and season with black pepper and salt. 3. Dip each piece into flour, then into egg mixture and then into breadcrumbs. 4. Put on the Smart Lid on top of the Ninja Foodi Steam Fryer. Move the Lid Slider to the "Air Fry/Stovetop". Select the "Air Fry" mode for cooking. Adjust the cooking temperature to 170°C. Cook for around 13 minutes. 5. Turn once during cooking.

Per serving: Calories 357; Fat: 16.1g; Sodium 80mg; Carbs: 26g; Fiber: 7.3g; Sugars 9.2g; Protein 29.4g

Fish Fingers

Prep Time: 10 minutes | Cook Time: 10 minutes | Serves: 2

- 250g codfish, sliced into strips
- 2 teaspoons mixed dried herbs
- 2 eggs
- ¼ teaspoon baking soda
- 1 teaspoon rice flour
- 2 teaspoons corn flour
- 2 tablespoons almond flour
- ½ lemon, juiced
- 1 teaspoon ginger garlic
- ½ teaspoon turmeric powder
- ½ teaspoon red chili flakes
- 2 teaspoons garlic powder
- 2 tablespoons olive oil
- 100g breadcrumbs
- Tartar sauce or ketchup

1. Place the Cook & Crisp Basket in your Pressure Cooker Steam Fryer. 2. Place fish fingers in a suitable bowl. Add a teaspoon of mixed herbs, 1 teaspoon of garlic powder, red chili flakes, turmeric powder, ginger garlic, lemon juice, salt and black pepper. Stir well and set aside for around 10 minutes. 3. In another bowl, mix almond flour, rice flour, corn flour and baking soda. Break eggs into this bowl. Stir well then add fish. Set aside for around 10 minutes. 4. Mix breadcrumbs and remaining 1 teaspoon of mixed herbs and 1 teaspoon of garlic powder. Cover fish with breadcrumb mixture. 5. Lay aluminum foil in the Cook & Crisp Basket. Lay the fish fingers in the basket and cover with olive oil. Put on the Smart Lid on top of the Ninja Foodi Steam Fryer. 6. Move the Lid Slider to the "Air Fry/Stovetop". Select the "Air Fry" mode for cooking. Adjust the cooking temperature to 180°C. 7. Cook for around 10 minutes and serve with tartar sauce or ketchup.

Per serving: Calories 541; Fat: 12.4g; Sodium 250mg; Carbs: 85.4g; Fiber: 21.3g; Sugars 6.1g; Protein 26.5g

Vegetable with Salmon Fillets

Prep Time: 20 minutes | Cook Time: 12 minutes | Serves: 2

- 60ml soy sauce
- ½ teaspoon salt
- 120ml fresh juiced orange
- 1 tablespoon avocado oil
- 1 tablespoon chopped ginger
- 2 minced garlic cloves
- 2 (125g) salmon fillets
- 2 teaspoons grated orange zest
- 3 tablespoons rice vinegar
- **For the Veggies**
- ½ teaspoon toasted sesame seeds
- 1 tablespoon sesame oil
- 50g stemmed dry shiitake mushrooms
- 2 halved heads baby bok choy
- Salt, to taste

1. Place the Cook & Crisp Basket in your Pressure Cooker Steam Fryer. 2. Using a suitable mixing bowl, add in the avocado oil, soy sauce, salt, vinegar, orange juice, zest, ginger, garlic and mix until mixed. 3. Divide the marinade into 2 and reserve one then add the salmon fillets into a Ziploc bag and pour the remaining soy sauce mix in to marinate for an hour. 4. Transfer the marinated salmon into the "cook & crisp basket" then put on the Smart Lid on top of the Ninja Foodi Steam Fryer. 5. Move the Lid Slider to the "Air Fry/Stovetop". Select the "Air Fry" mode for cooking. air fry for around 6 minutes at 200°C. 6. In the meantime, coat the mushroom and bok choy with the oil, season with the salt then set aside. 7. Add the vegetables into the "cook & crisp basket" along with the salmon fillets and cook for an extra 6 minutes. 8. Serve, drizzled with the reserved marinade, a garnish of the sesame seeds and enjoy.

Per serving: Calories 404; Fat: 19.4g; Sodium 187mg; Carbs: 5g; Fiber: 1.1g; Sugars 0.8g; Protein 52g

Breaded Salmon

Prep Time: 10 minutes | Cook Time: 20 minutes | Serves: 4

| 200g breadcrumbs | 4 salmon fillets | 2 eggs, beaten | 100g Swiss cheese, shredded |

1. Place the Cook & Crisp Basket in your Pressure Cooker Steam Fryer. 2. Dip each salmon filet into eggs. Top with Swiss cheese. Dip into breadcrumbs, coating entire fish. 3. Put into the Cook & Crisp Basket. Put on the Smart Lid on top of the Ninja Foodi Steam Fryer. Move the Lid Slider to the "Air Fry/Stovetop". Select the "Air Fry" mode for cooking. Adjust the cooking temperature to 200°C. 4. Cook for around 20 minutes.
Per serving: Calories 347; Fat: 17.7g; Sodium 1655mg; Carbs: 6.8g; Fiber: 1.2g; Sugars 2.8g; Protein 33.3g

Parmesan Tilapia

Prep Time: 10 minutes | Cook Time: 5 minutes | Serves: 4

| 1 tablespoon olive oil
4 tilapia fillets | 75g grated Parmesan cheese
1 tablespoon parsley, chopped | 2 teaspoons paprika
Pinch of garlic powder |

1. Place the Cook & Crisp Basket in your Pressure Cooker Steam Fryer. 2. Brush oil over tilapia fillets. Mix the remaining recipe ingredients in a suitable bowl. Coat tilapia fillets with parmesan mixture. 3. Line the Cook & Crisp Basket with parchment paper and arrange fillets. Place in Pressure Cooker Steam Fryer. 4. Put on the Smart Lid on top of the Ninja Foodi Steam Fryer. Move the Lid Slider to the "Air Fry/Stovetop". Select the "Air Fry" mode for cooking. 5. Adjust the cooking temperature to 175°C. Cook for around 5 minutes.
Per serving: Calories 323; Fat: 17.9g; Sodium 838mg; Carbs: 4.3g; Fiber: 1.5g; Sugars 1g; Protein 35.5g

Red Salmon Croquettes

Prep Time: 10 minutes | Cook Time: 10 minutes | Serves: 4

| 350g tin of red salmon, drained
2 free-range eggs | 5 tablespoons olive oil
50g breadcrumbs | 2 tablespoons spring onions, chopped | Black pepper and salt to taste
Pinch of herbs |

1. Place the Cook & Crisp Basket in your Pressure Cooker Steam Fryer. 2. Add drained salmon into a suitable bowl and mash well. Break in the egg, add herbs, spring onions, salt, pepper and mix well. In another bowl, mix breadcrumbs and oil and mix well. 3. Take a spoon of the salmon mixture and shape it into a croquette shape in your hand. Roll it in the breadcrumbs and place inside the Cook & Crisp Basket. 4. Put on the Smart Lid on top of the Ninja Foodi Steam Fryer. Move the Lid Slider to the "Air Fry/Stovetop". Select the "Air Fry" mode for cooking. 5. Set your Ninja Foodi Pressure Steam Fryer to 200°C for around 10 minutes.
Per serving: Calories 419; Fat: 15.8g; Sodium 3342mg; Carbs: 0.4g; Fiber: 0.2g; Sugars 0g; Protein 65.4g

Cajun Lemon Salmon

Prep Time: 10 minutes | Cook Time: 7 minutes | Serves: 1

| 1 salmon fillet
1 teaspoon Cajun seasoning | 2 lemon wedges, for serving
1 teaspoon liquid stevia | ½ lemon, juiced |

1. Place the Cook & Crisp Basket in your Pressure Cooker Steam Fryer. 2. Mix lemon juice and liquid stevia and coat salmon with this mixture. Sprinkle Cajun seasoning all over salmon. Place salmon on parchment paper in the Cook & Crisp Basket. 3. Put on the Smart Lid on top of the Ninja Foodi Steam Fryer. Move the Lid Slider to the "Air Fry/Stovetop". Select the "Air Fry" mode for cooking. Adjust the cooking temperature to 175°C. 4. Cook for around 7-minutes. Serve with lemon wedges.
Per serving: Calories 570; Fat: 29.3g; Sodium 845mg; Carbs: 5.8g; Fiber: 1.6g; Sugars 2.7g; Protein 68.6g

Crab Legs

Prep time: 3 minutes | Cook time: 3 minutes | Serves: 4

| 900g wild-caught Snow Crab legs | 240ml water
70g ghee or clarified butter | Lemon slices |

1. Place the Cook & Crisp Basket in the Ninja Foodi XL Pressure Cooker Steam Fryer with SmartLid cooking pot with 240ml water. Put the crab legs in the pot and seal the lid. 2. Lock lid; move slider to AIR FRY/STOVETOP. Select STEAM, and set time to 3 minutes. Press START/STOP to begin cooking. 3. When cooking is complete, let pressure release naturally. Melt the ghee or clarified butter in a microwave or on the stovetop. 4. Serve the legs with ghee and with lemon slices on the side.
Per Serving: Calories 221; Fat 11g; Sodium 256mg; Carbs 6g; Fiber 4g; Sugar 2g; Protein 9g

Salmon Cakes

Prep Time: 35 minutes | Cook Time: 15 minutes | Serves: 5

75g mashed avocado	teaspoons	1 ½ teaspoon yellow curry powder	**For the Greens**
10g chopped coriander, with extra	½ teaspoon salt	2 large eggs	½ teaspoon salt
10g tapioca starch, with 4 extra	40g coconut flakes	Avocado oil	2 teaspoons olive oil
	455g salmon		120g arugula and spinach mix

1. Place the Cook & Crisp Basket in your Pressure Cooker Steam Fryer. 2. Skin the salmon then chop into pieces and transfer into a suitable mixing bowl. 3. Add in the coriander, salt, curry powder, avocado and incorporate together. 4. Pour in the teaspoons of tapioca then mix until mixed then mold the patties into 10 even sizes. 5. Transfer the molded patties into a parchment paper prepared baking sheet then freeze for about 30 minutes. 6. In the meantime, mix the eggs in a suitable mixing bowl and pour the coconut flakes and tapioca into different bowls. 7. Coat the "cook & crisp basket" with oil. 8. Run the chilled patties through the tapioca until coated, then dredge in the egg mix and finally coat with the coconut flakes. 9. Transfer the covered patties into the basket then put on the Smart Lid on top of the Ninja Foodi Steam Fryer. 10. Move the Lid Slider to the "Air Fry/Stovetop". Select the "Air Fry" mode for cooking. Cook at 200°C for around 15 minutes until the crispy and tenderized. 11. Using a suitable pan, heat the olive oil up over medium heat then add in the spinach, arugula, salt and stir cook for a minute until wilted. 12. Serve the salmon cakes and greens together, enjoying with a garnish of coriander.
Per serving: Calories 367; Fat: 22.9g; Sodium 101mg; Carbs: 8g; Fiber: 1.9g; Sugars 3g; Protein 31.8g

Grilled Salmon

Prep Time: 10 minutes | Cook Time: 8 minutes | Serves: 2

2 salmon fillets	1 teaspoon liquid stevia	80ml of water
2 tablespoons olive oil	80ml of light soy sauce	Salt and black pepper to taste

1. Place the Cook & Crisp Basket in your Pressure Cooker Steam Fryer. 2. Season salmon fillets with black pepper and salt. Mix the rest of the recipe ingredients in a suitable bowl. 3. Allow the salmon fillets to marinate in mixture for around 2 hours. Drain salmon fillets. 4. Put on the Smart Lid on top of the Ninja Foodi Steam Fryer. Move the Lid Slider to the "Air Fry/Stovetop". Select the "Air Fry" mode for cooking. Adjust the cooking temperature to 180°C. 5. Air Fry for around 8 minutes.
Per serving: Calories 684; Fat: 30.1g; Sodium 1075mg; Carbs: 15.1g; Fiber: 1.5g; Sugars 10.1g; Protein 84.9g

Salmon Potato Patties

Prep Time: 10 minutes | Cook Time: 10 minutes | Serves: 2

3 large russet potatoes, boiled, mashed	1 egg	Parsley, fresh, chopped	½ teaspoon dill
1 salmon fillet	Breadcrumbs	Handful of parboiled vegetables	Black pepper and salt to taste
	2 tablespoons olive oil		

1. Place the Cook & Crisp Basket in your Pressure Cooker Steam Fryer. 2. Peel, chop, and mash cooked potatoes. Put potatoes in the Cook & Crisp Basket. 3. Put on the Smart Lid on top of the Ninja Foodi Steam Fryer. Move the Lid Slider to the "Air Fry/Stovetop". Select the "Air Fry" mode for cooking. Air Fry salmon for 5 minutes. 4. Use a fork to flake salmon then set aside. Add vegetables, parsley, flaked salmon, dill, salt, and pepper to mashed potatoes. 5. Add egg and mix. Shape the mixture into six patties. Cover with breadcrumbs. Cook at 180°C for around 10 minutes.
Per serving: Calories 403; Fat: 23.8g; Sodium 782mg; Carbs: 4.4g; Fiber: 1.9g; Sugars 0.7g; Protein 48.9g

Fried Prawns

Prep Time: 7 minutes | Cook Time: 10 minutes | Serves: 4

½ teaspoon oregano	1 teaspoon pepper	900g peeled and deveined jumbo cooked prawns	quartered lime
65g shaved parmesan cheese	1 teaspoon powdered onion	4 minced garlic cloves	Cooking spray oil
1 teaspoon basil	2 tablespoons sesame oil		

1. Place the Cook & Crisp Basket in your Pressure Cooker Steam Fryer. 2. Using a suitable mixing bowl, add in the oil, powdered onion, basil, oregano, pepper, parmesan cheese, garlic and mix everything together. 3. Add the cooked prawns into the mixture and toss until well coated. 4. Grease the "cook & crisp basket" with cooking spray oil then add in the coated prawns. Put on the Smart Lid on top of the Ninja Foodi Steam Fryer. 5. Move the Lid Slider to the "Air Fry/Stovetop". Select the "Air Fry" mode for cooking. 6. Air fry for around 10 minutes at 175°C. 7. Serve with a garnish of the lime juice and enjoy as desired.
Per serving: Calories 506; Fat: 23.9g; Sodium 197mg; Carbs: 3.6g; Fiber: 0.7g; Sugars 1.2g; Protein 66.1g

Mustard Coconut Prawns

Prep Time: 10 minutes | Cook Time: 20 minutes | Serves: 2

50g breadcrumbs	unsweetened	8 large prawns	160g orange jam, sugar-free
Salt and black pepper to taste	½ teaspoon cayenne pepper	1 tablespoon sugar-free syrup	1 teaspoon mustard
45g shredded coconut,	200g coconut milk	¼ teaspoon hot sauce	

1. Place the Cook & Crisp Basket in your Pressure Cooker Steam Fryer. 2. Place breadcrumbs, coconut, salt, pepper, and cayenne pepper in a suitable bowl and mix. 3. Dip the prawns in coconut milk first, then in breadcrumb mixture. 4. Line baking sheet and arrange prawns on it. Place in the Cook & Crisp Basket. Put on the Smart Lid on top of the Ninja Foodi Steam Fryer. Move the Lid Slider to the "Air Fry/Stovetop". Select the "Air Fry" mode for cooking. 5. Adjust the cooking temperature to 175°C. Cook for around 20 minutes. 6. Mix the orange jam, mustard, syrup, and hot sauce. Add the prawns to a serving platter and drizzle with sauce and serve.
Per serving: Calories 459; Fat: 3.6g; Sodium 1614mg; Carbs: 82g; Fiber: 11.5g; Sugars 8.3g; Protein 25.9g

Prawns Scampi

Prep Time: 5 minutes | Cook Time: 8 minutes | Serves: 4

455g raw prawns	1 tablespoon chopped chives	2 tablespoons chicken stock
1 tablespoon juiced lime	1 tablespoon fresh chopped	2 teaspoons red pepper flakes
1 tablespoon minced garlic	basil	4 tablespoons melted butter

1. Place the Cook & Crisp Basket in your Pressure Cooker Steam Fryer. 2. Add the pepper flakes, garlic and melted butter into the "cook & crisp basket". Put on the Smart Lid on top of the Ninja Foodi Steam Fryer. 3. Move the Lid Slider to the "Air Fry/Stovetop". Select the "Air Fry" mode for cooking. 4. Air fry at 200°C for a minute, until the butter, garlic and pepper are all incorporated. Add in the remaining recipe ingredients into the "cook & crisp basket" then mix together. 5. Air fry the prawns for around 7 minutes at 200°C. 6. Serve, garnished with extra herbs if desired and enjoy.
Per serving: Calories 340; Fat: 27.7g; Sodium 109mg; Carbs: 12.6g; Fiber: 0.3g; Sugars 3g; Protein 15.7g

Miso Salmon Fillets

Prep Time: 10 minutes | Cook Time: 10 minutes | Serves: 2

120ml boiling water	1 teaspoon sesame seeds	2 tablespoons white miso	Non-stick cooking spray
½ teaspoon cracked black pepper	1 teaspoons minced garlic cloves	2 chopped green spring onions	
1 teaspoon diced ginger	2 tablespoons soy sauce	2 tablespoons brown sugar	
		2 (125g) salmon fillets	

1. Place the Cook & Crisp Basket in your Pressure Cooker Steam Fryer. 2. Using a suitable mixing bowl, add in the pepper, ginger, garlic, miso, brown sugar, soy sauce and boiling water then mix together. 3. Using a flat work station, place the salmon fillets then cover with the sauce mixture, ensuring even amount of coating all over. 4. Grease the "cook & crisp basket" with cooking spray then add in the coated fillets. Put on the Smart Lid on top of the Ninja Foodi Steam Fryer. Move the Lid Slider to the "Air Fry/Stovetop". Select the "Air Fry" mode for cooking. Air Fry for around 12 minutes at 200°C. 5. Serve with a garnish of spring onions, sesame seeds and enjoy as desired.
Per serving: Calories 305; Fat: 16.7g; Sodium 148mg; Carbs: 2.5g; Fiber: 1.1g; Sugars 0.1g; Protein 36.5g

Delicious Umami Calamari

Prep time: 15 minutes | Cook time: 20 minutes | Serves: 4

1 tablespoon olive oil	including juice	1 teaspoon sea salt	455g calamari tubes, cut into ½ cm rings
1 small onion, peeled and diced	240ml chicken stock	½ teaspoon ground black pepper	25g grated Parmesan cheese
2 cloves garlic, minced	10g chopped fresh parsley	2 teaspoons anchovy paste	
60ml dry red wine	6 tablespoons chopped fresh basil, divided	1 bay leaf	
1 (360g) can diced tomatoes,			

1. Move the slider towards "AIR FRY/STOVETOP" and set Ninja Foodi XL Pressure Cooker Steam Fryer with SmartLid to SEAR/SAUTÉ mode. Adjust the temperature to "Hi5" by using up arrow. Press START/STOP to begin cooking. Add olive oil and heat. Add onion and sauté for 3–5 minutes until onions are translucent. Add garlic and sauté for an additional minute. Add red wine, press Adjust button to change temperature to less, and simmer unlidded for 5 minutes. 2. Add remaining ingredients except 2 tablespoons basil and Parmesan cheese. 3. Lock lid; move slider towards PRESSURE. Adjust pressure release valve in the SEAL position. Close pressure-release valve. The cooking temperature will default to HIGH, which is accurate. Set time to 3 minutes. Select START/STOP and start cooking. 4. When cooking is complete, let pressure release naturally for 10 minutes, then quick-release any remaining pressure by turning it into VENT position. 5. Remove bay leaf. Use a slotted spoon to transfer pot ingredients to four bowls. Garnish each bowl with equal amounts Parmesan cheese and ½ tablespoon basil.
Per Serving: Calories 194; Fat 6g; Sodium 481mg; Carbs 6g; Fiber 1.5g; Sugar 3g; Protein 27g

Delicious Louisiana Grouper

Prep time: 10 minutes | Cook time: 20 minutes | Serves: 4

2 tablespoons olive oil	and diced	1 teaspoon honey	into bite-sized pieces
1 small onion, peeled and diced	1 (375g) can diced tomatoes	Pinch of dried basil	½ teaspoon sea salt
1 stalk celery, diced	60ml water	2 teaspoons Creole seasoning	¼ teaspoon ground black
1 small green pepper, seeded	1 tablespoon tomato paste	4 grouper fillets, rinsed and cut	pepper

1. Move the slider towards "AIR FRY/STOVETOP" and set Ninja Foodi XL Pressure Cooker Steam Fryer with SmartLid to SEAR/SAUTÉ mode. Adjust the temperature to "Hi5" by using up arrow. Press START/STOP to begin cooking. Heat oil and add onion, celery, and pepper. Sauté for 3–5 minutes until onions are translucent and peppers are tender. 2. Stir in undrained tomatoes, water, tomato paste, honey, basil, and Creole seasoning. 3. Sprinkle fish with salt and pepper. Gently toss the fish pieces into the sauce in the Ninja Foodi XL Pressure Cooker Steam Fryer with SmartLid cooking pot. 4. Lock lid; move slider towards PRESSURE. Adjust pressure release valve in the SEAL position. Close pressure-release valve. The cooking temperature will default to HIGH, which is accurate. Set time to 5 minutes. Select START/STOP and start cooking. When cooking is complete, let pressure release quickly by turning it into VENT position. 5. Transfer fish to a serving platter. Move the slider towards "AIR FRY/STOVETOP" and set Ninja Foodi XL Pressure Cooker Steam Fryer with SmartLid to SEAR/SAUTÉ mode. Adjust the temperature to "Hi5" by using up arrow. Press START/STOP to begin cooking and simmer juices unlidded for 10 minutes. 6. Transfer tomatoes and preferred amount of sauce over fish. Serve immediately.
Per Serving: Calories 366; Fat 16.6g; Sodium 256mg; Carbs 7.5g; Fiber 0.2g; Sugar 0.3g; Protein 4.6g

Creamy Scallops

Prep Time: 5 minutes | Cook Time: 10 minutes | Serves: 2

½ teaspoon salt	1 teaspoon minced garlic	8 jumbo sea scallops	Black pepper and salt, to taste
½ teaspoon black pepper	1 tablespoon tomato paste	300g pack frozen spinach,	
180g heavy whipping cream	1 tablespoon chopped fresh	drained and thawed	
1 teaspoon coconut oil	basil	Nonstick cooking oil spray	

1. Place the Cook & Crisp Basket in your Pressure Cooker Steam Fryer. 2. Grease the "cook & crisp basket" then add in the drained and thawed spinach and keep to the side. 3. Generously season the scallops all over with oil, a sprinkle of black pepper and salt then place inside the pan on the spinach. 4. Using a suitable mixing bowl, add in the extra pepper, salt, basil, tomato paste, garlic, heavy cream and mix together. 5. Then pour the cream mixture over the scallops and place in the Ninja Foodi Pressure Steam Fryer. 6. Air fry the scallops for around 10 minutes at 175°C then serve and enjoy as desired.
Per serving: Calories 315; Fat: 15g; Sodium 91mg; Carbs: 0g; Fiber: 0g; Sugars 0g; Protein 42.3g

Garlicky Salmon Fillets

Prep Time: 5 minutes | Cook Time: 12 minutes | Serves: 4

½ lime juice	1 teaspoon powdered garlic	2 teaspoons lime pepper
½ lime wedges	455g diced salmon fillets	seasoning
1 tablespoon coconut oil	2 teaspoons seafood seasoning	Salt, to taste

1. Place the Cook & Crisp Basket in your Pressure Cooker Steam Fryer. 2. Ensure the salmon fillets are completely dry then mix the lime juice and coconut oil together. 3. Coat the dry salmon with the oil mixture then sprinkle with the salt and remaining seasonings. 4. Prepare the "cook & crisp basket" with parchment paper then place in the salmon fillets. Put on the Smart Lid on top of the Ninja Foodi Steam Fryer. Move the Lid Slider to the "Air Fry/Stovetop". Select the "Air Fry" mode for cooking. Air Fry at 180°C for around 12 minutes. 5. Allow the fillets to cool off for a bit then serve, garnished with the lime wedges and enjoy.
Per serving: Calories 786; Fat: 24.2g; Sodium 252mg; Carbs: 31.6g; Fiber: 3.9g; Sugars 22.8g; Protein 106.9g

Parmesan Cod

Prep Time: 5 minutes | Cook Time: 15 minutes | Serves: 4

4 cod fillets, boneless	taste	4 tablespoons balsamic vinegar	3 spring onions, chopped
Salt and black pepper to the	100g parmesan	A drizzle of olive oil	

1. Place the Cook & Crisp Basket in your Pressure Cooker Steam Fryer. 2. Season fish with salt, pepper, grease with the oil, and coat it in parmesan. Put the fillets in the Cook & Crisp Basket. 3. Put on the Smart Lid on top of the Ninja Foodi Steam Fryer. Move the Lid Slider to the "Air Fry/Stovetop". Select the "Air Fry" mode for cooking. Air Fry at 185°C for around 14 minutes. 4. Meanwhile, in a suitable bowl, mix the spring onions with salt, pepper and the vinegar and whisk. 5. Divide the cod between plates, drizzle the spring onions mix all over and serve with a side salad.
Per serving: Calories 636; Fat: 25g; Sodium 259mg; Carbs: 0.9g; Fiber: 0.5g; Sugars 0g; Protein 95.6g

Regular Pad Thai

Prep time: 8 minutes | Cook time: 25 minutes | Serves: 4

455g chicken breast, cut into 5 cm strips	thinly sliced	240ml chicken stock	65g light brown sugar
8 large prawns deveined, peeled and tailed	1 medium carrot, shaved into ribbons	75g unsalted roasted peanuts, crushed, for garnish	2 tablespoons fish sauce
200g. Thai Rice Noodles	185g bean sprouts	1 lime cut into wedges, for garnish	1 tablespoon fresh lime juice
60ml rapeseed oil	1½ teaspoons fresh garlic, chopped	**Pad Thai Sauce:**	1 tablespoon tomato paste
3 spring onions, topped and	2 eggs	3 tablespoons tamarind paste	1 teaspoon ground chili paste, like Sambal Oelek

1. Soak noodles in hot water for 1-2 minutes and drain; noodles should bend slightly. Add pad thai sauce ingredients to a glass mixing bowl and whisk until well-blended. Move the slider towards "AIR FRY/STOVETOP" and set Ninja Foodi XL Pressure Cooker Steam Fryer with SmartLid to SEAR/SAUTÉ mode. Adjust the temperature to "Hi5" by using up arrow. 2. Press START/STOP to begin cooking. Add olive oil, garlic, carrots, bean sprouts, and spring onions to cooking pot. Sauté for 1 minute. Add chicken and sauté for 1 minute. Push ingredients to one side of the cooking pot and crack eggs into the empty spot and scramble until almost firm. Fold into other ingredients. Add stock. Fold in Pad Thai sauce and stir until well-combined. Gently fold noodles into the sauce. 3. Lock lid; move slider to AIR FRY/STOVETOP. Select STEAM, and set time to 10 minutes. Press START/STOP to begin cooking. Open the lid and lay prawns on top of the Pad Thai. Place on Keep Warm for 5 minutes. 4. Plate Pad Thai and serve garnished with peanuts and a lime wedge.
Per Serving: Calories 181; Fat 8.8g; Sodium 230mg; Carbs 17g; Fiber 3.5g; Sugar 4.1g; Protein 11.1g

Mussels in White Wine

Prep time: 10 minutes | Cook time: 8 minutes | Serves: 4

2 tablespoons ghee	120ml dry white wine	1 teaspoon sea salt	4 tablespoons chopped fresh parsley
1 medium onion, peeled and diced	1 (360g) can diced tomatoes, including juice	Juice of 1 lemon	
3 cloves garlic, minced	1 teaspoon cayenne pepper	900g fresh mussels, cleaned and debearded	

1. Move the slider towards "AIR FRY/STOVETOP" and set Ninja Foodi XL Pressure Cooker Steam Fryer with SmartLid to SEAR/SAUTÉ mode. Adjust the temperature to "Hi5" by using up arrow. Press START/STOP to begin cooking. Add the ghee and melt. Add onion and sauté for 3–5 minutes until translucent. Add garlic and cook for an additional minute. Stir in white wine and let cook 2 minutes. Add tomatoes, cayenne pepper, salt, and lemon juice. 2. Insert Cook & Crisp Basket. Place mussels on top. 3. Lock lid; move slider towards PRESSURE. Adjust pressure release valve in the SEAL position. Close pressure-release valve. The cooking temperature will default to HIGH, which is accurate. Set time to 0 minutes. Select START/STOP and start cooking. When cooking is complete, let pressure release quickly by turning it into VENT position. 4. Remove mussels and discard any that haven't opened. Transfer mussels to four bowls and pour liquid from Pot equally among bowls. Garnish each bowl with 1 tablespoon parsley. Serve immediately.
Per Serving: Calories 251; Fat 10g; Sodium 233mg; Carbs 4g; Fiber 3g; Sugar 1g; Protein 8g

Bacon Wrapped Scallops

Prep Time: 15 minutes | Cook Time: 7 minutes | Serves: 4

1 teaspoon coriander	¼ teaspoon salt	100g bacon, sliced	
½ teaspoon paprika	400g scallops	1 teaspoon sesame oil	

1. Place the Cook & Crisp Basket in your Pressure Cooker Steam Fryer. 2. Sprinkle the scallops with coriander, paprika, and salt. Then wrap the scallops in the bacon slices and secure with toothpicks. Sprinkle the scallops with sesame oil. Put the scallops in the "cook & crisp basket". 3. Put on the Smart Lid on top of the Ninja Foodi Steam Fryer. Move the Lid Slider to the "Air Fry/Stovetop". Select the "Air Fry" mode for cooking. 3. Adjust the cooking temperature to 200°C. 4. Cook for them for around 7 minutes.
Per serving: Calories 278; Fat: 15.4g; Sodium 321mg; Carbs: 1.3g; Fiber: 0.5g; Sugars 0.1g; Protein 32.1g

Cod with Spring Onions

Prep Time: 5 minutes | Cook Time: 15 minutes | Serves: 2

2 cod fillets, boneless	taste	3 tablespoons ghee, melted	
Salt and black pepper to the	1 bunch spring onions, chopped		

1. In the Cook & Crisp Basket, mix all the recipe ingredients, toss gently. 2. Place the Cook & Crisp Basket in your Pressure Cooker Steam Fryer. Put on the Smart Lid on top of the Ninja Foodi Steam Fryer. 3. Move the Lid Slider to the "Air Fry/Stovetop". Select the "Air Fry" mode for cooking. Air Fry at 180°C for around 15 minutes. 4. Divide the fish and sauce between plates and serve.
Per serving: Calories 443; Fat: 16.3g; Sodium 305mg; Carbs: 37.4g; Fiber: 7.8g; Sugars 11.4g; Protein 38.5g

Salmon with Chives Sauce

Prep Time: 5 minutes | Cook Time: 20 minutes | Serves: 4

4 salmon fillets, boneless	120g heavy cream	1 teaspoon dill, chopped
A pinch of salt and black pepper	1 tablespoon chives, chopped	2 garlic cloves, minced
	1 teaspoon lemon juice	50g ghee, melted

1. In a suitable bowl, mix all the recipe ingredients except the salmon and mix well. Arrange the salmon in the Cook & Crisp Basket, drizzle the sauce all over. 2. Place the Cook & Crisp Basket in your Pressure Cooker Steam Fryer. 3. Put on the Smart Lid on top of the Ninja Foodi Steam Fryer. Move the Lid Slider to the "Air Fry/Stovetop". Select the "Air Fry" mode for cooking. Air Fry at 180°C for around 20 minutes. 4. Divide everything between plates and serve.
Per serving: Calories 423; Fat: 18.4g; Sodium 137mg; Carbs: 4.6g; Fiber: 1.9g; Sugars 0.8g; Protein 56.2g

Country Boil

Prep time: 10 minutes | Cook time: 5 minutes | Serves: 6

1 large sweet onion, peeled and chopped	sixths	455g frozen tail-on prawns	1 lemon, cut into 6 wedges
4 cloves garlic, quartered	3 ears corn, cut in thirds	1 tablespoon Old Bay Seasoning	15g chopped fresh parsley
6 small red potatoes, cut in	675g fully cooked andouille sausage, cut in 2.5 cm sections	480ml chicken stock	

1. Layer onions in an even layer in the Ninja Foodi XL Pressure Cooker Steam Fryer with SmartLid cooking pot. Scatter the garlic on top of onions. Add red potatoes in an even layer, then do the same for the corn and sausage. Add the prawns and sprinkle with Old Bay Seasoning. Pour in stock. 2. Squeeze lemon wedges into the Ninja Foodi XL Pressure Cooker Steam Fryer with SmartLid cooking pot and place squeezed lemon wedges into the pot. 3. Lock lid; move slider towards PRESSURE. Adjust pressure release valve in the SEAL position. Close pressure-release valve. The cooking temperature will default to HIGH, which is accurate. Set time to 5 minutes. Select START/STOP and start cooking. 4. When cooking is complete, let pressure release quickly by turning it into VENT position. Transfer ingredients to a serving platter and garnish with parsley.
Per Serving: Calories 440; Fat 17g; Sodium 590mg; Carbs 44g; Fiber 6g; Sugar 3g; Protein 27g

Mediterranean Spicy Cod

Prep time: 5 minutes | Cook time: 6 minutes | Serves: 2

2 (125g) cod fillets, divided	10 pitted kalamata olives, divided	divided
2 teaspoons olive oil, divided	1 small Roma tomato, diced,	3 tablespoons chopped fresh basil leaves, divided
1½ teaspoons sea salt, divided		

1. Place a piece of cod on a 25 cm × 25 cm square of aluminum foil. Drizzle with 1 teaspoon olive oil. Sprinkle with ½ teaspoon salt. Scatter 5 olives, ½ the tomatoes, and 1 tablespoon basil on top of fish. Bring up the sides of the foil and crimp at the top to create a foil pocket. 2. Repeat with remaining piece of fish. Place both fish packs in the Ninja Foodi XL Pressure Cooker Steam Fryer with SmartLid cooking pot. 3. Lock lid; move slider towards PRESSURE. Adjust pressure release valve in the SEAL position. Close pressure-release valve. The cooking temperature will default to HIGH, which is accurate. Set time to 6 minutes. Select START/STOP and start cooking. When cooking is complete, let pressure release quickly by turning it into VENT position. 4. Remove foil packets and transfer fish and toppings to two plates. Garnish each plate with ½ tablespoon basil and ¼ teaspoon salt.
Per Serving: Calories 340; Fat 18.5g; Sodium 396mg; Carbs 8g; Fiber 4g; Sugar 2g; Protein 35g

Lemon Salmon with Dill

Prep time: 5 minutes | Cook time: 5 minutes | Serves: 2

2 (125g) salmon fillets	4 lemon slices	240ml water
½ teaspoon sea salt	2 teaspoons chopped fresh dill	

1. Pat fillets dry with a paper towel and place on a Cook & Crisp Basket. Season salmon with salt. Place 2 lemon slices on each fillet. Sprinkle with chopped dill. 2. Place water in Ninja Foodi XL Pressure Cooker Steam Fryer with SmartLid cooking pot. Insert Deluxe reversible rack. Place Cook & Crisp Basket onto Deluxe reversible rack. 3. Lock lid; move slider towards PRESSURE. Adjust pressure release valve in the SEAL position. Close pressure-release valve. The cooking temperature will default to HIGH, which is accurate. Set time to 5 minutes. Select START/STOP and start cooking. When cooking is complete, let pressure release quickly by turning it into VENT position. 4. Remove fish to plates and serve immediately.
Per Serving: Calories 282; Fat 13g; Sodium 359mg; Carbs 6g; Fiber 2.5g; Sugar 1g; Protein 36g

Delicious Lobster Risotto

Prep time: 5 minutes | Cook time: 20 minutes | Serves: 4

4 tablespoons butter	300g Arborio rice	3 tablespoons grated Parmesan cheese	pepper
1 small onion, peeled and finely diced	240ml chardonnay	½ teaspoon salt	Meat from 3 small lobster tails, diced
2 cloves garlic, minced	720ml vegetable stock	¼ teaspoon ground black	10g chopped fresh parsley
	½ teaspoon lemon zest		

1. Move the slider towards "AIR FRY/STOVETOP" and set Ninja Foodi XL Pressure Cooker Steam Fryer with SmartLid to SEAR/SAUTÉ mode. Adjust the temperature to "Hi5" by using up arrow. Press START/STOP to begin cooking and add the butter. Heat until melted. Add onion and stir-fry for 3–5 minutes until translucent. Add garlic and rice and cook for an additional minute. Add white wine and slowly stir unlidded for 5 minutes until liquid is absorbed by the rice. 2. Add stock, lemon zest, Parmesan, salt, and pepper. 3. Lock lid; move slider to AIR FRY/STOVETOP. Select STEAM, and set time to 10 minutes. Press START/STOP to begin cooking. Carefully unlock lid. 4. Stir in lobster, garnish with fresh parsley, and serve warm.

Per Serving: Calories 461; Fat 21.5g; Sodium 652mg; Carbs 41g; Fiber 3.5g; Sugar 5g; Protein 26g

Mahi-Mahi with a Lemon-Caper Sauce

Prep time: 5 minutes | Cook time: 7 minutes | Serves: 2

2 (150g, 2.5 cm thick) mahi-mahi fillets	2 tablespoons capers	2 tablespoons butter, cut into 2 pats	parsley
2 tablespoons fresh lemon juice	1 teaspoon sea salt	1 tablespoon chopped fresh	
	1 teaspoon lemon zest		

1. Place a piece of foil on the Ninja Foodi XL Pressure Cooker Steam Fryer Cook & Crisp Basket. Set both fillets on the foil. Create a "boat" with the foil by bringing up the edges. Pour lemon juice on fish. Add capers. Season fish with salt and zest. Add a pat of butter to each fillet. Set Deluxe reversible rack in the Ninja Foodi XL Pressure Cooker Steam Fryer and place the Cook & Crisp Basket on the rack. 2. Lock lid; move slider towards PRESSURE. Adjust pressure release valve in the SEAL position. Close pressure-release valve. The cooking temperature will default to HIGH, which is accurate. Set time to 7 minutes. Select START/STOP and start cooking. When cooking is complete, let pressure release quickly by turning it into VENT position. 3. Transfer fish to two plates. Garnish each with ½ tablespoon chopped parsley.

Per Serving: Calories 436; Fat 26.5g; Sodium 616mg; Carbs 24g; Fiber 4g; Sugar 5g; Protein 28g

Steamed Prawns with Asparagus

Prep time: 5 minutes | Cook time: 1 minutes | Serves: 2

240ml water	1 teaspoon sea salt, divided	deveined	2 tablespoons butter, cut into 2 pats
1 bunch asparagus	455g prawns, peeled and	½ lemon	

1. Pour water into Ninja Foodi XL Pressure Cooker Steam Fryer with SmartLid cooking pot. Insert Deluxe reversible rack. Place Cook & Crisp Basket on rack. 2. Prepare asparagus by finding the natural snap point on the stalks and discarding the woody ends. 3. Spread the asparagus on the bottom of the Cook & Crisp Basket. Sprinkle with ½ teaspoon salt. Add the prawns. Squeeze lemon into it, then sprinkle prawns with remaining ½ teaspoon salt. Place pats of butter on prawns. 4. Lock lid; move slider towards PRESSURE. Adjust pressure release valve in the SEAL position. Close pressure-release valve. The cooking temperature will default to HIGH, which is accurate. Set time to 1 minutes. Select START/STOP and start cooking. When cooking is complete, let pressure release quickly by turning it into VENT position. 5. Transfer prawns and asparagus to a platter and serve.

Per Serving: Calories 45; Fat 3g; Sodium 100mg; Carbs 0.9g; Fiber 0g; Sugar 0g; Protein 3.5g

Steaming Clams

Prep time: 5 minutes | Cook time: 10 minutes | Serves: 4

900g fresh clams, rinsed and purged	1 tablespoon olive oil	diced	120ml chardonnay
	1 small white onion, peeled and	1 clove garlic, quartered	120ml water

1. Place clams in the Cook & Crisp Basket. Set aside. 2. Move the slider towards "AIR FRY/STOVETOP" and set Ninja Foodi XL Pressure Cooker Steam Fryer with SmartLid to SEAR/SAUTÉ mode. Adjust the temperature to "Hi5" by using up arrow. Press START/STOP to begin cooking. Heat olive oil. Add onion and sauté 3–5 minutes until translucent. Add garlic and cook another minute. Pour in white wine and water. Insert Cook & Crisp Basket. 3. Lock lid; move slider towards PRESSURE. Adjust pressure release valve in the SEAL position. Close pressure-release valve. The cooking temperature will default to HIGH, which is accurate. Set time to 4 minutes. Select START/STOP and start cooking. When cooking is complete, let pressure release quickly by turning it into VENT position. 4. Transfer clams to four serving bowls and top with a generous scoop of cooking liquid.

Per Serving: Calories 338; Fat 5.6g; Sodium 239mg; Carbs 5.5g; Fiber 0.6g; Sugar 0.6g; Protein 62.2g

Creamy Crab

Prep time: 5 minutes | Cook time: 8 minutes | Serves: 4

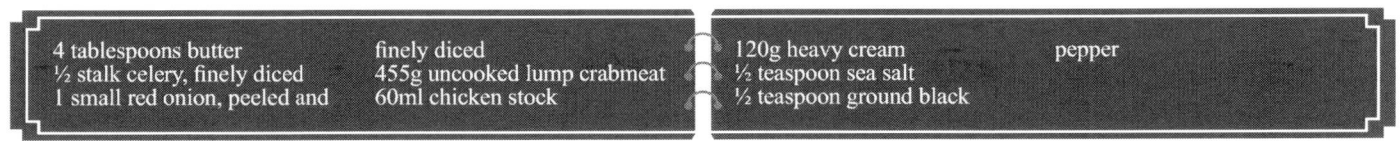

- 4 tablespoons butter
- ½ stalk celery, finely diced
- 1 small red onion, peeled and finely diced
- 455g uncooked lump crabmeat
- 60ml chicken stock
- 120g heavy cream
- ½ teaspoon sea salt
- ½ teaspoon ground black pepper

1. Move the slider towards "AIR FRY/STOVETOP" and set Ninja Foodi XL Pressure Cooker Steam Fryer with SmartLid to SEAR/SAUTÉ mode. Adjust the temperature to "Hi5" by using up arrow. Press START/STOP to begin cooking. Add the butter and melt. Add the celery and red onion. Stir-fry for 3–5 minutes until celery begins to soften. Stir in the crabmeat and stock. 2. Lock lid; move slider towards PRESSURE. Adjust pressure release valve in the SEAL position. Close pressure-release valve. The cooking temperature will default to HIGH, which is accurate. Set time to 3 minutes. Select START/STOP and start cooking. When cooking is complete, let pressure release quickly by turning it into VENT position. 3. Carefully stir in the cream, add salt and pepper, and serve warm.
Per Serving: Calories 273; Fat 9.9g; Sodium 258mg; Carbs 3.4g; Fiber 1.6g; Sugar 0.3g; Protein 39.8g

Cod with Olives and Fennel

Prep time: 15 minutes | Cook time: 25 minutes | Serves: 2

- 2 tablespoons olive oil
- ½ white onion
- 1 head garlic
- 240ml chicken stock
- 60ml olive brine
- 80g canned tomato purée
- Salt and pepper, to taste
- 35g green olives
- 1 head fennel
- One 300 g Alaskan cod fillet
- ¼ bunch basil

1. Cut the garlic head in half and cut cod fillet into 15 cm squares. Pit the olives and crush them, then cut the fennel into quarters. 2. Move the slider towards "AIR FRY/STOVETOP" and Set Ninja Foodi XL Pressure Cooker Steam Fryer with SmartLid to SEAR/SAUTÉ mode. Adjust the temperature to "Hi5" by using up arrow. 3. Press START/STOP to begin cooking and add the oil. Place the garlic and onion cut side down in the oil and sauté for a few minutes. When the garlic and onion start to brown flip them over and add the stock, olive brine and tomato purée to pot and turn it off. Add the olives and fennel to the pot and season with salt and pepper. 4. Lock lid; move slider towards PRESSURE. Adjust pressure release valve in the SEAL position. Close pressure-release valve. The cooking temperature will default to HIGH, which is accurate. Cook on LOW pressure for 10 minutes. Select START/STOP and start cooking. 5. When cooking is complete, let pressure release naturally. Season the cod with salt and pepper and put it in the pot. Seal the pot and cook the cod on Low pressure for 4 minutes. 6. Remove the fish and transfer it to serving bowls. Tear the basil leaves into the pot. Top the fish with the vegetables then spoon the basil stock over the fish to serve.
Per Serving: Calories 215; Fat 10.4g; Sodium 214mg; Carbs 23.1g; Fiber 1.8g; Sugar 2.8g; Protein 7.6g

Fish Chowder

Prep time: 10 minutes | Cook time: 5 minutes | Serves: 4

- 85g chopped bacon
- 1 shallot
- 2 ribs celery
- 1 carrot
- 2 cloves garlic
- 3 Yukon gold potatoes
- 960ml vegetable stock
- 2 tablespoons butter
- 455g frozen wild caught haddock fillets
- 170g frozen corn
- White pepper, to taste
- 480g heavy cream
- 1 tablespoon potato starch

1. Chop the vegetables and bacon and mince the garlic. Peel and cube the potatoes into small cubes. Move the slider towards "AIR FRY/STOVETOP" and set Ninja Foodi XL Pressure Cooker Steam Fryer with SmartLid to SEAR/SAUTÉ mode. Adjust the temperature to "Hi5" by using up arrow. 2. Press START/STOP to begin cooking and melt the butter. Add the bacon and cook until browned. Add the veggies and continue to cook until the vegetables begin to soften. Add the fish, corn, and stock to the pot and seal the pot. 3. Lock lid; move slider towards PRESSURE. Adjust pressure release valve in the SEAL position. Close pressure-release valve. The cooking temperature will default to HIGH, which is accurate. Set time to 5 minutes. Select START/STOP and start cooking. 4. When cooking is complete, let pressure release naturally. Mix the starch and cream in a small bowl then stir it into the pot. 5. Allow the mixture to thicken for a few minutes before serving.
Per Serving: Calories 133; Fat 7g; Sodium 236mg; Carbs 8.1g; Fiber 1.4g; Sugar 0.5g; Protein 10.5g

Steamed Crab

Prep time: 5 minutes | Cook time: 3 minutes | Serves: 2

- 240ml water
- 4 cloves garlic, quartered
- 1 small onion, peeled and diced large
- 1 tablespoon Old Bay Seasoning
- 2 sprigs fresh thyme
- 900g crab legs

1. Add water, garlic, onion, Old Bay Seasoning, and thyme to the Ninja Foodi XL Pressure Cooker Steam Fryer; stir to combine. 2. Insert Deluxe reversible rack. Add crab legs. 3. Lock lid; move slider to AIR FRY/STOVETOP. Select STEAM, and set time to 3 minutes. Press START/STOP to begin cooking. When cooking is complete, let pressure release quickly by turning it into VENT position. Carefully unlock lid. 4. Transfer crab legs to a serving platter.
Per Serving: Calories 251; Fat 14g; Sodium 411mg; Carbs 6g; Fiber 5g; Sugar 1g; Protein 12g

Curried Coconut Prawns

Prep time: 10 minutes | Cook time: 10 minutes | Serves: 4

455g prawns, shelled, deveined	½ teaspoon turmeric	1 teaspoon garam masala	
1 tablespoon ginger	1 teaspoon salt	120ml unsweetened coconut milk	
1 tablespoon garlic	½ teaspoon cayenne pepper		

1. Mince the ginger and garlic. Mix all the ingredients in a casserole dish. Put the Cook & Crisp Basket in the Ninja Foodi XL Pressure Cooker Steam Fryer with SmartLid cooking pot. 2. Pour 480ml of water in the pot and put the dish on the Cook & Crisp Basket. Cover the dish with foil and seal the pot. 3. Lock lid; move slider to AIR FRY/STOVETOP. Select STEAM, and set time to 4 minutes. 4. Serve with extra coconut milk if desired, poured over rice.
Per Serving: Calories 367; Fat 10.3g; Sodium 222mg; Carbs 3.5g; Fiber 1.6g; Sugar 2.3g; Protein 62.1g

Fish Stew

Prep time: 5 minutes | Cook time: 15 minutes | Serves: 4

4 tablespoons olive oil	200ml bottle clam juice	taste	2 tablespoons chopped fresh dill
1 red onion	480ml water	900g boneless, skinless sea bass fillets	
4 cloves garlic	455g diced tomatoes	2 tablespoons fresh lemon juice	
120ml dry white wine	Salt, pepper, and red pepper to		

1. Cut the bass into 5 cm pieces. Mince the garlic and thinly slice the onion. Move the slider towards "AIR FRY/STOVETOP" and set Ninja Foodi XL Pressure Cooker Steam Fryer with SmartLid to SEAR/SAUTÉ mode. Adjust the temperature to "Hi5" by using up arrow. 2. Press START/STOP to begin cooking and add 2 tablespoons of oil. Add the onions and cook until they begin to soften. Add the garlic and continue to sauté for another minute. Add the wine and scrape up any brown bits from the bottom of the pot. Mix in the clam juice, tomatoes, salt, and peppers. 3. Lock lid; move slider towards PRESSURE. Adjust pressure release valve in the SEAL position. Close pressure-release valve. The cooking temperature will default to HIGH, which is accurate. Set time to 5 minutes. Select START/STOP and start cooking. 4. When cooking is complete, let pressure release naturally. Add the fish and continue to cook on SEAR/SAUTÉ mode for about 5 minutes or until the fish is cooked. 5. Mix in the remaining oil, lemon juice, and dill before serving.
Per Serving: Calories 95; Fat 7g; Sodium 210mg; Carbs 8.4g; Fiber 3.6g; Sugar 4.7g; Protein 1.5g

Lobster with Butter Sauce

Prep time: 5 minutes | Cook time: 5 minutes | Serves: 4

1 tablespoon old bay seasoning	230g butter	½ teaspoon salt	2 teaspoons lemon juice
4 lobster tails	1 clove garlic	½ teaspoon pepper	1 teaspoon dill weed

1. Mince the garlic. Put 240ml water in the pot and mix in the old bay seasoning. Put the lobster in the Cook & Crisp Basket and put the basket in the pot. 2. Lock lid; move slider towards PRESSURE. Adjust pressure release valve in the SEAL position. Close pressure-release valve. The cooking temperature will default to HIGH, which is accurate. Set time to 4 minutes. Select START/STOP and start cooking. 3. When cooking is complete, let pressure release naturally. While the lobster cooks, heat 1 tablespoon of butter in a saucepan over medium heat until the butter starts to brown. Add the remaining butter and garlic and cook for another minute. 4. Mix in the remaining ingredients and transfer the melted butter to a bowl for serving. Serve the lobster with butter sauce.
Per Serving: Calories 210; Fat 19.2g; Sodium 410mg; Carbs 6.2g; Fiber 3.5g; Sugar 1.5g; Protein 6.7g

Prawns Scampi with Cheese

Prep time: 5 minutes | Cook time: 10 minutes | Serves: 6

2 tablespoons butter	½ teaspoon red pepper flakes	120ml milk	
455g prawns	½ teaspoon paprika	50g parmesan cheese	
4 cloves garlic	240ml chicken stock	Pepper, to taste	

1. Mince the garlic. Move the slider towards "AIR FRY/STOVETOP" and set Ninja Foodi XL Pressure Cooker Steam Fryer with SmartLid to SEAR/SAUTÉ mode. Adjust the temperature to "Hi5" by using up arrow. Press START/STOP to begin cooking and add the butter. Add the garlic and red pepper and sauté for 2 minutes. Add the paprika, prawns, stock, and pepper. 2. Lock lid; move slider towards PRESSURE. Adjust pressure release valve in the SEAL position. Close pressure-release valve. The cooking temperature will default to HIGH, which is accurate. Set and time to 2 minutes. Select START/STOP and start cooking. 3. When cooking is complete, let pressure release naturally. Select the SEAR/SAUTÉ mode again then stir in the half and half and parmesan until the parmesan is completely melted. 4. Serve over linguini.
Per Serving: Calories 216; Fat 7.9g; Sodium 147mg; Carbs 6.3g; Fiber 0.6g; Sugar 0.6g; Protein 0.2g

Prawns with tangy Risotto

Prep time: 10 minutes | Cook time: 30 minutes | Serves: 6

- 1 tablespoon olive oil
- 5 teaspoons butter
- 160g onion, chopped fine
- 75g red pepper
- 1 tablespoon lemon zest
- 200g Arborio rice
- 60ml white wine, like Sauvignon Blanc
- 720ml chicken stock
- 24 medium prawns, deveined, peeled and tailed
- 2 lemons, one juiced, one cut into wedges
- 50g parmesan cheese, grated
- ⅛ teaspoon coarse black pepper
- 1 tablespoon fresh parsley, chopped
- Olive oil, for drizzling

1. Move the slider towards "AIR FRY/STOVETOP" and set Ninja Foodi XL Pressure Cooker Steam Fryer with SmartLid to SEAR/SAUTÉ mode. Adjust the temperature to "Hi5" by using up arrow. Press START/STOP to begin cooking. 2. When the bottom of the cooking pot gets hot, add olive oil and butter. Add onion and red pepper when butter is melted and sauté for about 3 minutes or until softened. Stir in lemon zest. Fold in rice until completely coated. Sauté for about 5 minutes or until mostly translucent. Stir in wine and cook for 3 to 4 minutes or until evaporated. Stir in stock. 3. Lock lid; move slider to AIR FRY/STOVETOP. Select STEAM, and set time to 20 minutes. Press START/STOP to begin cooking. Open the lid and stir the risotto. Fold in prawns and lemon juice. Set STEAM for 5 minutes. Prawns should be pink and opaque; if risotto is too 'al dente' cook for an additional 5 minutes. Fold in parmesan and black pepper. 4. Serve garnished with parsley, lemon wedges, and an olive oil drizzle on top.

Per Serving: Calories 169; Fat 11.1g; Sodium 347mg; Carbs 1.7g; Fiber 0.6g; Sugar 1.1g; Protein 13.6g

Tilapia with Tomatoes

Prep time: 5 minutes | Cook time: 5 minutes | Serves: 4

- 4 tilapia fillets
- Salt and pepper
- 3 roma tomatoes
- 2 cloves garlic
- 10g basil
- 2 tablespoons olive oil
- Salt and pepper, to taste
- Balsamic vinegar
- Mince the garlic and chop the basil.

1. Season the fish with salt and pepper and place in a Cook & Crisp Basket Deluxe Reversible Rack. Place the basket in the pot with 120ml water. 2. Lock lid; move slider towards PRESSURE. Adjust pressure release valve in the SEAL position. Close pressure-release valve. The cooking temperature will default to HIGH, which is accurate. Set time to 4 minutes. Select START/STOP and start cooking. 3. When cooking is complete, let pressure release naturally. Dice the tomatoes, toss them in a bowl with garlic, basil, olive oil, salt, pepper, and vinegar. Transfer the fish to a serving plate. 4. Top with the tomato mixture and serve.

Per Serving: Calories 145; Fat 13.7g; Sodium 411mg; Carbs 6g; Fiber 1.7g; Sugar 3.5g; Protein 1.3g

Delicious Seafood Gumbo

Prep time: 10 minutes | Cook time: 10 minutes | Serves: 8

- 2100g sea bass fillets
- 3 tablespoons olive oil
- 3 tablespoons Cajun seasoning
- 2 yellow onions
- 2 peppers
- 4 celery ribs
- 720g tomatoes, chopped
- 65g tomato paste
- 3 bay leaves
- 480ml bone stock
- 900g medium raw prawns, deveined

1. Pat the fish dry and cut into 5 cm cubes. Chop the onions, peppers, and celery. Season the fish with salt, pepper, and half of the Cajun seasoning. 2. Move the slider towards "AIR FRY/STOVETOP" and set Ninja Foodi XL Pressure Cooker Steam Fryer with SmartLid to SEAR/SAUTÉ mode. Adjust the temperature to "Hi5" by using up arrow. 3. Press START/STOP to begin cooking and add the oil. Add the fish and cook for about 4 minutes, flipping a few times to make sure it's evenly cooked. 4. Remove the fish with a slotted spoon and set aside. Add the pepper, onions, celery, and remaining Cajun seasoning and Sauté for another few minutes. Return the fish to the pot and add the tomatoes, paste, stock, and bay leaves. 5. Lock lid; move slider towards PRESSURE. Adjust pressure release valve in the SEAL position. Close pressure-release valve. The cooking temperature will default to HIGH, which is accurate. Set time to 5 minutes. Select START/STOP and start cooking. 6. When cooking is complete, let pressure release naturally. Set Ninja Foodi XL Pressure Cooker Steam Fryer with SmartLid to SEAR/SAUTÉ mode again. 7. Add the prawns and cook for 4 minutes. Season with more salt and pepper to taste before serving.

Per Serving: Calories 271; Fat 12g; Sodium 354mg; Carbs 6g; Fiber 4g; Sugar 2g; Protein 11g

Chapter 7 Snack and Appetizer Recipes 57

101	Bacon Sprouts Wraps	103	Pickled Bacon
101	Tacon Mexican Muffins	104	Crusted Hot Dogs
101	Mushroom Basil Bites	104	Salmon Bites
101	Bacon Chaffle	104	Cashew Dip
101	Crispy Courgette Chips	104	Aubergine Chips
102	Cheddar Cheese Rounds	104	Meatballs
102	Parsley Olives Fritters	105	Beef Smokies
102	Avocado Wraps	105	Chicken Meatballs
102	Crusted Courgette Chips	105	Coconut Granola
102	Bacon Bites	105	Avocado Balls
103	Air-Fried Pork Rinds	106	Prawn Balls
103	Sushi	106	Turmeric Chicken Bites
103	Pork Meatballs	106	Duck Wraps
103	Cheese Sticks		

Bacon Sprouts Wraps

Prep Time: 5 minutes | Cook Time: 20 minutes | Serves: 12

- 12 bacon strips
- 12 Brussels sprouts
- A drizzle of olive oil

1. Place the Cook & Crisp Basket in your Pressure Cooker Steam Fryer. 2. Wrap each Brussels sprouts in a bacon strip, brush them with some oil, put them in the Cook & Crisp Basket. 3. Put on the Smart Lid on top of the Ninja Foodi Steam Fryer. Move the Lid Slider to the "Air Fry/Stovetop". Select the "Air Fry" mode for cooking. Air Fry at 175°C for around 20 minutes. 4. Serve as an appetizer.
Per serving: Calories 330; Fat: 29.1g; Sodium 348mg; Carbs: 12.6g; Fiber: 1.6g; Sugars 0g; Protein 7.7g

Tacon Mexican Muffins

Prep Time: 10 minutes | Cook Time: 15 minutes | Serves: 4

- 140g beef
- 1 teaspoon taco seasonings
- 50g Mexican blend cheese, shredded
- 1 teaspoon tomato sauce
- Cooking spray

1. Place the Cook & Crisp Basket in your Pressure Cooker Steam Fryer. 2. Meanwhile, in the mixing bowl mix up beef and taco seasonings. Grease the muffin molds with cooking spray. 3. Then transfer the beef mixture in the muffin molds and top them with cheese and tomato sauce. Transfer the muffin molds in the Cook & Crisp Basket. 4. Put on the Smart Lid on top of the Ninja Foodi Steam Fryer. Move the Lid Slider to the "Air Fry/Stovetop". Select the "Air Fry" mode for cooking. Adjust the cooking temperature to 190°C. 5. Cook for them for around 15 minutes.
Per serving: Calories 105; Fat: 2.4g; Sodium 812mg; Carbs: 12.2g; Fiber: 2.4g; Sugars 2.4g; Protein 9.5g

Mushroom Basil Bites

Prep Time: 5 minutes | Cook Time: 12 minutes | Serves: 6

- Salt and black pepper to the taste
- 150g coconut flour
- 2 garlic clove, minced
- 2 tablespoons basil, minced
- 225g mushrooms, minced
- 1 egg, whisked
- Cooking spray

1. Place the Cook & Crisp Basket in your Pressure Cooker Steam Fryer. 2. In a suitable bowl, mix all the recipe ingredients except the cooking spray, stir well and shape medium balls out of this mix. 3. Arrange the balls in the Cook & Crisp Basket, grease them with cooking spray. Put on the Smart Lid on top of the Ninja Foodi Steam Fryer. 4. Move the Lid Slider to the "Air Fry/Stovetop". Select the "Air Fry" mode for cooking. Air Fry at 175°C for around 6 minutes on each side. 5. Serve as an appetizer.
Per serving: Calories 151; Fat: 10.4g; Sodium 703mg; Carbs: 9.2g; Fiber: 0g; Sugars 8.7g; Protein 6g

Bacon Chaffle

Prep Time: 10 minutes | Cook Time: 25 minutes | Serves: 4

- 4 eggs, beaten
- 50g bacon, chopped, cooked
- 1 cucumber, pickled, grated
- 50g Cheddar cheese, shredded
- ¼ teaspoon salt
- ½ teaspoon black pepper
- Cooking spray

1. Place the Cook & Crisp Basket in your Pressure Cooker Steam Fryer. 2. In the mixing bowl mix up eggs, bacon, pickled cucumber, cheese, salt, and black pepper. Mix the mixture gently. 3. Then grease the Cook & Crisp Basket with cooking spray. Pour ¼ part of the liquid inside. 4. Put chaffle in the "cook & crisp basket". Put on the Smart Lid on top of the Ninja Foodi Steam Fryer. Move the Lid Slider to the "Air Fry/Stovetop". Select the "Air Fry" mode for cooking. 5. Adjust the cooking temperature to 200°C. 6. Cook for it for around 6 minutes. 7. Then transfer the cooked chaffle in the plate. 8. Repeat the same steps with the remaining chaffle batter. In the end, you should get 4 chaffles.
Per serving: Calories 209; Fat: 15.8g; Sodium 3342mg; Carbs: 0.4g; Fiber: 0.2g; Sugars 0g; Protein 5.4g

Crispy Courgette Chips

Prep Time: 5 minutes | Cook Time: 15 minutes | Serves: 6

- 3 courgettes, sliced
- Salt and black pepper to the taste
- 2 eggs, whisked
- 95g almond flour

1. Place the Cook & Crisp Basket in your Pressure Cooker Steam Fryer. 2. In a suitable bowl, mix the eggs with black pepper and salt. Put the flour in a second bowl. Dredge the courgettes in flour and then in eggs. Arrange the chips in the Cook & Crisp Basket. 3. Put on the Smart Lid on top of the Ninja Foodi Steam Fryer. Move the Lid Slider to the "Air Fry/Stovetop". Select the "Air Fry" mode for cooking. 4. Air Fry at 175°C for around 15 minutes and serve as a snack.
Per serving: Calories 270; Fat: 8.4g; Sodium 1761mg; Carbs: 35.7g; Fiber: 13.3g; Sugars 4.1g; Protein 4.8g

Cheddar Cheese Rounds

Prep Time: 10 minutes | Cook Time: 6 minutes | Serves: 4

100g Cheddar cheese, shredded	

1. Place the Cook & Crisp Basket in your Pressure Cooker Steam Fryer. 2. Then line the Ninja Foodi Pressure Steam Fryer basket with baking paper. Sprinkle the cheese on the baking paper in the shape of small rounds. 3. Put on the Smart Lid on top of the Ninja Foodi Steam Fryer. 4. Move the Lid Slider to the "Air Fry/Stovetop". Select the "Air Fry" mode for cooking. 5. Adjust the cooking temperature to 200°C. 6. Cook them for around 6 minutes or until the cheese is melted and starts to be crispy.
Per serving: Calories 291; Fat: 10.8g; Sodium 2153mg; Carbs: 12.1g; Fiber: 1.6g; Sugars 5.6g; Protein 7g

Parsley Olives Fritters

Prep Time: 5 minutes | Cook Time: 12 minutes | Serves: 6

Cooking spray	45g almond flour	3 spring onions, chopped	3 courgettes, grated
20g parsley, chopped	Salt and black pepper to the taste	70g kalamata olives, pitted and minced	
1 egg			

1. Place the Cook & Crisp Basket in your Pressure Cooker Steam Fryer. 2. In a suitable bowl, mix all the recipe ingredients except the cooking spray, stir well and shape medium fritters out of this mixture. 3. Place the fritters in the Cook & Crisp Basket, grease them with cooking spray. Put on the Smart Lid on top of the Ninja Foodi Steam Fryer. 4. Move the Lid Slider to the "Air Fry/Stovetop". Select the "Air Fry" mode for cooking. Air Fry at 195°C for around 6 minutes on each side. 5. Serve them as an appetizer.
Per serving: Calories 194; Fat: 2.6g; Sodium 1257mg; Carbs: 35.4g; Fiber: 3.7g; Sugars 3.1g; Protein 9.4g

Avocado Wraps

Prep Time: 5 minutes | Cook Time: 15 minutes | Serves: 4

2 avocados, peeled, and cut into 12 wedges	12 bacon strips	1 tablespoon ghee, melted

1. Place the Cook & Crisp Basket in your Pressure Cooker Steam Fryer. 2. Wrap each avocado wedge in a bacon strip, brush them with the ghee, put them in the Cook & Crisp Basket. 3. Put on the Smart Lid on top of the Ninja Foodi Steam Fryer. Move the Lid Slider to the "Air Fry/Stovetop". Select the "Air Fry" mode for cooking. Air Fry at 180°C for around 15 minutes. 4. Serve as an appetizer.
Per serving: Calories 137; Fat: 7.1g; Sodium 167mg; Carbs: 16.2g; Fiber: 3.8g; Sugars 4.7g; Protein 3.1g

Crusted Courgette Chips

Prep Time: 10 minutes | Cook Time: 13 minutes | Serves: 8

2 courgettes, sliced	50g Parmesan	½ teaspoon white pepper
4 tablespoons almond flour	2 eggs, beaten	Cooking spray

1. Place the Cook & Crisp Basket in your Pressure Cooker Steam Fryer. 2. In a suitable bowl, mix up almond flour, Parmesan, and white pepper. Then dip the courgette slices in the egg and coat in the almond flour mixture. Place the prepared courgette slices in the Cook & Crisp Basket in one layer. 3. Put on the Smart Lid on top of the Ninja Foodi Steam Fryer. Move the Lid Slider to the "Air Fry/Stovetop". Select the "Air Fry" mode for cooking. 4. Cook them at 180°C for around 10 minutes. Then flip the vegetables on another side. Cook for them for around 3 minutes more or until crispy.
Per serving: Calories 195; Fat: 12.7g; Sodium 1131mg; Carbs: 27.7g; Fiber: 3.5g; Sugars 5.9g; Protein 2.1g

Bacon Bites

Prep Time: 5 minutes | Cook Time: 10 minutes | Serves: 4

4 bacon slices, halved	260g dark chocolate, melted	A pinch of pink salt

1. Place the Cook & Crisp Basket in your Pressure Cooker Steam Fryer. 2. Dip each bacon slice in some chocolate, sprinkle pink salt over them, put them in the Cook & Crisp Basket. 3. Put on the Smart Lid on top of the Ninja Foodi Steam Fryer. Move the Lid Slider to the "Air Fry/Stovetop". Select the "Air Fry" mode for cooking. Air Fry at 175°C for around 10 minutes. 4. Serve as a snack.
Per serving: Calories 68; Fat: 7g; Sodium 475mg; Carbs: 1.8g; Fiber: 0.3g; Sugars 0g; Protein 0.5g

Air-Fried Pork Rinds

Prep Time: 10 minutes | Cook Time: 10 minutes | Serves: 3

| 150g pork skin | 1 tablespoon keto tomato sauce | 1 teaspoon olive oil |

1. Place the Cook & Crisp Basket in your Pressure Cooker Steam Fryer. 2. Chop the pork skin into the rinds and sprinkle with the sauce and olive oil. Mix up well. Place the pork skin rinds in the Ninja Foodi Pressure Steam Fryer basket in one layer. 3. Put on the Smart Lid on top of the Ninja Foodi Steam Fryer. Move the Lid Slider to the "Air Fry/Stovetop". Select the "Air Fry" mode for cooking. Adjust the cooking temperature to 200°C. 4. Cook for around 10 minutes. Flip the rinds on another side after 5 minutes of cooking.
Per serving: Calories 342; Fat: 0g; Sodium 1mg; Carbs: 10.6g; Fiber: 2g; Sugars 7.8g; Protein 0.2g

Sushi

Prep Time: 10 minutes | Cook Time: 10 minutes | Serves: 10

| 10 bacon slices | 2 tablespoons cream cheese | 1 cucumber |

1. Place the Cook & Crisp Basket in your Pressure Cooker Steam Fryer. 2. Place the bacon slices in the Cook & Crisp Basket in one layer. Put on the Smart Lid on top of the Ninja Foodi Steam Fryer. 3. Move the Lid Slider to the "Air Fry/Stovetop". Select the "Air Fry" mode for cooking. Cook for around 10 minutes at 200°C. 4. Meanwhile, cut the cucumber into small wedges. When the bacon is cooked, cool it to the room temperature and spread with cream cheese. 5. Then place the cucumber wedges over the cream cheese and roll the bacon into the sushi.
Per serving: Calories 110; Fat: 4.3g; Sodium 81mg; Carbs: 16.4g; Fiber: 5.4g; Sugars 6.1g; Protein 3.8g

Pork Meatballs

Prep Time: 5 minutes | Cook Time: 20 minutes | Serves: 12

455g pork meat, chopped	1 chili pepper, minced	1 and ½ tablespoons coconut aminos
3 spring onions, minced	1 tablespoon ginger, grated	A pinch of salt and black pepper
3 tablespoons coriander,	2 garlic cloves, minced	Cooking spray

1. Place the Cook & Crisp Basket in your Pressure Cooker Steam Fryer. 2. In a suitable bowl, mix all the recipe ingredients except the cooking spray, stir really well and shape medium meatballs out of this mix. 3. Arrange them in the Cook & Crisp Basket, grease with cooking spray. Put on the Smart Lid on top of the Ninja Foodi Steam Fryer. 4. Move the Lid Slider to the "Air Fry/Stovetop". Select the "Air Fry" mode for cooking. Air Fry at 195°C for around 20 minutes. 5. Serve as an appetizer.
Per serving: Calories 110; Fat: 3.4g; Sodium 1446mg; Carbs: 13.9g; Fiber: 5.4g; Sugars 3.8g; Protein 8.2g

Cheese Sticks

Prep Time: 10 minutes | Cook Time: 4 minutes | Serves: 4

| 1 egg, beaten | 1 teaspoon paprika | Cooking spray |
| 4 tablespoons coconut flakes | 150g Provolone cheese | |

1. Place the Cook & Crisp Basket in your Pressure Cooker Steam Fryer. 2. Cut the cheese into sticks. Then dip every cheese stick in the beaten egg. After this, mix up coconut flakes and paprika. Coat the cheese sticks in the coconut mixture. 3. Put the cheese sticks in the Cook & Crisp Basket and grease them with cooking spray. 4. Put on the Smart Lid on top of the Ninja Foodi Steam Fryer. Move the Lid Slider to the "Air Fry/Stovetop". Select the "Air Fry" mode for cooking. 5. Adjust the cooking temperature to 200°C. Cook the meal for around 2 minutes from each side. 6. Cool them well before serving.
Per serving: Calories 285; Fat: 7.5g; Sodium 367mg; Carbs: 50.6g; Fiber: 9.6g; Sugars 18.2g; Protein 4.4g

Pickled Bacon

Prep Time: 5 minutes | Cook Time: 20 minutes | Serves: 4

| 4 dill pickle spears, sliced in half and quartered | 8 bacon slices, halved | 240g avocado mayonnaise |

1. Place the Cook & Crisp Basket in your Pressure Cooker Steam Fryer. 2. Wrap each pickle spear in a bacon slice, put them in the Cook & Crisp Basket. Put on the Smart Lid on top of the Ninja Foodi Steam Fryer. 3. Move the Lid Slider to the "Air Fry/Stovetop". Select the "Air Fry" mode for cooking. Air Fry at 200°C for around 20 minutes. 4. Divide into bowls and serve as a snack with the mayonnaise.
Per serving: Calories 98; Fat: 7.2g; Sodium 475mg; Carbs: 8.7g; Fiber: 3.9g; Sugars 1.6g; Protein 2.2g

Crusted Hot Dogs

Prep Time: 15 minutes | Cook Time: 5 minutes | Serves: 4

| 4 hot dogs | 1 egg, beaten | 40g coconut flour | ½ teaspoon turmeric |

1. Place the Cook & Crisp Basket in your Pressure Cooker Steam Fryer. 2. In the bowl mix up egg, coconut flour, and turmeric. Then dip the hot dogs in the mixture. 3. Transfer the hot dogs in the freezer and freeze them for around 5 minutes. Place the frozen hot dogs in the Ninja Foodi Pressure Steam Fryer basket. 4. Put on the Smart Lid on top of the Ninja Foodi Steam Fryer. Move the Lid Slider to the "Air Fry/Stovetop". Select the "Air Fry" mode for cooking. Adjust the cooking temperature to 200°C. 5. Cook for them for around 6 minutes or until they are light brown.
Per serving: Calories 236; Fat: 8.1g; Sodium 14mg; Carbs: 42.1g; Fiber: 6.3g; Sugars 0.8g; Protein 2.3g

Salmon Bites

Prep Time: 5 minutes | Cook Time: 10 minutes | Serves: 12

2 avocados, peeled, pitted and mashed	boneless and chopped	1 teaspoon dill, chopped
100g smoked salmon, skinless,	2 tablespoons coconut cream	A pinch of salt and black pepper
	1 teaspoon avocado oil	

1. Place the Cook & Crisp Basket in your Pressure Cooker Steam Fryer. 2. In a suitable bowl, mix all the recipe ingredients, stir well and shape medium balls out of this mix. 3. Place them in the Cook & Crisp Basket. Put on the Smart Lid on top of the Ninja Foodi Steam Fryer. Move the Lid Slider to the "Air Fry/Stovetop". Select the "Air Fry" mode for cooking. Air Fry at 175°C for around 10 minutes. 4. Serve as an appetizer.
Per serving: Calories 122; Fat: 10.1g; Sodium 143mg; Carbs: 4.9g; Fiber: 1.2g; Sugars 1.1g; Protein 3.6g

Cashew Dip

Prep Time: 5 minutes | Cook Time: 8 minutes | Serves: 6

70g cashews, soaked in water for around 4 hours and drained	chopped	A pinch of salt and black pepper
3 tablespoons coriander,	2 garlic cloves, minced	2 tablespoons coconut milk
	1 teaspoon lime juice	

1. Place the Cook & Crisp Basket in your Pressure Cooker Steam Fryer. 2. In a blender, mix all the recipe ingredients, pulse well and transfer to the Cook & Crisp Basket. 3. Put on the Smart Lid on top of the Ninja Foodi Steam Fryer. Move the Lid Slider to the "Air Fry/Stovetop". Select the "Air Fry" mode for cooking. Air Fry at 175°C for around 8 minutes. 4. Serve as a party dip.
Per serving: Calories 187; Fat: 18.3g; Sodium 596mg; Carbs: 4.9g; Fiber: 1.1g; Sugars 0g; Protein 3.1g

Aubergine Chips

Prep Time: 10 minutes | Cook Time: 25 minutes | Serves: 4

| 1 aubergine, sliced | 1 teaspoon garlic powder | 1 tablespoon olive oil |

1. Place the Cook & Crisp Basket in your Pressure Cooker Steam Fryer. 2. Mix up olive oil and garlic powder. Then brush every aubergine slice with a garlic powder mixture. Place the aubergine slices in the Ninja Foodi Pressure Steam Fryer basket in one layer. 3. Put on the Smart Lid on top of the Ninja Foodi Steam Fryer. Move the Lid Slider to the "Air Fry/Stovetop". Select the "Air Fry" mode for cooking. Cook them at 200°C for around 15 minutes. 4. Then flip the aubergine slices on another side. Cook for around 10 minutes.
Per serving: Calories 36; Fat: 1g; Sodium 1159mg; Carbs: 2.1g; Fiber: 0.6g; Sugars 1.3g; Protein 3.9g

Meatballs

Prep Time: 5 minutes | Cook Time: 20 minutes | Serves: 6

| 455g beef meat, | 1 teaspoon garlic powder | pepper | Cooking spray |
| 1 teaspoon onion powder | A pinch of salt and black | 2 tablespoons chives, chopped | |

1. Place the Cook & Crisp Basket in your Pressure Cooker Steam Fryer. 2. In a suitable bowl, mix all the recipe ingredients except the cooking spray, stir well and shape medium meatballs out of this mix. 3. Place them in the Cook & Crisp Basket, grease with cooking spray. Put on the Smart Lid on top of the Ninja Foodi Steam Fryer. 4. Move the Lid Slider to the "Air Fry/Stovetop". Select the "Air Fry" mode for cooking. Air Fry at 180°C for around 20 minutes. 5. Serve as an appetizer.
Per serving: Calories 176; Fat: 9.6g; Sodium 122mg; Carbs: 15.7g; Fiber: 4.5g; Sugars 3.8g; Protein 7.8g

Beef Smokies

Prep Time: 15 minutes | Cook Time: 10 minutes | Serves: 10

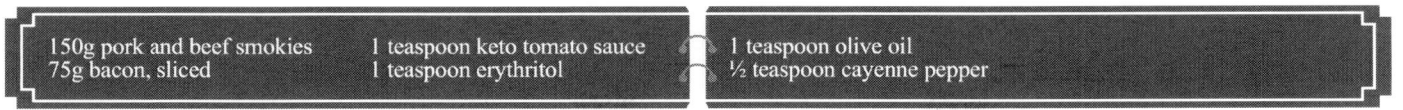

150g pork and beef smokies	1 teaspoon keto tomato sauce	1 teaspoon olive oil
75g bacon, sliced	1 teaspoon erythritol	½ teaspoon cayenne pepper

1. Place the Cook & Crisp Basket in your Pressure Cooker Steam Fryer. 2. Sprinkle the smokies with cayenne pepper and tomato sauce. Then sprinkle them with erythritol and olive oil. 3. After this, wrap every smokie in the bacon and secure it with the toothpick. Place the bacon smokies in the Cook & Crisp Basket. 4. Put on the Smart Lid on top of the Ninja Foodi Steam Fryer. Move the Lid Slider to the "Air Fry/Stovetop". Select the "Air Fry" mode for cooking. Adjust the cooking temperature to 200°C. 5. Cook for them for around 10 minutes. Shake them gently during cooking to avoid burning.
Per serving: Calories 171; Fat: 10g; Sodium 2629mg; Carbs: 18.6g; Fiber: 2.6g; Sugars 13.8g; Protein 4.3g

Chicken Meatballs

Prep Time: 5 minutes | Cook Time: 20 minutes | Serves: 12

900g chicken breast, skinless, boneless and	pepper	2 tablespoons ghee, melted	Cooking spray
A pinch of salt and black	2 garlic cloves, minced	6 tablespoons keto hot sauce	
	2 spring onions, chopped	75g almond meal	

1. Place the Cook & Crisp Basket in your Pressure Cooker Steam Fryer. 2. In a suitable bowl, mix all the recipe ingredients except the cooking spray, stir well and shape medium meatballs out of this mix. 3. Arrange the meatballs in the Cook & Crisp Basket, grease them with cooking spray. Put on the Smart Lid on top of the Ninja Foodi Steam Fryer. 4. Move the Lid Slider to the "Air Fry/Stovetop". Select the "Air Fry" mode for cooking. Air Fry at 180°C for around 20 minutes. 5. Serve as an appetizer.
Per serving: Calories 136; Fat: 14.3g; Sodium 9mg; Carbs: 3.5g; Fiber: 0g; Sugars 0g; Protein 0.3g

Coconut Granola

Prep Time: 10 minutes | Cook Time: 12 minutes | Serves: 4

1 teaspoon monk fruit	chopped	2 tablespoons pumpkin seeds, crushed	Cooking spray
1 teaspoon almond butter	1 teaspoon pumpkin puree	1 teaspoon hemp seeds	
1 teaspoon coconut oil	½ teaspoon pumpkin pie spices	1 teaspoon flax seeds	
2 tablespoons almonds,	2 tablespoons coconut flakes		

1. Place the Cook & Crisp Basket in your Pressure Cooker Steam Fryer. 2. In the big bowl mix up almond butter and coconut oil. Microwave the mixture until it is melted. 3. After this, in the separated bowl mix up monk fruit, pumpkin spices, coconut flakes, pumpkin seeds, hemp seeds, and flax seeds. Add the melted coconut oil and pumpkin puree. 4. Then stir the mixture until it is homogenous. Then put the pumpkin mixture on the baking paper and make the shape of the square. 5. After this, cut the square on the serving bars and transfer in the Cook & Crisp Basket. Put on the Smart Lid on top of the Ninja Foodi Steam Fryer. 6. Move the Lid Slider to the "Air Fry/Stovetop". Select the "Air Fry" mode for cooking. Adjust the cooking temperature to 175°C. Cook the pumpkin granola for around 12 minutes.
Per serving: Calories 194; Fat: 10.9g; Sodium 292mg; Carbs: 21.7g; Fiber: 6.4g; Sugars 9g; Protein 6.4g

Avocado Balls

Prep Time: 5 minutes | Cook Time: 5 minutes | Serves: 4

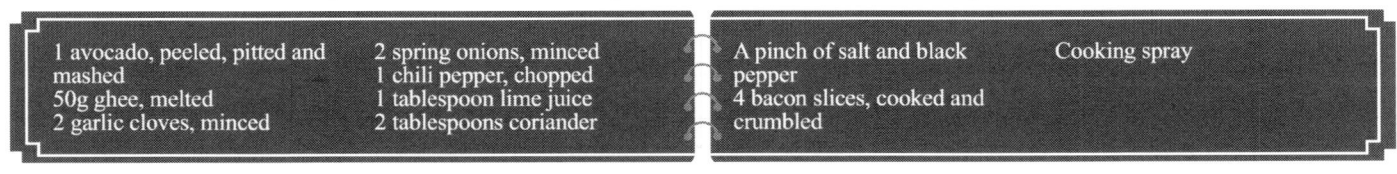

1 avocado, peeled, pitted and mashed	2 spring onions, minced	A pinch of salt and black pepper	Cooking spray
50g ghee, melted	1 chili pepper, chopped	4 bacon slices, cooked and crumbled	
2 garlic cloves, minced	1 tablespoon lime juice		
	2 tablespoons coriander		

1. Place the Cook & Crisp Basket in your Pressure Cooker Steam Fryer. 2. In a suitable bowl, mix all the recipe ingredients except the cooking spray, stir well and shape medium balls out of this mix. 3. Place them in the Cook & Crisp Basket, grease with cooking spray. 4. Put on the Smart Lid on top of the Ninja Foodi Steam Fryer. Move the Lid Slider to the "Air Fry/Stovetop". Select the "Air Fry" mode for cooking. Air Fry at 185°C for around 5 minutes. 5. Serve as a snack.
Per serving: Calories 52; Fat: 3.5g; Sodium 702mg; Carbs: 3g; Fiber: 1.4g; Sugars 0.1g; Protein 1.4g

Prawn Balls

Prep Time: 5 minutes | Cook Time: 15 minutes | Serves: 4

455g prawns, peeled, deveined and minced	3 tablespoons coconut, shredded	1 tablespoon avocado oil	
1 egg, whisked	60g coconut flour	1 tablespoon coriander, chopped	

1. Place the Cook & Crisp Basket in your Pressure Cooker Steam Fryer. 2. In a suitable bowl, mix all the recipe ingredients, stir well and shape medium balls out of this mix. Place the balls in the Cook & Crisp Basket. 3. Put on the Smart Lid on top of the Ninja Foodi Steam Fryer. 4. Move the Lid Slider to the "Air Fry/Stovetop". Select the "Air Fry" mode for cooking. 5. Air Fry at 175°C for around 15 minutes and serve as an appetizer.
Per serving: Calories 120; Fat: 2.3g; Sodium 2mg; Carbs: 24.1g; Fiber: 2.3g; Sugars 10g; Protein 3.6g

Turmeric Chicken Bites

Prep Time: 10 minutes | Cook Time: 12 minutes | Serves: 6

200g chicken fillet	½ teaspoon turmeric	½ teaspoon paprika	4 tablespoons almond flour
½ teaspoon black pepper	¼ teaspoon coriander	3 egg whites, whisked	Cooking spray

1. Place the Cook & Crisp Basket in your Pressure Cooker Steam Fryer. 2. In the shallow bowl mix up black pepper, turmeric, coriander, and paprika. Then chop the chicken fillet on the small cubes and sprinkle them with spice mixture. Stir well and add egg white. Mix up the chicken and egg whites well. 3. After this, coat every chicken cube in the almond flour. Put the chicken cubes in the Ninja Foodi Pressure Steam Fryer basket in one layer and gently spray with cooking spray. 4. Put on the Smart Lid on top of the Ninja Foodi Steam Fryer. Move the Lid Slider to the "Air Fry/Stovetop". Select the "Air Fry" mode for cooking. Adjust the cooking temperature to 190°C. 5. Cook the chicken popcorn for around 7 minutes. Then shake the chicken popcorn well. Cook for it for around 5 minutes more.
Per serving: Calories 139; Fat: 11.9g; Sodium 60mg; Carbs: 5.4g; Fiber: 3.1g; Sugars 1g; Protein 5g

Duck Wraps

Prep Time: 15 minutes | Cook Time: 6 minutes | Serves: 6

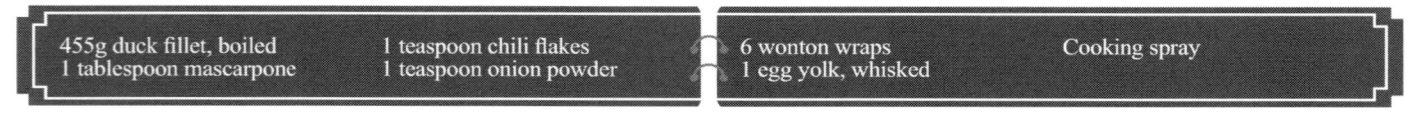

455g duck fillet, boiled	1 teaspoon chili flakes	6 wonton wraps	Cooking spray
1 tablespoon mascarpone	1 teaspoon onion powder	1 egg yolk, whisked	

1. Place the Cook & Crisp Basket in your Pressure Cooker Steam Fryer. 2. Shred the boiled duck fillet and mix it up with mascarpone, chili flakes, and onion powder. 3. After this, fill the wonton wraps with the duck mixture and roll them in the shape of pies. Brush the duck pies with the egg yolk. 4. Put the duck pies in the Cook & Crisp Basket and grease them with the cooking spray. Put on the Smart Lid on top of the Ninja Foodi Steam Fryer. 5. Move the Lid Slider to the "Air Fry/Stovetop". Select the "Air Fry" mode for cooking. Adjust the cooking temperature to 195°C. 6. Cook the snack for around 3 minutes from each side.
Per serving: Calories 72; Fat: 5g; Sodium 70mg; Carbs: 0.4g; Fiber: 0g; Sugars 0.4g; Protein 6.3g

Chapter 8 Dessert Recipes

108	Cranberry Cake		115	Raspberry Pineapple Sundaes
108	White Chocolate Cookies		115	Chocolate Cookie Cups
108	Macadamia Cookies		115	Chia Pudding Tarts
108	Chocolate Cake		115	Spiced Pumpkin Pudding
109	Pudding with Sultanas		116	Chocolate Pudding Cake
109	Soft Raisin Muffins		116	Carrot Cake
109	Pineapple with Macadamia Batter		116	Nutty Cake
109	Frosted Blackberry Shortcake		116	Lemon Cheesecake
110	Cranberry Brownies		117	Regular Chocolate Pudding
110	Almond Cookies		117	Sweet Raspberry Curd
110	Prune Cookies		117	Coconut Custard
110	Sweet Lemon Bars		117	Berries Mug Cake
111	Sweet Pecans		118	Yellow Marmalade
111	Clafoutis		118	Caramel Pear Pudding
111	Orange Cake		118	Delicious Banana Bread
111	Chocolate Egg Rolls		118	Red Cherry Compote
112	Apricots in Whiskey Sauce		119	Sweet Quiche
112	Cracker S'mores		119	Tangy Fruit Salad Jam
112	Cinnamon Pear Clafoutis		119	Nutty Chocolate Candy
112	Crispy Profiteroles		119	Poached Spiced Pears with Pomegranate
113	Blueberry Oats Crisp		120	Delicious Blueberries Yogurt
113	Peach Walnut Parfaits		120	Vegan Coconut Yogurt
113	Cinnamon Flour Twists		120	Sweet Tapioca
113	Flaxseed Carrot Cake		120	Creamy Raspberry Jam
114	Flaxseed Cookies		121	Syrupy Crème Brulee
114	Confetti Cake		121	Matcha Cake
114	Vegan Apple Pies		121	Flan
114	Cinnamon Stuffed Apples		121	Delicious Cranberry Pudding

Cranberry Cake

Prep Time: 10 minutes | Cook Time: 20 minutes | Serves: 8

- 100g almond flour
- ⅓ teaspoon baking soda
- ⅓ teaspoon baking powder
- 1 tablespoon Truvia for baking
- ½ teaspoon cloves
- 50g cranberries, fresh or thawed
- 2 eggs, 1 egg yolk, beaten
- ½ teaspoon vanilla paste
- 115g butter
- ½ teaspoon cardamom
- ⅓ teaspoon cinnamon
- 1 tablespoon browned butter

1. In a suitable bowl, mix the flour with baking soda, baking powder, Truvia, cloves, cinnamon, and cardamom. 2. In another bowl, add stick of butter, vanilla paste, mix in the eggs and mix until light and fluffy. Add the flour or sweetener mixture to butter or egg mixture and fold in cranberries and browned butter. 3. Add the mixture into the greased Cook & Crisp Basket. Place the Cook & Crisp Basket in your Pressure Cooker Steam Fryer. 4. Put on the Smart Lid on top of the Ninja Foodi Steam Fryer. Move the Lid Slider to the "Air Fry/Stovetop". Select the "Air Fry" mode for cooking. Adjust the cooking temperature to 180°C. Air Fry for around 20 minutes.
Per serving: Calories 192; Fat: 6.6g; Sodium 15mg; Carbs: 34.5g; Fiber: 4g; Sugars 27.3g; Protein 2.9g

White Chocolate Cookies

Prep Time: 10 minutes | Cook Time: 11 minutes | Serves: 10

- 2 eggs, beaten
- 200g white chocolate, chopped
- ¼ teaspoon fine sea salt
- ⅓ teaspoon nutmeg, grated
- ⅓ teaspoon allspice
- ⅓ teaspoon anise star,
- 2 tablespoons Truvia
- 40g quick-cooking oats
- 215g almond flour
- 170g butter

1. Put all the recipe ingredients, except 1 egg, into a suitable mixing bowl. Knead with hands until a soft dough is formed. Place the prepared dough into fridge for around 20 minutes. Roll the chilled dough into small balls; flatten the balls in the Cook & Crisp Basket. 2. Make and egg wash by using the remaining egg. Then, glaze the cookies with the egg wash; Place the Cook & Crisp Basket in your Pressure Cooker Steam Fryer. 3. Put on the Smart Lid on top of the Ninja Foodi Steam Fryer. 4. Move the Lid Slider to the "Air Fry/Stovetop". Select the "Air Fry" mode for cooking. 5. Adjust the cooking temperature to 175°C. Cook for around 11 minutes.
Per serving: Calories 385; Fat: 28.3g; Sodium 80mg; Carbs: 27.4g; Fiber: 0.7g; Sugars 16.7g; Protein 4.6g

Macadamia Cookies

Prep Time: 10 minutes | Cook Time: 25 minutes | Serves: 10

- 180ml coconut oil, room temperature
- 185g coconut flour
- 155g macadamia nuts, unsalted and chopped
- ½ teaspoon pure vanilla extract
- ⅓ teaspoon baking soda
- ½ teaspoon baking powder
- ⅓ teaspoon cloves,
- ¼ teaspoon nutmeg, freshly grated
- 2 tablespoons Truvia for baking
- 200g almond flour
- 3 eggs and egg yolk, whisked
- ½ teaspoon pure coconut extract
- ⅛ teaspoon fine sea salt

1. In a suitable bowl, mix both types of flour, baking soda and baking powder. In suitable bowl, beat the eggs with coconut oil. Mix the egg mixture with the flour mixture. Add other ingredients and shape into cookies. 2. Transfer them to the Cook & Crisp Basket. Place the Cook & Crisp Basket in your Pressure Cooker Steam Fryer. 3. Put on the Smart Lid on top of the Ninja Foodi Steam Fryer. Move the Lid Slider to the "Air Fry/Stovetop". Select the "Air Fry" mode for cooking. Air Fry at 185°C for around 25 minutes.
Per serving: Calories 433; Fat: 26.6g; Sodium 694mg; Carbs: 36.8g; Fiber: 2.8g; Sugars 28.4g; Protein 17.3g

Chocolate Cake

Prep Time: 10 minutes | Cook Time: 20 minutes | Serves: 4

- ⅛ teaspoon fine sea salt
- 1 tablespoon candied ginger
- ½ teaspoon cinnamon
- 2 tablespoons cocoa powder
- 75g almond flour
- 1 egg 1 egg white, whisked
- 55g unsalted butter, room temperature
- 2 tablespoons Truvia for baking
- **For Filling:**
- 150g raspberries, fresh
- 1 tablespoon Truvia
- 1 teaspoon lime juice, fresh

1. Place the Cook & Crisp Basket in your Pressure Cooker Steam Fryer. 2. Then, spritz the inside of two cakes pans with buttered-flavored cooking spray. In a suitable mixing bowl, beat Truvia and butter until creamy. 3. Then, stir in the whisked eggs. Stir in the cocoa powder, flour, cinnamon, ginger and salt. Press the prepared batter dividing it evenly into cake pans; use a wide spatula to level the surface of batter. Put the cake pan on the Cook & Crisp Basket. 4. Put on the Smart Lid on top of the Ninja Foodi Steam Fryer. Move the Lid Slider to the "Air Fry/Stovetop". Select the "Air Fry" mode for cooking. Adjust the cooking temperature to 155°C. Air Fry for around 20 minutes. 5. While your cake is baking, stir the ingredients for filling in a suitable saucepan. Cook over high heat, stirring often and mashing; bring to a boil and decrease the temperature. 6. Cook for about 7 minutes or until mixture thickens. Allow filling to cool at room temperature. 7. Spread half of raspberry filling over first cake, then top with other cake and spread the remaining raspberry filling on top.
Per serving: Calories 592; Fat: 40g; Sodium 104mg; Carbs: 65.1g; Fiber: 13.2g; Sugars 41.2g; Protein 18.6g

Pudding with Sultanas

Prep Time: 10 minutes | Cook Time: 25 minutes | Serves: 8

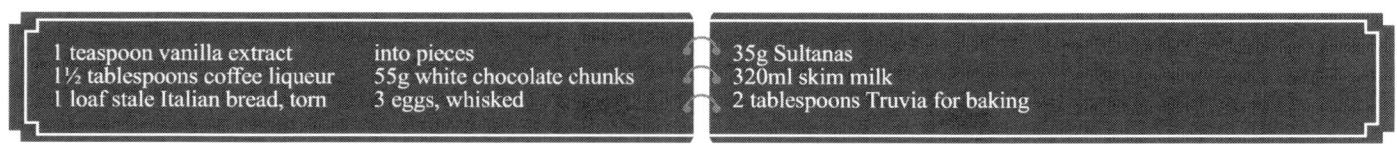

1 teaspoon vanilla extract	into pieces	35g Sultanas	
1½ tablespoons coffee liqueur	55g white chocolate chunks	320ml skim milk	
1 loaf stale Italian bread, torn	3 eggs, whisked	2 tablespoons Truvia for baking	

1. Place the Cook & Crisp Basket in your Pressure Cooker Steam Fryer. 2. Prepare two mixing bowls. Dump bread pieces into first bowl. In the second bowl, mix the remaining ingredients, except the white chocolate and Sultanas; mix until smooth. 3. Pour the egg or milk mixture over the bread pieces. Allow to soak for around 20 minutes; using a suitable spatula gently press down. 4. Now, scatter chocolate chunks and Sultanas over the top. Divide the bread pudding between two mini loaf pans. Transfer them to the Cook & Crisp Basket. 5. Put on the Smart Lid on top of the Ninja Foodi Steam Fryer. Move the Lid Slider to the "Air Fry/Stovetop". Select the "Air Fry" mode for cooking. Air Fry for around 25 minutes at 160°C.
Per serving: Calories 320; Fat: 28.8g; Sodium 1mg; Carbs: 18.2g; Fiber: 4.2g; Sugars 11.6g; Protein 1.8g

Soft Raisin Muffins

Prep Time: 10 minutes | Cook Time: 15 minutes | Serves: 6

¼ teaspoon salt	⅓ teaspoon allspice,	1¼ teaspoons baking powder	2 tablespoons Truvia for baking
½ teaspoon lemon zest, grated	2 eggs	240g sour cream	110g raisins
⅓ teaspoon anise star	200g almond flour	120ml coconut oil	

1. Place the Cook & Crisp Basket in your Pressure Cooker Steam Fryer. 2. In a suitable bowl, mix flour, baking powder, Truvia, salt, anise star, allspice and lemon zest. In another bowl, mix coconut oil, sour cream, eggs, and mix to mix. Now, add the wet mixture to the dry mixture and fold in the raisins. 3. Press the prepared batter mixture into a greased muffin tin. Transfer them to the Cook & Crisp Basket. Put on the Smart Lid on top of the Ninja Foodi Steam Fryer. 4. Move the Lid Slider to the "Air Fry/Stovetop". Select the "Air Fry" mode for cooking. Air Fry at 175°C for around 15 minutes.
Per serving: Calories 490; Fat: 37g; Sodium 183mg; Carbs: 29.7g; Fiber: 7.8g; Sugars 11.6g; Protein 19.3g

Pineapple with Macadamia Batter

Prep Time: 10 minutes | Cook Time: 7 minutes | Serves: 8

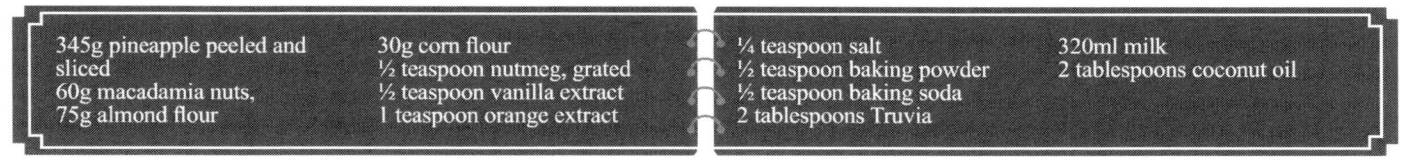

345g pineapple peeled and sliced	30g corn flour	¼ teaspoon salt	320ml milk
60g macadamia nuts,	½ teaspoon nutmeg, grated	½ teaspoon baking powder	2 tablespoons coconut oil
75g almond flour	½ teaspoon vanilla extract	½ teaspoon baking soda	
	1 teaspoon orange extract	2 tablespoons Truvia	

1. Place the Cook & Crisp Basket in your Pressure Cooker Steam Fryer. 2. To make batter mix all the recipe ingredients, except for pineapple, in a suitable mixing bowl. Dip the slices of pineapple into batter. 3. Transfer them to the Cook & Crisp Basket. Put on the Smart Lid on top of the Ninja Foodi Steam Fryer. 4. Move the Lid Slider to the "Air Fry/Stovetop". Select the "Air Fry" mode for cooking. Adjust the cooking temperature to 195°C. Air fry for around 7 minutes or until golden.
Per serving: Calories 257; Fat: 16.5g; Sodium 1031mg; Carbs: 23.6g; Fiber: 3.4g; Sugars 6.1g; Protein 4.7g

Frosted Blackberry Shortcake

Prep Time: 10 minutes | Cook Time: 12 minutes | Serves: 4

125g plain flour	⅛ teaspoon salt	510g fresh blackberries	refrigerated overnight
2 tablespoon granulated sugar	2 tablespoon coconut oil	**For the Cream**	1½ tablespoon icing sugar
1½ teaspoon baking powder	60ml unsweetened soy milk	400g canned coconut milk,	2 teaspoons orange zest

1. To make the cream, mix coconut milk with the icing sugar and orange zest and mix until fluffy. 2. In a suitable bowl, mix the flour, granulated sugar, baking powder, and salt. Add the coconut oil and use a pastry cutter to work the oil into the flour until distributed throughout the dry recipe ingredients. 3. Add the soy milk and use clean hands to gently mix. Be careful not to overmix. Gently press the prepared dough into the Cook & Crisp Basket. 4. Place the Cook & Crisp Basket in your Pressure Cooker Steam Fryer. 5. Put on the Smart Lid on top of the Ninja Foodi Steam Fryer. Move the Lid Slider to the "Air Fry/Stovetop". Select the "Air Fry" mode for cooking. Adjust the cooking temperature to 160°C. 6. Air Fry until the edges are golden, about 12 minutes. 7. Remove from the "cook & crisp basket" and allow the shortcake to cool for around 10 minutes. 8. Place the baked shortcake onto a serving platter and cut into 4 slices. Top each slice with 2 tablespoons of cream and an equal amount of the blackberries before serving.
Per serving: Calories 256; Fat: 3.5g; Sodium 7mg; Carbs: 54.2g; Fiber: 10.7g; Sugars 32.2g; Protein 4.9g

Cranberry Brownies

Prep Time: 10 minutes | Cook Time: 35 minutes | Serves: 8

1 teaspoon pure rum extract	2 eggs and an egg yolk, whisked	3 tablespoons coconut flakes	3 tablespoons whiskey
¼ teaspoon cardamom	120ml coconut oil	75g almond flour	35g cranberries
2 tablespoons Truvia for baking		200g white chocolate	

1. Place the Cook & Crisp Basket in your Pressure Cooker Steam Fryer. 2. Microwave white chocolate and coconut oil until melted. Allow mixture to cool at room temperature. Next, mix eggs, Truvia, rum extract, and cardamom, mix well. 3. Add the rum mixture to the chocolate mixture, stirring in flour and coconut flakes. Mix the cranberries with whiskey let soak for around 15 minutes. Fold them into the prepared batter. Press the butter into buttered Cook & Crisp Basket. 4. Put on the Smart Lid on top of the Ninja Foodi Steam Fryer. Move the Lid Slider to the "Air Fry/Stovetop". Select the "Air Fry" mode for cooking. 5. Air-fry for around 35 minutes at 170°C. Allow them to cool on a wire rack before serving.
Per serving: Calories 194; Fat: 13g; Sodium 208mg; Carbs: 30.6g; Fiber: 5.6g; Sugars 20.7g; Protein 9.1g

Almond Cookies

Prep Time: 10 minutes | Cook Time: 13 minutes | Serves: 8

55g slivered almonds	2 tablespoons Truvia	40g coconut flour	1 tablespoon candied ginger
115g butter, room temperature	35g almond flour	⅓ teaspoons cloves	¾ teaspoon pure vanilla extract

1. In a mixing dish, beat Truvia, butter, vanilla extract, cloves, and ginger until light and fluffy. Then, throw in the both kinds of flour and slivered almonds. Continue to mix until soft dough is formed. Cover and place into fridge for around 35 to minutes. 2. Roll the prepared dough into small cookies and place them on the Cook & Crisp Basket; gently press each cookie using the back of a spoon. Place the Cook & Crisp Basket in your Pressure Cooker Steam Fryer. 3. Put on the Smart Lid on top of the Ninja Foodi Steam Fryer. Move the Lid Slider to the "Air Fry/Stovetop". Select the "Air Fry" mode for cooking. Adjust the cooking temperature to 155°C. 4. Air Fry cookies for around 13 minutes.
Per serving: Calories 221; Fat: 3.9g; Sodium 154mg; Carbs: 50g; Fiber: 3.4g; Sugars 26.1g; Protein 1.8g

Prune Cookies

Prep Time: 10 minutes | Cook Time: 20 minutes | Serves: 10

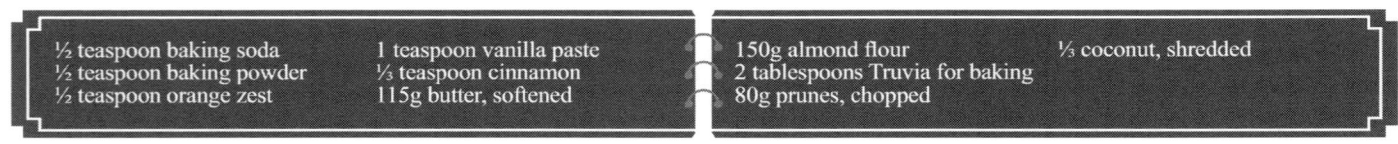

½ teaspoon baking soda	1 teaspoon vanilla paste	150g almond flour	⅓ coconut, shredded
½ teaspoon baking powder	⅓ teaspoon cinnamon	2 tablespoons Truvia for baking	
½ teaspoon orange zest	115g butter, softened	80g prunes, chopped	

1. Mix the butter with Truvia until mixture becomes fluffy; sift in the flour and add baking powder, as well as baking soda. Add the remaining recipe ingredients and mix well. Knead the prepared dough and transfer it to the fridge for around 20 minutes. 2. To finish, shape the chilled dough into bite-size balls; arrange the balls on the Cook & Crisp Basket and gently flatten them with the back of a spoon. Place the Cook & Crisp Basket in your Pressure Cooker Steam Fryer. 3. Put on the Smart Lid on top of the Ninja Foodi Steam Fryer. Move the Lid Slider to the "Air Fry/Stovetop". Select the "Air Fry" mode for cooking. Air fry for around 20 minutes at 155°C.
Per serving: Calories 375; Fat: 28.4g; Sodium 128mg; Carbs: 22.4g; Fiber: 6.3g; Sugars 9.7g; Protein 14.9g

Sweet Lemon Bars

Prep Time: 10 minutes | Cook Time: 22 minutes | Serves: 6

4 tablespoon coconut oil, melted	1 teaspoon pure vanilla extract	60ml freshly squeezed lemon juice	120g canned coconut cream
	100g granulated sugar		4 tablespoon corn flour
¼ teaspoon 1 pinch of salt	2 tablespoons plain flour	Zest of 1 lemon	Icing sugar

1. In a suitable bowl, mix the coconut oil, ¼ teaspoon of salt, vanilla extract, and 3 tablespoons of sugar. Mix in the flour until a soft dough forms. Transfer the mixture to the Cook & Crisp Basket and gently press the prepared dough to cover the bottom. 2. Place the Cook & Crisp Basket in your Pressure Cooker Steam Fryer. 3. Put on the Smart Lid on top of the Ninja Foodi Steam Fryer. Move the Lid Slider to the "Air Fry/Stovetop". Select the "Air Fry" mode for cooking. Air Fry at 175°C until golden, about 10 minutes. Remove the crust from the "cook & crisp basket" and set aside to cool slightly. 4. In a suitable saucepan on the stovetop over medium heat, mix the lemon juice and zest, coconut cream, the pinch of salt, and the remaining 100 g of sugar. Mix in the corn flour and. cook for until thickened, about 5 minutes. Pour the lemon mixture over the crust. 5. Place them in the "cook & crisp basket". Put on the Smart Lid on top of the Ninja Foodi Steam Fryer. Move the Lid Slider to the "Air Fry/Stovetop". Select the "Air Fry" mode for cooking. Adjust the cooking temperature to 175°C. 6. Cook for until the mixture is bubbly and almost completely set, about 10 to 12 minutes. 7. Remove them from the "cook & crisp basket" and set aside to cool completely. Transfer to a dish and put in the refrigerator for at least 4 hours. 8. Dust with the icing sugar and slice into 6 bars before serving.
Per serving: Calories 194; Fat: 2.6g; Sodium 1257mg; Carbs: 35.4g; Fiber: 3.7g; Sugars 3.1g; Protein 9.4g

Sweet Pecans

Prep time: 15 minutes | Cook time: 15 minutes | Serves: 2

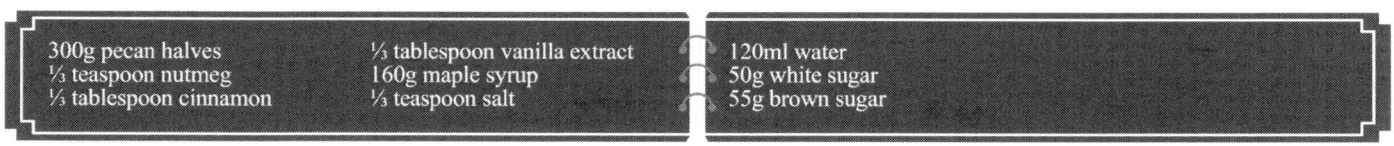

300g pecan halves	⅓ tablespoon vanilla extract	120ml water
⅓ teaspoon nutmeg	160g maple syrup	50g white sugar
⅓ tablespoon cinnamon	⅓ teaspoon salt	55g brown sugar

1. Move the slider towards "AIR FRY/STOVETOP" and set Ninja Foodi XL Pressure Cooker Steam Fryer with SmartLid to SEAR/SAUTÉ mode. Adjust the temperature to "Hi5" by using up arrow. Press START/STOP to begin cooking. In the Ninja Foodi XL Pressure Cooker Steam Fryer cooking pot, combine the pecans, nutmeg, cinnamon, vanilla, maple syrup and salt. Stirring constantly, cook for 7-10 minutes, until the pecans are tender. Press the START/STOP to stop the SAUTÉ function. Pour in the water. 2. Lock lid; move slider towards PRESSURE. Adjust pressure release valve in the SEAL position. Close pressure-release valve. The cooking temperature will default to HIGH, which is accurate. Set time to 20 minutes. Select START/STOP and start cooking. 3. When cooking is complete, let pressure release quickly by turning it into VENT position. Pour the pecans mixture onto the Cook & Crisp Basket. 4. Lock lid; move slider to STEAMCRISP. Select STEAM & BAKE, set temperature to 190°C, and set time to 10 minutes. Press START/STOP to begin cooking. Bake for 5 minutes then flip and cook for another 5 minutes. 5. Transfer the pecans to the bowl and let them cool for 10 minutes. Add sugar and mix well. Serve.

Per Serving: Calories 354; Fat 7.9g; Sodium 704mg; Carbs 6g; Fiber 3.6g; Sugar 6g; Protein 18g

Clafoutis

Prep Time: 10 minutes | Cook Time: 25 minutes | Serves: 6

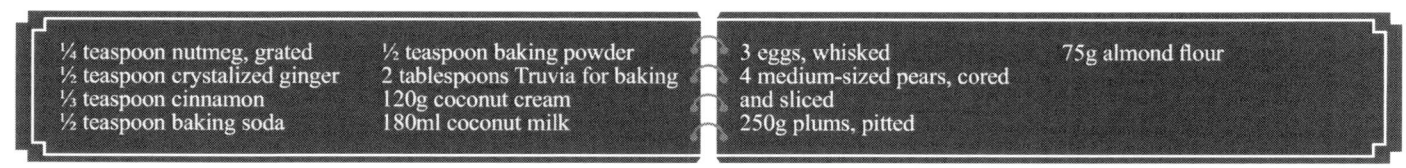

¼ teaspoon nutmeg, grated	½ teaspoon baking powder	3 eggs, whisked	75g almond flour
½ teaspoon crystalized ginger	2 tablespoons Truvia for baking	4 medium-sized pears, cored and sliced	
⅓ teaspoon cinnamon	120g coconut cream		
½ teaspoon baking soda	180ml coconut milk	250g plums, pitted	

1. Place the deluxe reversible racking your Pressure Cooker Steam Fryer. 2. grease 2 mini pie pans using a non-stick cooking spray. Lay the plums and pears on the bottom of pie pans. In a suitable saucepan that is preheated over medium heat, warm the cream along with the coconut milk until heated. Remove the pan from heat; mix in the flour along with baking soda and baking powder. 3. In a suitable bowl, mix the eggs, Truvia, spices until the mixture is creamy. Add the creamy milk mixture. Carefully spread this mixture over your fruit in pans. Put the pans on the rack. 4. Put on the Smart Lid on top of the Ninja Foodi Steam Fryer. Move the Lid Slider to the "Air Fry/Stovetop". Select the "Air Fry" mode for cooking. Air Fry at 160°C for around 25 minutes.

Per serving: Calories 281; Fat: 6.7g; Sodium 187mg; Carbs: 52.7g; Fiber: 6.6g; Sugars 29g; Protein 5.1g

Orange Cake

Prep Time: 10 minutes | Cook Time: 20 minutes | Serves: 6

45g almonds, chopped	½ teaspoon allspice,	150g almond flour	pans
3 tablespoons orange marmalade	½ teaspoon anise seed,	2 tablespoons Truvia for baking	
115g butter	½ teaspoon baking powder	2 eggs 1 egg yolk, beaten	
	1 teaspoon baking soda	Olive oil cooking spray for	

1. Place the deluxe reversible rack in your Pressure Cooker Steam Fryer. 2. Grease cake pan with olive oil cooking spray. Mix the butter and Truvia until nice and smooth. Fold in the eggs, almonds, marmalade; beat again until well mixed. Add flour, baking soda, baking powder, allspice, star anise and cinnamon. 3. Put the cake pan on the rack. Put on the Smart Lid on top of the Ninja Foodi Steam Fryer. Move the Lid Slider to the "Air Fry/Stovetop". Select the "Air Fry" mode for cooking. Air Fry at 155°C for around 20 minutes.

Per serving: Calories 361; Fat: 31.3g; Sodium 385mg; Carbs: 13.8g; Fiber: 7.3g; Sugars 2.5g; Protein 9.7g

Chocolate Egg Rolls

Prep Time: 10 minutes | Cook Time: 6 minutes | Serves: 4

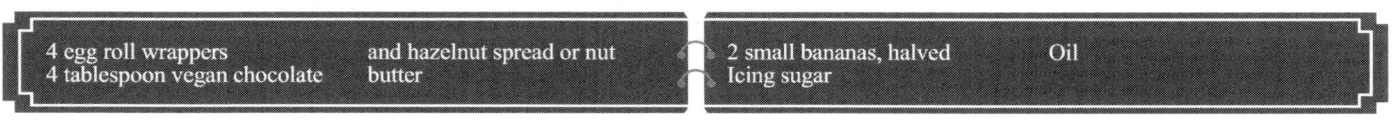

4 egg roll wrappers	and hazelnut spread or nut butter	2 small bananas, halved	Oil
4 tablespoon vegan chocolate		Icing sugar	

1. Place the Cook & Crisp Basket in your Pressure Cooker Steam Fryer. 2. Place 1 wrapper on a flat surface, with the pointed end facing up. Spread the butter in the middle and top with half a banana. Fold in the sides over the filling and then roll up from bottom to top. Repeat this step with the remaining wrappers and filling. Grease the egg rolls with oil. 3. Place the egg rolls in the "cook & crisp basket". Put on the Smart Lid on top of the Ninja Foodi Steam Fryer. Move the Lid Slider to the "Air Fry/Stovetop". Select the "Air Fry" mode for cooking. Adjust the cooking temperature to 185°C. 4. Cook for 5 to 6 minutes until golden brown. 5. Transfer the egg rolls to a platter and allow to cool for at least 10 minutes. Dust with the icing sugar before serving.

Per serving: Calories 149; Fat: 15.4g; Sodium 313mg; Carbs: 1.1g; Fiber: 0.1g; Sugars 0.1g; Protein 2.2g

Apricots in Whiskey Sauce

Prep Time: 10 minutes | Cook Time: 35 minutes | Serves: 4

455g. apricot, pitted and halved	1 teaspoon pure vanilla extract	170g maple syrup sugar-free
60ml whiskey	55g butter, room temperature	

1. In a suitable saucepan over medium heat, heat the maple syrup, vanilla, butter; simmer until the butter is melted. Add the whiskey and stir to mix. Arrange the apricots on the bottom of greased Cook & Crisp Basket. 2. Pour the sauce over the apricots; scatter whole cloves over the top. Then, place the Cook & Crisp Basket in your Pressure Cooker Steam Fryer. 3. Put on the Smart Lid on top of the Ninja Foodi Steam Fryer. Move the Lid Slider to the "Air Fry/Stovetop". Select the "Air Fry" mode for cooking. 4. Air-fry at 195°C for around 35 minutes.
Per serving: Calories 469; Fat: 36.5g; Sodium 46mg; Carbs: 31.4g; Fiber: 4.5g; Sugars 17.9g; Protein 9.1g

Cracker S'mores

Prep Time: 10 minutes | Cook Time: 3 minutes | Serves: 4

4 squares vegan dark chocolate	4 large vegan marshmallows	4 full graham crackers, halved

1. Place the Cook & Crisp Basket in your Pressure Cooker Steam Fryer. 2. Place 1 chocolate square and 1 marshmallow on 1 cracker half. Repeat this step with 3 more cracker halves. 3. Place the s'mores in the "cook & crisp basket". Put on the Smart Lid on top of the Ninja Foodi Steam Fryer. Move the Lid Slider to the "Air Fry/Stovetop". Select the "Air Fry" mode for cooking. Adjust the cooking temperature to 175°C. 4. Cook for until the marshmallow is puffed and golden, about 2 to 3 minutes. 5. Transfer the s'mores to a platter. Top each with a remaining cracker half and serve immediately.
Per serving: Calories 363; Fat: 10.7g; Sodium 253mg; Carbs: 63.7g; Fiber: 3.8g; Sugars 22.9g; Protein 4.9g

Cinnamon Pear Clafoutis

Prep Time: 10 minutes | Cook Time: 25 minutes | Serves: 4

320g medium pears, finely chopped	100g granulated sugar	⅛ teaspoon salt	1 tablespoon rapeseed oil
juice of ½ lemon	30g whole wheat pastry flour	½ teaspoon cinnamon	
	1 teaspoon baking powder	120ml unsweetened soy milk	

1. In the Cook & Crisp Basket, mix the pears, lemon juice, and 2 tablespoons of sugar. 2. In a suitable bowl, mix the pastry flour, baking powder, salt, and cinnamon. Add the soy milk, rapeseed oil, and the remaining 6 tablespoons of sugar. Mix until a smooth batter forms. Pour the prepared batter over the pears. 3. Place the Cook & Crisp Basket in your Pressure Cooker Steam Fryer. 4. Put on the Smart Lid on top of the Ninja Foodi Steam Fryer. Move the Lid Slider to the "Air Fry/Stovetop". Select the "Air Fry" mode for cooking. Adjust the cooking temperature to 170°C. 5. Air Fry until the cake is puffed and golden, about 20 to 25 minutes. 6. Remove the cake from the "cook & crisp basket" and allow the cake to cool before serving.
Per serving: Calories 420; Fat: 17.1g; Sodium 282mg; Carbs: 65.7g; Fiber: 4.5g; Sugars 35.1g; Protein 7g

Crispy Profiteroles

Prep Time: 10 minutes | Cook Time: 10 minutes | Serves: 2

2 tablespoon vegan butter	substitute	**For the Cream**	**For the Drizzle**
60ml unsweetened soy milk	125g plain flour	400g canned coconut milk, refrigerated overnight	40g vegan chocolate chips
1 teaspoon pure vanilla extract	1 teaspoon baking powder	1½ tablespoon icing sugar	½ teaspoon coconut oil
1 tablespoon maple syrup	¼ teaspoon salt		
3 tablespoon liquid egg	Nonstick cooking spray		

1. Place the Cook & Crisp Basket in your Pressure Cooker Steam Fryer. 2. Grease the "cook & crisp basket" with nonstick cooking spray. 3. In a suitable saucepan on the stovetop over medium-low heat, melt the butter. Add the soy milk, vanilla extract, maple syrup, and egg. Mix to mix. Add the flour, baking powder, and salt. Mix well with a wooden spoon until a sticky dough forms. Turn off the heat and allow to cool for around 2 minutes. Add the warm dough to a piping bag with a wide tip. 4. Pipe the prepared dough directly into the Cook & Crisp Basket, forming 10 mounds the size of golf balls. Dampen your finger with water and gently press down the top of each mound to prevent burning. Put on the Smart Lid on top of the Ninja Foodi Steam Fryer. 5. Move the Lid Slider to the "Air Fry/Stovetop". Select the "Air Fry" mode for cooking. 6. Adjust the cooking temperature to 190°C. 7. Cook until puffed and golden, about 10 minutes. 8. Transfer the profiteroles to a platter and allow to cool. 9. Add the coconut cream, and icing sugar to bowl and mix until fluffy, about 2 to 3 minutes. Set aside. 10. Place the chocolate chips and coconut oil in a microwave-safe dish. Microwave for around 60 to 90 seconds. Stir until mixed and glossy. 11. Use a serrated knife to slice each profiterole in half and fill with a heaping spoonful of cream. (You'll have about half the cream left over. Refrigerate for up to 3 days for another use.) Drizzle the profiteroles with the chocolate sauce and serve immediately.
Per serving: Calories 130; Fat: 3.9g; Sodium 3mg; Carbs: 21.6g; Fiber: 1.6g; Sugars 9.8g; Protein 3.6g

Blueberry Oats Crisp

Prep Time: 10 minutes | Cook Time: 17 minutes | Serves: 4

295g fresh blueberries	2 teaspoon corn flour	40g rolled oats	2 tablespoon coconut sugar or granulated sugar
Juice of ½ orange	1 tablespoon vegan butter	25g almond flour	Pinch of salt
1 tablespoon maple syrup	(Earth Balance recommended)	½ teaspoon cinnamon	

1. In the Cook & Crisp Basket, mix the blueberries, orange juice, maple syrup, and corn flour. Mix well. 2. In a suitable bowl, mix the butter, oats, almond flour, cinnamon, sugar, and salt. Use clean hands to mix until a soft, crumbly dough forms. Evenly sprinkle the prepared dough over the blueberries. 3. Place the Cook & Crisp Basket in your Pressure Cooker Steam Fryer. 4. Put on the Smart Lid on top of the Ninja Foodi Steam Fryer. Move the Lid Slider to the "Air Fry/Stovetop". Select the "Air Fry" mode for cooking. Adjust the cooking temperature to 185°C. 5. Air Fry until the topping is crispy and the berries are thick and bubbly, about 15 to 17 minutes. 6. Remove the crisp from the "cook & crisp basket" and allow the crisp to cool for at least 10 minutes before serving.
Per serving: Calories 360; Fat: 7.8g; Sodium 280mg; Carbs: 74.4g; Fiber: 8g; Sugars 47.4g; Protein 2.7g

Peach Walnut Parfaits

Prep Time: 10 minutes | Cook Time: 12 minutes | Serves: 2

3 tablespoon light brown sugar	¼ teaspoon sea salt	removed
40g chopped walnuts	4 peaches, halved and pits	170g dairy-free plain yogurt

1. Place the Cook & Crisp Basket in your Pressure Cooker Steam Fryer. 2. In a suitable bowl, mix the brown sugar, walnuts, and salt. Mix well. 3. Place the peaches in the Cook & Crisp Basket. Evenly sprinkle the walnut mixture over the peaches. 4. Put on the Smart Lid on top of the Ninja Foodi Steam Fryer. 5. Move the Lid Slider to the "Air Fry/Stovetop". Select the "Air Fry" mode for cooking. 6. Adjust the cooking temperature to 175°C. 7. Cook until the peaches are tender and the sugar has begun to caramelize, about 10 to 12 minutes. 8. Transfer the peaches to a platter to cool slightly. Top with the yogurt before serving.
Per serving: Calories 488; Fat: 34.3g; Sodium 130mg; Carbs: 42.4g; Fiber: 1.7g; Sugars 21.5g; Protein 4.8g

Cinnamon Flour Twists

Prep Time: 10 minutes | Cook Time: 12 minutes | Serves: 20

240g plain flour, more	120ml rapeseed oil	50g granulated sugar
½ teaspoon salt	5 to 8 tablespoon cold water	1½ teaspoon cinnamon

1. Place the Cook & Crisp Basket in your Pressure Cooker Steam Fryer. 2. In a suitable bowl, mix the flour and salt. 3. In a separate medium bowl, mix the oil and 5 to 6 tablespoons of the water. Make a well in the center of the flour mixture and pour in the oil mixture. Mix with a fork until just mixed. Add 1 to 2 more tablespoons of water as needed. 4. In a suitable bowl, mix the sugar and cinnamon. 5. On a floured surface, roll out the prepared dough into a 25 cm round. Cut the prepared dough into 10 strips and then cut each strip in half. Sprinkle the sugar and cinnamon mixture on both sides and gently twist each strip. 6. Working in batches, place 10 twists in the "cook & crisp basket". Put on the Smart Lid on top of the Ninja Foodi Steam Fryer. Move the Lid Slider to the "Air Fry/Stovetop". Select the "Air Fry" mode for cooking. Adjust the cooking temperature to 165°C. 7. Cook for until golden brown, about 5 to 6 minutes. 8. Transfer the cinnamon twists to a platter and allow to cool before serving.
Per serving: Calories 182; Fat: 0.7g; Sodium 7mg; Carbs: 46.3g; Fiber: 6.2g; Sugars 40.7g; Protein 1.9g

Flaxseed Carrot Cake

Prep Time: 10 minutes | Cook Time: 30 minutes | Serves: 6

1 tablespoon flaxseed	½ teaspoon cinnamon	75g grated carrots	**For The Glaze**
3 tablespoon water	100g granulated sugar	2 tablespoon raisins	40g icing sugar
60g cake flour	60ml rapeseed oil	2 tablespoon chopped walnuts	½ teaspoon pure vanilla extract
¼ teaspoon baking soda	½ teaspoon pure vanilla extract	Nonstick cooking spray	2 teaspoons dairy-free milk (soy recommended)
Pinch of salt	65g unsweetened applesauce		

1. Spray the Cook & Crisp Basket with nonstick cooking spray. Set aside. 2. In a suitable bowl, mix the flaxseed and water. Set aside for at least 5 minutes. 3. In a suitable bowl, mix the cake flour, baking soda, salt, and cinnamon. Add the sugar, rapeseed oil, vanilla extract, applesauce, and flaxseed mixture. Mix well. Fold in the carrots, raisins, and walnuts. Place the prepared batter in the Cook & Crisp Basket. 4. Place the Cook & Crisp Basket in your Pressure Cooker Steam Fryer. 5. Put on the Smart Lid on top of the Ninja Foodi Steam Fryer. Move the Lid Slider to the "Air Fry/Stovetop". Select the "Air Fry" mode for cooking. Adjust the cooking temperature to 155°C. Air Fry until a toothpick comes out clean from the center, about 25 to 30 minutes. 6. Transfer the cake to a serving platter and allow to cool completely. 7. In a suitable bowl, make the glaze by whisking the ingredients. Drizzle the prepared glaze over the cake and allow to set. 8. Cut the cake into 6 slices before serving.
Per serving: Calories 344; Fat: 3g; Sodium 603mg; Carbs: 73.8g; Fiber: 11.5g; Sugars 8.6g; Protein 9.4g

Flaxseed Cookies

Prep Time: 10 minutes | Cook Time: 10 minutes | Serves: 18

1 tablespoon flaxseed	255g creamy peanut butter	80g plain flour	½ teaspoon salt
3 tablespoon water	160g light brown sugar	1 teaspoon baking soda	Nonstick cooking spray.

1. Place the Cook & Crisp Basket in your Pressure Cooker Steam Fryer. 2. In a suitable bowl, mix the flaxseed and water in a suitable bowl. Mix and set aside for around 5 minutes. 3. In a suitable bowl, mix the peanut butter and brown sugar. Add the flaxseed mixture, flour, baking soda, and salt. Mix until a soft dough forms. Refrigerate the prepared dough for at least 20 minutes. 4. Grease the "cook & crisp basket" with nonstick cooking spray. 5. Use a suitable scoop or tablespoon to roll the prepared dough into 18 equally sized balls. Use a fork to press a diagonal hash mark into each ball. 6. Working in batches, place 9 balls in the "cook & crisp basket". 7. Put on the Smart Lid on top of the Ninja Foodi Steam Fryer. Move the Lid Slider to the "Air Fry/Stovetop". Select the "Air Fry" mode for cooking. Adjust the cooking temperature to 165°C. Cook for until golden, about 5 minutes. 8. Serve.
Per serving: Calories 105; Fat: 2.4g; Sodium 812mg; Carbs: 12.2g; Fiber: 2.4g; Sugars 2.4g; Protein 9.5g

Confetti Cake

Prep Time: 10 minutes | Cook Time: 30 minutes | Serves: 4

180g vegan vanilla cake mix	2 tablespoon colored sprinkles	(Earth Balance recommended)	1 to 2 tablespoon unsweetened
190g unsweetened applesauce	Nonstick cooking spray	125g icing sugar	soy milk
2 tablespoon rapeseed oil	**For the Frosting**	½ teaspoon pure vanilla extract	
60ml water	3 tablespoon vegan butter	Pinch of salt	

1. Spray the Cook & Crisp Basket with nonstick cooking spray. 2. In a suitable bowl, mix the cake mix, applesauce, rapeseed oil, and water. Fold in the sprinkles. Place the mixture in the Cook & Crisp Basket. 3. Place the Cook & Crisp Basket in your Pressure Cooker Steam Fryer. 4. Put on the Smart Lid on top of the Ninja Foodi Steam Fryer. Move the Lid Slider to the "Air Fry/Stovetop". Select the "Air Fry" mode for cooking. Adjust the cooking temperature to 155°C. Air Fry until the top is golden and a toothpick comes out clean from the center, about 30 minutes. 5. In a suitable bowl, make the frosting by beating the butter, icing sugar, vanilla extract, and salt until well mixed. Continue to mix while adding 1 to 2 tablespoons of soy milk to reach the desired consistency. 6. Remove the "cook & crisp basket" and allow the cake to cool completely. Spread the buttercream over the cake before serving.
Per serving: Calories 93; Fat: 1.6g; Sodium 465mg; Carbs: 15.2g; Fiber: 5g; Sugars 3.8g; Protein 4.5g

Vegan Apple Pies

Prep Time: 10 minutes | Cook Time: 10 minutes | Serves: 4

1 medium apple (Gala or Granny Smith recommended), peeled and finely diced	Juice of ½ orange 2 tablespoon granulated sugar ½ teaspoon cinnamon	2 teaspoon corn flour 285g vegan pie dough All-purpose flour

1. Place the Cook & Crisp Basket in your Pressure Cooker Steam Fryer. 2. In a suitable bowl, mix the apple, orange juice, sugar, cinnamon, and corn flour. Mix well. 3. Roll out the prepared dough on a floured surface. Cut the prepared dough into 4 rounds. Place 2 tablespoons of the apple mixture in the center of each. Fold the prepared dough in half and seal the edges with a fork. Make a suitable slit in the top for steam to escape. 4. Place the pies in the "cook & crisp basket". Put on the Smart Lid on top of the Ninja Foodi Steam Fryer. Move the Lid Slider to the "Air Fry/Stovetop". Select the "Air Fry" mode for cooking. Adjust the cooking temperature to 175°C. 5. Cook for until golden brown, about 10 minutes. 6. Transfer the pies to a wire rack to cool before serving.
Per serving: Calories 339; Fat: 14g; Sodium 556mg; Carbs: 44.6g; Fiber: 6.4g; Sugars 3.8g; Protein 10.5g

Cinnamon Stuffed Apples

Prep Time: 10 minutes | Cook Time: 20 minutes | Serves: 4

2 small red or green apples, halved horizontally 4 teaspoon vegan butter (Earth	Balance recommended) ¼ teaspoon cardamom 2 teaspoon cinnamon	30g chopped walnuts 40g raisins Pinch of salt

1. Remove the seeds and core from both halves of each apple and place all 4 halves cut side up in the Cook & Crisp Basket. Pour about 2.5 cm of water into the bottom of the basket. 2. In a suitable bowl, mix the butter, cardamom, cinnamon, walnuts, raisins, and salt. Mix well. Equally divide the filling among the apple halves. 3. Place the Cook & Crisp Basket in your Pressure Cooker Steam Fryer. 4. Put on the Smart Lid on top of the Ninja Foodi Steam Fryer. Move the Lid Slider to the "Air Fry/Stovetop". Select the "Air Fry" mode for cooking. Adjust the cooking temperature to 175°C. 5. Air Fry until the apples are tender, about 20 minutes. 6. Remove the apples from the "cook & crisp basket" and allow the apples to cool for around 10 minutes before serving.
Per serving: Calories 241; Fat: 9.8g; Sodium 605mg; Carbs: 29.8g; Fiber: 8.5g; Sugars 1.1g; Protein 9.8g

Raspberry Pineapple Sundaes

Prep Time: 10 minutes | Cook Time: 5 minutes | Serves: 4

| 420g diced pineapple | ½ teaspoon granulated sugar | 180g dairy-free ice cream | Granola |
| ½ teaspoon cinnamon | 125g raspberries | 55g Agave and Pistachio | Nonstick cooking spray |

1. Place the Cook & Crisp Basket in your Pressure Cooker Steam Fryer. 2. Grease the "cook & crisp basket" with nonstick cooking spray. 3. In a suitable bowl, mix the pineapple, cinnamon, and sugar. Toss well to coat. 4. Place the pineapple in the "cook & crisp basket". Put on the Smart Lid on top of the Ninja Foodi Steam Fryer. Move the Lid Slider to the "Air Fry/Stovetop". Select the "Air Fry" mode for cooking. Adjust the cooking temperature to 200°C. Cook for until sizzling and the sugar begins to caramelize, about 5 minutes. 5. Remove the pineapple from the "cook & crisp basket" and allow to cool slightly. Serve the pineapple over the ice cream. 6. Top each sundae with an equal amount of Agave and Pistachio Granola and raspberries.
Per serving: Calories 49; Fat: 3.8g; Sodium 638mg; Carbs: 3g; Fiber: 1.6g; Sugars 0.4g; Protein 2.1g

Chocolate Cookie Cups

Prep Time: 10 minutes | Cook Time: 10 minutes | Serves: 4

1 tablespoon flaxseed	½ teaspoon baking powder	2 tablespoon coconut oil, melted	Nonstick cooking spray
3 tablespoon water	¼ teaspoon salt		
125g plain flour	3 tablespoon maple syrup	40g vegan chocolate chips	

1. Place the Cook & Crisp Basket in your Pressure Cooker Steam Fryer. 2. Spray 4 ramekins with nonstick cooking spray. Set aside. 3. In a suitable bowl, mix the flaxseed and water. 4. In a suitable bowl, mix the flour, baking powder, and salt. Add the flaxseed mixture, maple syrup, and coconut oil. Mix until just mixed. Fold in the chocolate chips. Add an equal amount of batter into each ramekin. 5. Place the prepared ramekins in the Cook & Crisp Basket. Put on the Smart Lid on top of the Ninja Foodi Steam Fryer. Move the Lid Slider to the "Air Fry/Stovetop". Select the "Air Fry" mode for cooking. Adjust the cooking temperature to 170°C. Air Fry until puffed and golden, about 8 to 10 minutes. 6. Remove the ramekins from the "cook & crisp basket" and allow the cookie cups to cool before serving.
Per serving: Calories 195; Fat: 7.3g; Sodium 592mg; Carbs: 31.8g; Fiber: 4.7g; Sugars 0.6g; Protein 1.8g

Chia Pudding Tarts

Prep Time: 10 minutes | Cook Time: 10 minutes | Serves: 6

| 240ml chocolate soy milk | 1 tablespoon orange zest | 240g flour | 120ml rapeseed oil |
| 40g chia seeds | Pinch of sea salt | ½ teaspoon salt | 8 tablespoons cold water |

1. In a 475-milliliter glass jar, mix the soy milk, chia seeds, orange zest, and sea salt. Allow the prepared mixture to sit for around 10 minutes before whisking again. Cover and refrigerate for at least 6 hours. In a suitable bowl, mix the flour and salt. 2. In a separate medium bowl, mix the oil and 5 to 6 tablespoons of the water. Make a small well in the center of the flour mixture and pour in the oil mixture. Mix with a fork until just mixed. Add 2 more tablespoons of water as needed. Shape the prepared dough into a ball. 3. Roll out the prepared dough between 2 sheets of wax or parchment paper. Use a 5cm ring mold to cut out 6 rounds. Transfer the prepared dough to ramekins and press in gently to form the cups. 4. Place the prepared ramekins in the Cook & Crisp Basket. Place the Cook & Crisp Basket in your Pressure Cooker Steam Fryer. 5. Put on the Smart Lid on top of the Ninja Foodi Steam Fryer. Move the Lid Slider to the "Air Fry/Stovetop". Select the "Air Fry" mode for cooking. Adjust the cooking temperature to 175°C. 6. Air Fry until the crust is golden, about 10 minutes. 7. Remove the ramekins from the "cook & crisp basket" and allow the cups to cool completely. Transfer the cups to a platter. Fill the cups with the chia pudding and serve immediately.
Per serving: Calories 336; Fat: 9.9g; Sodium 1672mg; Carbs: 42.6g; Fiber: 1.7g; Sugars 2.1g; Protein 12.3g

Spiced Pumpkin Pudding

Prep time: 2 minutes | Cook time: 6 minutes | Serves: 4

| 1 tablespoon vanilla | 2 eggs | 3 tablespoons corn flour | 300ml can evaporated milk |
| 1 teaspoon pumpkin pie spice | 50g sugar | 375g can pumpkin puree | |

1. Beat the eggs in a medium bowl. Mix in half the milk, the pumpkin puree, and the vanilla into the eggs and set aside. Mix the sugar, spice, and starch together in the cooking pot. 2. Move the slider towards "AIR FRY/STOVETOP" and set Ninja Foodi XL Pressure Cooker Steam Fryer with SmartLid to SEAR/SAUTÉ mode. Adjust the temperature to "Hi5" by using up arrow. Press START/STOP to begin cooking. Slowly stir in the remaining milk to the pot. Continue stirring on Sauté for about 3 minutes. 3. Press the START/STOP and mix in the pumpkin spice mix. Turn the pot back to SEAR/SAUTÉ and stir continuously for another 3 minutes. 4. Remove from heat and allow to cool before eating. Add a dollop of whipped cream or vanilla ice cream for a treat.
Per Serving: Calories 350; Fat 22.5g; Sodium 166mg; Carbs 38g; Fiber 1g; Sugar 25g; Protein 1g

Chocolate Pudding Cake

Prep time: 15 minutes | Cook time: 15 minutes | Serves: 2

185g butter	2 tablespoons instant coffee crystals	4 tablespoons unsweetened cocoa powder	⅛ teaspoon salt
50g unsweetened chocolate	1 teaspoon vanilla extract	80g almond flour	5 eggs
120g heavy cream			135g sugar

1. Move the slider towards "AIR FRY/STOVETOP" and set Ninja Foodi XL Pressure Cooker Steam Fryer with SmartLid to SEAR/SAUTÉ mode. Adjust the temperature to "Hi5" by using up arrow. Press START/STOP to begin cooking. 2. Add the butter and chocolate. Stir continuously until melted then remove from heat. In one small bowl mix together the heavy cream, coffee crystals, and vanilla. 3. In a separate small bowl mix the cocoa, flour, and salt. In a third small bowl beat the eggs then mix in the sugar. Mix the eggs into the pot. Add the cocoa, stirring continuously. Add in the cream mix stirring continuously until an even batter forms. 4. Lock lid; move slider to STEAMCRISP. Select STEAM & BAKE, set temperature to 200°C, and set time to 9 minutes. Press START/STOP to begin cooking.
Per Serving: Calories 173; Fat 13.6g; Sodium 281mg; Carbs 3g; Fiber 1g; Sugar 1g; Protein 10g

Carrot Cake

Prep time: 10 minutes | Cook time: 50 minutes | Serves: 8

3 eggs	1 teaspoon baking powder	120g heavy whipping cream	
120g almond flour	1½ teaspoons apple pie spice	110g shredded carrots	
130g sugar	60ml coconut oil	60g chopped walnuts	

1. Mix together all the ingredients with a hand whisk. Grease the Cook & Crisp Basket and pour the mixture into the Cook & Crisp Basket. 2. Cover the basket with foil and place on the Deluxe Reversible Rack of Ninja Foodi XL Pressure Cooker Steam Fryer. Add the pot with 480ml water. 3. Lock lid; move slider towards STEAMCRISP. Select STEAM & BAKE, set temperature to 200°C, and set time to 40 minutes. Press START/STOP to begin cooking. 4. Serve by itself or with a scoop of vanilla ice cream.
Per Serving: Calories 217; Fat 7.9g; Sodium 998mg; Carbs 17g; Fiber 4g; Sugar 8g; Protein 19g

Nutty Cake

Prep time: 10 minutes | Cook time: 40 minutes | Serves: 8

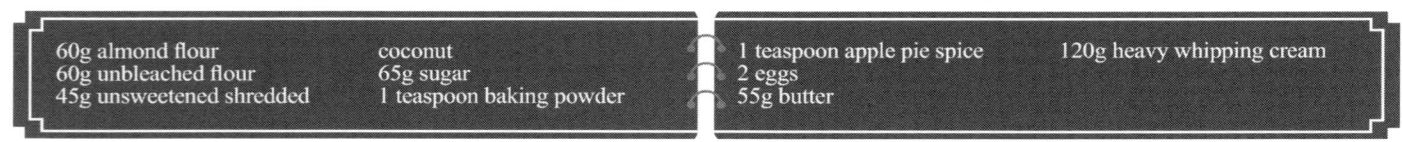

60g almond flour	coconut	1 teaspoon apple pie spice	120g heavy whipping cream
60g unbleached flour	65g sugar	2 eggs	
45g unsweetened shredded	1 teaspoon baking powder	55g butter	

1. Blend the dry ingredients in a medium bowl. Mix the wet ingredients in the bowl one at a time. Pour the mix into a greased cake pan and cover with foil. Pour 480ml water into the pot. Put the cake pan on the Deluxe Reversible Rack and lower it into the pan in Ninja Foodi XL Pressure Cooker Steam Fryer. 2. Lock lid; move slider towards PRESSURE. Adjust pressure release valve in the SEAL position. Close pressure-release valve. The cooking temperature will default to HIGH, which is accurate. Set time to 40 minutes. Select START/STOP and start cooking. 3. When cooking is complete, let pressure release naturally for 10 minutes. Remove from the pot and allow to cool an additional 15 minutes before serving.
Per Serving: Calories 118; Fat 7.2g; Sodium 232mg; Carbs 14g; Fiber 1g; Sugar 11g; Protein 2g

Lemon Cheesecake

Prep time: 10 minutes | Cook time: 35 minutes | Serves: 8

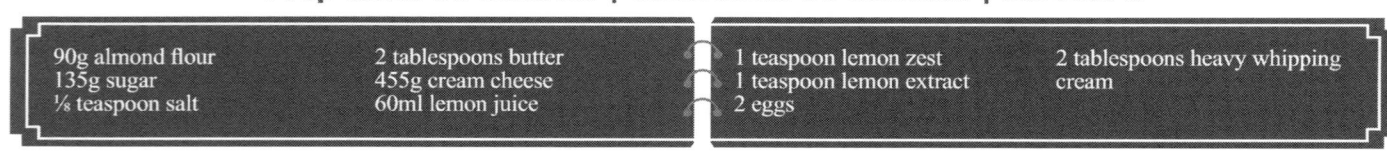

90g almond flour	2 tablespoons butter	1 teaspoon lemon zest	2 tablespoons heavy whipping cream
135g sugar	455g cream cheese	1 teaspoon lemon extract	
⅛ teaspoon salt	60ml lemon juice	2 eggs	

1. Line Cook & Crisp Basket with greaseproof paper and set aside. Melt the butter in a bowl and mix in the salt, almond flour, and 2 tablespoons sugar to make crust mixture. Press the crust into the Cook & Crisp Basket and set aside. 2. Beat the cream cheese in a medium bowl until smooth, then mix in the lemon juice, zest, and extract. Beat in the eggs one at a time. Beat in the cream then pour the mixture onto the prepared crust. 3. Wrap the Cook & Crisp Basket in foil and place it on the Deluxe Reversible Rack. Pour 240ml water into the pot and lower the Deluxe Reversible Rack into the pot. 4. Lock lid; move slider towards PRESSURE. Adjust pressure release valve in the SEAL position. Close pressure-release valve. 5. The cooking temperature will default to HIGH, which is accurate. Set time to 35 minutes. Select START/STOP and start cooking. 6. When cooking is complete, let pressure release naturally. Transfer the cake to the refrigerator for a few hours before serving.
Per Serving: Calories 429; Fat 32g; Sodium 325mg; Carbs 5g; Fiber 1g; Sugar 3g; Protein 5g

Regular Chocolate Pudding

Prep time: 15 minutes | Cook time: 15 minutes | Serves: 2

360ml water	150g bittersweet chocolate slivers	2 teaspoon vanilla extract	55g brown sugar
360g whipping cream	5 egg yolks	Dash of salt	
120ml milk		¼ teaspoon cinnamon	

1. Prepare the Ninja Foodi XL Pressure Cooker Steam Fryer by adding the water to the pot and placing the Deluxe Reversible Rack in it. 2. In a saucepan, combine the cream and milk and bring to a simmer. Remove from heat. Add the chocolate. Stir until the chocolate is melted. In a bowl, whisk together the egg yolks, vanilla extract, salt, cinnamon and sugar until combined. Stirring constantly, add hot chocolate to yolk mixture. Pour the mixture in the Cook & Crisp Basket. Cover the pan tightly with aluminum foil. 3. Lock lid; move slider towards PRESSURE. Adjust pressure release valve in the SEAL position. Close pressure-release valve. The cooking temperature will default to HIGH, which is accurate. Cook on LOW pressure for 20 minutes. Select START/STOP and start cooking. 4. When cooking is complete, let pressure naturally release for 5 minutes, then quickly release any remaining pressure by turning it into VENT position. Remove the Cook & Crisp Basket from the pot. 5. Let it cool to room temperature, cover and chill at least 4 hours or up to 2 days. Serve.
Per Serving: Calories 354; Fat 7.9g; Sodium 704mg; Carbs 6g; Fiber 3.6g; Sugar 6g; Protein 18g

Sweet Raspberry Curd

Prep time: 5 minutes | Cook time: 25 minutes | Serves: 8

1200g. raspberries	3 tablespoon lemon juice	3 tablespoon butter
300 g sugar	3 egg yolks	

1. In the Ninja Foodi XL Pressure Cooker Steam Fryer, combine the raspberries, sugar and lemon juice. Lock lid; move slider towards PRESSURE. Adjust pressure release valve in the SEAL position. Close pressure-release valve. The cooking temperature will default to HIGH, which is accurate. Set time to 2 minutes. Select START/STOP and start cooking. 2. When cooking is complete, let pressure release naturally for 5 minutes, then quickly release by turning it into VENT position. Open the lid. 3. Use the mesh strainer to puree the raspberries and remove the seeds. In a bowl, whisk egg yolks and combine with the raspberries puree. Return the mixture to the pot. 4. Move the slider towards "AIR FRY/STOVETOP" and set Ninja Foodi XL Pressure Cooker Steam Fryer with SmartLid to SEAR/SAUTÉ mode. Adjust the temperature to "Hi5" by using up arrow. Press START/STOP to begin cooking. 5. Bring the mixture to a boil, stirring constantly. Press the START/STOP key to stop the SAUTÉ function. Add the butter and stir to combine. Serve chilled.
Per Serving: Calories 354; Fat 7.9g; Sodium 704mg; Carbs 6g; Fiber 3.6g; Sugar 6g; Protein 18g

Coconut Custard

Prep time: 5 minutes | Cook time: 30 minutes | Serves: 4

240ml unsweetened coconut milk	3 eggs	4 drops pandan extract
	65g sugar	

1. Combine all of the ingredients and pour them into a casserole dish and cover with foil. Add the Deluxe Reversible Rack and 480ml of water to the cooking pot of Ninja Foodi XL Pressure Cooker Steam Fryer. 2. Place the casserole dish on the Deluxe Reversible Rack. 3. Lock lid; move slider towards PRESSURE. Adjust pressure release valve in the SEAL position. Close pressure-release valve. The cooking temperature will default to HIGH, which is accurate. Set time to 30 minutes. Select START/STOP and start cooking. 4. When cooking is complete, let pressure release naturally. Then transfer to the fridge until the custard sets.
Per Serving: Calories 381; Fat 36g; Sodium 2mg; Carbs 16g; Fiber 1g; Sugar 13g; Protein 0g

Berries Mug Cake

Prep time: 5 minutes | Cook time: 10 minutes | Serves: 1

40g almond flour	1 tablespoon maple syrup	⅛ teaspoon salt
1 egg	½ teaspoon vanilla	75g blueberries

1. Combine all of the ingredients in a bowl. Transfer to a 200g mason jar and cover with foil. Add the Deluxe Reversible Rack in Ninja Foodi XL Pressure Cooker Steam Fryer and a 180ml of water to the pot. Place the jar on the Deluxe Reversible Rack and seal the pot. 2. Lock lid; move slider towards PRESSURE. Adjust pressure release valve in the SEAL position. Close pressure-release valve. The cooking temperature will default to HIGH, which is accurate. Set time to 10 minutes. Select START/STOP and start cooking. 3. When cooking is complete, let pressure release naturally. Serve while still warm.
Per Serving: Calories 106; Fat 6.9g; Sodium 1mg; Carbs 12g; Fiber 2g; Sugar 10g; Protein 0g

Yellow Marmalade

Prep time: 15 minutes | Cook time: 15 minutes | Serves: 6

| 455g lemons, quartered, deseeded, and sliced with a mandolin | 120ml water | 900g sugar |

1. Add the lemons and water to the Ninja Foodi XL Pressure Cooker Steam Fryer. 2. Lock lid; move slider towards PRESSURE. Adjust pressure release valve in the SEAL position. Close pressure-release valve. The cooking temperature will default to HIGH, which is accurate. Set time to 2 minutes. Select START/STOP and start cooking. 3. When cooking is complete, let pressure release naturally for 10 minutes. Uncover the pot. Add the sugar and stir for 2 minutes until the sugar melts. 4. Move the slider towards "AIR FRY/STOVETOP" and set Ninja Foodi XL Pressure Cooker Steam Fryer with SmartLid to SEAR/SAUTÉ mode. Adjust the temperature to "Hi5" by using up arrow. Press START/STOP to begin cooking. 5. Bring to a boil, cook for 5 minutes. Transfer the mixture into clean or sterilized jars. Serve chilled or store in the refrigerator.
Per Serving: Calories 354; Fat 7.9g; Sodium 704mg; Carbs 6g; Fiber 3.6g; Sugar 6g; Protein 18g

Caramel Pear Pudding

Prep time: 15 minutes | Cook time: 15 minutes | Serves: 2

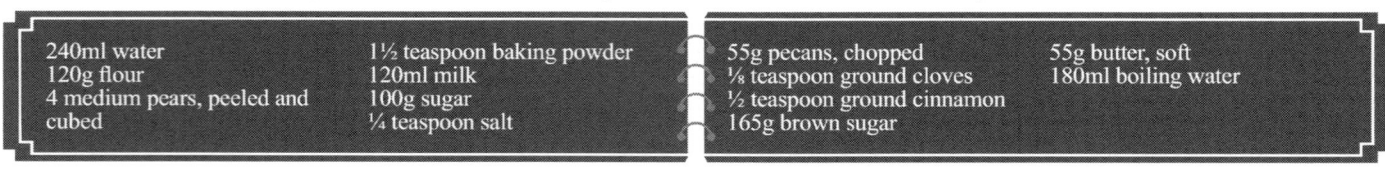

240ml water	1½ teaspoon baking powder	55g pecans, chopped	55g butter, soft
120g flour	120ml milk	⅛ teaspoon ground cloves	180ml boiling water
4 medium pears, peeled and cubed	100g sugar	½ teaspoon ground cinnamon	
	¼ teaspoon salt	165g brown sugar	

1. Prepare the Ninja Foodi XL Pressure Cooker Steam Fryer by adding the water to the pot and placing the Deluxe Reversible Rack in it. 2. In the Cook & Crisp Basket, combine the flour, pears, baking powder, milk, sugar, salt, pecans, cloves, and cinnamon. In a bowl, whisk together the butter, sugar and boiling water until combined. Pour this mixture into the Cook & Crisp Basket, don't stir. Place the Cook & Crisp Basket on the Deluxe Reversible Rack. 3. Lock lid; move slider towards PRESSURE. Adjust pressure release valve in the SEAL position. Close pressure-release valve. The cooking temperature will default to HIGH, which is accurate. Set time to 35 minutes. Select START/STOP and start cooking. 4. When cooking is complete, let pressure quickly release by turning it into VENT position. 5. Let the pudding cool, and then refrigerate before serving.
Per Serving: Calories 354; Fat 7.9g; Sodium 704mg; Carbs 6g; Fiber 3.6g; Sugar 6g; Protein 18g

Delicious Banana Bread

Prep time: 15 minutes | Cook time: 1 hour 10 minutes | Serves: 6

120g unbleached flour	½ teaspoon baking soda	150g ripe bananas, mashed	1 egg
100g sugar or sugar substitute	½ teaspoon vanilla extract	75g softened butter	30g walnuts, chopped
2 teaspoons baking powder	½ teaspoon sea salt	60ml milk	

1. Combine the flour, sugar, baking powder, baking soda and salt in a large mixing bowl; whisk until the ingredients are well mixed. Fold in the bananas, butter, milk, egg and vanilla extract. 2. Use an electric mixer to mix until the batter has a uniform thick consistency. Fold in chopped walnuts. Grease the bottom of the cooking pot with non-stick cooking spray. Pour batter into cooking pot. 3. Lock lid; move slider to AIR FRY/STOVETOP. Select STEAM, and set time to 30 minutes. Press START/STOP to begin cooking. Cook for 30 minutes more. 4. Transfer to plate and let cool for one hour before serving.
Per Serving: Calories 105; Fat 5g; Sodium 233mg; Carbs 7g; Fiber 2g; Sugar 4g; Protein 8g

Red Cherry Compote

Prep time: 15 minutes | Cook time: 15 minutes | Serves: 2

| 460g cherries, fresh or frozen | 1 tablespoon coconut oil | 1½ tablespoon maple syrup | 2 tablespoon corn flour |
| 110g apples, peeled and diced | 180ml water | A pinch of salt | |

1. In the Ninja Foodi XL Pressure Cooker Steam Fryer, combine the cherries, apples, coconut oil, water, maple syrup, and salt. 2. Lock lid; move slider towards PRESSURE. Adjust pressure release valve in the SEAL position. Close pressure-release valve. The cooking temperature will default to HIGH, which is accurate. Set time to 4 minutes. Select START/STOP and start cooking. 3. When cooking is complete, let pressure quickly release by turning it into VENT position. Carefully unlock the lid. Stir well. 4. Move the slider towards "AIR FRY/STOVETOP" and set Ninja Foodi XL Pressure Cooker Steam Fryer with SmartLid to SEAR/SAUTÉ mode. Adjust the temperature to "Hi5" by using up arrow. Press START/STOP to begin cooking. 5. Add the corn flour, and stirring occasionally, bring the mixture to a boil. Press the START/STOP to stop the SAUTÉ function. Let the compote cool for 10 minutes. Serve.
Per Serving: Calories 354; Fat 7.9g; Sodium 704mg; Carbs 6g; Fiber 3.6g; Sugar 6g; Protein 18g

Sweet Quiche

Prep time: 5 minutes | Cook time: 35 minutes | Serves: 2

3 large eggs	Salt and ground black pepper	1 tablespoon chives, chopped	Cooking spray
60ml milk	to taste	50g cheddar cheese, shredded	240ml water

1. In a medium bowl, whisk together eggs, milk, salt, pepper, and chives until combined. Grease the Cook & Crisp Basket with cooking spray. Add the cheese to the Cook & Crisp Basket. 2. Pour the egg mixture into the pan and spread evenly. Pour the water into the Ninja Foodi XL Pressure Cooker Steam Fryer and set a Deluxe Reversible Rack in the pot. Place the Cook & Crisp Basket on the rack. 3. Lock lid; move slider towards PRESSURE. Adjust pressure release valve in the SEAL position. Close pressure-release valve. The cooking temperature will default to HIGH, which is accurate. Set time to 30 minutes. Select START/STOP and start cooking. 4. When cooking is complete, let pressure quickly release by turning it into VENT position. Carefully unlock the lid. Serve.
Per Serving: Calories 30; Fat 13g; Sodium 12mg; Carbs 49g; Fiber 4g; Sugar 6g; Protein 3g

Tangy Fruit Salad Jam

Prep time: 15 minutes | Cook time: 15 minutes | Serves: 2

150g blueberries	1 medium apple, diced	1 teaspoon lemon zest	360ml water
1 medium orange, peeled	200g sugar	½ teaspoon cinnamon	

1. In the Ninja Foodi XL Pressure Cooker Steam Fryer, combine the blueberries, orange, apple, sugar, lemon zest, cinnamon and water. 2. Lock lid; move slider towards PRESSURE. Adjust pressure release valve in the SEAL position. Close pressure-release valve. The cooking temperature will default to HIGH, which is accurate. Set time to 4 minutes. Select START/STOP and start cooking. 3. When cooking is complete, let pressure release naturally for 10 minutes, then quickly release any remaining pressure by turning it into VENT position. Carefully unlock the lid. 4. Move the slider towards "AIR FRY/STOVETOP" and set Ninja Foodi XL Pressure Cooker Steam Fryer with SmartLid to SEAR/SAUTÉ mode. Adjust the temperature to "Hi5" by using up arrow. Press START/STOP to begin cooking. 5. Simmer the sauce until thickened. Let it cool and serve.
Per Serving: Calories 354; Fat 7.9g; Sodium 704mg; Carbs 6g; Fiber 3.6g; Sugar 6g; Protein 18g

Nutty Chocolate Candy

Prep time: 15 minutes | Cook time: 15 minutes | Serves: 2

1100ml condensed coconut milk	150g dark chocolate chips	90g almonds, chopped
	480ml	

1. In the Cook & Crisp Basket, combine the chocolate chips and coconut milk. Cover the Cook & Crisp Basket tightly with aluminum foil. Place the Deluxe reversible rack in the bottom of cooking pot. Place the Cook & Crisp Basket on the rack. 2. Lock lid; move slider towards PRESSURE. Adjust pressure release valve in the SEAL position. Close pressure-release valve. The cooking temperature will default to HIGH, which is accurate. Set time to 3 minutes. Select START/STOP and start cooking. 3. When cooking is complete, let pressure release quickly by turning it into VENT position. Carefully unlock the lid. Add the almonds and mix well. Line a sheet pan with a parchment paper. 4. With a tablespoon, drop the candy onto the paper. Slip the pan into the freezer for about 10-20 minutes. Serve.
Per Serving: Calories 354; Fat 7.9g; Sodium 704mg; Carbs 6g; Fiber 3.6g; Sugar 6g; Protein 18g

Poached Spiced Pears with Pomegranate

Prep time: 10 minutes | Cook time: 55 minutes | Serves: 4

2 firm Anjou or Bosc pears, peeled, halved, and cored	2 cinnamon sticks	1 pinch of freshly shaved nutmeg	Vanilla ice cream, optional
480ml pomegranate juice	1 large orange peel, about 2.5 cm thick	1-piece fresh ginger peeled, cut into thin slivers	
480ml apple cider	2 whole cloves		

1. Add all ingredients to the cooking pot of the Ninja Foodi XL Pressure Cooker Steam Fryer. 2. Lock lid; move slider to AIR FRY/STOVETOP. Select STEAM, and set time to 30 minutes. Press START/STOP to begin cooking. Cook for 20 minutes more. 3. Open the lid and flip the pears over; let rest for 1 hour. Turn pears over again and let sit for another hour. 4. Serve warm with vanilla ice cream, or refrigerate overnight for a more intense flavor and color.
Per Serving: Calories 200; Fat 15.6g; Sodium 165mg; Carbs 5g; Fiber 1g; Sugar 2g; Protein 10g

Delicious Blueberries Yogurt

Prep time: 15 minutes | Cook time: 15 minutes | Serves: 4

50g sugar	½ teaspoon balsamic vinegar	480g drained low-fat yogurt	and diced
295g blueberries	1 tablespoon lime juice	1 tablespoon pistachios, shelled	

1. In the Ninja Foodi XL Pressure Cooker Steam Fryer, combine the sugar, blueberries, vinegar and lime juice. 2. Lock lid; move slider towards PRESSURE. Adjust pressure release valve in the SEAL position. Close pressure-release valve. The cooking temperature will default to HIGH, which is accurate. Set time to 10minutes. Select START/STOP and start cooking. 3. When cooking is complete, let pressure release naturally for 10 minutes by turning it into VENT position. Uncover the pot. Prepare the yogurt jars. Pour 60 g of yogurt into each jars. Then add 2 tablespoon of blueberry sauce into jars. Make another layer of yogurt and top with blueberry sauce again. 4. Sprinkle with pistachios at the end. Refrigerate until ready to serve.
Per Serving: Calories 354; Fat 7.9g; Sodium 704mg; Carbs 6g; Fiber 3.6g; Sugar 6g; Protein 18g

Vegan Coconut Yogurt

Prep time: 15 minutes | Cook time: 15 minutes | Serves: 2

3 cans coconut milk	4 capsules probiotics	1 tablespoon maple syrup	2 tablespoon gelatin

1. Remove the top cream from the coconut milk and add to the Ninja Foodi XL Pressure Cooker Steam Fryer. 2. Lock lid; move slider to AIR FRY/STOVETOP and select the YOGURT. The default temperature setting will display. Use the up and down arrows to the left of the display to select "FEr". Press START/STOP to begin cooking. Bring the milk to a boil. Then press START/STOP to stop cooking. 3. When the temperature drops to 40°C, open the probiotics capsules and add to the milk. Stir until combined. Close and lock the lid. Select the YOGURT again and set the cooking time for 8 hours. 4. Open the lid. Add the maple syrup and gelatin and gently stir well. Pour equally into the jars. Let it cool completely and refrigerate for 1-2 hours before serving.
Per Serving: Calories 354; Fat 7.9g; Sodium 704mg; Carbs 6g; Fiber 3.6g; Sugar 6g; Protein 18g

Sweet Tapioca

Prep time: 15 minutes | Cook time: 15 minutes | Serves: 2

150g pearl tapioca, rinsed	2 teaspoon ginger, grated	4 egg yolks	½ teaspoon salt
1.2L coconut milk	15 cm lemongrass, diced	200g sugar	130g cashew nuts, toasted

1. In the Ninja Foodi XL Pressure Cooker Steam Fryer, combine the tapioca and coconut milk. Add the ginger and lemongrass, stir. 2. Lock lid; move slider to AIR FRY/STOVETOP. Select STEAM, and set time to 6 minutes. Press START/STOP to begin cooking. Uncover the pot. In a bowl, whisk together the egg yolks, sugar and salt until combined. 3. Move the slider towards "AIR FRY/STOVETOP" and set Ninja Foodi XL Pressure Cooker Steam Fryer with SmartLid to SEAR/SAUTÉ mode. Adjust the temperature to "Hi5" by using up arrow. Press START/STOP to begin cooking and add the egg mixture. 4. Simmer until the mixture has thickened. Sprinkle with toasted cashew nuts and serve.
Per Serving: Calories 354; Fat 7.9g; Sodium 704mg; Carbs 6g; Fiber 3.6g; Sugar 6g; Protein 18g

Creamy Raspberry Jam

Prep time: 5 minutes | Cook time: 25 minutes | Serves: 8

490g raspberries (fresh or frozen)	200g sugar or 225g light honey	1½ tablespoon corn flour
	3 tablespoon lemon juice	1½ tablespoon water

1. In the Ninja Foodi XL Pressure Cooker Steam Fryer, combine the raspberries, sugar and lemon. Stir well. 2. Lock lid; move slider towards PRESSURE. Adjust pressure release valve in the SEAL position. Close pressure-release valve. The cooking temperature will default to HIGH, which is accurate. Set time to 3 minutes. Select START/STOP and start cooking. 3. When cooking is complete, let pressure release naturally for 10 minutes, then quickly release by turning it into VENT position. 4. Uncover the pot. In a cup, whisk together the corn flour and water until combined. Pour this mixture in the pot and stir. 5. Let the jam cool and use up within a week, or freeze for later.
Per Serving: Calories 354; Fat 7.9g; Sodium 704mg; Carbs 6g; Fiber 3.6g; Sugar 6g; Protein 18g

Syrupy Crème Brulee

Prep time: 15 minutes | Cook time: 15 minutes | Serves: 2

240ml water	¼ teaspoon ground cinnamon	300g heavy whipping cream, warm	½ teaspoon maple extract
3 large egg yolks	105g brown sugar		1½ teaspoon sugar

1. Pour the water into the Ninja Foodi XL Pressure Cooker Steam Fryer and set a Deluxe Reversible Rack in the pot. In a medium bowl, whisk together egg yolks, cinnamon and sugar until combined. 2. Add the warm cream and stir well. Add the maple extract, stir. Divide the mixture between the ramekins and sprinkle sugar for the topping. Place the ramekins on the Deluxe Reversible Rack. 3. Lock lid; move slider to AIR FRY/STOVETOP. Select STEAM, and set time to 30 minutes. Press START/STOP to begin cooking. 4. Let the ramekins cool, and then refrigerate them for 10-15 minutes. Serve.
Per Serving: Calories 354; Fat 7.9g; Sodium 704mg; Carbs 6g; Fiber 3.6g; Sugar 6g; Protein 18g

Matcha Cake

Prep time: 8 minutes | Cook time: 30 minutes | Serves: 4

2 large eggs	100g sugar	1 tablespoon green tea matcha powder	½ teaspoon baking powder
120g unbleached flour	115g butter		

1. Combine all of the ingredients in a large mixing bowl. Grease the cooking pot of the Ninja Foodi XL Pressure Cooker Steam Fryer with non-stick cooking spray. 2. Add the cake mix to the cooking pot. Lock lid; move slider to STEAMCRISP. Select STEAM & BAKE, set temperature to 200°C, and set time to 30 minutes. Press START/STOP to begin cooking. 3. Open the lid. Transfer to a plate to cool for 20 minutes and serve!
Per Serving: Calories 138; Fat 10.6g; Sodium 102mg; Carbs 1g; Fiber 0g; Sugar 1g; Protein 9g

Flan

Prep time: 15 minutes | Cook time: 1 hour 10 minutes | Serves: 4

6 egg yolks	1 (150g) can condensed milk	50g granulated sugar, for caramel sauce	One flan mold
1 (150g) can evaporated milk	1 teaspoon pure vanilla extract		

1. Gently combine the egg yolk, condensed milk, evaporated milk and vanilla in a large mixing bowl and set aside. Add granulated sugar to a saucepan and heat on a stove at medium-low, while stirring; turn off the heat when sugar is melted and caramel colored, and assemble flan. Pour the custard into the flan mold. 2. Add caramel sauce evenly over custard. Place flan in the Cook & Crisp Basket. 3. Lock lid; move slider to AIR FRY/STOVETOP. Select STEAM, and set time to 30 minutes. Press START/STOP to begin cooking. Cook for 30 minutes more. 4. Let it cool completely, transfer to a plate, and serve!
Per Serving: Calories 311; Fat 6g; Sodium 112mg; Carbs 15g; Fiber 6g; Sugar 12g; Protein 2g

Delicious Cranberry Pudding

Prep time: 15 minutes | Cook time: 15 minutes | Serves: 2

240ml water	100g sugar, granulated	1 teaspoon vanilla extract	105g bread cubes
3 large eggs, beaten	480ml milk	35g dried cranberries	35g pecans, chopped

1. Prepare the Ninja Foodi XL Pressure Cooker Steam Fryer by adding the water to the pot and placing the Deluxe Reversible Rack in it. 2. In a bowl, whisk together the eggs, sugar and milk until combined. Add the vanilla, stir. Grease the Cook & Crisp Basket and add the cranberries and bread cubes. Pour the egg mixture in the Cook & Crisp Basket. Cover tightly with tin aluminum foil. Place the dish on the Deluxe Reversible Rack. Close and lock the lid. 3. Lock lid; move slider to AIR FRY/STOVETOP. Select STEAM, and set time to 25 minutes. Press START/STOP to begin cooking. Open the lid, uncover the Cook & Crisp Basket and sprinkle with pecans. 4. Serve or cover and chill up to 24 hours.
Per Serving: Calories 354; Fat 7.9g; Sodium 704mg; Carbs 6g; Fiber 3.6g; Sugar 6g; Protein 18g

Conclusion

In this fast-paced world, everything moves quickly, and your lifestyle needs to match that. For this reason, many cooking appliances are made to make it easier and take less time to make a tasty, healthy, and nutritious meal. Ninja Foodi XL Pressure Cooker Steam Fryer is one of the best appliances for today's fast-paced world because it lets you cook quickly, gives you a healthy meal that meets your dietary needs, and doesn't break the bank. With this appliance, you can quickly cook, bake, slow cook, and steam food.

The Ninja Foodi XL Pressure Cooker Steam Fryer cookbook is the perfect guidance that shows you how to use your device like a pro and gives you quick, easy, and healthy recipes. You can spend your time in the kitchen and do other things simultaneously. You and your family can enjoy a fantastic meal when you're done.

This fantastic cookbook has recipes for food from all over the world. Even if you don't cook often or professionally, it's easy to make food. This fantastic cookbook shows you how to prepare and cook your meal like a pro. So, guys, let's start our Ninja Foodi XL Pressure Cooker Steam Fryer journey and enjoy our fast-forward life with delicious food.

Appendix 1 Measurement Conversion Chart

VOLUME EQUIVALENTS (LIQUID)

US STANDARD	US STANDARD (OUNCES)	METRIC (APPROXIMATE)
2 tablespoons	1 fl.oz	30 mL
¼ cup	2 fl.oz	60 mL
½ cup	4 fl.oz	120 mL
1 cup	8 fl.oz	240 mL
1½ cup	12 fl.oz	355 mL
2 cups or 1 pint	16 fl.oz	475 mL
4 cups or 1 quart	32 fl.oz	1 L
1 gallon	128 fl.oz	4 L

VOLUME EQUIVALENTS (DRY)

US STANDARD	METRIC (APPROXIMATE)
⅛ teaspoon	0.5 mL
¼ teaspoon	1 mL
½ teaspoon	2 mL
¾ teaspoon	4 mL
1 teaspoon	5 mL
1 tablespoon	15 mL
¼ cup	59 mL
½ cup	118 mL
¾ cup	177 mL
1 cup	235 mL
2 cups	475 mL
3 cups	700 mL
4 cups	1 L

TEMPERATURES EQUIVALENTS

FAHRENHEIT(F)	CELSIUS (C) (APPROXIMATE)
225 °F	107 °C
250 °F	120 °C
275 °F	135 °C
300 °F	150 °C
325 °F	160 °C
350 °F	180 °C
375 °F	190 °C
400 °F	205 °C
425 °F	220 °C
450 °F	235 °C
475 °F	245 °C
500 °F	260 °C

WEIGHT EQUIVALENTS

US STANDARD	METRIC (APPROXINATE)
1 ounce	28 g
2 ounces	57 g
5 ounces	142 g
10 ounces	284 g
15 ounces	425 g
16 ounces (1 pound)	455 g
1.5 pounds	680 g
2 pounds	907 g

Appendix 2 Air Fryer Cooking Chart

Vegetables	Temp (°F)	Time (min)
Asparagus	375	4 to 6
Baked Potatoes	400	35 to 45
Broccoli	400	8 to 10
Brussels Sprouts	350	15 to 18
Butternut Squash (cubed)	375	20 to 25
Carrots	375	15 to 25
Cauliflower	400	10 to 12
Corn on the Cob	390	6
Eggplant	400	15
Green Beans	375	16 to 20
Kale	250	12
Mushrooms	400	5
Peppers	375	8 to 10
Sweet Potatoes (whole)	380	30 to 35
Tomatoes (halved, sliced)	350	10
Zucchini (½-inch sticks)	400	12

Frozen Foods	Temp (°F)	Time (min)
Breaded Shrimp	400	9
Chicken Burger	360	11
Chicken Nudgets	400	10
Corn Dogs	400	7
Curly Fries (1 to 2 lbs.)	400	11 to 14
Fish Sticks (10 oz.)	400	10
French Fries	380	15 to 20
Hash Brown	360	15 to 18
Meatballs	380	6 to 8
Mozzarella Sticks	400	8
Onion Rings (8 oz.)	400	8
Pizza	390	5 to 10
Pot Pie	360	25
Pot Sticks (10 oz.)	400	8
Sausage Rolls	400	15
Spring Rolls	400	15 to 20

Meat and Seafood	Temp (°F)	Time (min)
Bacon	400	5 to 10
Beef Eye Round Roast (4 lbs.)	390	45 to 55
Bone to in Pork Chops	400	4 to 5 per side
Brats	400	8 to 10
Burgers	350	8 to 10
Chicken Breast	375	22 to 23
Chicken Tender	400	14 to 16
Chicken Thigh	400	25
Chicken Wings (2 lbs.)	400	10 to 12
Cod	370	8 to 10
Fillet Mignon (8 oz.)	400	14 to 18
Fish Fillet (0.5 lb., 1-inch)	400	10
Flank Steak (1.5 lbs.)	400	10 to 14
Lobster Tails (4 oz.)	380	5 to 7
Meatballs	400	7 to 10
Meat Loaf	325	35 to 45
Pork Chops	375	12 to 15
Salmon	400	5 to 7
Salmon Fillet (6 oz.)	380	12
Sausage Patties	400	8 to 10
Shrimp	375	8
Steak	400	7 to 14
Tilapia	400	8 to 12
Turkey Breast (3 lbs.)	360	40 to 50
Whole Chicken (6.5 lbs.)	360	75

Desserts	Temp (°F)	Time (min)
Apple Pie	320	30
Brownies	350	17
Churros	360	13
Cookies	350	5
Cupcakes	330	11
Doughnuts	360	5
Roasted Bananas	375	8
Peaches	350	5

Appendix 3 Recipes Index

A

Air Fried Bacon Slices 66
Air Fried Grapefruit 14
Air Fried Turkey Breast 50
Air-Fried Bacon Slices 64
Air-Fried Brown Mushrooms 29
Air-Fried Brussels Sprouts 31
Air-Fried Chicken Breasts 50
Air-Fried Chicken Legs 50
Air-Fried Pork Rinds 103
Air-Fried Turkey Wings 55
Almond Cookies 110
Apricots in Whiskey Sauce 112
Artichoke Hearts and Chicken 56
Artichoke Pizza 15
Artichoke Stuffed Aubergine 36
Asian Style Sea Bass 88
Asian-Spiced Duck 51
Aubergine Chips 104
Avocado Balls 105
Avocado Wraps 102

B

Bacon and Sausage Omelet 14
Bacon Bites 102
Bacon Chaffle 101
Bacon Cups 64
Bacon Knots 14
Bacon Red Cabbage with Cheese 32
Bacon Sprouts Wraps 101
Bacon Wrapped Scallops 94
Baked Cheesy Hash Brown Bake 25
Baked Egg 27
Baked Eggs 18
Barbecue Spicy Meatloaf 71
BBQ Baby Ribs 67
Bean Ham Soup 83
Beef and Tomatillo Stew 78
Beef Carne Asada 63
Beef Meat Loaf 65
Beef Reuben Fritters 67
Beef Smokies 105
Beef Steak Nuggets 62
Beef Taco Pasta 71
Beefy Minestrone Soup 84
Beefy Poppers 64
Beer–Braised Short Ribs 72
Berries Mug Cake 117
Blueberry Morning Muffins 19
Blueberry Oats Crisp 113
Boiled Eggs 21
Bratwurst with Sauerkraut 73
Breaded Salmon 90
Breakfast Scotch Eggs 18
Broccoli Cranberry Salad 34
Broccoli Quiche 15
Burrito Bowls with Chicken And Beans 59
Buttery Egg Noodles 42

C

Cajun Lemon Salmon 90
California-style Pot Roast 69
Caramel Pear Pudding 118
Carrot Cake 116
Cashew Dip 104
Cayenne Parsnip Burgers 33
Cheddar Cheese Rounds 102
Cheese Broccoli Pizza 30
Cheese Sticks 103
Cheese Stuffed Peppers 33
Cheesy Bacon Muffins 19
Cheesy Bacon Quiche 26
Cheesy Meaty Sausage Frittata 23
Cheesy Philly Steaks 72
Chia Pudding Tarts 115
Chicken and Vegetable Stock 84
Chicken BBQ Burgers 51
Chicken Egg Roll 54
Chicken Fritters 49
Chicken Meatballs 105
Chicken Mushroom Kabobs 48
Chicken Parmesan 49
Chicken Pepper Fajitas 55
Chicken Soup 85
Chicken Taquitos 54
Chicken Tenders 48
Chicken Thighs with Salsa 56
Chicken Wing Stir-Fry 49
Chicken with Broccoli Stir-Fry 48
Chicken with Dumplings 81
Chicken with Marinara Sauce 57
Chicken with Mushrooms 52
Chicken with Pineapple 54
Chile Verde 59
Chinese Braised Pork with Aubergine 74
Chocolate Cake 108
Chocolate Cookie Cups 115
Chocolate Egg Rolls 111
Chocolate Pudding Cake 116
Chocolate Rolls 17
Chow Relish 39
Cinnamon Flour Twists 113
Cinnamon Pear Clafoutis 112
Cinnamon Stuffed Apples 114
Cinnamon-Spiced Beef Noodle Soup 76
Citrus-Glazed Pork Chops 62
Clafoutis 111
Clam Chowder 83
Clam Corn Chowder 81
Classical Hard-Boiled Eggs 17
Classical Poached Eggs 19
Coconut Custard 117
Coconut Granola 105
Cod with Grapes 88
Cod with Olives and Fennel 97
Cod with Spring Onions 94
Colourful Burgundy Mushrooms 35
Colourful Ratatouille Stew 34
Colourful Vegetable Rice 43
Confetti Cake 114
Corn Chowder with Potatoes 81
Corn on The Cob 31
Country Boil 95
Crab Legs 90
Cracker S'mores 112
Cranberry Brownies 110
Cranberry Cake 108
Cranberry Nutty Grits 24
Cranberry-citrus Sauce 41
Creamy Cauliflower Puree 40
Creamy Corn 40
Creamy Corn with Crabmeat 42
Creamy Crab 97
Creamy Raspberry Jam 120
Creamy Scallops 93
Crispy Courgette Chips 101
Crispy Fish Sticks 89
Crispy Fried Chicken 46
Crispy Honey Chicken Wings 45
Crispy Parmesan Artichokes 37
Crispy Profiteroles 112
Crispy Sweet Brussels Sprouts 38
Crispy Sweet Potatoes 30
Crusted Aubergine 31
Crusted Chicken Fingers 50
Crusted Courgette Chips 102
Crusted Hot Dogs 104
Crusted Lamb Chops 65
Crusted Portobello Mushrooms 34
Cumin-Spiced Beef and Potato Stew 79
Curried Coconut Prawns 98

D

Delicious Arroz Con Pollo 52
Delicious Banana Bread 118
Delicious Beef Stroganoff 70
Delicious Blueberries Yogurt 120
Delicious Collard Greens 41
Delicious Cranberry Pudding 121
Delicious Lamb Gyros 77
Delicious Lobster Risotto 96
Delicious Louisiana Grouper 93
Delicious Minestrone 84

Delicious Moroccan Carrot Soup 86
Delicious Moroccan Meatballs 79
Delicious Mushroom Frittata 24
Delicious Mustard Potato Salad 32
Delicious Pork Vindaloo 77
Delicious Portobello Pot Roast 35
Delicious Seafood Gumbo 99
Delicious Sesame Chicken 55
Delicious Teriyaki Chicken 47
Delicious Umami Calamari 92
Delightful Eggs 23
Dijon Glazed Pork Loin 61
Duck Wraps 106

E

Easy Pork Chops 63
Egg Quesadillas 21
Eggs Dish 25

F

Fajita Rollups 46
Fig-Glazed Ham with Potatoes 76
Fish Capers Cakes 89
Fish Chowder 97
Fish Fingers 89
Fish Stew 98
Flan 121
Flaxseed Carrot Cake 113
Flaxseed Cookies 114
Flaxseed Muffins 21
Fried Beans 36
Fried Chicken 56
Fried PB&J Sandwich 26
Fried Prawns 91
Frosted Blackberry Shortcake 109

G

Garlic and Chive Fries 33
Garlicky Mashed Vegetables 39
Garlicky Roasted Cauliflower 38
Garlicky Salmon Fillets 93
German Roulade 64
Gingered Potatoes 40
Green Beans Salad 38
Green Rice 43
Grilled Salmon 91
Grilled Salmon with Capers 88

H

Ham Casserole 26
Ham Eggs 14
Ham Polenta Muffins 15
Hamburgers 68
Hawaiian Roll Sliders 53
Healthy Blueberry Oat Mini Muffins 24
Healthy Egg Muffins 24

Healthy Three Bean Chili 86
Healthy White Chicken Chili 85
Herbed Lamb Chops 69
Herby Pork Chops with Squash 73
Honey Bratwurst with Brussels Sprouts 61
Hush Puffs 15

I

Indian Chicken Marsala 47
Indian Lamb Steaks 63
Italian Pork Loin 66
Italian Sauce 70

J

Jelly stuffed Muffins 23
Jerk-Spiced Chicken Wings 49

K

Kale Sausage Soup 85
KFC Chicken 48
Korean Wings 45

L

Lemon Cheesecake 116
Lemon Chicken with Herbed Potatoes 58
Lemon Salmon with Dill 95
Lemony Broccoli Salad 36
Lemony Brussels Sprout Salad 37
Limey Duck Breast 55
Lo Mein 58
Lobster with Butter Sauce 98

M

Macadamia Cookies 108
Madeira Glazed Ham 62
Mahi-Mahi with a Lemon-Caper Sauce 96
Maple Carrots with Dill 29
Matcha Cake 121
Mayo Chicken Salad 54
Mayo Egg Salad 25
Meatball Lettuce Wraps 67
Meatballs 104
Meatballs with Creamy Pan Sauce 71
Meatloaf 63
Mediterranean Chicken Fillets 53
Mediterranean Spicy Cod 95
Mexican Burgers 46
Miso Salmon Fillets 92
Moroccan Meat Soup with Chickpeas and Lentils 76
Muffin Burgers 61
Mushroom 'Pot Roast' 42
Mushroom Basil Bites 101

Mushroom Boat Eggs 19
Mushroom Burgers 69
Mushroom Cheese Loaf 38
Mussels in White Wine 94
Mustard Coconut Prawns 92

N

Nutty Cake 116
Nutty Chocolate Candy 119

O

Oat Muffins 20
Omelet Cups 20
Orange Cake 111

P

Pakistani Spiced Beef Stew 78
Paprika Cabbage Steaks 40
Paprika Chicken Cutlets 53
Parmesan Bread 13
Parmesan Cauliflower 32
Parmesan Cod 93
Parmesan Green Bean Casserole 39
Parmesan Potatoes 34
Parmesan Tilapia 90
Parsley Olives Fritters 102
Parsnips Meal 32
Peach Vanilla Fritters 13
Peach Walnut Parfaits 113
Pearl Couscous Salad 39
Pepper Bread 16
Pepper Cups 20
Pepperoni Cheese Pizza 17
Persian Beef and Kidney Bean Stew 77
Pesto Turkey Meatballs with Pasta 59
Pickled Bacon 103
Pineapple with Macadamia Batter 109
Pita Bread 13
Poached Spiced Pears with Pomegranate 119
Pork Bun Thit Nuong 66
Pork Chops with Beans 73
Pork Cutlets 61
Pork Meatballs 103
Pork Quiche Cups 27
Pork Ragu with Gnocchi 74
Porridge 22
Pot Pie Soup 86
Potato Salad 33
Potato Soup with cheese 83
Prawn Balls 106
Prawns Scampi 92
Prawns Scampi with Cheese 98
Prawns with tangy Risotto 99
Prune Cookies 110
Pudding with Sultanas 109
Pulled Pork Barbecue 72

R

Raspberry Pineapple Sundaes 115
Red Cherry Compote 118
Red Salmon Croquettes 90
Refreshing Chicken Tacos 59
Refreshing Steamed Broccoli 41
Regular Chicken Stock 82
Regular Chocolate Pudding 117
Regular Pad Thai 94
Regular Vegetable Stock 82
Roasted Broccoli 29
Roasted Country-Style Vegetables 29
Roasted Peppers 30
Roasted Red Hummus 37

S

Salisbury Steak with Mushroom Gravy 66
Salmon Bites 104
Salmon Cakes 91
Salmon Potato Patties 91
Salmon with Chives Sauce 95
Salmon with Courgette 88
Salsa Chicken 56
Savoury Beans 43
Sesame Carrots 37
Shakshuka 27
Short Rib Bibimbap 74
Shredded Greek-Style Chicken 58
Smoked Salmon and Veggie Quiche Cups 22
Smoky Barbecue Chicken 58
Smoky Beef Tacos 70
Soft Eggs 22
Soft Raisin Muffins 109
Spelt with Berries and Walnuts 21
Spiced Chicken Thighs 50
Spiced Pumpkin Pudding 115
Spicy Bacon Pieces 67
Spicy Buffalo Chicken Wings 45
Spicy Buffalo Wings 47
Spicy Chicken Alfredo 45
Spicy Curried Cauliflower Soup 85
Spicy Lamb Tagine 75
Spicy Potatoes 29
Spicy Teriyaki Chicken 53
Spinach- Rollups 17
Spinach-Feta Cups 20
Sriracha Glazed Ribs 61
Steak Bulgogi 65
Steamed Crab 97
Steamed Prawns with Asparagus 96
Steaming Clams 96
Strawberry Morning Toast 18
Stuffed Turkey Breast with Gravy 57
Stuffed Venison Tenderloin 68
Sushi 103
Swedish Beef Meatloaf 62
Sweet and Sour Beef Brisket 68
Sweet Barbecue Spareribs 78
Sweet Lemon Bars 110
Sweet Pecans 111
Sweet Potato Toast 16
Sweet Quiche 119
Sweet Raspberry Curd 117
Sweet Tapioca 120
Swiss Chard and Vegetables in Cheesy Sauce 30
Syrupy Crème Brulee 121
Szechuan Beans 36
Szechuan-Style String Beans 42

T

Taco Seasoned Meatballs 65
Tacon Mexican Muffins 101
Tangy Fruit Salad Jam 119
Tasty Tomato Spinach Quiche 26
Thai Chicken Rice 57
Thanksgiving Turkey 51
The Baked Beans 31
Tilapia with Tomatoes 99
Toast Sticks 16
Tomato and Spinach Healthy Breakfast 25
Tomato Soup with basil 83
Tortellini Soup with pesto 82
Traditional Beef Chili 82
Traditional French Eggs 23
Tropical Oats 22
Turkey Sausage Roll-Ups 16
Turkey with Gravy 51
Turkey with Mustard Glaze 46
Turmeric Chicken Bites 106
Turnips with Greens 41
Tuscan Beef Stew 75
Tuscan Chicken 52

V

Vegan Apple Pies 114
Vegan Coconut Yogurt 120
Vegetable with Salmon Fillets 89
Vietnamese Beef Soup 75

W

Walnut Apple Muffins 18
Warm Lentils 43
White Chocolate Cookies 108

Y

Yellow Marmalade 118
Yellow Pea Curry 35

Printed in Great Britain
by Amazon